WITHAM 11/14

Please return this book on or before the date shown above. To renew go to www.essex.gov.uk/libraries, ring 0845 603 7628 or go to any Essex library.

Essex County Council

Ess...

301...

D1330139

DIANA COOPER

Darling Monster

The Letters of Lady Diana Cooper to her
son John Julius Norwich 1939–1952

EDITED BY
John Julius Norwich

VINTAGE BOOKS
London

Published by Vintage 2014

2 4 6 8 10 9 7 5 3 1

First published in Great Britain in 2013 by
Chatto & Windus

Vintage
Random House, 20 Vauxhall Bridge Road,
London SW1V 2SA

www.vintage-books.co.uk

Addresses for companies within The Random House Group
Limited can be found at: www.randomhouse.co.uk/offices.htm

The Random House Group Limited Reg. No. 954009

A CIP catalogue record for this book
is available from the British Library

ISBN 9780099578598

The Random House Group Limited supports the Forest Stewardship
Council® (FSC®), the leading international forest-certification
organisation. Our books carrying the FSC label are printed on
FSC®-certified paper. FSC is the only forest-certification scheme
supported by the leading environmental organisations, including
Greenpeace. Our paper procurement policy can be found at
www.randomhouse.co.uk/environment

MIX
Paper from
responsible sources
FSC
www.fsc.org
FSC® C018575

Typeset in Sabon by Palimpsest Book Production Limited,
Falkirk, Stirlingshire

Printed and bound in Great Britain by
CPI Group (UK) Ltd, Croydon, CR0 4YY

To my grandchildren
Who would have loved their great-grandmother
As she would have loved them

Contents

Introduction

She was an inveterate letter-writer. I can see her now, sitting bolt upright in bed, cross-legged, a pad of paper balanced on her right knee, a pencil in her hand – always pencil, so as not to get ink on the sheets. Bed was the bridge, the control tower, the centre of operations. On it was the telephone, the writing paper, the addresses, the engagements. Never did I see her sitting at a desk or other table if bed was within range.

She always maintained that she could never keep a diary; it was no fun writing to herself. So she wrote to other people instead – to my father if he was away somewhere, to her old friend Conrad Russell, or to me, her son. And she told us everything that happened, writing in a style that was entirely her own – there was no way that any letter of hers could be mistaken for anyone else's. The writing was effortless; an hour would produce five or six long pages; then she would fold them rather roughly, give the envelope a quick lick, address it – still in pencil – and, as often as not, start on another.

Never did she seem remotely conscious of the fact that she was a celebrity; but a celebrity she was. First of all there was the startling beauty; second, she was a member of the high aristocracy – in those days still an advantage – born on Monday 29 August 1892 and brought up in one of England's most spectacular country houses, Belvoir Castle, as the youngest daughter of the eighth Duke of Rutland. (Her adoring public would have been horrified to learn that she was in fact the result of a long and passionate affair between the Duchess and the Hon. Harry Cust, from the neighbouring estate at Belton.[1]) But there was more to it than that. Ever since her presentation at court in 1911, she had been the darling of the society and gossip columns; and when she married my father, Duff Cooper – a penniless commoner of whom no one had ever heard – at St Margaret's, Westminster, a body of mounted police had to be brought in to control the adoring crowds outside.

She would have married him in any event; she was to love him to distraction until the day he died. But by then marriageable young men were thin on the ground. At the outbreak of the First World War my father, as a member of the Foreign Service, had been exempt from the call-up – a fact for which I am heartily thankful, since had he not been I should almost certainly not be here today – but most of his friends had not been so lucky. So much has been written of the massacre of that war – particularly of the young officers – that it seems superfluous to add anything further; but I remember my mother telling me that by the end of 1916, with the single exception of my father, every man she had ever danced with was dead.

In December 1916 Herbert Asquith resigned as Prime Minister, to be succeeded by David Lloyd George, one of whose first actions – in view of what was becoming a serious shortage of manpower at the front – was to extend conscription to several of the 'reserved professions', including the Foreign Service. My father, who had been increasingly embarrassed by what he saw as his enforced inactivity while nearly all his contemporaries were in France, felt nothing but relief.

The training, he always maintained, was the worst part. It had been described by his friend Eddie Grant as 'being stuck in a six-foot bog, trained like an Olympian athlete and buggered about like a mulatto telegraph boy', and he hated it. He loved to tell the

---

1 There have long been persistent rumours that another recipient of Mr Cust's attentions was a member of the domestic staff at Belton who later became the maternal grandmother of Lady Thatcher, and that our former Prime Minister is consequently my first cousin. I should dearly love to know, but have never had the courage to suggest DNA.

story of a certain evening in early July when he briefly escaped to London from his training camp at Bushey in Hertfordshire, only to discover that no one he knew, male or female, was in town. For once, he felt genuinely depressed; there was nothing for it but to go to his club – the Junior Carlton in those days, rather than the beloved White's of his later years – and to order the best dinner he could get, washed down with a pint of champagne. From the library he took down a copy of *Through the Looking-Glass*, always one of his favourite books. 'Then,' he wrote, 'as if by enchantment my melancholy left me and I knew that I should not be unhappy again.'[2] On 27 April 1918 he left for France.

Even there, his high spirits did not desert him. 'From a comfortable dug-out' he reported to my mother that 'the horrors of war have been much exaggerated', and offered to send her a food parcel; but he soon had reason to change his mind. At 5 a.m. on 21 August he and his company went over the top in a heavy mist, and before long his platoon became separated from the rest. They reached their objective of the Arras–Albert railway line – the only platoon to do so – but immediately ran into heavy fire from a German machine-gun post. He went forward to destroy it, not knowing that all the men following him had been killed, and on his arrival – almost miraculously unscathed – shot one man and called upon the others, in what German he could still remember, to surrender. Believing themselves to be outnumbered, to his intense surprise they did; and so it happened that a callow young second lieutenant with practically no experience of battle managed to capture eighteen Germans single-handed. He was recommended for the Victoria Cross, but had to settle for the Distinguished Service Order which, particularly when awarded to a subaltern, was generally considered to be the next best thing.

Only two nights later his company attacked again. This time he described it as 'one of the most memorable moments of my life . . . a thrilling and beautiful attack, bright, bright moonlight

2 Duff Cooper, *Diaries*.

and we guided ourselves by a star . . . it was what the old poets said it was and the new poets say it isn't'. After one more battle 'the sun rose beautifully and the enemy fled in all directions including ours with their hands up, and one had a glorious Ironside feeling of Let God Arise and let His Enemies be Scattered. And then they came back again over the hill and one was terrified and had a ghastly feeling of God is sunk and His enemies are doing nicely.' Fortunately 'the battle rolled away'. It was his last engagement. Meanwhile my mother – much against my grandmother's wishes – the Duchess could not bear the thought of her favourite child washing the wounded and emptying bedpans – had become a nurse at Guy's Hospital. For the past year she and my father had been growing closer; only he, it seemed, could provide the strength and consolation she so desperately needed.

They were married seven months after the Armistice, on 2 June 1919. Just three years later, at the age of thirty and to the undisguised horror of her parents and their friends, she became a film star, taking the lead in two films – silent of course – for the then celebrated though now long-forgotten producer J. Stuart Blackton. In one, *The Virgin Queen*, she played Queen Elizabeth I; alas, all the prints have been lost. Of the other, a swashbuckling seventeenth-century drama called *The Glorious Adventure*, I possess a copy. It is not, I think, likely to be revived. These two films did little for my mother's reputation in London society; but they led to something far more important. They brought her to the attention of the world-famous Austrian theatre producer Max Reinhardt, who was seeking actresses for the two leading parts in his forthcoming new production of *The Miracle*. This free adaptation of a medieval miracle play had had considerable success at London's Olympia shortly before the First World War; Reinhardt now proposed to take it to New York and to give it a completely new and far more ambitious production at the Century Theater. If successful there it would tour America.

The action of *The Miracle* is set in a vast medieval abbey, which houses a convent of nuns. It also possesses a life-size statue of the Virgin and Child credited with miraculous properties. The plot, in brief, tells of a beautiful young nun who prays before the statue for her freedom – at which the Virgin slowly descends from her niche, dons the nun's habit and thenceforth takes her place, leaving the niche empty. The poor girl has gained her liberty, but her venture into the outside world proves disastrous: she is betrayed, abused, corrupted; and a year or two later she makes her way back to the abbey broken in body and spirit, a dying baby in her arms. While all the other nuns are congregated in prayer, one of their number suddenly rises from their midst, removes her habit – which she gives back to the girl – takes the baby, now dead, from her and slowly returns with it to the niche, where it becomes the Christ-child.

Reinhardt's production was a triumph. The theatre was dark for six months while it was transformed into a Gothic abbey, the bells of which rang for half an hour every evening before the performance. During the long New York run, my mother played sometimes the nun and sometimes the Virgin – the latter being by far the more taxing as she had to stand motionless in her niche, holding a heavy wooden baby, for some fifty minutes before slowly coming to life. When the run was over, she stayed on with the company for its nationwide tour of America. Later they did two more tours, the first through central Europe, the second through England and Scotland.

I have told the story of *The Miracle* at some length because it was immensely important in her life. This importance was to a large extent financial; as – in theory at least – the fifth child and third daughter of the Duke, she stood to inherit virtually nothing. She had been expected to find a rich husband; instead, she had picked a comparative pauper who had little to live on except his Foreign Office salary. They married on £1,100 a year – obviously a good deal more than it is today, but still far from princely; and my grandmother, who had had visions of Belgravia or Mayfair, was appalled when they settled at No. 90 Gower Street, Bloomsbury.

But *The Miracle* also gave my mother something else: experience of other worlds totally foreign to her own. For what must have been a total of six or seven years she lived in the world of theatre – and not the English theatre either, but the Austrian-American-Jewish theatre, which was something quite different again. It was a milieu that she would love for the rest of her life. This explains, in the earlier years covered by these letters, the presence of the near-ubiquitous Dr Rudolf Kommer (Kaetchen) who had been Reinhardt's factotum and was to be my guardian during my wartime stay in America. On the other hand, the long enforced absences that my parents were called upon to suffer with the broad Atlantic between them could easily have destroyed their marriage, particularly in view of my father's constant infidelities. In fact it did nothing of the kind. They both saw the *Miracle* money as an investment – one that would enable my father to throw up the Foreign Office and its salary of £900 a year and launch himself into the political career on which he had set his heart.

In the letters that follow, he plays a supporting role only; yet one feels his presence all the time. Commoner he may have been, but his lineage was not altogether without distinction. He was, in fact, the great-great-grandson of King William IV, who had no fewer than nine illegitimate children by Mrs Dorothy Jordan, the leading *comédienne* of her day. One of their countless grandchildren, Lady Agnes Hay, married James, fifth Earl of Fife – curiously enough, at the British Embassy in Paris – and had four children, the youngest of whom was named Agnes like her mother.

Lady Agnes grew up to be extremely attractive but more than a little flighty, and in 1871 at the age of nineteen eloped with the young and dashing Viscount Dupplin. Two years later she gave birth to a daughter, Marie, who married into the family of Field Marshal von Hindenburg and settled in Germany. A romantic novelist, she loved to talk about what she called 'the Jordan blood', and no wonder: when she was only two years old her mother eloped for the second time, on this occasion with a young man called Herbert Flower, whom she married in 1876 as soon as Lord

Dupplin had been granted a divorce – on the grounds, it need hardly be said, of his wife's adultery. The Flowers went off on a world cruise, but their idyll was to be all too short: just four years later in 1880, Herbert died at the age of twenty-seven.

Agnes was heartbroken; he was the love of her life. She herself was still only twenty-eight, but what was she to do? Her family had disowned her; she was virtually penniless; and after two elopements and a divorce not even an earl's daughter with royal connections – her brother Alexander had married the eldest daughter of the future King Edward VII – could hope to be accepted into society. But she had never lacked spirit. In the hopes of becoming a nurse, she took a menial job in one of the major London teaching hospitals, and there, in 1882, it is said while she was scrubbing the floor, she caught the eye of one of the consulting surgeons, Dr Alfred Cooper.

Now Dr Cooper was a good deal more interesting than he sounds. Born in 1838 in Norwich to a family of lawyers, he had completed his medical studies at St Bartholomew's in London and by the mid-1860s had built up a highly successful practice in Jermyn Street. According to the *Dictionary of National Biography*:

> Cooper, whose social qualities were linked with fine traits
> of character and breadth of view, gained a wide knowledge of
> the world, partly at courts, partly in the out-patient rooms of
> hospitals, and partly in the exercise of a branch of his profession
> which more than any other reveals the frailty of mankind.

It did indeed. That branch was, moreover, forked: syphilis and piles. Within a short time my grandfather and grandmother together were said to know more about the private parts of the British aristocracy than any other couple in the country. Despite this – or perhaps because of it – he quickly made his name in London society, becoming a member of all the right clubs and an ever-popular guest at dinner parties, country houses and even on grouse moors. Among his patients he numbered Edward, Prince of Wales, whom in 1874 he accompanied to St Petersburg.

(From which of the above two distressing complaints His Royal Highness suffered is not known; the Palace announced at the time that Dr Cooper was treating him for a form of bronchitis – but what else could the Palace have said?) The two remained friends, and in 1901, when the prince succeeded his mother on the throne and became King Edward VII, he was to award my grandfather a knighthood in his Coronation Honours.

Dr Cooper had done well: well enough to send his only son Duff[3] – there were also three daughters – to Eton and Oxford where, according to his biographer John Charmley, 'he trailed clouds of dissipation', drinking, gambling and pursuing regiments of women, whom he wooed – on the whole successfully – not only by his charm and wit but also by bombarding them with sonnets, for which he had a quite extraordinary facility. These were a by-product of a genuine passion for literature, in particular poetry and nineteenth-century novels in both English and French; by the end of his life it was almost impossible to find one of these that he had not read and remembered.

After the war he did indeed give up the Foreign Office, embarking instead on a political career, in the course of which he became Secretary of State for War in 1936 and First Lord of the Admiralty – effectively Secretary of State for the Navy – in 1937. He loved the latter post, which included the use of the Admiralty yacht, a converted destroyer called HMS *Enchantress*; but he did not enjoy it for long. At the end of August 1938 Nazi troops had begun to mass along Germany's frontier with Czechoslovakia. Prime Minister Neville Chamberlain and his Foreign Secretary Lord Halifax were prepared to see the destruction of what Chamberlain famously described as 'a far-away country' and 'people of whom we know nothing'; my father took a stronger line. He wanted us to make it absolutely clear to Hitler that if he marched into Czechoslovakia the result would be war. At first, he wrote, the

3 In later years the press tended to give him (and my mother) a hyphen, making 'Duff' part of the surname. This was unwarranted: he was christened Duff, his mother's family name. It was never my mother's and has never been mine.

alternatives seemed to be 1) peace with dishonour – allowing Hitler to take over Czechoslovakia; 2) war. But then Chamberlain made three flights to Germany to see Hitler; and when he returned after their last meeting, having accepted virtually all Hitler's demands, my father saw that there was now a third possibility staring us in the face: war with dishonour – betraying Czechoslovakia and still having to fight, since Hitler was clearly not going to be satisfied. He could bear it no longer, and on 1 October submitted his resignation.

This, then, is the background to the letters that follow. They were written over a thirteen-year period, between 1939 and 1952. When I received the first I had recently celebrated my tenth birthday; the last found me a married man with a child of my own on the way, soon to be twenty-three and to enter the Foreign Service myself. For both my mother and me, these were eventful years. Their beginning virtually coincided with the outbreak of the Second World War. For her, this was followed by a lecture tour that my father undertook in America, the London Blitz, the establishment of a smallholding farm in Sussex, a five-month posting to Singapore involving extensive tours of South-East Asia, nine months with General de Gaulle in Algiers, three years at the British Embassy in post-liberation Paris and, finally, retirement in a house just outside Chantilly. For me, they saw my evacuation in 1940 to the United States, eighteen months' education in Toronto, a return to England in 1942 on a Royal Navy cruiser, four years at Eton, two on the lower deck of the Navy and, to finish off, three years at New College, Oxford.

During that time, my mother wrote me several hundred letters, sometimes daily, hardly ever less frequently than two or three times a week. Despite repeated injunctions to keep them carefully, I fear that the very occasional bundle has been lost – almost certainly my fault. One particularly sad casualty is that which concludes the American lecture tour in the very first chapter. But the vast majority – at least 90 per cent – have survived, and it is the best of these that you now hold in your hands. They have in some cases been slightly abridged, but only to spare the reader those paragraphs which would have bored him or her stiff, or which I myself, after so long an interval, find incomprehensible. There are, alas, far too many names. Most of them are identified in the footnotes or – also by Christian names and nicknames – in the List of Names at the end of the book. Of those which are not, some are made sufficiently clear by the context, others are too well-known to need additional explanation. The remainder are left unexplained because I have no idea who they are.

Particularly during the early years, I was a far less dutiful correspondent than she – and, as her letters make abundantly clear, she never let me forget it. ('This one only told me that your gym master had been ill.') Increasing maturity showed a welcome improvement, and by the time I reached the Navy and had a good deal of time on my hands I was writing regularly, sometimes at inordinate length. The results you have been spared; but, simply to give a taste of the two-way correspondence, one of my own letters, ruthlessly abridged, has been included as a sort of prelude to each chapter, to be ignored at will.

1

'Pray for Hitler's sharks not to catch us'

USA, OCTOBER 1939–FEBRUARY 1940

My darling Mummy and Papa,

We are not snowed up any more, I am glad to say, but there is still a lot about.

The new music teacher, who plays the organ in church, is very nice. I have her twice a week, for half an hour, and am getting on fine.

We had films last night. One was about owls, hawks and things. It was frightfully good, showing hawks in midair, catching bones. Film No. 2 was pure humour but it kept going wrong. It was a maid who dropped all the best china, and it came to life and tortured her. I did not like it and you would have loathed it.

The master, Mr. Clinch, is an owner of performing fleas. We are going to have a demonstration this afternoon. He is also going to try to get a scout troop, and is teaching us many knots. Still, to go on with fleas. They are called performing livestock, since 'fleas' sounds too undignified. They are called Oscar and Cuthbert, and Mr. Clinch got them from the Sahara Desert.

I now know about thirty verses from Horatius.[2] When I have learned it all, you will owe me £3 10s, since there are seventy verses.

Lots and lots of love,

John Julius

---

1 The boarding school to which my London day school, Egerton House, had been evacuated on the outbreak of war.

2 The long narrative poem by Lord Macaulay. Learning and reciting poetry by heart was my only source of pocket money.

Having resigned from the Chamberlain government in October 1938, my father found himself at a loose end. When, therefore, towards the end of the year, he was invited to lecture in America, he did not turn the suggestion down flat. He replied that given the existing situation he could not possibly commit himself at that time; he might, however, be able to do so in the following year, 'if conditions were favourable'. He was in fact fairly certain that they would not be; but the inactivity that had continued month after month in 1939 had proved almost more than he could stand. War was declared on 3 September 1939. He knew there was no hope for a ministerial post while Neville Chamberlain remained in power; at the same time he did not feel that he could leave England without the Prime Minister's approval. On 21 September he managed an interview; but, as he noted in his diary, 'Chamberlain merely suggested that in six weeks' time, when "things will be getting pretty hot here", a man of my age might be criticised for leaving the country. I said that that was my own responsibility and was a question that I could settle for myself. After some humming and hawing he said that it would be a good thing for me to go – and so I left him. I wasn't with him for more than ten minutes and I left with a feeling of intensified dislike.'

His mission, if he went, would be clear enough. He must do his best to persuade America that the isolationist policies then being advocated by Colonel Charles Lindbergh – and a good many others in high places – would prove disastrous to both our countries. The cause of Great Britain was not everywhere popular in the United States. There was in particular a deep suspicion of the Empire; not 1 per cent of his audiences, wrote my father, believed that the Dominions were really self-governing; nor did they have any idea of the bloodshed that was bound to follow a British withdrawal from India, which most of them wholeheartedly advocated. Above all, they had to be made to understand that the western world was fighting for its life. Without American help, the battle might well be lost.

He decided to go; my mother, as she always did, went with him; and the letters begin.

———

In the train to Southampton
October 12th, 1939

Papa and I have barged and battered our way through a mob of passengers and seers-off and are at last seated (not everybody is) in a Pullman car with eggs and strawberry jam. There was a crowd of photographers hunting Papa like sleuths, but I implored them not to take us as we don't want the enemy to send a special torpedo. We gave a party last night at the Savoy and tried to forget we were going, not that I mind much except for leaving you. I'll write, no cable you as soon as I arrive in N.Y. but I don't suppose it will be for ten or twelve days. Work hard, play hard and *don't change* till I come back anyway. Be just as I left you, gay and brave and good and sensible. Don't forget that there's a war being fought and that it's *got to be won* and that your contribution towards winning it is to be better, more hardworking, more thoughtful and braver than usual . . . I love you very much.

S.S. Manhattan
Halfway over

The sea is rather Cape Wrathish[3] and I have forgotten the terror of the torpedoes in my efforts to cope with standing upright. Everybody except Papa and me is sleeping five and six in a cabin on cots like you slept on in the *Enchantress* and all the big saloons are dormitories of fifty unfortunates all sicking together. We have a film every afternoon and we have to go and sit on our places two hours before it starts. The news that you will delight in is that we shall actually see the World's Fair.[4] I'll send you pictures and details. The deck is black with children which makes me want you very much. They play a nice dart game on deck which I'll send you for Christmas if I can get it over.

We get very little English news. What comes through is on a radio at its most confused and raucous worst. I'm trying to remember what Belvoir was like when I was half your age, with no taps, no electric light, no motors, but instead lamp-men and water-men carrying gigantic cans. Drives in the afternoon with Grandpapa in a big landau with a big fat coachman on the box driving a pair of spanking horses and a footman in a long coat and top hat who leapt down and opened a gate and scrambled up to the box again and did nothing else in life. If I can put it all together and make it interesting enough I might make a radio talk in America, and make some money to give to the Red Cross. I'll stop now and add a bit more to this letter before we land.

Saturday. We are due to land tomorrow. It got lovely and calm again yesterday and there was a good film called *Stanley and Livingstone*[5] and in the evening we gave a dinner party of two other people . . .

3 In August–September 1937, when my father was First Lord of the Admiralty, we had sailed in the *Enchantress* around the north of Scotland from Holyhead to Rosyth, and had run into dreadful weather round the aptly named Cape Wrath.

4 The New York World's Fair was staged at Flushing Meadows in 1939 and 1940.

5 Twentieth Century Fox, 1939. The two name parts were played by Spencer Tracy and Cedric Hardwicke respectively.

Shall hope to see old Kaetchen at 9 a.m. tomorrow morning. I shall be happy to arrive, the perils of the sea behind us for a bit. I shall be thinking about you all the time and longing for letters, nothing too silly to tell me about, remember that as I shall be hungry for news of you – air raid warnings, outings with Nanny.

October 27th, 1939
New York

I've been to the World's Fair for the first time – not, you will be sorry to hear, to the Amusement Park. I go there tomorrow, but I've been inside the Perisphere. It's that large globe one sees in the pictures. One goes in the door at the foot of the pyramid and there's a blue-lit, rather sinister moving staircase which shoots you off into the inside of the globe on to a revolving platform that carries you round the circle while you look down upon the city of the future – done like panoramas are done. The dome above you looks just like the real sky and changes to night and stars and the model city lights up. I did the English Pavilion – good but dull – and the French one – good and exciting – and the Russian one, immense and made of marble and showing with tremendous pride things the U.S.S.R. has made and invented and developed since their new regime – all the things we've had for years, such as an underground railway. The Exhibition doesn't look half as lovely as the Paris one – fountains much less good, but one doesn't get so tired as there are little motors and little chairs a man pushes you in. I saw too a room of *minute* babies in incubators. That was fascinating, and you would have very much liked the Palace of Health, with transparent men with pulsating kidneys and brains, etc. I'll write you about the Amusements next time.

It seems dreadful being so far from you and the family and unhappy England. No news from anyone yet, only stories of Germany's hatred of England. It makes one desperately sad. Here the cry is 'Keep out of the war'. A few years ago America passed a law called the Neutrality Act which meant that they might not *sell* any armaments or aeroplanes or oil or steel to countries that were at war. Now there is a big fight going on because Roosevelt, the President, wants to repeal that law, to tear it up and allow any nation at war to buy what they want, as long as they can fetch it in their own ships and pay cash down for it. ('Cash and Carry' it's called.) He wants this because he is very pro-England and France, and he knows that the repeal of the law would advantage us, who have ships and money and the command of the seas. So we must pray that the President pulls it off, and now you know what the Repeal of the Neutrality Act is, or you ought to if you're not a tiny idiot or if I am incapable of making myself clear. We are going to Washington next week and I hope to see my darling President in his White House.

Goodbye, my beloved. Don't forget to say your prayers at night under the clothes – you needn't kneel if the other boys don't, but say them please.

British Embassy
Washington D.C.
November 3rd, 1939

You will be very sorry to hear that I never again got to the Fair. I'd promised myself two days – the last two before the Fair closed – to do all the parachutes and heart-stoppers. And on those two days the heavens opened and torrential rains that drowned every-thing, and now it's shut till next year and it's just too bad. We came to Washington D.C. yesterday to see our Ambassador there, Lord Lothian, and this evening – great excitement – we are to go to the White House and see the President, so I won't finish this letter till later so that I can tell you what he is like. I've always loved him as you know, but he is unpopular with the very rich because he taxes them mercilessly and a good job too. He's very pro-Ally and does not really think that America should be an 'isolationist' country that takes no part in the rest of the world's troubles. He would like to come to our help and has already done so by getting the Neutrality Law repealed (it was done yesterday just as we arrived, by a big majority of votes). So now we can buy all the arms we can pay for from the U.S.A. and so can France, and Hitler won't like it one little bit. That will do for my lecture bit of this letter.

Papa makes his first lecture next Monday at Columbia University – that's New York – and three days later he makes one in New Jumper – I mean New Jersey, which is the next state. Papa has gone very American – he has given up carrying a stick or umbrella, he is very energetic and full of hustle as though he thought 'time was money'. He speaks through his nose and soon he will be wearing pince-nezes and smoking a cheroot, and may even grow a little goatee beard. I'm going out now to the Capitol and to look at a colossal Abraham Lincoln made of marble sitting in a chair. I pray every night that you are happy and well. By the time you get this there will be only about three weeks more of school. Perhaps you'll be preparing a play. I haven't heard a word of you yet.

Saturday 4th. Well, the White House was a big success. Mr. President was gleeful over his repeal and didn't pretend to be neutral at all. I was a bit nervous and didn't do very well with him, but he did very well with me. If his legs had not been paralysed he'd have danced a war dance. Before the tea with the President we went to see the Hoover Institute of Criminal Investigation.[6] You would so have loved it. When the gangsters and racketeers were at their worst and the kidnappers, Mr. Hoover was put in charge of the Police Department and made the 'G-men'. (G stands for Government.) They are a severely trained body of men who know the law, who are husky and strong, and who are taught to shoot straight and carry guns. The result has been miraculous. The headquarters are at Washington and there

6 Now the FBI.

you can see all the relics of the gangsters, their blood-stained bits, their death masks, their sawn-off shotguns, notes written by kidnapped children, millions of indexed fingerprints. To finish up you are taken to the shooting gallery where you are first shown how the different kinds of machine-guns and repeaters of all sorts are operated with tracer bullets that show in the dark, and then you can try them yourself on the target of a life-sized man. I did pretty well and kept my riddled man for you. I'll send it if I can.

On to Williamsburg today to see what a colonial town in Virginia in the time of Queen Anne looks like. They have restored it to look exactly as it did. New York next day.

Kiluna Farm,
Manhasset, Long Island
November 12th, 1939

This letter will probably get to you before the last one I wrote you about Washington because I'm giving it to Ronnie Tree who leaves on the Clipper[7] tomorrow. It's a month since I left, and I haven't had a letter from anyone except Conrad,[8] and one from Hutchie[9] by air. I really can't wait to hear something of you. Tomorrow we are off to the Southern States for ten days and there will be seven lectures and seven or eight nights in the train. When we get back to N.Y. we shall be wrecks. I spend half my day at the washing basin scrubbing Papa's socks and drawers and pyjamas and handkerchiefs, and the other half ironing them and perpetually burning them. You will say why don't you send them to a laundry. The answer is that everything in this country is so expensive that it hurts my sensitive Scotch soul, and what Papa flings away on

---

7   A transatlantic airline using flying boats.
8   Conrad Russell. Bachelor friend of my mother (see Directory of Names).
9   St John Hutchinson, K.C. (See Directory).

tips and leaving money about, and not taking the trouble to learn the currency and so giving 50 cents instead of 10 cents, I try to make up for by pathetic economies. We had a very successful lecture at Summit, New Jersey, the state on the other side of the Hudson river from N.Y. They've built a splendid tunnel, bigger and better and faster and generally more impressive than the Mersey Tunnel. We had dinner before the speech with an old American family, good and noble and high-principled and delightful. Grace before our dinner which was at half-past six. We had to eat the food though I wanted to regurgitate. I thought of you. Papa likes a drink before a lecture, but this home disapproved of anything but water!

This home, which belongs to Mr. Paley, the President of the Columbia Broadcasting, has too much alcohol on the other hand. Result – I've got a headache today and wish that I was back with the fine American middle-class family in spite of their abstinence.

I enclose the man I shot at in the Criminal Investigation Department with a hand machine-gun. My Washington letter will explain.

British Embassy
Washington
November 19th, 1939

At last I've got a scrubby little letter from you dated 29 October. You are the nastiest little pig I know and I despise the school for not urging you to be a little less beastly. Do you realise that you let eighteen days pass without giving your poor frightened exiled mother a thought? Please, darling horror, don't do it again. Write as often as you can. It's so sad waiting for letters that don't come and are not even written.

I'm writing on very thin loo paper because airmail is so expensive and it goes by weight. Papa and I spend every night in the train, Papa up above monkeywise. He's more like a monkey

than I was because up above there is a criss-cross arrangement
of green tape like a cage to keep him from being shot out. Most
nights he lectures and yesterday at Pittsburgh, a huge town where
they make steel (their Sheffield) he had to speak for an hour at
10 a.m. They gave him in return a large ivory penknife with the
giver's name which happened to be Duff engraved upon it. I should
claim it from him when we get home. He's more likely to cut
himself than you are. It's hot as summer and Washington is all
avenues of trees and spaces and big beautifully designed offices
for Government. Tonight it's the train again for Charlotte, N.
Carolina, and the next night train again to New York, three days
break and off to Canada. I love my darling boy. Don't treat me so
badly again or I'll have your lights and liver when I get home.

November 29th, 1939

Here we are at Ottawa where the Governor General of Canada
lives in kingly splendour. He's called Lord Tweedsmuir and we
curtsey to him as though he were the King himself. Last evening
Papa was on his legs bawling away at Boston Massachusetts and
at 11 p.m. we got into our train bed and got out again at Utica,
N.Y. State. There we waited an hour and had a glorious breakfast
if rather curious, i.e. coffee, grapefruit juice, drop scones made
of buckwheat, sausages, bacon and over the lot maple-sugar syrup.
On again in a boiling train that went about three miles an hour
and stopped with a sickening jolt at every station. My feet swelled
with the heat and my back ached and we were both in a kind of
coma, like people in a submarine that's gone wrong. At last we
came to the majestic St. Lawrence river that divides Canada from
U.S. and where there is no frontier nonsense, no soldiers or forts
or things like *Mussolini ha sempre ragione*[10] (do you remember?).

---

10 *Mussolini is always right.* When my mother had taken me skiing two years before,
we had seen these words in huge letters at the Italian frontier.

Canada and the U.S.A. understand and trust each other, hence the simplification.

Don't forget to love me. I feel so far from you and frightened that you'll grow away from me. Be determined not to, for if you did it would break my heart.

Deshler–Wallick Hotel
Columbus, Ohio
About December 7th, 1939

This will probably be your Christmas letter and where am I to imagine you as being? Where will you be delving into a bulging stocking? I hope at Belvoir. Wherever you are I want you to have a lovely lovely Christmas full of fun and presents and treats, and for war to be forgotten, anyway for the day. It's the first Christmas I shall not be with you and I mind it dreadfully. Please pray hard that we'll be together next year and that Hitler will be defeated, and that we'll all be trying to mend our poor England. I shan't be much of a mender because I'm so tired and weak, but you'll have to do a lot about it, and so will Papa.

What a day we had yesterday. We tumbled out of the train at 6.30 a.m. at Cleveland, Ohio, and there were the merciless photographers and reporters. At 11 a.m. Papa gave a lecture. Then came a luncheon of 500 strangers at the end of which Papa had to answer their questions about the European situation. Then a two-hour motor drive with strangers and dinner with them and another lecture, and then an endless supper with a different lot of strangers at a place called Canton, Ohio. Then a two-hour motor drive to a place called Youngstown, and at last we tumbled back into the train at 1.30 a.m. – nineteen hours running without a break. We woke up next morning in Toronto, Canada, where everyone is in khaki and off to the war. Now we're at Troy, N.Y. State, very unlike my idea of Troy, no Greeks, no gods, no visible heroes. These Trojans make shirts for all America to wear. Tomorrow we shall be in Boston, and so it goes on.

Just arrived Boston and found a wonderful account written by Martin of his torpedoing. Also three letters from Conrad and one from Hutchie and a scrubby little bit from you. Really your letters are too horrid, one side of a sheet, not one word of affection or love. This one only told me your gym master had been ill. It was not even signed. You can't think how disappointing it is to get a letter like that. You used to write lovely long ones before you went to school.

Sunday, December 17th, 1939

Our mad bout of travelling is ending for a bit. In three days we shall get two weeks without lectures. Papa is like you and wants to sit quiet in town and go to the theatres and eat and drink and play cards, and wink at the lovely ladies, while I, as you know me, am trying to put a bit more enterprise and adventure into it. I am drawn to the snows, or to the hot beaches of Florida, or to cowboys or Indians or something. Papa will win.

The other night when we arrived at the lecture hall in Brooklyn we saw it to be completely surrounded by policemen with bludgeons. We were half an hour too early, so we went and sat at a café opposite and watched developments. It was raining and soon sad bedraggled young men began to appear carrying placards which read '*Send Duff Home*', '*We Won't be Dragged into War*', '*Don't Listen to English Lies*' and so on, but no one was paying the slightest attention to them. When we got inside there were still more cops but nothing happened at all – no demonstration, no row. The only effect it had was to give us a friendly crowd at the stage door when we left. They cheered us.

I'm not expecting to get any Christmas presents. I hope you get a great many, you darling little boy. Write *by air* on a typewriter. There is sure to be one at Belvoir if you can get around the secretary. You write longer and better letters on the machine, I think.

The Ambassador Hotel
Park Avenue, New York
January 3rd, 1940

We had a lovely New Year's Eve sitting up in a large kitchen till 5 o'clock a.m. cooking eggs and bacon and people were still dropping in when I left, treating night as day. I wonder how it all went at Belvoir, and if it's all very different to normal times.

Yesterday I went to the Natural History Museum. It's as lovely here as ours in London is awful. I missed you a lot. There were so many revolting exhibits you would have rejoiced in. One extraordinary peepshow was how a room, for instance, looks to you and how it looks to a dog. A dog sees no colour, whereas a fly sees more colours than we do. A hen sees other hens bigger or smaller according to the other's pecking abilities and she sees the cock-a-doodle-doo *enormous*, though how they can tell I don't know. No more do I believe they do.

The streets are still covered with ice and the roofs with snow. Tomorrow we start on our travels again. In two months we shall be starting home. I haven't heard from you in a long, long time. All the ships are delayed and the Clippers too. Label your letters 'Clipper' and get them stamped. It's 1/6d the ½ oz.

Hotel Oliver
South Bend, Indiana
January 14th, 1940

We are keeping our peckers up splendidly. Sometimes it is gloomy and dull and other days the town is bright, the hotel lovely and the people full of life and fun, and everything seems good. South Bend, Indiana, is the worst we have been to, whereas Toledo, Ohio, was heavenly. At Akron, Ohio, there was a restaurant called the Hawaiian Room. It would have amused you, I think. It was very very dark with a sort of witch-doctory light on the tables.

The bar was a native hut, but the fun was that one wall was a panorama scene of a coral reef – a sandy bay edged with palm trees. Suddenly, though no one was there except Papa and me and a group of very old ladies having lunch together, the panorama darkened and flooded itself with torrential rain. The artificial thunder and blinding lightning deafened us for ten minutes . . .

Now I must get up and wash Papa's vest and drawers and socks and pack and have lunch and listen to the lecture and catch a train to Chicago where with any luck there will be a letter from you.

Fort Worth, Texas
('Where the West Begins')
January 28th, 1940

I've had lovely letters from you lately. Belvoir sounds a hatful of fun and the letters were long and full of the kind of thing I like. What luck to have ice! It's been ridiculously cold here but I haven't smelt a ski or a skate. It was 22 below zero in Minneapolis, Minnesota, and snowing in Alabama, which should be as hot as summer, and at Palm Beach, Florida – where I have always been too hot in January, swimming and sweating alternately – it was so cold that they had to shut all the schools. They have no heating arrangements as it's always hot, so they thought the children would suffer and get ill. Palm Beach is known as the 'millionaires' playground'. Lorna Mackintosh's[11] father runs a bar there called the 'Alibi' Bar, his name being Ali. I think Ali-Bar-Bar would have been a funnier name.

Believe it or not I went flying yesterday.[12] A man who had a two-engined, two-piloted plane offered to take us for a joyride. The conditions seemed perfect – no wind and perfect visibility

11 A childhood friend.
12 She was always terrified of flying. This was her first flight.

– ground flat as a pancake and few buildings, so I thought it a golden opportunity of breaking the ice. Oh John Julius, how I hated it! I had to stay up an hour and twenty minutes and I was agonised with fear all the time, but of course couldn't say so and the owner thought I was liking it and kept telling the pilot to go further and to circle round things. When you turn in a plane you tip right over and see the ground alongside you, and you feel you're going about five miles an hour because nothing passes you in the way of hedges or traffic. So if it wasn't alarming it would be boring and I shan't go up again ever for fun. All the old ladies travel by air in this country and nobody thinks anything of it, but your mother is a shuddering funky old mouse and you must make the best of her.

Kansas City, Missouri
('The Heart of America')

I got a delightful letter from you yesterday, still from Belvoir. How can you explain your letters being so *horrible* to start with, and so nice now? Was it, is it, the dreadful influence of school, do you suppose? We went to see *Gone with the Wind* at Oklahoma City, and when we got into the theatre all the audience stood up and 'God Save the King' was played. The Americans are all very pro-Ally, thank goodness, but they are also determined not to get into the war. Someone in the question period after the lecture always asks 'Why didn't England stop Germany sooner?' and Papa answers 'Because all our actions and all our policy was affected by wishing to keep out of the war. There is no policy more dangerous – every insult will be put upon you if the offender knows you will not fight, and in the end you are forced into it.' That makes them think a bit. I wonder often if all our dear sailors of the *Enchantress* are safe. Hitler's sharks are so hungry.

One more stop in Amarillo, Texas, and then the real West. San

Francisco next. Papa has gone American, but not much hope I fear of his going cowboy. He's been given a white Texan hat, but not what they call a ten-gallon Tom Mix one.[13] Still, he wears it with a certain swagger.

February 7th. We're in the desert now, in Arizona – distant spiky mountains and all the rest desert covered with a grey-blue-lavender sort of bush and tiny stunted palm plants; soon there will be cactuses like this:

February 8th. The cactuses have come and gone.

February 9th. We woke up, still in our train, to find the world changed from desert to garden. California is as green as England in May and laden with flowers and fruit – orange trees, mimosa, eucalyptus trees, grapefruit, vines. It's a paradise of sun and sea and plenty – the Promised Land, milk and honey everywhere. I've seen it before but Papa hadn't, so he is doing a Cortez. If you don't know what that means get a book of well-known poems and look at a sonnet by Keats called 'On first looking into Chapman's Homer'.

El Mirasol
Santa Barbara
California
February 1940

I'm in Hollywood you'll be thrilled to hear and who should I sit next to the other night but your favourite Errol Flynn. He certainly is very good-looking but I'm sorry to tell you I took a violent dislike to him. First of all he was disgustingly anti-English, which being an Australian-Irishman he should not be, and secondly he's got an awful lot of 'side', and kept on pointing

13 A cowboy hero of the silent films.

out other men as giving themselves airs. Another night I sat beside Charlie Chaplin. He has dyed his grey hair black to look like Hitler in the new film[14] he has just finished. They say that he has made dictators so ridiculous that we ought to show the picture on a screen opposite the German trenches and thereby stop the war.

Marlene Dietrich we often see – she wears a velvet trouser suit with Fauntleroy collar and cuffs. Laurence Olivier and Vivien Leigh are here. She's made the greatest success ever known in *Gone with the Wind*. My favourite is a young man called James Stuart. I saw him acting in the studios yesterday. All the time I wish I had you with me. It would amuse you so much to see the sets indoors and out. I saw for instance yesterday the inside of Waterloo Station and a trainload of Tommies steaming out of it. You turn a corner and there is Peking under snow and a London street next to Tarzan's jungle. The quite big trees are on flat wooden trays so they can be transplanted on wheels. I lunched there in the studio restaurant among Austrian peasants, Nazis in uniform, Victorian young ladies, Napoleonic young men. Another thing that you'd love is films called 'blow-outs' of 1938 or 1939. These are all the pieces cut out of films because actors either forget their words, or drop something, or fall down. They always swear of course, and those are the bits you see. We are staying with Mr and Mrs Jack Warner in great luxury. He is the head of Warner Bros. We've been over the Metro-Goldwyn studios and tomorrow we go over Warner's.

Back next month. Pray for us both – pray for Hitler's sharks not to catch us.

14 *The Great Dictator.*

2

'No country for vile invaders' feet'

LONDON, JULY 1940–SEPTEMBER 1940

Kiluna Farm, Manhasset,
Long Island, New York
July 1940

My darling Mummy and Papa,

I do hope you are well, happy and free from bombs. I am having a lovely time here. As I got up at 5.30 a.m. on Saturday the 13th I was so excited, and at about 6.30 passed Brooklyn, Ellis Island, New Jersey and the Statue of Liberty. It was so lovely, but as we were queuing up to have our passports, etc., examined, lots of reporters came on board. We kept them off for about twenty minutes but they knew I was there, and they were so persevering, getting me over the heads of the crowd that at last we were forced to surrender to them.

When we got off, Kaetchen was there on the dock, waiting. We were in New York only two hours and then we went to the Paleys. Mr. Paley has arranged for a tennis pro, Mr. Farrell, to come and teach me. He says I am very good indeed and that I shortly will be playing marvellous tennis.

Lots and lots of love,
John Julius

On their return to London my parents 'camped out', as my mother put it, for three months in my grandmother's old house at No. 34 Chapel Street. I'm not sure what had happened to Gower Street and why they didn't move back there – Admiralty House, after all, was never going to be more than temporary. I can only assume that they had decided to sell it and finally to settle in Chapel Street instead; with its huge library it certainly had far more space for my father's books. After my Easter holidays – spent with my mother at our seaside house near Bognor Regis[1] in Sussex – I returned to Westbury Manor. Soon after the summer term began, however, it became clear to a good many of us that the young schoolmaster who had just arrived to teach us English was in fact a German spy. We took turns to keep a watch on him, and it was one evening when two of us were shadowing him to what was clearly the hiding place of his short-wave transmitter that I suddenly felt hideously sick and threw up in the bushes. On my return to the house I was found to be running a high temperature, and on the following day measles was diagnosed. Of the next fortnight I remember scarcely anything – which is a pity, since it means that I have totally forgotten the fall of France and the Dunkirk evacuation. Then one Sunday, when I was on my feet again but still shaky, my mother appeared and took me out to lunch at a hotel in Buckingham.

From the moment we sat down I could see that she was worried; at one moment I thought she was going to cry. Then she told me that I was being sent to America, and that I should

---

1 West House, Aldwick, was two or three miles from Bognor Regis. As pretty – its garden led straight out on to the beach – as it was uncomfortable, it had been my parents' country retreat since their marriage.

be leaving in three days. My reaction was far from what she had expected. She had thought I would burst into uncontrollable tears, fling my arms round her neck and say I wanted to stay with her for ever; but no – for me, America was simply the most exciting place in the world. It meant New York and skyscrapers, and cowboys and Indians, and grizzly bears and hot dogs, and Hollywood, where I should at last meet my hero Errol Flynn. I couldn't wait to be off. The next afternoon I was put on the train to London, and two nights later Nanny and I left Chapel Street on the first stage of our adventure – far more frightening for her than it was for me – first by train to Holyhead and thence on the night ferry to Dublin.

There, early the following morning, we were met by someone from the American Embassy and taken to breakfast with the Ambassador, Mr David Gray, an old friend of my parents. We were then bundled into another car and driven straight across Ireland – with the occasional stop for me to be sick – to Galway, where the gigantic SS *Washington* awaited us, the largest Stars and Stripes I have ever seen painted all over its hull in order to leave German U-boats in no doubt of its neutrality. We landed a week later in New York, whence we were driven to the house of Mr and Mrs William S. Paley, who had very kindly agreed to take care of me for as long as was necessary. Bill Paley was President of the Columbia Broadcasting System; his house on Long Island was not uncomfortable.

My father, meanwhile, was having a distinctly rough passage of his own. His old friend Winston Churchill, who in May 1940 had succeeded Neville Chamberlain as Prime Minister, had appointed him to a new post which he had just invented, that of Minister of Information. The appointment was not a success. He alone had been responsible for arranging – in the teeth of violent Foreign Office opposition – for General de Gaulle to make his historic broadcast to the French nation after the fall of France; but the press, terrified of censorship and led by Lord Beaverbrook's *Daily Express*, mounted a virulent campaign against him, and the news that he was sending his son to safety in America provided them with just the ammunition they wanted.

Left to himself, my father would never have considered the idea for a second; but my mother was adamant. Was it not true, she argued, that hundreds – perhaps thousands – of other English children were being similarly evacuated in American ships? All the signs were that London would, over the next few months, be bombed to smithereens; alternatively, Hitler might at any moment invade. Would my father – whose name was among the top half-dozen on the Nazi hit list – ever forgive himself if his only son were killed – or, perhaps worse, taken hostage to ensure his father's good behaviour? And so he allowed himself to be persuaded – with my mother in her present mood he had very little choice. There were one or two indignant questions in Parliament; but the Government had a few rather more important matters to concern itself with, and the storm soon blew itself out.

Within a few days of my departure my parents locked up Chapel Street – this was no time to begin all the trouble and expense of setting up in a new house, particularly if it was shortly to be bombed to bits. Instead they hunkered down for the winter in two rooms on the eighth – and top – floor of the Dorchester Hotel. They got them cheap, since few people were prepared to live so close to the roof.

The large London hotels were very popular during the earlier stages of the war. Their very size spelt a sort of safety; private houses were a good deal more vulnerable, besides being impossible to heat. Domestic staff were hard to find – nearly all had been swept up in the war effort. Moreover, commuting in wartime was a nightmare: buses and taxis were scarce, while the tube stations were themselves used as air raid shelters; everyone tried to sleep as near as possible to their place of work. Inevitably, different people favoured different hotels; but Claridge's and the Ritz were relatively old and fragile buildings, while the Dorchester on the outbreak of war was only eight years old and appeared to be made entirely of concrete.

Like all her friends, my mother spent her days doing war work. At one time she was on the top floor of the Army & Navy Stores making camouflage nets; at another she was involved – I can't remember how – with the distribution of gas masks; on yet other occasions she worked in canteens, sometimes for the forces, sometimes in factories or hospitals or the YMCA. The great thing, she used to say, was to keep busy – which she certainly did.

═══

The Dorchester
July 5th, 1940

I'm going to try to write to you every day even if it's only a scrap and even though it's about things that won't interest you a great deal. That way there will be a record of these hideous days and I shall feel I am in touch with you and you with me. You had rather a pale little face at the train window but I hoped that was excitement and not sadness. I went back to dinner with the parent Trees[2] and talked about sinking and capturing the French Navy.[3] Everyone is glad, even if some of them are horrified at the same time – horrified at firing on one's allies the French. I did not feel horrified. It was vital that the Germans should not possess the strips to use against us and the French had broken every pledge in signing them away to their enemies. I woke sadly early this morning July 5, and thought about you hard. Phyllis[4] looked in and Conrad on his way back to the farm to lift his last load of hay. Jones[5] writes that they were nearly blown out of bed by five bombs

---

2 Ronald and Nancy Tree, whose son Jeremy had also travelled to New York on the *Washington*.

3 On 3 July 1940, the British fleet attacked the French navy in the harbour of Mers-el-Kebir, Algeria, to prevent the French ships falling into German hands; three battleships were sunk.

4 Countess de Janzé (see Directory).

5 The Gardener at Bognor.

falling on the beach. Soldiers are in possession of the long strip of grass along our sea front and are digging up the tamarisk hedge, for what purpose I forget, trenches or guns or a loo or what-not.

July 6th. I went to [censored, but I knew it was Rottingdean] this morning to see poor Maurice.[6] He is half the size he used to be. A bright blue budgerigar sits on his shoulder always chattering into his ear, pecking his cheek and making little messes. He claims Dempsey (that's his name) talks. I doubt it. I wasn't allowed to drive along the front where the camouflaged six-inch guns are. Now we're establishing ourselves in the Dorchester high up, for England, on the eighth floor. We can see all London beyond the green sea of Hyde Park.

When the parachutists land in their thousands they will probably be wearing battle dress indistinguishable from our own soldiers. The confusion ensuing is what they rely on to gain an advantage, so I was thinking all day in the train what one could do to mark our own men. If they had armlets the Huns could take them off the dead or wounded ones and wear them themselves. The same would apply to any badge or flag. I suddenly thought of warpaint. Paint all our boys' faces blue one day, scarlet the next, tiger stripes another day, or snow white. I don't see how the enemy could catch up on that, so if you hear of it being done you will know that it was Mummy's idea.[7]

July 7th. It's rather lovely living at the Dorchester. Here I feel as free of possessions as a bird – just the clothes I am wearing, the book I am reading, the letter that has to be answered and a few preparations for sudden descent into the shelter. Wadey[8]

---

6 Maurice Baring, writer.

7 A rather better idea proposed at that time was to recite to suspects the following limerick:

> *A young engine-driver named Hunt*
> *Once took out his engine to shunt;*
> *Saw a runaway truck*
> *And by shouting out 'Duck!'*
> *Saved the life of the fellow in front.*

and to see whether they laughed.

8 My mother's maid (see Directory).

suggested that I should wear a particularly comic robe that I bought in America, and when I said 'Oh no, I'd look too funny' she said 'I didn't think you minded that.'

Conrad has had bombs ¾ of a mile from Mells. He's stuck posts and wire all over his big field to stop aeroplanes landing – his own idea and at his own expense. I can't understand why every soul in the country isn't hammering or digging or drilling against the invasion. The Army and Navy and Air Force are hard at it but the ordinary countrymen and women don't seem to do much. The tables are laden with food, taxis buzz about. Last war we never could get anything like petrol or meat or butter. We expect the greatest struggle ever known and possible catastrophe. We imagine it in every detail and in every horror, and yet we all seem as cool as cucumbers.

July 8th, 1940

Well my darling, I've just heard that you did not leave till Sunday afternoon.[9] What a late date. I wonder if you stayed on in Dublin or waited on the ship. In the old days when the world was like home, we should have been able to wireless to each other every day, now the sea is silent for all but wrecks and disasters. I have remembered too that I never warned you about the press reporters, who will have swarmed on to the ship on your arrival in New York. I meant to tell you to avoid them if possible, and if brought face to face with them to say the minimum with the maximum civility. However, it's too late now, though I cabled to Kaetchen to do his best. Reporters are nice boys if well treated, but I am fearful that English children arriving in the U.S. will be written up as indications that we expect to lose the war.

July 10th. This evening I dined with your old friend Mason[10] who had got a famous writer called Somerset Maugham who had

9   7 July.
10   AEW Mason, novelist.

just landed from the south of France off a coaling ship with no water, no food, no loo, no nothings. He broadcast his ordeals but I didn't hear it unfortunately. Papa tells me nothing. It's been a grievance for twenty years. Today Venetia[11] said 'I love the letters I get from Duff. I always feel they are addressed to me personally, though of course "Dear Madam" gives it away.' Only then did I learn that he sends a fortnightly letter to all people who by their position or profession see a great many other people, i.e. doctors, schoolmasters, clergymen, etc. I enclose one of them.

July 11th. A day of rage. All morning it was Mumble at Rottingdean, no lunch, debris-righting at Chapel Street. Exhausted and hungry I bought myself a strawberry ice cream at Gunters, also a strawberry tart in a paper frill, and took them to the house of Jimmy Sheean[12] so that I might eat them in company there. I found a German. Now a lot of yesterday I had been wrestling with the police and the Prisoners of War department under which internees come, in a great struggle to get some unfortunates liberated. My heart was torn by the poor alien anti-Nazi women whose husbands have been interned, and who are as demented as I should be if Papa were taken and I left, not knowing sometimes where they are or if they will ever connect up with them again. However, after half an hour's talk with the German so-called anti-Nazi man, I found myself wanting to intern him and all his kind for ever. He felt so violently against us for daring to intern him or any anti-Nazi and could not see that even though the innocent suffer temporarily we cannot risk a lot of the fifth column spies and Nazi propagandists *sent* as refugees to this country being at large, weaving insults to tangle us.

I left the house furious and when I got back to Dodgems[13] what did I find but all the air gone from my tyres. I bawled for the policeman who I saw walking away rather fast. He came back sheepishly and I

11 Venetia Montagu, very old friend of my mother.
12 An American journalist.
13 Her tiny wartime car – an Austin 7 as I remember.

asked him what had caused him to be such a brute. 'You should lock your doors,' he replied. 'If you will look at my doors you will see they have no locks. It's a 1909 model,' I said with pardonable exaggeration. 'Try and start it,' I said, 'here is the ignition key, get in and try and start it.' I had been to all the pains of taking out the distributor, which means plunging oneself into the engine and covering one's clean summer dress with oleaginous muck.[14] He apologised and looked guilty and ashamed, but that didn't help me. I had to telephone a garage and get a man with a pump and there was no vengeance that I could take upon the policeman.

July 12th. A further rage day. I wake up to find my letter to you written a week ago returned to me by the Censorship Office, because I had denied a rumour which is what we are told to do. The rumour and its denial are also in the paper. The censorship comes under the M. of Information so I am the boss's wife and wrote my name outside the envelope. I shan't do that again because I suppose they think they will not be considered thorough if they let my letters pass. Again furious and with no redress. The letter will have missed the boat and you will think I have neglected you. I hope you will guess what the words are in the heavy blackouts. I went to lunch with Winston. There, instead of it being four or five of us which is what I'm used to and which is like a holiday on a mountain for me, I found a large spread, with a lot of people I don't like at all, but the P.M. was his brave confident self and said that production was splendid and with America's help – and it was coming over in mass – we won't be beaten and we'll save the world yet.

I still continue to get letters from you and Nanny from different parts of Ireland. Thank her very very much – her letters tell me just what I want to hear and are very sweet too. I think about you and wonder, wonder all the time.

July 14th. Quatorze juillet. On this day 150ish years ago the tyrannous Bastille fell and the Frogs thought they had won freedom

14 The law required that – to frustrate possible parachutists – every car left unattended must be immobilised by removing the distributor head or by some other approved method.

for ever. Freedom takes a lot of maintenance. Yesterday I went to Ditchley and was greeted with the news of your arrival. Ronnie Tree had had a telegram from Jeremy. It was a real joy to hear of you in America and to picture Kaetchen on the dock, where I have so often seen his good dear face after long peering from the deck at the masses. Coalbox[15] was there and Noël Coward and your great-aunt Norah Lindsay, and a beautiful American called David Bruce, and Bobbety and Betty Cranborne. The country, which one goes to for a rest, is so much noisier than London. The planes are deafening and always it may be an enemy one. No one quakes. It's strange. One used to be told that the people in the Spanish Civil War got completely callous to the danger and I can believe it now.

The censorship had no more right to open my first letter to you than the policeman had to deflate my tyres. They have grovelled and in future I shall use the word parachutist when and how the fancy takes me. This morning I read with pride the enclosed cutting. You did very well, better than I would have no doubt.[16]

July 15th. Nothing happened today to amuse you or me. It rained in torrents and I got soaked to the skin in Dodgems because (a) it is not watertight and (b) I had to spend so long under the waterspout taking its appendix out. All the American journalists went to meet the Queen today.[17] Jimmy Sheean did a big personal reconstruction and Mr. Stoneman – whom I call 'Lava' because he said all Europe will shortly be lava – bought a new shirt and had a shave and a shine. They fell for the plump little siren as all men do, and I hope after all their efforts they impressed her.

July 16th. Jones writes from Bognor that the military – the licentious soldiery – are making havoc at home. They broke into the house too, but Jones thinks took nothing. They steal cushions and

---

15 Lady Colefax (see Directory).

16 On landing in New York I had indeed been surrounded by journalists. To the question 'Do you think England will win the war?' I was quoted, somewhat imaginatively, as answering with the words 'I am convinced that she most assuredly will' – which would have been an insufferable remark from a ten-year-old.

17 Queen Elizabeth, married to King George VI, mother of Queen Elizabeth II.

mattresses chiefly and then books. I so sympathise with both these needs that I can't resent their intrusions. I got a telegram from Raimund[18] and one from Henri Bernstein and one from Dorothy Paley all saying they had seen you and that you were well and happy.

July 20th, 1940

The blow[19] hasn't fallen yet – it's always to be next Tuesday or next weekend. Still, however, it is calm in London town and people go about their work and play with strong bright faces, and the inhabitants of the little houses that are blown to fine powder drink a glass of ale on the ruins. I saw this on the newsreel. I hope it's seen over there. It's an answer to those who say 'You don't *realise*.' One realises all right if one's house falls on top of one but one still smiles apparently, so why not smile before it falls? Great excitement as I write, the telephone rings and it is St. George's Hospital telling me to come and give my blood. I'm thrilled and only hope I shan't go green in the face and sweat with cold fear when the moment arrives.

July 21st, 1940

After lunch a lot of us went to Warner's Theatre to see *The Sea Hawk*, with your admired Errol Flynn acting a privateer's part. I expect you will have seen it. If not do, it's rather your affair. Papa is having a rough passage in the press. They got it into their hysterical heads that he wanted to put a stricter censorship upon them. He never did, but they went off the deep end and attacked him on everything – on the Silent Column,[20] and on you going

18 Raimund von Hofmannsthal (see Directory).
19 The expected German invasion.
20 A highly successful campaign designed to stop alarmist rumours.

to the U.S. Now that it is all settled and they know that they are not going to be muzzled and never were, they will think that their abuse and baiting have gained their point. It's a hard life, politics, and one must have all the things in 'If'.[21] Papa has most of them and is unaffected by bludgeonings but your poor Mummy has none of them and is not unaffected.

I've just come back from the hospital minus a pint of my rich blue blood. I was shown into a fine empty ward and led to a bed surrounded by screens. Now being an old hospital bird, I know that screens are put round beds only for the gravest cases and death. So that gave me a bit of a gasp but having just had a nip of brandy I was feeling in good heart and in good tongue. A young doctor came and pinched my forearm, and another one a bit older said 'How are her veins – nice and big?' 'No, I'm afraid they're very small' said the younger doctor. Now funnily enough I was glad they were small, in spite of the fact that being small they would less willingly release their blood. It sounded more charming, more graceful, more delicate, finer workmanship. Next they gave me an injection with a fine needle that doesn't hurt of novocaine which numbs the spot. Then into my frail flesh was jabbed a needle the size of a skewer which turned into a rubber tube that ran into a pint bottle.

They wiggled about for a long time to get it into the vein. Once it was in I had to open and shut my hand (*gi-me gi-me gi-me*) to expedite the precious flow. When the bottle was full it was corked up and sent to an ice box where it is good for three weeks. If we have a lot of raid casualties then they will have a good supply ready. Meanwhile they use what will not last on ordinary hospital cases who would before now have had salt and water dripped into their veins. Blood is much better for people who are desperately weak, collapsing or dying. They then bound my arm up, made me drink tea which I hate, so as to get the amount of liquid I had lost back into my system, and forced me to stay resting on the

21 Kipling's poem.

bed. At last the ordeal was over for good but their last words were 'We shan't need you for another three months.'

July 22nd. A letter this morning from Nanny. I was so delighted to get it. The ship sounds great fun – games – boys – no sickness – but no word yet of how you were impressed by New York. Also this morning the *Mirror* has a picture of you sitting on your pathetic bottom on your pathetic trunk – I nearly howled. You looked like all the refugees of the world rolled into one wistful little victim of the Nazis' Follow-my-Leader.

July 24th. Went to Brighton to see the paralysed Major.[22] Found him in high spirits. Owing to being in acute pain, he said. His blue budgerigar was pecking hairs out of his ears and talking to him incessantly. The visit passed in a flash. We both felt so gay, sipping sherry and nibbling chocolates and arguing about the Pope. Last night at about 1 a.m., when Papa was asleep and I was reading, a gentlemanly voice on the telephone said 'I'm speaking from Hoxton' (Hoxton is a sadly poor quarter of Greater London) 'and a great many parents in Hoxton would like to come and see you because they resent your having sent your son to America.' I was nice to him but cross in myself partly at the time of day he'd chosen to telephone and partly at the general injustice. I said I'd be delighted to see the parents and what day would he come. He chose a day and let me choose the hour 'between 8.30 and 9 a.m.' I said sharply. I thought he'd gasp a bit and sure enough he did. He wanted to think I wasn't called till noon and didn't of course know of the hard school of frozen legs greeting my waking moments at 7.30. He agreed reluctantly to the hour and I insisted that he should ring me an hour before the date, because in my heart I did not believe the thing. No one serious rings up at that hour.

July 25th. Another voice bawls into my ear at seven this evening that it is speaking from Deptford and that the parents in Deptford would like to come and have a look at me too. He knew about the

22 Maurice Baring.

man from Hoxton, so I said 'Do you know I was afraid he could not have been quite sober, ringing me up at that hour?' 'Not sober!' yelled the voice. 'Mr Wingfield is a teetotaller. He thought you were at the theatre.' Why not call before the theatre (which I was not at) or next morning? I said he could bring his parents. Both men suggested bringing fifty strong. I said I didn't see how a hundred adults were going to get into my small room but they could try, and there was always the passage to surge into. I don't know what I shall say to them and I'm really shaking in my shoes, as I stutter and stammer and gobble and gulp if I have to speak to more than two people at once.

The canteen[23] has folded up on me so now instead of having a happy afternoon tearing and bustling around giving and taking orders, the morning's telephoning goes on all day except when I go and argue unsuccessfully with the Home Office or the War Office or Scotland Yard. I try cajolery and blackmail and braggadocio and bootlicking and I'm only very seldom successful in increasing efforts to have men put in prison or taken out or children sent to New Zealand or Canada. Papa is attacked daily with great malice by my oldest demon-friend Lord Beaverbrook. He announced to a dinner party of his own adherent yes-men and to two outsiders who blabbed that he was not going to stop until he got Papa and the Minister for Air – Archie Sinclair – out of office. Papa weathers it well but it makes me sick and ill and sleepless all night and yawny all day.

Today I got a cable from Kaetchen about your going to school at Aikin.[24] I hope you will think I was right to say you had better stick to Canada. After all it's your own country, which in peacetime I wouldn't think an important factor, but in wartime an Englishman had better, I think, be in a country that is at war with his enemy, don't you. In Canada you will become a great skater and perhaps

23 She had been working every afternoon at a YMCA canteen.
24 A huge school in South Carolina. I don't believe the possibility of my going there was ever mentioned to me.

a second Grey Owl.[25] The U.S. will take you back for holidays. I should like it above all things, that way you'll learn about both countries. I don't like to look too far ahead because I want you back so dreadfully and so I don't want to envisage terms and holidays and more terms, all divided from me by a waste of seas.

I'll post this now and tell you if the hundred mothers engulf me or if they are just a hoax. Get hold of a typewriter when you can because you write with much great abandon on the machine, unlike everyone else.

July 27th, 1940

Darling Monster, the deputation of Hoxton and Deptford mothers never came. I fussed a good deal from 7.30 on but by ten I felt safe from the visitation. It's been a good day. When Papa came in he brought a letter from an unknown colonel who said 'Your wife has been the victim of a hoax. The secretary of the man who rang up and purported to be from Hoxton is a swine of a *nouveau riche*.'[26] Now I am dying for the hoaxer to ring up again, and I am going to say 'I am rather upset about what happened. I feel I ought to warn you of the danger you are in. What at first I took to be a joke, as you must have realised when I said I thought the Hoxton man was drunk, has now become through my talking and laughing about it a rather serious matter and quite out of my control. All Mr. Cooper's telephones are naturally tapped by Scotland Yard, and I have every reason to believe that they have traced you.' The other good news of the day was that the Queen has settled to adopt the Queen's Messenger idea which I sent her (not alas my own). It seems that special women with their headquarters in Buckingham Palace and armlets round their arm arrive at the home of anyone whose child

25 A pseudo-Red Indian (as we called them in those days) who lived on a lake in Saskatchewan and wrote several books about 'his people' and beavers. He was a hero of my childhood, but was later found to have been born in Hastings.

26 I don't know what this means.

has been killed or wounded by air raids and bring comfort, help, sympathy and a roll on which to inscribe the child's name, and some token from the Queen – like soldiers get medals.

There is a famous American called Wild Bill Donovan, who was a colonel in the last war commanding the 59th Division. (They made a film about him which you may see.) He was awfully good to Papa in N.Y. last time and gave him two or three dinners of representative men – lawyers, journalists, financiers, politicians, heads of enterprises, writers, everything. Now he has arrived in London practically straight from the President's arms, to see and report on how things are shaping over here. I asked him to dinner tomorrow and got Winston to come and meet him. The only fly in the day's ointment was when Wild Bill rang me up and said he simply could not get out of dinner with Joe Kennedy the Ambassador. I've heard since that Joe is in such a rage over his coming to England that he threatened to resign. 'If-he-can't-report-to-the-President-then-he'd-better-go-and-Bill-can-do-it-himself' line. So I've got Winston up from the country under false pretences, but he'll be just as happy and less strained.

July 28th. Dinner was a great success. Rex[27] and Caroline[28] came too, Rex with a tough military moustache. He says that there are not so many hairs, but each one is thick as a hedge, so they make a brave show. He was dreadfully funny about his agonies as an inexperienced subaltern of the Guards. He was told suddenly to form his men up and march them to church. Every order he shouted produced greater chaos, soldiers scuttling in opposite directions forming sixes and sevens instead of fours, or is it threes now? At last he found himself isolated in the middle of the parade ground. One day's more experience would have taught him when in doubt to say 'Carry on, Sergeant-Major.' Standing in a row to be inspected, he realised he'd forgotten his collar. The colonel inspecting felt it so apoplectically that he was robbed of speech, which didn't return to him till he came to the next officer, who got the whole blast of

27 Rex Whistler, the painter.
28 Lady Caroline Paget (see Directory).

blimp rage for having a loose shoelace. Poor Rex – he's not suited to the life. He can't paint, so he has no money at all because the little pay accorded to him by a country at war has to keep the wolf from his mother's door. This is a sad bore at the bar, and Rex likes a bar as much as you do and drinks of a strengthening nature a good deal more than you do, and now the tired youth has to pretend to like a glass of rain best.

I just turned on the radio and by ill luck got the news in Welsh. It was so funny, like this: 'Llanfair Duffcooper pwelliwin gegerereth duffcooper sinscreillio gogooth Duffcooper.' Torture, too, not knowing what they were saying about poor Papa. Poor Papa indeed, the papers get worse every day. He made a very very good speech in the House. I went to listen and he counter-attacked the press, which is bound to have the result of more mud in Papa's eye, but things will be better after this outburst, I am sure. Perhaps invasion will put it right.

Today England was white with German leaflets. Everyone delighted, because we love to see any inefficiency on the part of the Germans, and to think that they should go to the expense and danger of sending us only what we ourselves have published causes great rejoicing. Martin looked in this morning, all the better for having been torpedoed – at least he looked it. He is a captain now, so is Mr. Wu.[29] Charles, too, an exquisite grenadier,[30] often comes to see me. I thought it was love at first, but I'm not sure that it isn't for my petrol coupons that he comes. Dodgems is so abstemious that I don't use half my ration. Miss Marler is married to Mr. Wakefield, an engineer. She is Daphne to me now. Her husband has to open dud German bombs that drop about very often. The last one he opened was stuffed not as you might have thought with explosive matter, but with old Berlin newspaper. So someone in Germany disapproves of the policy of his country. I wonder how it seems to you, looking at us from the outside – very different from the inside view? I expect so.

29 Evelyn Waugh.
30 Unidentified.

Tell America we'll hold on all right with our arms and teeth and nails, but tell her too to hurry up. Always my grateful love to Dorothy, Bill and Kaetchen. Write often. Don't forget it's a hard world – in America one is apt to, especially staying with the Paleys. Your report has come. I'll copy it out for you next time. This term doesn't really count. Because the term was measle-term, but not keeping your mind on things seems your greatest crime. Tell Kaetchen to teach you concentration. He's failed with me but you are younger.

August 4th, 1940

Your godfather Lord Beaverbrook was yesterday made a member of the War Cabinet. From the hour of his promotion he changed his tune about Papa. Orders from his boss, no doubt, to cease bludgeoning a colleague. The sheepish press will take his lead, and so the assault I hope is over. Today in the *Sunday Pictorial* is a Duff Cooper ballot – a coupon to be cut out and sent back to the editor. There is a picture of Papa as a debauched criminal and the coupon says 'He gets £5000 a year for being Minister of Information. Do you think he should hold the office? Yes or no.' Now only cross people who hate you or are indignant fetch a pair of scissors, cut it out and buy a stamp and send it off, and those women who are in love with you, but they are very few. The large majority who are quite satisfied with you and think the press is making a fool of itself always and anyway just dismiss the idea and of course don't look for the scissors. So today I started buying *Sunday Pictorial*s at the street corner – never more than four or six could I get. Suddenly at St. Pancras Station I found 240, so I shamelessly bought the lot and shall send them scissored and enveloped to friends to send in. It probably won't make any difference because by next Sunday Hitler may be here, or interest may be quite dead, or anyway they probably don't play fair. For all that I enjoyed collecting them on a Sunday. It was like digging for gold – so many disappointments and then striking a seam.

August 5th. A lovely long letter from the Cat[31] this morning and one from George · Moore* enclosing a photograph of you and him and Kaetchen on the top of the Empire State. You look very happy and indeed the letters tell me how good and nice you are. It all sounds like a fairy story for you, and I am as jealous as a prisoner. Today is a Bank Holiday and I never realised it. Business as usual, the shops open and hundreds of gentle-ish-men with their coats off digging in that patch of earth opposite St. George's Hospital. The Battle of the Press versus Ministry of Information is completely over. Olive branches are waving everywhere. Papa has won, but he must see that this does not happen again. We always knew the Ministry was a hideous shapeless chaotic mess and a lot of people are being sacked and one can only hope the new ones won't be worse.

I lunched with the Cranbornes and dined with three American journalists – Sheean, Helen Kirkpatrick and Mr. Robertson representing *P.M.*[32] here. We went to the Players Club and to the Savoy and to a flat, jabbering and drinking till the small hours. Papa meanwhile was jabbering and drinking with sixteen English pressmen, chiefly editors who had been abusing and insulting him, guying him and spitting ink in his face for the last ten days. This 'get-together' meal was arranged in the height of the fight by Frank Owen (*Evening Standard* editor). They all told Papa what a good chap he was and that they approved wholeheartedly of the snoopers[33] and that all newspapers used the method. All of which makes me think most journalists exceedingly low.

August 6th. More squaring of the press today. A dinner party in our sky [eighth floor] sitting room for Lord and Lady Camrose, owner of the *Daily Telegraph*, Lord Ashfield too and Shakespeare Morrison (Postmaster General). Eight of us, and I ordered grouse – half each at fantastic expense as it's the first day of shooting,[34]

---

31 Kaetchen (see Directory).
*   See page 254.
32 An American evening newspaper.
33 'Duff Cooper's Snoopers', allegedly employed by my father.
34 Grouse shooting had begun a week earlier than usual.

and then Papa brought Crinks Johnson (Department of Trade) in as a ninth and with a mouth drooling like a retriever dog's I had to say 'No' to mine. 'O no, thank you, as a matter of fact' swallowing the mouth-water with squelchy noise, 'I never liked grouse.' Papa told us of a man, an English aviator he had seen, who had been obliged to bale out and as he got near the ground he could see only guns and shotguns pointing out of every hedge. Tortured by fear he guided his parachute, in the limited way one can, to the bang centre of a cornfield hoping that would give him a little time, but no, on landing there was an old farmer a few yards away drawing a relentless bead upon him and a soldier following up. He had a horrible feeling that something was behind him and flashing an eye round saw a burly man with a large iron railing in his hands, just about to crown him with it. He managed to convince them he was a friend and not a foe, but the farmer was so disappointed he kept his gun aimed at the unfortunate, and went on saying 'I'd like to shoot your bloody head off!' I dread to think what would have happened to a Polish flier in our service with at best a few words of German and a flood of Polish. 'Dead for a ducat', as Shakespeare would say.

August 8th. All the people I love and respect are longing for the invader to come. Your poor Mother was never as brave as that. I would rather victory was achieved by famine and revolt in Europe than by hideous hordes in England. The people sing and hammer and swear that here at last the enemy will meet with a new and devastating experience – defeat. Good, but still the war goes on, and they write their loss off and call it a preliminary skirmish. That august man I went yachting with in '36[35] says he thinks every soul in England is *mad* not to see that we are doomed. Well, maybe.

August 10th, Sunday. I went yesterday to consult Mrs. Massey (wife of Vincent Massey, the High Commissioner for Canada in this country, brother of Raymond Massey the actor) about your new life in Canada. Upper Canada College, Toronto, is your destination, poor puppet. I think though that it sounds good and that you will be happy

35 The Duke of Windsor.

there. Milo[36] and probably many other English boys will be there, and everything they told me sounded right for you, but of course it's only hearsay, so you must promise to tell me exactly how you feel about it when you get there. I know that you are good and naturally happy and brave and good at making the best of bad jobs, so I shall believe and approve your judgment and move you only if after a real effort to adapt yourself you are unhappy.

I fear my letters are very dull and uneventful. Coming from the war, they should read much more blood and thundery, but it's only outside this inner fortress of London that the air is disturbed. We live on 'report' and thank God we believe it. Daily the battle intensifies. 'Is this really [the invasion]?' is the commonest question. One dares not hope that it is. Tonight Papa and I go to Woodford, a town in Winston's constituency, for a large meeting. It is in Essex, though not quite in the front line. Still it's a likely place for a dive-bomber. He'd catch a few thousand people closely packed, plus that old warmonger your father. The best answer to be given to Papa's attackers (and remember it in case of need) is – those that Hitler hates most are Churchill, Duff Cooper and Eden. Judge from this fact how far they should be trusted.

Monday August 12th. We should be shooting grouse over bonnie purple heather today instead of stewing in offices, but the poor birds paid their debt to nature and sport a week ago. It shows when such traditions break that there's a war on. They didn't bomb us last night at Woodford. It was a terrific to-do – the band and the Mayor in scarlet and his aldermen and his mace, and the Home Guard, and the V.A.D.s and A.R.P.s,[37] all in procession, and crowds in thousands. The speech relayed to crowds outside the hall and everyone cried and cheered and yelled 'Good old Duff.' We drove home in brilliant moonlight through the suburbs to the heart of this strange city. It doesn't seem strange any more – as

36 Milo Cripps (see Directory).

37 VADs: members of the Women's Voluntary Aid Detachment; ARPs meant Air Raid Precautions. It was never normally used in the plural, as here. She must mean Air Raid Wardens.

normal it is to me as the lights and Rollses and the displays in shops seem to you in N.Y. I lunched with Rex Benson[38] and Lesley. He had been around inspecting foreign troops and he told me (what was news) that we have part of the real Foreign Legion in this country – wonderful troops, he said, as highly disciplined as the Guards and of every nationality – many Germans among them. The Poles are next best, Belgians worst, Dutch medium. I went next to Olympia where I was told help was urgent. The Free French are billeted here – the free and the keen-fighters. The 'free anti-fighters' are at the White City, huddled and bored and frightened. I found nothing to do except to sew tricolors on to the shoulders of new arrivals, speak French to them in my inimitable way, sell them toothpaste and bootlaces, and promise to procure two girl-friends for two particularly nice very young Frogs. I shan't go again, not enough doing.

There are two schools of thought in England about the invader's reception – shall every man and woman shoot to kill and poison and trap and snipe and stab in sleep every Hun they come across, or shall only the Army and the Home Guard deal death? I'm for the former method of ending the war, though whether my courage would stand up till the end I can't think. I think the majority think my way. Another poor airman falling in a home ditch found an old woman with a scythe bearing down on him – Dame Death no less.

August 15th. Lunched with Oggie,[39] where I saw Cecil Beaton just down from a north-eastern town where he'd been photographing. He was sent there as being one of the towns most harassed. He was surprised to find how little damage there was – only two-storey houses that crumple and crumble into such fine debris that wonderfully few people are hurt even if they fall upon them. No military objectives, no big buildings. He'd been too to see the patients in hospital and moved me to tears by telling of their fortitude and

38 Brother of Guy Benson, husband of my mother's sister Letty.
39 Olga Lynn (see Directory).

cheerfulness. One poor woman had had her daughter killed and was rather badly hurt herself. She started to talk of it to Cecil, and the nurse said 'No, Mrs Brown, you know you mustn't think about it.' 'No, I know I mustn't,' she said and changed the subject. Everyone is self-disciplined and even sorrow is checked.

I took Bloggs[40] and the farmer[41] and Katherine Asquith to *Thunder Rock.*[42] It's the fourth time I have seen it. Tell Kaetchen – he will laugh at me as I have so often laughed at him for the same idiocy. That was yesterday. This evening was quite another picnic. At 7.30 the farmer and I were sitting in my room talking about a course of guerrilla warfare he is to take next week at [*censored*]. (Too funny thinking of Conrad on all fours in a ditch or dropping sugar into petrol tanks when not observed) when he said 'There goes the raid warning.' Some people, though sharp-eared, can't hear a bat – it is out of their ear's register. I have that peculiarity when it comes to air raid warnings. I took his word for it and down we went to the lounge. I fetched out the dispatch case with the diamond dolphins and trembling diamond spray and other precious stones and essential papers and passports, £200, powder, rouge, brows and lashes, a comb – but forgot book, knitting, gas mask and tin hat. It didn't matter because it only lasted a quarter of an hour, but I was ashamed of my lack of method. The lounge was full of quite gay[43] people ordering tea and cigarettes. A few street-sters came in and many freaks came out of their rooms for the first time. Even the elevator boys said they had never taken them up. I suppose some went to the shelter below but I think very few. Wadey was in her element, all smiles, and went up first to the roof before taking to the cellars. When we all got back to our eighth floor Wadey pointed out an enormous column of black smoke about ten miles away. I don't know yet what it was.

---

40 Wyndam Baldwin (see Directory).

41 Conrad Russell.

42 An intensely anti-isolationist play by Robert Ardrey, starring Michael Redgrave.

43 In the old sense of the word, of course.

This raid happened on a day when I could almost have welcomed a bomb to destroy me utterly, because at five minutes to midnight I had said, to please Desmond MacCarthy[44], that I would broadcast in a programme called *And So To Bed* in which people read and comment upon a favourite verse or piece of prose. I settled that I would give them the *Battle Hymn of the Republic*. It pleased my own American complex of love. I thought twenty lines and the five verses would last five minutes all right. Papa wouldn't or couldn't help me so I sweated in blood to put the twenty lines together. When at last I thought it could go at that, I found that reading slowly it took just two minutes. I tore off to the shutting London Library and got a life of the authoress and against time dug out of the two fat volumes two episodes that I hoped would pass muster. At 11.45 I was at the B.B.C. with my pathetic script rustling in my moist hands. No sooner had I got to my studio on the third floor than there was what is called a 'purple light' – almost the red which means 'take cover' – so down we went to the basement studios. I swear to you that I was longing for the purple to turn red, in the belief that such trivial talks as mine would give way before Government directions. The light didn't change, so I was for it. I can't tell you how it went – I think not badly, anyway I made no boggle or splutter, and my tongue though too big for my mouth did not twist.

Papa listening at home said it was all right, but Wadey asked me what programme I'd been on. I told her and she said she'd listened to the news at 12 but she hadn't heard me. I said she must have. She said no. She'd heard a woman talking about the war but it wasn't me. I let it go, but of course it *was* me but I suppose the old rasp was quite unrecognisable – all to the good.

August 16th. The column of smoke was, they say, a scent factory – somebody's Lavender Water. Good, I say, but not so good if one thinks that some of the sensational conflagrations our airmen see as a result of a successful bomb on German soil may be eau

44 Author and critic; an old friend.

de cologne only. I went to see a man at the Ministry about getting some rooms in the actual building for me and Duff to live in when he said 'I'm afraid that's the warning.' I began to be frightened for my hearing – again I was aware of nothing. The whole million souls who occupy the M. of I. all trooped down to the basement, where the big boys conduct business as usual. One dreads, curiously enough, once reasonably safe, not bombs but boredom, and the fear that it may last four or five hours. There were tin-hatted decontaminators, Red Cross nurses, fire-fighters, all grades of A.R.P. Papa was sitting in a soundproof room with his big shots around him and fifty telephones and maps and signals and lamps and gadgets. He might have been conducting a war from G.H.Q.

I got some friends to talk to and was jabbering away when a male voice shouted 'Quiet please.' Silence followed, and then 'All firemen upstairs.' Of course I thought the bomb had hit us. Next order after the jabbering was again quieted was 'This passage to be kept clear for Red Cross ambulances.' Corpses next, I thought, but it was the All Clear next, thank God, and so far no news of anything dropped.

The M. of I. has put out a new short film to encourage the sale of War Savings Certificates and you will be glad to hear that the cast consists of Mr. and Mrs. Ramsbottom and young Albert.[45] Albert sells everything he's got including his beloved stick with the 'orse's 'ead 'andle to buy savings certificates, and then he gets so bitten with the idea that he sells his father's 'smoking set' and the stuffed birds from the parlour. Stanley Holloway says the words and you never see Albert's face actually; only the back of him is shown and very unlovable he looks.

7.30 same day. Just had our second raid warning today. It's most tedious but I'll get used to it. This time I happened to be in Chapel Street so I dropped into No. 34[46] and joined Daisy and Claud Russell and three foreigners – nationalities indistinct

---

45 *Albert and the Lion* and other verses by Marriott Edgar were superbly read on the old 78 rpm records by Stanley Holloway, in a strong northern accent.

46 The house was now occupied by Daisy Fellowes.

– in our passage shelter. Daisy has filled it with green linen mattresses. It looked like a little Arabian room and we sat cross-legged and smoked and ate chocolates. We were there about an hour and it was wearisome in the extreme. Londoners will get used to it like the people in Dover have, and when they do life will just go on as though nothing were happening, but the orders of taking cover have been so drummed into us law-abiders that we suffer the ghastly waste of time and acute boredom to boot.

August 17th. I went to see poor shrivelling shrinking shaking Mumble at Rottingdean today. I took my tin hat along. The high white cliffs are bristling with guns. I can't see how even the Huns are to scale that height of chalk. I fully expected some excitement but got none and saw nothing. I found myself unwilling to hang about the stations, so made a bolt in and out of trains. The thought of the glass roof falling on one is so unpleasant.

No fighting today. I think it's a shade ominous, but the general spirit here is one of victory and Londoners seem pleased to have received their baptism of bombs. The provincials and bumpkins can't jeer at us for being scrimshankers in cotton wool any more. Papa broadcast this evening. I couldn't hear it because I had a dinner party downstairs here, thirty-two-strong, for overseas officers. I took my little receiving set to hold to my ear, but Ursula[47] put it out of action by dropping it within five seconds of my asking her to hold it. The overseas high-grade officers had a great time. I got lovely women and famous men to meet them and we are to do it twice a week and have different hosts and hostess at each, but it's quite exhausting.

I read this letter to Papa and he says you won't understand one word of it. He got me so discouraged that I thought I'd tear the damned thing up, but I don't think it's so obscure and Kaetchen can help deciphering and explaining.

August 18th. Two air raid warnings today, but we rose above them and sat lunching in the Chapel Street garden for the first one and

47 Lady Ursula Manners (see Directory).

did not leave our roof sitting room for the second. There's a completely demolished house with only its garden gate intact. The owner had stuck a collection box on it with a sign saying *Fund for Spitfires*.

August 20th, 1940

I enclose my broadcast, not that I'm in any way proud of it but that I like you to know as much as possible what I am doing so that we may not lose touch with one another. It's so easy with a waste of seas between us. Space makes faces and memories dim as well as time. Please to remember this and not forget me when you are in Canada and if you were as Scotch as your grandmother you could say this poem. The author is unknown and it's lovely, I think, and bad Beaverbrook's favourite:

> From the low sheiling of the misty island
> Mountains divide us, and a waste of seas
> Yet still the blood is strong, the heart is Highland
> And we in dreams behold the Hebrides.[48]

22nd and 23rd were days of maddening internee trouble.[49] All my time and all my patience get exhausted. I suppose, if I live, a harvest will be reaped one day. Papa and I are like slum children about going away for a weekend. It's about two months since we saw the country (I don't count the Mumble visits). Tomorrow we actually go to Lavington.[50] I believe it's a curtain of fire but heavens we're all so brave these days.

24th. Big day. It's the hols! It opened with a bang or rather

---

48 The so-called 'Canadian Boat Song' has been attributed to half a dozen different writers, including Scott, Hogg and Lockhart.

49 She was desperately trying to arrange for the release of refugees – mostly Jewish – from Germany and Austria who had been interned on the Isle of Man and elsewhere.

50 Home of Euan and Barbie Wallace.

with a siren shrieking its soul out like a baffled banshee. That didn't last long and at eleven we were off in Dodgems, who's taken on a new and speedy lease of life since I spent 17/6 on her. England looked most lovely. Every child seemed to look like you to my hungry eye, corn being lifted, trees and hedges heavy with fruit and berries, dahlias and hot-coloured flowers, bees and flowerpots – no country for vile invaders' feet.

Once at Lavington one might as well be in a hive. The planes (nationality always unknown) buzz around one like bees. Very high though tiny silver midges that one wouldn't see in peacetime because one wouldn't peer so hard. After lunch Papa and I set off for West House.[51] A raid was on but then it always is. The first thing I saw grinning like a jackass was Mr. Uncles.[52] He genuinely felt you were missing something. 'Wouldn't John just love it,' he said about forty times. 'There's a German plane lying at Rose Green and another in Pagham harbour. They haven't dared go near 'em for fear of delayed action bombs. The dead Germans are still lying there. Smell something frightful they do. Wouldn't John just love it?' I felt he was right because anything that makes me feel sickish you like so much.

Then we went on to the house. We found it undamaged by soldiers, but O the Prom![53] It's a fortress. It's Carcassonne. I suppose there are forty blocks of concrete about four feet square and five feet high almost meeting right along, with just room for a gun between each. It seems to be the only part of the coast really fortified. I was alarmed, but impressed and proud rather. Mr. Uncles must get it photographed for me to send you. The Joneses were being themselves, dreamy and pleasant. They are like Adam and Eve, I think, splendid gardeners and loving of each other but they have learnt nothing of the past or progress or science. They'd never seen electric light or a tap when they came to us, and he looked aghast when we asked him if he had

51 Bognor.
52 Our local newsagent.
53 A long stretch of grass dividing our garden from the beach.

a Kodak or if he knew of anyone who had. I might have asked him if he'd got a gyroscope on him from his expression.

Like you, drawn rather to the horror of the smell of dead Germans, we thought we'd go and look for them in Pagham harbour. When I say we – Papa dragged behind like a tired donkey – we walked along the dykes round the water. It looked so beautiful and desolate and untouched by human hand, no stacks, no cars or cottages, only reeds and gulls and tough grass. The All Clear siren rent the air and wailed off, adding to the idea of peace and purity. Suddenly we found the broken monster. No dead Germans, only a sad torn sock to show that men had brought it to this quiet field. Contorted and twisted, not a bone intact, it looked more like a mutilated brontosaurus than a super-modern weapon of death. Back to supper and bed, and a night punctuated by guns and bombs, none of which I heard, thank God.

25th. At crack of dawn Barbie and I stocked up the mobile canteen with forty dozen cakes, matches, cigs, tea, lemonade and Wrigley's[54] and stamps, stationery, and soap – and bumped off very slowly to the airfield [Tangmere]. I was a bit nervous but didn't show it, and when I saw it my heart stopped. It is conceded that it has had a 'dusting' from the enemy. Not one hangar has missed that duster, and when a hangar gets an explosion of course it looks far worse than a house. It's large and thin and empty with no floors or thickness or beams or concrete, and it just caves in. Well! The place was a shambles, but yet it has made absolutely *no difference* to the working of the aerodrome. The planes were of course *not* in the hangars and they lost a few, a very few testing bombers, and surprisingly few people, and they were all as perky and gay as be damned. It's great fun, the mobile canteen. I should dearly love to live at Lavington and do it daily but we know that I can't desert Mr. Micawber. You bump round from group to isolated group; as they see you coming thirty men rush at you as

54 Chewing gum.

they would for the last bus and fall on the tea and doughnuts and cigarettes. These are the 'few' that many are so grateful to.

At one outpost the loudspeaker suddenly blared out something. I feared it would be 'Enemy aircraft above' but instead it was the new awards given to that squadron for valour, endurance, courage, wisdom and the rest of it. I liked hearing that so much. They cheered from their hearts and guts. I must say that with aircraft perpetually swooping down and taking off, etc. and with perpetual appalling explosions due to dynamiting the damaged hangars, one was perpetually in and out of one's skin. Billy Wallace was on the field with the canteen for the dusting. They popped him into a trench and put a board over him and there he stayed crouched for an hour. They all think the work dreadfully tiring but compared to my London Y.M.C.A. it's a rest cure and fun and beautiful and out of doors, and no jam or egg or marge or knives to scrape and clean.

That night the Wing Commander C.O. of three squadrons came to dinner. He is known as the 'Phizzer' and a phizzer he was. I like him awfully – complete confidence in the world, the war and himself, but no side or swank – that's a great combination. One of his squadrons had brought down seventeen that afternoon with loss of one, the squadron leader himself who with a shattered wing rammed into a Messerschmitt and into certain death. After dinner the butler came in to say a raid was on as usual and also a gas alert. 'What do we do now?' was everyone's question, so no one did anything. Bombs fell in the distance but I need hardly say I didn't hear them. Surreptitiously I slid out of the house and groped my way in total blackout to Dodgems where I sneaked the gas masks out. Wadey had fastened the most inappropriate pink chiffon flower on to mine to distinguish it from Papa's. No more was heard of the gas. Rumour had it that it was coming in from the sea. This sounded too fantastic to swallow, so to bed we went.

August 26th. I motored up alone and when I got to Cobham the policeman stopped me and said 'There's a raid on, you know' (I needn't tell you that I hadn't heard the warning). 'What do I do?' I said. 'Optional – you can proceed if desired or take shelter fifteen yards ahead in the public shelter.' I was torn between wanting to see a public shelter so as to tell you about it, and not wanting to be late for a quiet lunch with Papa in our room, so that he might have a siesta afterwards. He sleeps so badly, not of course because of bombs but because of his office and his scurvy critics.

You will be proud to hear that the old funk 'proceeded' in her muslin dress, with now a tin hat added, and Dodgems had the road practically to herself. I ran out of the raid at Kingston. One knows a raid is on by the fact that the traffic almost stops and everybody is out of their house Johnny-head-in-airing. When the All Clear goes, back they go to their dinners and off puff the cars again. We got through the afternoon all right but of course in the middle of dinner it all began again. I was dining with Coalbox and about ten other distinguished guests. The servants are sent to the basement and the guests serve the food. The raid got quite forgotten. It reminded me of an old friend of mine, long dead, called Harry Cust.[55] He was having a men's dinner, Bernard Shaw was there, and H.G. Wells. His house caught fire. The engines arrived and soused the house. Dinner went on. They sent for bath towels to put round their necks against the drip from the upper floors. The house burnt merrily. H.G. said 'Where's your fiddle, Harry?' It's all told in one of Wells's books, *The New Machiavelli* I think.

August 29th, 1940

My birthday and a sweet telegram from you to wake me, one from Kaetchen too and some flowers from Hutchie and some more from Euan and a cartload from brute Beaverbrook. Last night we had one of our overseas dinners and at midnight Papa gave me a £100 note. Of course it has to go straight into the pile I'm collecting to pay the taxes with, still it was nice to handle it for a short while. A raid was on from 9 p.m. till 4 a.m. but we paid no attention

55 At that time I had no idea that he was in fact her father.

and I slept through the All Clear. The sirens go so incessantly that one gets confused as to which went last.

August 30th. We had a nice dinner with H.G. and Bedbug and Erica Mann[56] last night and a long sleep and no warnings, though I heard the intermittent drone of the enemy wing all night. Phyllis and Juliet[57] got a big bomb about fifty yards from them and are atrocious bores about it. No one wants to hear of other people's bombs. Only one's own interests one.

Raids twice today. The second found me for the first time in a shop – John Lewis's – trying to buy a purple felt. To my horror I discovered that unless one tore to the door one was locked in until the All Clear and that the nervous pedestrians are locked *out* of the good shelter. There must clearly be changes. All arrangements are made of course for a devastating knock-out raid and not of course for these sc-air [scare] raids, but things will get adjusted. I lunched with Hilary[58] and drove him back in Dodgems to his club in Pall Mall. As he got out with fearful difficulty something happened that only happens in the cheaper kind of music halls – an undiscoverable nail in the dilapidated upholstery caught his threadbare alpaca pants just exactly where he sits and tore three sides of a square exposing a yard of shirt and a great deal of real pink flesh. Poor old man – on the steps of his smart club too. I could not follow in to sew him up either. The indignity was complete. He had to limp up a long flight of outside steps with in one hand a whacking shillelagh and the other spread across his shameless behind.

Papa and I left London to the tune of the siren in our pram,[59] filled to brimming with trunks, books, gas masks, tin hats, guns and cartridges, my yachting cap and a Mexican sun hat. It was raid warning till we got to High Wycombe – everyone at his doorstep, an army of A.R.P. men with tin hats and armlets appear

---

56 Daughter of the German novelist Thomas Mann.

57 Juliet Duff (see Directory).

58 Hilaire Belloc.

59 Dodgems, which was about the same size as a pram.

like the dragon's teeth did out of the ground. Planes overhead but one can't tell what's Jerry and what isn't. No gunfire. We came at last to Milo's house, where were only Fred and Violet Cripps and Maureen Stanley. A night free from sirens but the dark skies buzz always.

August 31st. Such shameful shooters I never saw. There had been of course talk of an early start. Partridges fly better early, but they didn't muster till 10.30. They dragged themselves out about eleven. At 12.30 Violet came to me to say that a message had come − would we fetch them home in cars? We came upon them in some stubble, each dragging one weary middle-aged foot behind the other. Papa might have had a swim in the Serpentine. His thick tweed jacket was *drenched*. It's rather pathetic. For a year now none of them has had any exercise at all. Fred sits in the N. corner of Scapa Flow in an office without a friend. Papa hasn't left London till last week since I can remember. They fell on their lunch and put the afternoon's shooting out of their heads for the rest of the day. Maureen Stanley, Papa and I then came on here − Ditchley. Air activity as usual, but I have had a very happy pre-war day going round this lovely country swishing into other people's drives.[60] A nice American from the Embassy called Butterworth produced unlimited petrol. I was really quite happy and forgetful of the war. Tomorrow Papa is to shoot again and leave afterwards for the London front in Dodgems. I'm sad that the holiday is over, but I'm hoping to return next Sunday as Papa has a speech to make in Oxford. The country is laden with fruit, the branches bow, the fields are very dry and the stubble yellow.

September 1st. The air activity is frightful in these parts but no warnings, which makes a delightful change. The English don't know when they're beaten. That's why they win − ignorance is bliss. All this is a prologue to the announcement that in the middle of the Battle for Britain, Brendan[61] has bought himself a country

60 A weakness of my mother's. She could not see an open drive gate without swishing into it to have a look at the house to which it led. It was this habit of hers which led to her discovery, a few years later, of our house at Chantilly.

61 Brendan Bracken MP.

house. I've long had my eye on it. The poor old sweet is very ill with antrum and sinuses, black decay and pus pockets, and squirts and nose-blows and general bloat and sleeping dope. He is thin and pale and his blazing pate is silvered. He was so excited about his new acquisition and we had to motor for two hours across country without signposts to see it. And at last there and showing the garden and rooms and river, I could see that he didn't like it any more, but that's human nature. He'll like it again the next time he's there.

September 2nd. Papa has to speak on the Children's Hour programme. I've never seen him more hot and fussed and sleepless over a speech. I wonder so much if you'll hear him. The Empire will, but perhaps not the U.S.

September 3rd. Drove all the way home through an air raid. I didn't like it. One's mood makes one brave or jittery. All Clear at noon and no guns. A nice letter from Hilary not referring to his trousers, but none alas from you.

3

'Only one thing matters – not to
be overcome'

My darling Mummy and Papa,

I do so hope you are still well and happy. I am writing this on that memorable 15th of September, my birthday, and the first I have ever had at school. Isn't it awful? What is worse I am not allowed out this weekend. Apparently I shall have to have an enormous birthday cake for tea and ice creams.[1] Still, it is Sunday and we are going to church, and so I think it will go quite quickly. I hope so, anyway.

We do not seem to be doing much work yet. Just arithmetic tests and the reading of the Iliad, which the masters don't seem to care about. They just say 'Read the Iliad' in the tone of voice which doesn't seem to mind whether you like it or not. But still, it is not for me to talk yet, as we have not properly got into the term so far.

There is a sweet shop on the school grounds and it absolutely ruins me as it is about the only thing to spend money on and we are allowed 25 cents a week.

I have lots more to say, but I shall have to stop as we only get ¾ of an hour to write letters in, and now we have to go to church.

Lots of love,

John Julius

---

1 I dreaded birthdays as a child, finding them acutely embarrassing and hating being the centre of attention.

M y parents had devoted much thought to the question of my education during my absence in the New World, and since my father's heart was set on my going to Eton in September 1942 it was decided that I should go to school in Canada, where the curriculum was based on the British model. The Preparatory School of Upper Canada College was finally chosen; accordingly, after a happy summer with the Paleys and their two small children in Long Island and in Maine, in early September I was put on the night sleeper to Toronto. The pattern was henceforth established. School meant Toronto; holidays were always to be spent in the USA.

But this chapter is not about my schooling; it is about the Blitz on London; and, as a description not just of the event itself but of what it felt like to have to endure it night after night, it seems to me that it could hardly be bettered. And the letters never lose their humour. October 20th, 1940 is, I think, a case in point.

━━━

September 5th, 1940

This is my first letter to Upper Canada College and I hope to heavens it will still find you as happy as can be expected. The first day, even weeks, must be a bit difficult but you have always met obstacles and disappointments and troubles of all kinds with a smile, and I think you will always do that. Keep it up and remember that if you are really unhappy things can be changed.

I'm dreadfully tired. Last night I never closed an eye. I went to dine at Coalbox's. We were ten strong and after dinner she had the highest class of what is called chamber music – a violin, a viola and a piano. At nine the warning went and I felt a little jumpy on account of Box's house being as frail as a pack of cards, and Queen Anne[2] cards at that. We hoped the music, Bach and Handel and Mozart, might drown the bombs. It was stifling hot with windows blacked out, and clothes sticking to our backs and behinds and legs. We sat with rapt musical faces but every time the thud of a bomb was heard, we'd all surreptitiously give each other a meaning look and being timorous I would sweat a little more. I left about 1 a.m. There seemed to be a lull in the noises.

I got home by taxi to find Papa fast asleep. I undressed in the dark and dared not turn the light on to read, which would have encouraged sleep to come to me. The All Clear wouldn't go and the wakefulness was supported by the watcher on the Dorchester roof walking up and down so very near my head. It kept me aware of how little covering there was above us. At five the All Clear blazed away and I thought 'Now I'll sleep', but within a very few minutes heard a salvo of bombs and shortly after that the old wailing warning started again. At 6.30 the All Clear and at nine another warning. It's exhausting if you are not fear-proof, as we should all be by now.

We lunched with old Hilary who never mentioned his trousers and later Papa went to Oxford on a job and I motored myself down to a house Barbara Rothschild is living in nearby. Hutchie and Mary were there and we had a cosy evening, occasionally breaking talk off to listen to the unmistakable intermittent drone of a German plane high overhead. When the devils fly over us they desynchronise their engines. This makes it much more difficult for the detectors to pick them up. We do the same over Germany, so both countries can recognise the enemy by its broken buzz, like a much more drawn-out telephone 'engaged' signal. I slept

2 The house was in Queen Anne's Gate.

soundly till 9.30 because of not fussing about whether Papa was sleeping soundly. And now it's

September 7th and I'm at Ditchley again. Papa met me here. He'd been discussing the propaganda of war aims and the future with Professor Toynbee at Oxford. After dinner the butler came in and said the Home Guard was being called out. Talk and games continued and Ronnie Tree went to telephone to Oxford. He came back with about as long a face as you can pull without it breaking and said 'It looks like the real thing this time. The Home Guard is called out and the church bells have been told to ring[3] by the code word.' Nobody seemed to believe it much. Papa got on to the over-calm Ministry who said they knew of no invasion. Many parts of the country had had the order and it was a mistake. The London docks had had a knocking about, and the raid was still on. Now I'm in bed and I've just broken a valuable lamp, and so that is weighing on me as well as the war. I'll have to confess my clumsiness to the hostess in the morning. O dear O damn.

September 8th and a bad news Sunday. The raid last night as you will have read was on a far bigger scale than we have had before – damage and death and fire and I fear much agony. Hannah Hudson, the wife of the Minister of Agriculture, who lives at the gate, has heard that her little house in Smith Square has collapsed. The two maids in the basement she spoke to were quite unharmed and unflustered. Chapel Street may be a heap of ruins for all I know with your little barrel-organ and my ski-boots hanging incongruously from a beam. I went to church by myself. It was an Intercession Sunday with prayers against dismay and cowardice and many other things, but I prayed hardest against those things knowing my need of their opposites.

No alarums or excursions this Sunday evening, though Randolph's wife[4] straight from Chequers told me that invasion

---

3 This was the agreed signal for the expected invasion. A code word would be circulated by radio and all the church bells – silent since the beginning of the war – would start ringing.

4 Pamela Churchill, later Harriman.

was fully expected now, that Saturday night there was every indication, including isolated parachutists. Four Germans too had arrived in a rubber boat and said they were going to fight for us and that they abhorred Hitler and all he stood for. We were just going to take them to our bosoms when parts of a powerful receiving set were found on their persons. She told me the Ministries were to leave London – this I *knew* to be untrue so after that I didn't believe anything she said. Mrs Hudson's boy arrived to say the house in Smith Square had *not* crumbled to pieces, only glass and doors broken, but the brand new French Officers' Club in the same square, also the Melchetts' house, were no more.

Sept. 9th. Another appalling raid in London last night and it's there I'm repairing today. The days have an autumn nip in them and a later sunrise – cobwebs and dew and a yellowing leaf – all too beautiful and always cloudless. London looked just the same. Conversation is restricted entirely to bombs. Phyllis has had her pathetic house burgled in the blackout and all her furs, her rat-coats and cat-coats and stoat and weasel coats and tippets all taken. What *will* the thief do with them? I had a dinner party tonight for the American Ambassador – Oliver Stanley and Jean Norton[5] and Pam Berry and Hutchie and Jimmy Sheean. There's a bad A.A. gun just outside that bangs away and bombs drop *all* the time but our talk drowned some of the noise and a glass of wine gave me a bit of Dutch courage. It's really not the place to sleep, the eighth floor. I never closed an eye but Papa sleeps like a baby in a pram. One hears that vile machine and the whistling and the thuds and then one starts waiting for the next and counting the watch-out man's steps overhead. I cannot bear to look out of the window. There seem always to be great fires in a dotted ring all round you. The All Clear goes when light comes, and at last one sleeps for an hour and then one looks out on to the next day and there are no fires and one cannot believe so much can have gone on and yet so much be standing.

5 Lord Beaverbrook's mistress.

Sept. 10th. You are at school now, you darling child. I do hope
it isn't too bad and that you are seeing it as an adventure. Anyway
you seem to have had the most glorious summer and mind you
write an enthusiastically thanking letter to the Paleys. Here there
are five or six raids a day. One copes with them fairly well. People
say 'you know there's a delayed bomb in Montagu Square or
Buckingham Palace' or 'Lansdowne House has gone – hadn't you
heard?' One could bear it better if one could see any end to it.
Of course it's there – the end I mean – but one can't see it yet.
Is it the beginning of an invasion scheme or is it just to break our
spirit? It won't do that. The taxi man who took me to Liz's[6] house,
the windows of which have gone, said with a grin from ear to ear
'There's nothing left of my home. This is nothing.' I agreed it
wasn't much but I felt as the glass was out I'd better get in and
remove anything good she might have left.

You would have laughed to see me and Rex carrying out his
clothes individually and stuffing them into Dodgems, scarlet slippers and collars and shiny pumps dropping about and a bouncing
billycock and scattering single socks. Liz had only left some lovely
linen so I stuffed that into a huge linen basket and put that on to
Dodgems's roof which is slightly rounded so Rex had to hold it
steadyish with his crooked stick stuck through a chink of the newly
discovered sunshine roof. There was a big row tonight between
Papa and me undressing and in different stages of nudity. The gun
was banging away outside, and the thuds were hideous to hear and
I said we *must* go down to the basement. I'd always meant to all
the day and had taken precautions to stop arguments such as 'I
haven't got a suitable dressing gown' by buying him a very suitable
inconspicuous navy blue alpaca one with dark red pipings. 'I think
you're too unkind' I'd say, pulling off a stocking. 'We *can't* go
down, I'm too tired, besides it doesn't make any difference where
you are.' I was beginning to cry and to give in when the guns gave
a particularly violent salvo and the look-out man popped his

6 Lady Elizabeth von Hofmannsthal, married to Raimund (see Directory).

tin-hatted head in at the door saying excitedly 'You're advised to take cover.' That was a break for me and it settled Papa, who then donned the new robe with the slowness of a tortoise and down we went. I'd arranged with the management that if I did achieve my purpose we could have two rest beds in the Turkish Bath. So there we lay in comfort and in my mind much greater security. There is the nice friendly noise of the dynamo that makes the electric light or the air conditioning or what not that drones on all the time and you hear practically nothing else and I had a wonderful night and feel much better.

Today, Sept. 11th, Ursula came panting in early in the morning, pea-green in the face and utterly whacked, but grinning and cheerful. She is a nurse in Battersea Hospital and has had a gruelling time. She had not been to bed for three nights and the bombs had been clustering round them in their efforts to hit the power station. Last night a delayed action bomb fell beside them so all the patients had to be evacuated to another hospital, and once done she had twenty-four hours to rest. She's a fine good girl and so is Caroline, who is driving a stretcher ambulance all night and picking up casualties from the seat of the disaster.

September 11th, 1940

Well there it is, my darling little boy, whatever your troubles are in your new world and your new school tie it doesn't really compare with ours, but I'm praying and trusting that you are coping well. This London front is a bit wearing but we make out as best we can. Papa and I sleep in the Turkish Bath and that is the nicest bit, because the air-conditioning dynamo makes such a nice *Enchantress* or Clipper noise that you can't hear the bombs and hardly our own big Hyde Park gun, which once above ground blows your head off. Still, we are all encouraged by its bombast because we feel it's some kind of answer, and the noise exhilarates. Everybody is exceedingly brave. Caroline drives a stretcher-bearing car and is out in the thick of it. She lunched with me today and I put her on my roofy bed and she slept like a bear in winter all afternoon. She looks so lovely and is so brave that a lump in my throat stops me telling her of my love and admiration.

September 12th. We had raids all day today. Papa and I had to lunch at the Spanish Embassy. I felt there was no choice, although the bombs were an excuse for not attending, but to offset that I felt Englishwomen's honour was at stake, the Spanish women having risen above dangers for three years. The big restaurant and the grill at the Dorchester where people have eaten since the beginning in, as they thought, relative security have just been discovered by the clients to have glass roofs with nothing above them. So the eaters have now been put into the heart of the ground floor. I have got nothing to grumble about really, still I do a good bit of it. Tomorrow we leave the front line for two days' rest and I'm looking forward to it madly. What stories I shall have to tell when it's all over. Nobody who has been through it will listen to me, but you'll get an earful.

Sept. 13th and a Friday. Invasion seems very probable but on this ugly date both sides can't be unlucky and we have a stronger hope than they have. It seems fairly certain to come. 'But when will it bee?' said the bells of Stepnee. 'I'm sure I don't know' said the Big Bell of Bow. Poor bells, they don't say it any more. Their tongues are held till the parachutists come, but it's what they *would* be saying.

Sept. 15th. It's in a way worse to watch London from a distance. Always I have felt superstitiously that as long as you keep your eye on something you are keeping it safe. Now that I'm away I imagine it being blown to pieces without my protection. I realise how dreadfully the papers must read over there with one's imagination to colour the hideous news. When one is in the heart and core of it one is so taken up with getting through with it and holding on and it being less bad perhaps than one feared, that one doesn't see it as a whole.

It's your birthday and I can't send a wire till tomorrow and you will think that I've forgotten your entrance into this hard world, and all the happy birthdays we have had. I haven't really, but things are sometimes disorganised – though wonderfully little considering. Telegrams are one. Everyone telegraphs to ask how their relatives are, and the little offices can't deal with the flood, so I must wait to get to London and a Western Union. Anyway let's feel sure that next year can't be as bad as this and that we shall be together and laughing at past anguish as we light twelve candles.

Sept. 16th. A raid needless to say in progress. I've discovered how to find out when one is on, since from a motor car one may well have heard no warning. All the policemen (who now wear tin hats with 'Police' written on them) and wardens carry their gas masks on their chests instead of on their backs. In the Dorchester hall they have it written up in large letters, either AIR RAID WARNING or ALL CLEAR.

I had to lunch with Coalbox in the house of cards, and the guns were blazing away and she wanted to go down to the basement, and the guests wouldn't because they knew they'd be no safer there. H.G. Wells was bawling away about God and Noah and the parlour maid was fixing boards up over the windows. After lunch I tried to do a few jobs but everything shut down and there's nothing to do but go home and write to you.

Ursula rushed in to say her Battersea Hospital had folded up on her – too many bombs and delayed bombs strewn all around, so the patients were evacuated for good. She's going straight into St. George's tomorrow. She's a good girl. Ministers have been told that the intensive bombing expected for several weeks (!) should alter Ministers' hours, and meals should be earlier, entrance to their quarters earlier and sleeping underground advised. This order lightens my task. Mr. Bonn the manager now tells me secretly that the Turkish Bath, in which I'd felt as secure as the good earth, was none too safe – nothing much above it – and that he proposed to put six or eight of us into the gymnasium when it's fixed up. How long will that take? He's managed to disturb my nights again. When will one learn to think less about one's own skin? Soon I think, but I'll always fuss about Papa's. He is so very foolish, while you I think will look after yourself and really have much more sense.

Sept. 17th. A terrific night of bombardment. A bomb fell in Park Lane not fifty yards away, another blew all the glass out of Berkeley Square. Papa has just gone to the meeting of the House of Commons. There's a raid on as usual and I'm terribly afraid of the Huns bombing it and getting a rich bag. They have a double warning and on the second one they dodge down to the shelter but Brendan has just told me that the shelter is made of paper. It's 4.45. Winston should have just begun to make his statement. I do hope he cuts it short.

September 18th, 1940

I hope you are happy. No news yet from Toronto. A nice letter from New York after the World's Fair. I wonder if they let you do the 'Parachute Jump'. I fear not. I would have let you, with my new doctrine of 'Fear nothing'. I wonder too if you did the 'Bobsled Run'. That I did with Papa and adored it, and he was so appalled and terrified by it. When I think of you in your brave new world I forget for a few moments our struggles here. They are pretty trying. One sleeps very little and that makes one more jumpy than if one felt more rested. At 11 p.m. we go down to our Turkish Bath cubicle and from this underground den the guns are much deadened, but a bomb gives us a good shaking and there's no more sleep for me. At six the cleaners come in and turn on a blaze of light. 'That's good,' I say, 'they can't have hit the power station.' Sometimes at that hour the lift isn't working and a long procession of exhausted blear-eyed men and women, weighed down and impeded by armfuls of pillows, eiderdowns, lilos, dogs, water bottles, jewel cases, night conveniences of all kinds, drag their way up flight after flight. It's eleven flights for us, but we have little paraphernalia, and one is so thankful that another night is past and the sun rising and the sky for the time being free of the enemy.

Thursday September 19th. We are getting so dreadfully tired of the inmates of our hotel; it's getting fuller and fuller and one must always dine in, as to get home means a shower of shrapnel even if one misses the bombs. Anyone sleeps anywhere. Hutchie and Mary came last night to dine, pyjamas in hand, and dossed down in the lobby of a friend's suite. The mews that we looked out on when standing at the buffet at weddings in Audley Square[7] has been bombed to blazes and I found poor Ursula struggling with two Hungarian maidservants, all the back windows of the house glassless and the basement full of rubble and damage. We got a pantechnicon with great difficulty and parked all the furniture and pictures and rugs and Ursula herself into it, and off to Belvoir.

Friday Sept. 20th. Last night we dined with a lot of Froggies and Madame Curie and M. Palewski, an ex-politician, all violent de Gaullites. The guns and bombs and orchestra and people's jabber deafen and bewilder, and the more you try to escape the danger and noise of war with light and music and food and wine, the more you think of the East End and the homeless and the fires raging nearby. Comfort we have to find in the argument that only one thing matters — not to be overcome. While the Huns are turning London's heavens into hell they are not doing much harm to our factories or war production. Therefore unless our resistance breaks, and there is no chance of that, they are wasting their pilots, their ammunition and their confidence.

Meanwhile we try and collect mattresses and pillows and rugs to put into basements for the homeless and the workers, and thousands a day of children and mothers are being got out of London. It seems so absurd that when we got all those congested areas cleared into the country last September we should ever have allowed them to go back to the slums. 'Couldn't stop them' is the answer, I suppose, not without compulsion, and we are so

7 The Rutlands' London house.

loath to do anything by compulsion. Even now they are unwilling to go, and act very strangely when they get to the outer country. At Mells for instance ten or twenty women arrived at noon. They had been all night in the train, four hours in a church at Frome four miles away during the early morning, and the first thing they asked Katherine was 'Is there a Lyons[8] here?' When she said 'No' they gasped and said 'What, no *Lyons*? How often does the bus go to Frome?' 'Twice a week' they were told. Well, believe it or not, no sooner had they swallowed their dinner than half of them walked the four miles back to Frome to get back to streets and see the shops. Another twenty arrived at Daphne Weymouth's and asked for shelter. Although her house is packed already with evacuated crippled children, she said she would manage somehow and tore off to the local town to buy them blankets and pots and stoves, etc. £8 she spent and when she returned staggering under her load, they'd all gone – vanished and no word left in explanation.

Sat. Sept. 21st. Last evening at five I suddenly thought why should we have a hideous night unnecessarily? Loelia Westminster has a house on the top of a Surrey hill about an hour away from London, and so we buzzed down. It was further than we thought and night fell and we got lost in little lanes filled with fast-moving lightless lorries. At last we were in a wood with soldiers holding shaded lanterns. They asked for our identity cards and there was a general fumble and fluster. I was so happy. Nothing mattered once out of London. The house loomed out of the blackness and we felt in sanctuary and went to bed at eleven and slept till eleven the next morning. Loelia says we can stay if I sleep on a sofa, so Papa has gone up at cockcrow and will come down again this evening. I don't mind so much not being near in the daytime. It's the night that I know he will not take cover without me. The day is a blaze of sun and blue. I feel like a child, full of peace and joy. To think that there are two days ahead and two long nights. Of course I don't say

8 A chain of cheapish restaurants.

that one can't hear old Jerry overhead if one wakes, but the smell of the Surrey woods, and the space, and no wounds or gashes to be seen on this very wide landscape, make one feel full of life and love again. Papa came back all right and now it's Sunday.

September 22nd. I've had another long night. I've written a letter to Nanny and one to the dear Kat and it's still pouring with rain, but I wouldn't mind if it was snowing ink. Anything, anything not to be in London. I don't think I shall ever want to live there again – never – never. Eve Curie told me that she had been on a tour with Lady Reading to all the provincial A.R.P. shelters. All the little children of five have Micky Mouse gas masks. They love putting them on for drill and at once start trying to kiss each other. Then they all march into their shelter and sing 'There'll always be an England'.

September 23rd. Back again in London, to find our Ministry has been repeatedly hit last night. We motored up in the early a.m. all dew and sun and peace, and now the siren has gone and everything is hideous again.

September 29th, 1940

I couldn't keep up my daily letter this week. Things have been too disturbed – too many sirens, too much noise, no possibility of concentration. Now I'm relatively out of harm's way and will try to remember what happened. We were anxious and fretful about Dakar.[9] It was a big failure and we must make the best of it. Poor de Gaulle is a smirched flag, but perhaps we can hoist him again. If you look from my top window at the Dorchester you can't see anything wrong with our London, but walking in the streets is more melancholy. 90 Gower Street is no more. Papa says it's thoroughly gutted. I won't go and look. It would make me too sad. Buck's Club also was said to have 'gone' but is mendable. John

9 The Navy had landed at Dakar (Senegal) in an unsuccessful attempt to detach the local French authorities from their loyalty to Vichy France and get them to declare for de Gaulle.

Lewis and D.H. Evans and Peter Robinson are burnt out. There's a big gap in Dover Street through to Albemarle Street.

The East End is beyond anything – quite demolished. A good thing if it wasn't for the sad inhabitants. We are getting basements going in the West End for them and the people in the ministries now sleep where they work – three nights a week they work almost double hours and after three days go home for three workless ones. This means less danger for them getting to and fro, fewer hours wasted in shelters and less congestion on the buses and undergrounds which are now public shelters at night. Families go in at about five with bedding, babies, buns and bottles and settle down to community singing, gossip, making new friends, exchanging bomb stories. I should rather like it together, but can you imagine Papa's reaction if he had to join the party?

There is a nice story being told this week of a letter coming from an English prisoner in Germany. It said 'I am having a wonderful time here. The prison is most comfortable, not to say luxurious, the food is excellent and plentiful. We are treated with every consideration and kindness. I should like you to tell all my friends that and the Forces too. Tell the Army, tell the Navy and R.A.F. and above all tell the Marines.'

All my supports are leaving. Jimmy Sheean has gone. H.G. Wells has flown to America. Somerset Maugham does the same tomorrow. We had our first night in the reconstructed gymnasium this week – eight nice little beds behind screens, all the camels and horses and bicycles and rowing apparatus removed. Unfortunately it has a hollow wood uncarpeted floor and three swing doors with catches on them, and the room is treated like a passage. I never got a wink, but Papa was the proverbial log and had sheets and a table and a lamp. No one else had a lamp. The next night a great improvement took place – a carpet to muffle the many fewer footsteps. Conversations are conducted in whispers that take me straight back to childhood and to you. Sir George Clark asking Major Cazalet if he knows what the time is etc. No one snores. If Papa makes a sound I'm up in a flash and rearrange his position. Perhaps Lady Halifax is doing the same to His Lordship.[10]

Between 6 and 6.30 a.m. we start getting up one by one. We wait till they have all gone. They each have a flashlight to find their slippers with and I see their monstrous profiles projected caricaturishly on the ceiling, magic-lantern-wise. Lord Halifax is unmistakable. We never actually meet. It's certainly more pally in the underground. Nothing seems disorganised, and in shops and in food there seems to be no difference at all. Taxis and cars are everywhere. Tin hats are like jewels, but they'll be purchasable soon. Mine (stolen last week) has been returned. Bertram[11] is brave as a lion and is loved by all beautiful women and sensible men. They have put up a plaque in St. Paul's to an American called Fish who was killed fighting in the R.A.F. It says 'To an American citizen who gave his life that England might live' or something like that. I thought it so moving.

Friday was a horrid day. At 9 a.m. the siren went and was followed immediately by a bombardment of guns. I was out of bed and halfway down the stairs in a flash because I heard above the blast and shock of the guns an approaching thunder of squadrons of aeroplanes that could only be German. Pam Berry had a room on the first floor so I sought sanctuary there and ate a couple of eggs and drank some coffee. They brought 133 down that day and I think I saw one being despatched to its death. I certainly saw a machine trailing a cloud of smoke, miles and miles above and obviously losing height. Later that day I was at Molyneux's buying a dress to spend the entire winter in when the same thing happened again and down the lot of us scampered, very quickly too, into the basement. Bridget Paget who works there tells me that really and truly the alarms, sirens, bombs and guns do not affect her at all, at all. She sleeps alone in her house and sleeps through it all and has no sense of fear. She ought not to be working at Molyneux in that case but sitting instead in the tail of a bomber

---

10 Lord Halifax, Neville Chamberlain's Foreign Secretary.
11 Bertram Cruger, an American friend of my mother.

and getting bars to a V.C. We came down here[12] to get a rest from the raids for two nights, but as bad luck would have it, the brutes concentrated on Surrey last night and the droning of their infernal machines kept me awake most of the night and bombs fell right and left without however doing much damage.

I have such acute bombitis of the ears now that if my inside rumbles I jump out of my skin and think it's air activity, which indeed it is.

I got a lovely letter from you (the second from school). You sounded cheerful and happy, and I love you for it. There'll be bad moments for you. There are bound to be. Bear with them, for they get right. Send postcards to the Paleys and to Kaetchen. Are you allowed a typewriter at school – if so ask Kaetchen to send you a cheap one at my expense.

You can't think how much I love you.

October 1st, 1940

I've had a wonderful letter from Nanny all about your school. What a good time they gave her but now she has left you, poor monster. It was very wrong of whoever told you that the Dorchester had been bombed. It was quite untrue. We've only had an incendiary bomb on the grass in front of it, which left a lot of black burn. It was said to have landed on the roof and been dealt with by the look-out man immediately, but incendiaries don't count if there is someone there to bury them in sand, or anyway I could find no black patch anywhere.

Today, October 2nd, we moved down to the fourth floor and I shall feel safer in the daytime. At night I feel quite secure in the gym and sleep like a log. A man called Sir Hugh Seely had a birthday party on the first floor and we all got very merry and enjoyed ourselves. Tomorrow Maureen Stanley gives another one,

12 To Loelia Westminster's house.

and I'm quite looking forward to it. The guns bang in the daytime now, but that's the only difference. At night Jerry isn't quite so active in the centre of London. Sometimes the All Clear goes in the middle of the night and some idiots trudge up to their upstairs beds and get comfy only to be woken an hour later by a siren and trudge down again. I wish, I wish it was all over – Hitler defeated, the lights up again and the guns still.

October 3rd. I'm crippled with lumbago, which seems an additional fleabite to all the troubles. Maureen's party was enjoyable enough. General Dill, the C.I.G.S. (Chief of Imperial General Staff), was there and I sat next Lord Halifax, who although I share the gym with him I seldom clap eye on. He was not very inspiring and told me all the things I know about Winston – how like a boy he is, etc. etc. He said too that he had read a telegram from Switzerland (I discovered later it came from Carl Buckhardt) describing the tortured state Hitler was in – moody and depressed, seeking always seclusion, antagonistic to his advisers, whom he now blamed for having turned him from his instincts and his astrological belief not to pit himself against England. It was encouraging to hear, but I seemed to have heard it very often before. Papa dined at the Other Club,[13] which I don't like because I hate him going about with the air thick with shrapnel. He won't put his tin hat on. I do always when the guns are giving tongue. It looks awfully funny with a silver fox cape, but soon they'll finish the modiste's trade.

October 4th. I walk across the park now at 6.45 a.m., lumbago and all, past the Achilles statue. The railings are all down and the ground is deep in leaves that have fallen fast this year. It's cold but it exhilarates me after a night below ground. I walk as far as our garage, and pick up Dodgems and go on to the Y.M.C.A. canteen. At 11.30 I come back and read the paper and letters, and go out to lunch. The days are terribly alike. I've brought the picture

13 A political dining society founded in 1911 by Winston Churchill and F. E. Smith.

of Noona by Queen Victoria and myself by Sargent, and the wax bust of Nelson, and the ivory ship and two photographs of you and one of Noona, so the new room looks a bit more personal. Send me all the snaps you can and don't marry before I see you again.

October 5th from Lavington. We came here last night and Papa has gone up to London for the day. It's the same story – one comes away from the bombs, but they rain round one just the same in the country. This morning I went out with the mobile canteen to the airfield again, not Tangmere this time, another one. It's lovely because the R.A.F. men rush the van and are jokey and grateful for hot teas and doughnuts, Mars bars and fruit gums. One whizzes round to lonely men sitting solitary in a pillbox with an anti-aircraft gun. 'Me and my gun's they are called, and it must be gloomy for them now and in winter it will be hell. One lot headed by a middle-aged Pole (now a Royal Engineer) has been put in a disused lunatic asylum, so the poor creatures are literally behind bars and we have to push the buns through the cage and shove the mug underneath through the wet grass. The Pole was a winner of the Davis Cup tennis at Wimbledon.

October 7th. Back in battered London. It is such a beautiful day. What is so disgusting about war is that when the sky is clear and peaceful and utterly heavenly, one says 'We ought to get a lot down today.' This time last year you had come for the first time to Westbury Manor and I was dreadfully unhappy in London pasting paper on windows, packing up treasures and thinking of America. Be happy and hard-working, be good and above all truthful, my darling John Julius. I had a letter from Dorothy Paley and one from the Doll[14] and they both talk of you as John without the Julius. I do wish they wouldn't.

14 Iris Tree, my mother's oldest friend (see Directory)

October 10th, 1940

I've given up writing every day because my days are so horribly alike and dreary. They always start at 6.30 a.m. and now it's pretty dark at that time. I don't get home much before twelve and lunch with a friend. Sometimes a few bombs fall in the morning and that I dislike most. In the evening we dine with people or people dine with us, and Papa wears a face of utter and acute boredom and hates every minute of it. Then there is the night with Lord Halifax in the gym, and 6.30 begins the next. We go away Saturday to Monday to escape the bombs but generally get them just the same. This week we are going to a little house taken by Maureen Stanley west of Windsor. She says it's very nice and very cheap and the only house in England not yet taken. There is obviously something very wrong with it. We shall see. I wonder whether you would notice very much difference in our part of London if you could see it. I think you might even be a bit disappointed in not seeing more devastation. When a house is hit it looks as bad as anything you can imagine – just matchwood and crumbles and feather-fans and loos still sticking to the wall of the next house, but no *street* looks the least demolished.

*October 14*th. Well, we saw what was the matter with Maureen's house. It was practically on an airfield and a target for bombs. The first night three fell about half a mile away and shook me and the house to bits and last night one fell just outside in the lane and blew the whole of Maureen's bow window away, and I, believe it or not, never woke. I'm thankful for it.

October 15th. Another shocking night in London last night. Hutchie arrived to take up his quarters in the Dorchester. His room bursts into my sitting room, so perhaps he'll buck me up a bit. He certainly was bursting with buck at dinner last night. He'd had a tremendous drive through bombs and barrages from Liverpool Street to Park Lane. Piccadilly was blazing, he said, the Pavilion Theatre too and the Carlton Club. He seemed to think it all most exciting, but it merely made me want to be sick. All afternoon I went round the demolished pieces of Pimlico and to schools and other buildings where homeless people are put till they can be billeted in other houses, or sent to the country. Mr. Coombs, Papa's political agent, was my guide and spared me nothing. I was quite happy to talk to the people and hear their stories and wonder at their serenity and stand aghast at their sincere desire to stay in London and not be evacuated, but I didn't see why I should have to look at the craters and the ruins. Mr. Coombs appeared to think it was a treat and probably you would have thought the same. The truth is I don't like realities. I like dreams and snows and plans for the future and storybooks and music and jokes. Best of all though I love you and Papa and you are both realities, so my argument collapses.

You talk of my coming over, but I don't see how I am to. God, how I should adore it. If only Lord Athlone would go home and Papa got made Governor General of Canada; you might start praying for that, though I can't see what in the world would take Lord A. home.

Tuesday, October 14th, 1940

Hutchie has moved in and is a great solace to me. His chambers have been bombed, also the beautiful Middle Temple Hall. In this most exquisite room the first performance of *Twelfth Night* was given in front of Queen Elizabeth herself. Every day something beautiful is destroyed utterly. What can we do to stop it? I sent a telegram to Kaetchen, my traditional helper in all trouble. I told him to get a suggestion to the President that he should appeal to the Pope to advise the belligerents to cease from this idiotic bombing of capital cities, the demolition of which will gain neither capitulation nor advantage to either side. I know that Rome and the Vatican are particularly terrified of destruction of their national monuments. The Dorchester stands up well so far. The water flows well, whereas at Claridge's no one has had a bath for a week. Gas is said to be off, but it is unnoticeable as they have substituted coal fires and the food is improved by it.

I can't remember if I told you about my unfortunate experience when the Westminster Hospital asked me to run round and give a pint of my good red blood for transfusions for the wounded. Three months ago I did it at St. George's with no pain and no trouble. This time they advanced upon my poor arm with a needle the size of a big blunt bodkin. I asked humbly if I was not to get a little injection of pain-killer first. 'No,' he said, 'it only means two pricks instead of one.' I did not dare insist. For more than a minute he shoved and pushed and thrust completely unsuccessfully to get the needle into my vein. The tears ran out of my eyes in torrents. 'Does it really hurt so much?' said the Dr. but I couldn't answer for tears. At last he had to give it up saying that the vein had probably closed up after the last draining and he'd try again with another one in the same arm. I could just say 'Couldn't it be the other arm?' and 'Couldn't I have a drop of novocaine?' So I got it and all was well and he drew off what looked like a bottle of burgundy. He comforted my shame of breaking down by telling me that everybody's nerves were very much affected by the raids and reacted quite differently to three months ago. Still my burgundy would be used that very night, so I felt it was well worth a flood of tears. Tonight I dined, none the worse, with Lord and Lady Willingdon – fine tough old birds out to S. America now on a mission, about sixty-five and seventy-three they are and they don't give the bombs a thought. They came out to dinner tonight (one of the heaviest bombings we have borne) he in a white waistcoat and she in purple satin, and they sleep in their own beds in their own bedrooms – no tin hats, masks or fuss.

Wed. 17th. The canteen still has no gas or water and the frenzy of giving 400 men breakfast is pretty funny. There is a huge 'hunter's moon' that lights my 6.45 walk. I look a bit queer and wish the moon wasn't there to show me up – brown shoes, bare legs, the old blue Navy coat, old *Enchantress* cap with yacht-club badge in front, and only a spot of very slap-dash make-up applied in the dark for fear of waking Papa, who tumbles into bed the moment we get up from the gym to our own bedroom. He tries to keep his eyes shut all the way up.

I lunched with Barbara Rothschild. She told me of how she had given her parents a really good shelter, gas-proof, reinforced and equipped with beds and comforts. Shortly after they had taken it into use, Hutchie came to her and said 'Um-m-m I want you to say something to Mary. I daren't speak to her myself as she'll fly into such a white rage, but really I can't sleep in the shelter if she goes on snoring that way. She's just like an old man.' The same day Mary came with exactly the same complaint – she never got a wink because of the appalling snorting and snoring and gulping and porpoising that Hutchie kept up.

Thursday Oct. 17th. Last night I dined about fourteen strong and sat next the Free French Admiral Muselier – rather an attractive man, I thought, full of humour and interest. He looks a ruffian, very dark with a funny feathery growth of black fluff on his high bald forehead that gives him an unshaven appearance. All the French say he is a ruffian and a crook and everything else against him, but no Frenchman ever had a word of good to say of another one. De Gaulle has never spoken to him.

Wadey and I worked like blacks packing Papa's books.[15] No book shop would do it because they can't use deal cases, so we are making paper parcels and packing them into a van and sending them direct to Belvoir (that is if the bombs give us a chance and a little time). Chapel Street still has its windows unbroken, though a large piece of shrapnel went through the skylight in the passage behind the library. None of my excellent ideas are accepted, and my latest is against these land mines which come down very slowly on parachutes. I suggest that they should put some very strong magnates [*sic*] in open spaces – parks and even squares to which they would be attracted. Perhaps it's impossible.

Papa has just rung me up to say he's dining at 10 Downing Street, which has put me into a fever of course, as it means the

15 They were in the library of 34 Chapel Street.

sirens will go any minute. It's just seven so that he'll have to drive home mid shot and shell. I talked to a huge Grenadier private soldier this morning at the canteen. I was laying ten tables against time and he liked the sound of his own voice. The outcome of it all was that he wished he was back fighting in France. He hadn't been frightened there, but in London, boy oh boy, he couldn't stand it. It made me feel quite heroic.

Friday October 18th Papa came home all right at about nine, as Winston dines at seven in a little blue sort of workman's overall suit. He looks exactly like the good pig who built his house of bricks. It wasn't a bad night because of mist and fog. It seems to have put them off a bit. Someone has urged indiscriminate bombing of Berlin, but Winston argued that 'business should come before pleasure'. Conrad came up today and Venetia, and at five we are to go to Loelia Westminster's so I've come to love a Friday and be terrified of something interfering with my departure.

October 19th. Ewhurst.[16] We got here and O! the peace and O! the dear mists of October which cloak that revealing moon. We had a lovely night with hardly the buzz of a plane, but Papa got up early and went back to the front and came back at tea time. It's hot and lovely and the woods are all copper and gold, and I went faggot–collecting and really felt quite serene for a few hours. I got my letter from you. I'd like to hear more troubles and who is nice and who is beastly and what you like most doing and what you hate most.

October 20th. A lovely summer's day. I was able to enjoy it. In the evening the other guests played bridge and I went to bed early. The planes were buzzing unintermittently overhead and I got more and more lonely and more and more wishful for them to come up to bed. So I got up and crept along to the room over where they were playing and gave one tremendous jump. Instantaneous effect. One of them immediately came to the door, came upstairs and looked round to see if anything had been hit by an incendiary bomb. Finding all quiet, for I had scuttled back to bed, he went

16 A large house in Surrey. I am not sure who was living there at the time.

down again. I left it for a quarter of an hour and this time took the biggest jump safety would allow from the top of the table to the floor. That brought the lot up. I pretended to be asleep and I heard Papa say 'It *was* bombs. Diana is asleep.' I never let on.

October 30th, 1940

I've neglected you this week, not because I haven't loved you as much as ever but because my days have been so terribly taken up, canteening from dawn till lunch and packing Papa's books in a hundred cardboard boxes all afternoon. I come in utterly exhausted, as the siren goes and just as I settle down to write the room fills with Hutchie who talks without drawing a breath. Phyllis looking funnier than ever now that the war allows her still more latitude in dress, Hubert,[17] Maureen Stanley, Eve Curie, some Frog gentlemen. Jean Norton also exhausted from canteen work and asking for a bath, Baroness Bedbug asking for a drink, Bertram, a few journalists from America, etc. Papa has got such a sickener of the restaurant and insists now on dining upstairs in the sitting room with two or three guests. It's awfully expensive and the guns bang away and make me jump. We've got four or five women dressed as real soldiers too – Monica Sheriffe[18], Lady Carlisle, Violet Cripps, Mrs. Carnegie. One huge one is dressed as a Khaki Highlander with kilt and knees. Sometimes the place looks like a barrack of women.

At the weekend we got away to Ditchley and had a most difficult drive. First we started late and then found Western Avenue utterly jammed up on account of a bomb having just fallen on the bridge, so after endless detours the blackout came upon us. Then I missed the difficult turn off the high road and we got completely lost – no signposts, no light in the houses, no one but evacuees to ask, who of course couldn't know the way. The climax came in the last lap through a forest – one couldn't see the demarcation of the road and

17 Hubert Duggan, her lover
18 Family friend, great lover of the Turf.

there was always the trunk of a tree looming up on the car bonnet. One curious new thing we saw – namely an enormous red light, like a timberyard on fire, lighting the whole sky and horizon. It would die down to nothing and then blaze up again in a sort of rhythm. When we came up near to it it turned out to be a sort of ten-foot-high lighthouse, sending up a blaze of red light every minute. Later we were told it was a mobile 'decoy' to lure German planes with.

Sunday I took a motor canteen to an aerodrome. It was a heavenly day. The country was as brightly coloured by the autumn as a parrot and I felt almost happy – no planes but our own, and the R.A.F. so gay and encouraging. The news never gets any better. France joins the Axis. Italy attacks the innocent Greeks. They won't bomb the Parthenon, I suppose, for fear of the Greeks bombing the Colosseum. Why should every capital but ours be respected? The French were so terrified of Paris being destroyed that it helped their collapse. The other countries think most of their capital and forfeit the future to present the past.

Liz's house having had all the windows blown out has now had an incendiary upon it. I went there yesterday. Never have I seen anything so dejected. Luckily there was practically no furniture in it, but what there was and the carpets are soused in a porridge of soot and water – quite irreparable. Poor Liz. Still, lucky she wasn't in it.

Soon it will be Christmas. I hope you will have a lovely one with the Paleys. Too many presents – last year I thought there was a glut.[19] They were too tired of opening them to go on. I wish O God I wish I was going to be with you. I want you to have a typewriter. I did write it before to you or Kaetchen, because you write me longer and funnier letters with a machine than you do with your poor fist.

The van takes the books to Belvoir tomorrow, thank God, and then I shall start the diary method again. A bomb fell at the feet

19 She and my father had spent Christmas with the Paleys during their American lecture tour.

of the Abraham Lincoln statue and only twenty yards from me in
the canteen. I didn't half jump.

> *November the 5th, 1940*
> *(please to remember it)*

They are electing the President at this moment. I pray to God
Roosevelt wins. I've come to think of Willkie[20] as Hitler's
candidate, more especially as we hear he is backed by Lindbergh
and Ford and Father Coughlin.[21] I wonder how excited Canada
gets and if the U.S. frenzy spreads over the border or across the
Great Lakes. You never tell me of these things. Do please try to.
I can't get back to my nice diary ways. I never seem to have a
spare minute. It's that fatal early rise, and no leisured morning
in bed with telephones and pencils and newspapers and the cold
cold legs of John Julius. Instead the cold cold street, gashed with
mutilations and this morning a cold cold rain to walk through
and the darkness of midnight.

After I got what proved to be nearly four tons of books off to
Belvoir on Friday, I had an ecstasy of achievement and relief.
Friday is such a good day anyway, as with any luck we shall leave
this dreadful city by five, and last Friday we left and went to Barbara
Rothschild's in a little woodman's cottage she has fixed up in the
park of Tring, once the family seat of the Rothschilds. She had
made it very attractive and there were no bombs, so I felt very
happy. Quite soon she is to have another baby, so she sits there
quietly and Victor works in London on something exceedingly
hush–hush and sleeps at Tring. On Saturday we had a duck shoot,
but there were practically no duck and it rained and blew a
hurricane, and after lunch we proceeded to Ditchley, my earthly

---

20 Wendell Willkie, the Republican candidate for the US Presidency in the 1940 election.

21 A rabidly anti-Semitic and pro-Axis Roman Catholic priest, whose weekly radio
    broadcasts were listened to by millions. At one time he was described as the second
    most important political figure in America.

Paradise. The house was packed with nice people with nice manners[22] including Brendan and Bertram. Both nights I slept fourteen hours running, so I felt fine and dandy and put Monday out of my mind as long as I could. Still it had to come, even as night does, so here I am. Talking of Bertram, he is going back to N.Y. for Christmas and you'll doubtless see him and he'll tell you all about us and how we live and how the poor town looks. He is America's best ambassador in this country.

Lord Lothian[23] is here at present. I wish to heavens he could be translated to something even higher and that Papa could have his place at Washington.

We are full of praise for the Greeks and perhaps wrongly sneering at the Wops. They say their tanks have six gears, five in reverse and one forward in case they are attacked from behind.

Write often. I get so sick for you sometimes, and when Winston talks of the preparations for 1943 and 1944 my heart sinks. The other night the All Clear went at 9 p.m. and that beast Papa made me go upstairs to sleep; of course the raid started again at 3 a.m. and the bombardment shook me to pieces, so I never slept another wink. I love you more than I can tell you. It would be selfish and worse to say I wish I'd never sent you away, but now that we think less of invasion, it sometimes overcomes me but I'm glad *really* because after all it's an adventure and I like to think you know the Old and New Worlds equally.

November 7th, 1940

I passed Egerton House[24] today. It hasn't got a pane of glass and looked quite blasted. The front of Chips's house[25] I hear is blown

22 Title of a then popular song.
23 British Ambassador in Washington.
24 My old preparatory school at 20 Dorset Square.
25 5 Belgrave Square.

in. It's very cold. Has the ice come to you, I wonder? It's lucky that you have always skated a bit and so will not start too handicapped. Perhaps you'll become an international ice hockey champion.

November 8th. I got into Dodgems with Venetia after my canteen and buzzed down to Chequers to have lunch with Clemmie Churchill, Mary her daughter and Judy.[26] Chequers was given twenty years ago by a rich peer to the Prime Minister of England. Money was settled upon it and so all Prime Ministers can go there at any time with all their family and friends and advisers and find a smoothly running house with food and staff and heating and flowers and soap and linen. Of course the Germans are always having a shot at it. It is a large pink brick Elizabethan house on a spur of the Chiltern Hills.

Our excitement after lunch was when the Chief Constable walked heavily into the white panelled drawing room and asked us all to vacate the house and to open all doors and windows as the Bomb Disposal Squad was going to explode the mine lying about a hundred yards away. We ran out. The bomb lay in a hole about twenty feet deep. (How people ever discover them when they don't explode I can't make out.) We were made to go a long way away, about 300 yards, then we heard the posse of men grouped round the hole blow whistles. We saw them jump into a car and a few seconds later a bang that split the heavens, a flash and a gigantic cloud of green and yellow and black smoke and flame as high as one could wish. We ran then to the huge crater it had made but there was nothing interesting about that. I suppose the bomb disposal men don't think it more frightening than anything else, and have quite accustomed themselves to the danger, just as we have (or *nearly* in my case have) living in London.

Nov. 9th. I'm at a house called Waddesdon near Aylesbury, the huge seat of James Rothschild. It is filled now with children under five, but they have kept a little freezing-cold wing to live

---

26 Montagu, daughter of Venetia Montagu, one of my mother's oldest friends, and inseparable friend of Mary Churchill.

in. We knit. Venetia and Judy are here and an old sister of the owner who has had to flee from the Paris she lived in and feels, poor creature, a burden to her brother – which indeed she is.

Nov. 11th. I motored up alone this morning and could not resist turning off the main road at Tring Park (a house Victor's family owned) where I had seen a tiny broken little house on the side of the wooded park, well situated to face a lovely prospect of a wide vale below it. All the park gates were locked but I found one to admit me though not Dodgems. The ground was atrociously soggy and I was wearing smart London shoes as high as stilts, but I ran hard through the pathless wood catching in brambles and bogs and came suddenly upon a disused avenue with a Cleopatra's Needle at the end and the most charming little temple façade of the broken house, the back of which faced the vale. All windows were broken, all doors open to the touch, a tiny tall sitting room with bay window and a room each side of it, one could be a bedroom with a bathroom built on and the other a dining room- kitchen, with a pantry-scullery built out. It belongs to Victor and if he will only mend it up and put the water in, I should so adore to have it for the war to sleep in. I confided my hopes to Hutchie who said 'But you wouldn't ask Duff to do *that?*' 'Why?' I said. 'Well you can't expect him to spend every evening alone with you. He likes bridge and fun.' 'Yes,' I said, 'but he likes the country and reading and quiet from bombs also.' 'Well I think that's *really* asking too much of him.' I have never felt more humiliated.

A dreadful afternoon at Liz's house with a charming little cousin of Raimund's.[27] O it does get me down. There is no roof, the rain cascades in to join the slush the fire-pumps have inundated the soot and debris with, nothing is worth salvaging, everything sodden and weighted with black saturation. No light of course and we groped about, candles in hand, when we left the daylight the open roof affords, to try to find things worth saving.

---

27 Raimund von Hofmannsthal, an American citizen, had gone back to join the army, taking his wife Liz with him.

A few bombs dropped some way away and made the ruins shudder. I hope poor Liz won't mind too much. I can't imagine anybody wanting to live in London again and now she will have to pay no rent or rates. I don't remember if I told you how lawless and rebellious Egerton House looks, as though the boys had mutinied, nothing but broken glass and things fluttering in the wind. It had no hit, only blast.

Nov. 12th. There was practically no raid last night. The All Clear went so early, and when Papa and I went down to the gym it was empty quite, so we talked for half an hour in ordinary voices and discussed a multitude of things and people, and joked in our own domestic way with phrases and nonsense language, and time-worn but loved ridiculousness. When nobody appeared to be coming down I got up and went round turning out the lights by the other beds. To my horror by a bed that had no light and which is rarely if ever occupied, I saw the bright beady eyes of Miss Cazalet darting out of the face with interest and horror at our conversation.

Monday, November 14th, 1940

Tremendous excitement about the battering of the Italian fleet at Taranto.[28] Really good news at last – everyone's spirits good. Conrad came to London and we went to the only play in London – only matinée. It is called *Diversions* and is a series of songs and sketches, in fact a revue of sorts – Edith Evans, Dorothy Dickson and five or six old favourites from the Players Club.[29] I was excited as a child by the smell of the theatre after so long. Edith Evans does a sketch of a London hop-picker who has had her home bombed on her way to her job in the train – excellent.

28 On 11–12 November British carrier-launched aircraft torpedoed the Italian fleet, at anchor in the harbour of Taranto. Italy lost half its capital ships in a single night.

29 A super-sophisticated re-creation of a Victorian music hall under Hungerford Bridge.

15th. Very bad news today about Coventry. The first news is that the factories are scarcely damaged but that the town itself is cruelly smashed and many killed. London of course had a quieter night, and I was beginning to get quite brave again. Poor Coventry. People are dashing off there with their mobile canteens to feed the homeless and hungry. I don't suppose there's gas or water or light.

This is a funny little house Helen[30] has bought on the golf course near Ascot. It's like a musical comedy cottage with thatch and a seat and a pump and pigeons and creepers. Rather common and absolutely delightful. Helen is as cheerful as ever, rather fat and exceedingly happy. They have a lot of bombs scattered about and Esmond Harmsworth, who lives next door in a smaller gimcrack little cottage he has rented for safety, is so terrified that one can't help teasing him about it. He goes green and shudders. Two fell in his garden and a big bit of shrapnel came through the wall of his bedroom just above his head and hit the opposite wall – *not* funny.

16th. Papa went to London for the day. It appears they had an appalling night in London last night – one of the worst. I'm thankful I missed it. It's like Long Island in this house and neigh-bours are in and out. The housemaid treats me as if I were a china invalid baby. She sits me up in bed and gets me someone else's fur jacket, she brings me little nips and snacks and hot water bottles at odd times. When I comment upon the attention she says anyone coming from London deserves it, so I feel heroic without reason.

Black Monday 18th. I'm afraid I shall end by getting on Papa's nerves. He so hates to dine in the restaurant and to sleep downstairs. I really *must* sleep down, otherwise it's no sleep. How could a bear hibernate if it had an immense naval gun within a few yards pounding away incessantly? I don't like eating in our sitting room for the same reason and also because bombs come

---

30 Helen Fitzgerald, a friend.

in broadside. The consequence is he's always pulling against me and sometimes I regret to say winning, poor Papa. He has more strains and worries than he tells of, but I feel exaggeratedly that my fears and troubles are worse than his and therefore should be given in to.

I had Albert and Bertram and the farmer and Papa and Jean[31] to dinner. Even Papa enjoyed it though we were downstairs. Lord Ashfield says that so much less real damage is done by bombs than appears to the eye. He gave as an example his own workshops which are all over London, his power station, etc. Since ten weeks (or is it eleven?), although repeatedly hit, not one of these premises isn't working 100 per cent.

London, Friday, December 13th, 1940

An ugly date my darling, but a day of great calm on our front and one laden with good news.[32] The Wops flee: 'Let God arise and let his enemies be scattered.' We are ringing the bells of our hearts, as our church bells are dumb till the invaders come.

In the midst of our uplift came the news of Lord Lothian's death. I'm ashamed to say my second thought was – might Duffy be given the job? What a vista of hope and light I floated down. I should – just to begin with – see you again as a bachelor and not as a man with a beard and family, out of the darkness, out of the fear, the shame of leaving others to face what I was missing mitigated by being *ordered* away, plus the Clipper terrors. I must not write of the hope nor think of it, as the odds are much against it. No use planning whether to take Wadey, or if I'd be well advised to take the old brown boots, or whether to have my hair permanently waved this side or that. Enough, enough.

---

31 Jean Norton, close friend of Lord Beaverbrook.
32 Major allied advances in North Africa.

December 20th, 1940

Papa read my last letter to you and tried to stop me sending it. He said it was quite unintelligible to a boy of eleven, or to an adult for that matter. I can't believe he is right. It seemed to me as clear as a nursery rhyme, not that a nursery rhyme makes much sense, but one knows them since childhood and you've known me since childhood and before, so we must hope you like to get a bit of news from this dear city. The proud city has had another rather easy week. The joy I should have taken in the relative calm was utterly marred by your dear Papa waking up on Wednesday after a healthy dinner and good sleep with 103 temperature. You can imagine my fuss and to-do! I of course feared for his life and also was greatly upset to think he would miss the Christmas week at Ditchley we had so greatly looked forward to, as a restorative and a delight. I thought of the weeks at the Admiralty where he had tossed with influenza-bronchitis from dolphin to dolphin[33] till my courage fainted. However, with intensive cosseting, two nurses, physicking, heating, sweating, cooling, plus a lot of praying and purging we have thrown the germ off, I trust, in four days and we shall go to our Christmas on Sunday.

So Lord Halifax is to go to Washington instead of me. I was never too hopeful, and I suppose there will be a prejudice against him because he was a Munich man, but America will like him very much when they know him. He has infinite charm and his predecessor had a worse name for appeasement when he was made Ambassador and yet he made a very good name for himself and was much praised. His only fault was to let the Huns have all the propaganda in the U.S.A. to themselves.

Ditchley, Dec. 22nd. We've got here, thank God. You should have seen the party leaving the Dorch. Wadey staggering under sordid paper parcels, last-minute sponges and slippers poking

---

33 My parents' bed at the Admiralty was supported on gilded dolphins.

out, two tin hats, two gas masks, guns, ammunition, a Christmas tree in a red box, another Ministry red box, big boxes, little boxes, fur gloves, a terribly intimate hot water bottle of a poisonous green, and Papa himself twice the size of Mr. Michelin in two coats under his fur coat and a muffler round his throat, another over his head and ears, and a hat on top of that, only one bright little blue eye goggling out. I've got lovely Christmas presents for the house party – picture of me by Noona for Brendan, another of Chicago for Ronnie Tree. Our old white Christmas tree I am going to candle up (one can't get *any* baubles here) with books for the boys etc. I'm quite excited about it. Velvet flowers in glass boxes for the smart ladies. The Hutchies and Barbara are a few miles away and Pam Berry not far either.

I'm glad to be able to picture you so well at the Paleys. I have a lovely present for them but needless to say it's not ready. We know our Rex. Papa has given him his ultra-smart Guardsman's evening great-coat – a relic of the last war – horizon-grey, waisted, gilt-buttoned, lapelled in flamboyant style, lined vermilion. It fitted him like fruit peel and he looked a fair treat.

Johnny Manners is here. They say he's a wild boy. I've only seen him, not spoken to him yet. A nice boy Ben Robertson leaving tomorrow will bring Noona's drawings for Kaetchen and Bertram and a little later will bring you a poor present from me. I've marked it London 1940. That's the point of it – no other except use, but it's like sending a postcard from the top of the Eiffel Tower, or from heaven or hell if one got to either, to send something from London. Chapel Street still stands, so does the Dorch. We had a big bomb in Curzon Street.

I wish I had you to hug and I simply hate seeing funny things that you would like and not being able to buy them. Hutchie is nearby and Barbara, who may have a baby any minute.

I love you my darling, don't forget me and try and love me in spite of the time and space.

Dorchester
January 1st, 1941
(the first time I write it)

I do so hope this year brings us together. It must if I have to take wings to you. Ditchley interlude came to an end like good things do. I nearly forgot the war for a week, because nothing much happened those days, and I didn't hear the barbarians had methodically burnt the monuments of London till Monday morning when I got home. They run so true to form, those Huns, for centuries they have never been able to resist burning and sacking beauty when they saw it, and now they can do it without seeing or looting it, so there isn't even hot-blood excuse.

I returned to my old canteen and had a gratifying reception, but I felt so ill (I couldn't say how) that I had to come home and go to bed. I feared that I couldn't manage New Year's Eve. Ann O'Neill had asked us to a party in a private room and I was loath to miss the celebrations. So at 8 o'clock and no siren sounding, I flogged my weary limbs up and into a bath and into the old gypsy dress. I found myself quite well, thank you, and was prepared for a good time. Of course we found ourselves thirteen thanks to Edward Stanley's muddles and bad manners, so I nobly said I'd dine downstairs with Oliver Stanley. Down we went and of course there wasn't a chink of room, real carousing was in course. So up again we toiled and had a separate little table till the bearded Ed. Stanley turned up and put us all to rights. At 12 o'clock we did our stuff, and Papa and I talked of you and thought of you and wondered if at the moment you were seeing a movie – a newsreel perhaps of London.

Someone at the party said they had seen pipers piping down-stairs, so a piper had to be sent for. Up he came – a god of beauty seven foot high, golden-haired, with skirts skirling, bonnet at a brave angle, ribbons flying and that appalling noise coming from the pigskin under his arm. Then everyone swoons and says there's nothing like the pipes (there isn't, thank God) and then someone always asks him to play the tune he's just played and that doesn't surprise him as it's invariable, since no one can possibly recognise a tune on the bagpipes, or at best three notes of one that put the idea into their heads. So round and round the small room he tramped, sometimes slow, sometimes quick march, and then he played a reel and no one could dance it but me and Ann O'Neill so off the old girls swirled, and the weight lifted from my heart for a while. So maybe there is something to be said for the pipes after all.

We went to bed then, Papa and I, but the party went on for a bit and then the hostess took some friends down and goodbyed them into the street, and coming back at 3 she found the bearded missing link Ed. Stanley sitting in a heap with the piper also sitting and still piping, from a semi-inflated bag and drinking from a very empty whisky bottle. The new Lord Rothermere was screaming from an adjoining bedroom 'Take that Scot Away' so Edward dragged him off to a night club called the 400 where I hope they remained until the blackout was over. What a scene! Like Trinquillo [Trinculo] and Stephano in *The Tempest*. Meanwhile the old crowds were assembled round Eros in Piccadilly Circus doing the old stuff – 'Auld Lang Syne' with crossed hands – although you can't see as much as a feather of his wing for the sandbags protecting him, and anyway it was as black as pitch. The nights that have no moon are so incredibly dark. I never get used to it. In the country where one is used to being out in the dark there is so much more sky than earth that always it seems to have some glow, but in a tall town the blackness can be blindness.

Jan 2nd. It's cold as charity. I tore off in Dodgems to the tiny folly in Tring Park, which Victor has agreed to do up and rent to me if I will take all the trouble. I don't know what to say. I could live there for £1 a week as against £15 here and I could feed myself and Papa on £3 a week and wash him and soap him and light him to bed and give him Vichy water and his *Times* for another £1 making altogether £5 a week, instead of feeding and warming masses of people and letting the hotel wash us and water us and light us to bed which works out at £40 a week. What's to be done with Wadey though? She'd be too lonely in the country with no companion. Send her to her sister, I think, and meet her in my London house once a week to get myself patched up. How does it all sound to you? Rather dull I expect, but I could run a communal feeding place or something in Tring all day and plant some onions and put the dinner on and what is more essential than all – pay the taxes which for the moment is utterly impossible – to meet them with 20 per cent is difficult.

Jan 3rd. We never sleep down now, raid or no raid, so Papa and I have ceased to quarrel. The days too should be getting longer though I can't detect it yet. The snow is falling. I'm home from the canteen and writing to my darling little boy who I had a cable from yesterday. This afternoon I hope to go to Gilbert Russell's till Monday. Tell that dear Christmas Katinka[34] to shake her Russian slay [*sic*] bells and lick the cream off the bortsch from her whiskers, pick up her Fabergé pen and stop not writing to me *at all*.

Eve Curie and Bertram will bring you my love and England's. Who are you sending home to me? H.G. Wells and Jimmy Sheean I'm hoping for. Ben Robertson is a darling. I hope you see him. He did the kindest deed, refused by all the other kind friends, in taking some of Noona's drawings to Kaetchen, in the great hopes that he might sell some of them to the rich, i.e. Mary Pickford and Gertie Lawrence. The paper stops me. Write to me on a typewriter, my pretty citizen.

Dorchester Hotel
January 7th, 1941

It is snowing here – not nice crisp clean American snow, but dirty old bread and milk snow. It keeps the Huns away a bit, so mustn't grumble but everybody's falling on their behinds, no one with

34 Kaetchen.

such a bump as me, so if we were undressed we should all look like mandrills.

We are all bursting with pride today on account of the Wops' surrender at Bardia.[35] Papa did a nice broadcast which you may or may not have heard.

Here's a nice story David Niven told me about the exploit of a 'Commando'. Commandos, you must know, are a new group of soldiers, very hush-hush, who operate with fleet and Air Arm no one quite knows where or how. Mr. Wu is one, so is Randy. Well, they settled that the enemy must be harried and if possible blown up in one of the Channel Isles. They had no idea how many soldiers and officers were in the garrison, so the first move was to send a single man to reconnoitre. Everyone volunteered, but Mr. Crosby (that is not his real name) a quiet little man of thirty-eight, was the most insistent. He said he had a plan and was confident of success. If he failed, they could always send someone else.

So off he started at dead of night, dressed believe it or not like an Englishman on the American stage, grey flannel trousers, loose tweed jacket and *regimental tie*. A submarine shot him up in a little rubber boat and he battled his way to the beach. In stockinged feet he crept to a gorse bush, where he hid till a reasonable morning hour. He then, looking smart as paint and just about as fresh, walked up to the German sentry at the gate and asked peremptorily to see the mess sergeant with a 'Come on, man, I have no time to waste' tone. (I forgot to say that one of the obstacles to his going was that he did not speak one word of German or French, French being the language of the Isles.) The sentry, bluffed, sent for someone who spoke English. The German who spoke English sent for the mess sergeant. Mr. Crosby civilly but firmly explained to the mess sergeant that the regiment, if they were employing M. Joubet as a caterer, were being sadly robbed. 'M. Joubet robbed the English soldiers, and he will rob you worse. Now my firm is

---

35 A city on the Libyan coast, heavily defended by the Italians. The city had fallen to the Australians – their first battle of the Second World War – on 4 January.

prepared to make you a very reasonable offer.' The mess sergeant, naturally pleased, said he would like to have an estimate.

'How many men?' says Crosby. 'Four hundred and eighty-two', says the sergeant. 'How many officers?' asks Mr Crosby. 'Thirty', said the sergeant. 'All at these barracks, or should I have to send in several directions?' 'All here', says the sergeant. 'I will let you have an estimate tomorrow' says Mr. Crosby. He then goes back to his gorse bush, waits till night falls, puts his stockings over his boots, blows up his rubber boat and paddles into the darkness to be picked up by the faithful submarine. Isn't it a nice story?

It is one o'clock and I am off to lunch with Winston. There is a blanket of snowy cloud and the guns are banging away very disagreeably. It may be the invasion but I doubt it.

Dorchester Hotel
January ?10th

I cried with laughter over Papa's censored letter.[36] It was like something you cut out for Christmas decorations. I never write to you without his telling me my letters are unintelligible, indecipherable and censorable, so my triumph over him is complete. I thought you forged his name with rather too much skill. Don't get into the habit.

January 24th, 1941

I went and had dinner with Lord Beaverbrook the other night. He told somebody that I wasn't at all suited to the Blitz, although I haven't seen him since the bombs arrived. I knew him to be a bit scared himself and I thought he was delighting in the idea that

36 My father had written me a letter which arrived so cut up by the wartime censor that it looked like lace. I sent it back to my parents to show them. As Minister of Information, he was responsible for all censorship at the time.

there was somebody *more* scared, so this led me to write him a letter in which I said I knew it was no good asking him out at night, but that I would love to come round and dine with him in the evening. By great good fortune there was no bombardment that night, so I didn't really appear very gallant. He has built himself a strongbox in the middle of the ruins of the *Evening Standard* offices. It is completely proof against everything, including air, though there is a little synthetic breathing material, mixed with something that helps his asthma, pumped in invisibly. It is enormous, with four or five bedrooms and baths, and generally splendatious. I can't but like him, although he is a big bad wolf and *will* not remember that you are his godson.

I have asked Mr. Wendell Willkie to dine with us. Will he, I wonder? I met him once. I shan't know what to say because what will be on the tip of my tongue will be 'I am so glad they didn't elect you President.' It is great fun, though, hearing people's impressions of London when they first arrive. They vary a great deal, some thinking it a complete ruin, others noticing nothing unusual, just depending of course on their characters, like you and me. You would never notice any disasters and I have double vision of them.

February 5th, 1941

The other day in the big gun works in Grantham, where Ursula works, a bomb exploded and another one fell, unexploded, in a workshop. They sent for the bomb disposal expert and your old friend, poor Perry Brownlow, had to take him to inspect the bomb. Perry's knees were shaking and his teeth chattering like castanets, while the expert knelt down with a stethoscope and applied it to the bomb's lungs. He then got up and said he would like to go and think about it for half an hour. Perry offered him a drink, thinking he would say brandy, but he asked instead for a cup of tea. Half an hour later he went back and deftly removed the pin and the detonator, boiling hot, which he placed in Perry's hands. He could scarcely hold them. The expert said every bomb is different and needs careful thought and diagnosis before dealing with it, like a human patient. When it was over, he asked for another cup of tea and went away thinking no more of it than we do of picking daisies.

London was excited and electrified by the Wendell Willkie visit. He has gone down like a dinner with the crowds. They shout and cheer and say 'Tell them we can take it' and 'Send us everything you can!' and this elephantine figure with a painted white tin helmet seems to amuse and impress them. I gave a dinner party for him, only ten of us in a private room in the Dorchester. He was treated like a king and a film star rolled into one, the papers told us what he ate for breakfast and what size boots he wore. Now he has gone. I waved him goodbye last night and pray God he will give a good account of this country and our needs and our hopes when he comes to testify in the Senate.

Victor and Barbara have behaved like unutterable beasts and have snatched my little house in the forest from me just as the builders were to move in. I was most cruelly disappointed and said so with tears and threats. This morning there seems to be a ray of hope – maybe they are remorseful.

We are all told to expect invasion. It's difficult to imagine it. People like to say 'I wish they'd come and get it over' but I feel every day they don't come brings us more help from America and Canada.

It's bitter cold and snowy.

I knew when Kaetchen telegraphed asking me if I had received his letter of Nov. 14th that he had not written since. Isn't he a beast? There is a lot to remind me of prison in living here now, especially for those like me who are used to travelling a lot, and one feels cruelly confined and the monotony and darkness and lack of art and theatre, so that letters from a bright continent and from one's nearest and dearest are a great joy, so it's beastly to be niggardly in writing to poor people doing time.

February 19th, 1941

Great excitement last weekend. We went to Ditchley where Winston was staying. Golly, what a to-do! To start with, the P.M. has a guard of fully equipped soldiers – two sentries at every door of the house to challenge you. I look very funny in the country these days in brightly coloured trousers, trapper's fur jacket, Mexican boots and refugee headcloth, so that on leaving the house I grinned at the sentries and said 'You will know me all right when I come back.' However, when I did return, the guard, I suppose, had been changed. I grinned at what I took to be the same two soldiers and prepared brazenly to pass when I was confronted with two bayonets within an inch of my stomach. They thought, no doubt, that I was a mad German assassin out of a circus.

Winston does nearly all his work from his bed. It keeps him rested and young, but one does not see so much of him as in the old Bognor days. There is also a new reverence for so great a leader and that creates an atmosphere of slight embarrassment until late in the evening. Also instead of old friends the guests included people called D.M.O. and D.M.I (Director of Military Operations and Director of Military Intelligence) and an enchanting Commander-in-Chief of the Air Force, Sir Charles Portal, with a wizened little wife with whom I used to play as a child because she lived at Denton near Belvoir. Brendan of course was there and Venetia, and Winston's wife and his daughter Mary.

Then on Sunday a flood of Poles rushed in – Sikorski, the President, and the Polish Ambassador and some other splendid Polaks. After lunch a little procession, headed by Winston, followed by the upstanding Poles and brought to a finish by your exceedingly reluctant and rather sleepy Papa, walked off to a private room for a conference on Polish publicity. It took an interminable time and when it ended and the Poles were due to move home the P.M. suddenly thought that the President should have a Guard of Honour. Secretaries and A.D.C.s went tearing about trying to find the Captain of the Guard, but he was sleeping or walking and could not be found, so Winston himself finally routed out some rather raw, inexperienced soldiers, who had never formed a Guard of Honour before. Meanwhile the patient Poles were sitting on the doorstep waiting for their Guard to arrive, and the President said: 'Mr Churchill is so great a man that we must let him do what amuses him.'

I tried to remember things that the P.M. said to interest you, but my poor brain is like a sieve and I can only think of something he said which I thought very touching and disclaiming of his power. When I said that the best thing he had done was to give the people courage, he said 'I never gave them courage, I was able to focus theirs.'

We had two lovely films after dinner – one was called *Escape* and the other was a very light comedy called *Quiet Wedding*. There were also several short reels from Papa's Ministry. Winston managed to cry through all of them, including the comedy.

The days are getting longer very quickly – no blackout till seven and not dark until 7.30. They talk of making another summertime hour on top of the one we have kept all winter – that would mean it would not be dark in June till 11.15 p.m. (There goes the All Clear.) Crocuses in the park at the feet of black tree trunks, no railings left, a gigantic mound of rubble, bricks, beams and parts of demolished houses grows in bulk daily near Kensington Gardens. Enough rubble to build an Egyptian pyramid of. Perhaps they will – it would be a fine warning never again to trust Germans. We might insert a special brick or stone in every house that weathers the battle. If we forget for a moment after peace comes – they'll do it again.

4

'A happy Easter, dear egg'

BOGNOR, FEBRUARY–JULY 1941

My darling Mummy and Papa,

I don't know whether I have told you or not, but Fara's[1] flat is full of pets. There is one white rat, two mice, a turtle and a bowl of goldfish. Anyhow, the poor things had been starved over the weekend and the rat had got out, eaten the turtle and most of Fara's hat. We usually kept him in with a bit of wire netting over the top of his bowl and The Last of the Mohicans on top of that, but now we find that The Last of the Mohicans is too light, and he can get out, so now we use Gone with the Wind . . .

Now we have left off carpentry and are doing art. I am drawing a beautiful Surrealistic for a play which the form is doing at the end of term, and I am awfully proud of it as it is the best Surrealistic I have ever done. Of course, now I have been told how to do them roughly by the master.

Lots and lots of love,

John Julius

---

1 Fara Bartlett, young and attractive, had accompanied Milo Cripps to Canada as guardian-governess and had taken a flat in Toronto.

The early summer of 1941 and the two long summers of 1942 and '43 were, my mother used to say, the happiest time of her life. Serving in canteens, doling out gas masks and making camouflage nets were all very well, but she had now decided that the cultivation of our pathetically few acres of Sussex – about four – while raising as many farm animals as she could, would be a far more useful contribution to the war effort. She had no knowledge of agriculture or husbandry, but she learned fast, relying on innumerable pamphlets from the Ministry of Agriculture and the expert advice of her devoted Conrad Russell. This tall, slow-moving, slow-speaking bachelor with his thatch of thick white hair – the Gothic Farmer, she used to call him – had run his own farm in Somerset for a quarter of a century and had practical experience of everything she needed to know. Having loved her for ten years but being, like her, perfectly content that their relationship should remain platonic, he would come to Bognor for two or three nights a week and would advise on the growing of cabbages or kale, on milking and cheese-making, on the proper composition of poultry meal or pig swill. There would be a cheese made every other day, Cheddar alternating with Pont-l'Evêque.

She had no helper except Conrad on his visits and me when I was there. Jones the gardener – now in his late sixties – rallied only if summoned in a crisis, and her old maid Miss Wade concerned herself exclusively with the chickens and ducks. Our one remaining family of evacuees from the East End of London were of no use at all; the country frightened them so much that they hardly ever left the house. My father meanwhile was still a distinctly reluctant Minister of Information, commuting daily to

London and – except on those occasions when he was obliged to stay at the Dorchester for the night – returning in time for dinner.

=====

Bognor, April 10th, 1941

I have to do all the marketing as there is no more delivering. I enjoy it enormously, not that there is any choosing and no pinching of chickens' breasts, no picking out brown eggs, or settling which biscuits to buy. You just take what you are given and like it, but there's the big excitement of suddenly seeing a bunch of leeks or some mushrooms and falling – no, pouncing – upon the find. Mr. Parfrement[2] sold me his old hen house for 30/- and said 'I hope you'll give me all the patronage you can. I can supply any fish you want as well as meat and poultry.' 'I always do, Mr. Parfrement' I said. 'I notice that you had a parcel from Ragler's in your car', he said. I went as scarlet as a turkey cock and mumbled something about it not happening again.

Conrad came down and together we made a cheese of cow's milk. It's a fascinating occupation and takes hours of standing with your arms deeply plunged into ever-warming curds and whey. It is so winter cold that I was grateful for the heat, and we put the whey into a dear little press and made a most professional-looking little cheese. Holbrook's[3] pantry is the dairy and I hope to make about sixty cheeses as a contribution to next winter's food, but it's the goats that evade me. They are unprocurable. I've telephoned all over the country to famous herds, and scoured every village and farm in Sussex. Mr. Owen, who sold me the two old goats years ago from Rose Green, has two milky animals and I go daily and practise my hand at milking

2 The local butcher.
3 My parents' pre-war butler.

and 'stripping' the udders. I can do it quite well now, but I feel I'll never get goats.

There was quite a struggle to get the laying pullets, but by dint of walking into every farm between here and Chichester, I bought six from a very eccentric farmer. He always complained of being half asleep and he wouldn't give me any guarantee that they'd lay eggs. I liked his lack of salesmanship and preferred it to the kind of man that tells you how lucky you are to have come to him, so the next day I went to collect. He complained again of my having woken him and we popped the panic-stricken six into my shut car. They were fluttering all round me as I drove home, clucking and making messes and obstructing the view of the road, but an egg was laid in the car and three more appeared in the egg nests before night, so Wadey and I were thrilled.

I collect pails of disgusting scraps from neighbouring houses, boil them and then with my hands break the pulp up small and mix it with rationed meal. They fall on the muck and it's a great pleasure as we had only three old foreign eggs the first week. Now I hope to have fifty a week when Conrad brings me another six hens, and we shall sell them easily. The pigs are being bought before I write again. The bombs fall pretty fast and the planes are incessantly over very low day and night. We had a stick of them in Bognor the other night all around the station. They didn't do a great deal of harm and only killed one person, but it's a different kind of blitz to get used to. Always in London and other parts I have been, balloons or barrage have kept them in the upper sky. Here at night with our paper, leaking roof I feel there is nothing to divide the enemy from me.

Papa commutes. He likes it very much and he catches the 7.45 train in the morning and gets back at 8 or 9 p.m. according to how busy he is. We have dinner like we did last year over the drawing room fire, cooked by a daily 'general' who looks like an elderly Marie Antoinette, but I can boss her and the food is delicious. I like being in the country a hundred times better than London but I miss you, my darling. On Sundays we go over to

Bosham and have lunch at the Ship Inn Club. It's most charming. The water laps the houses at high tide and there's a little bar after your own heart. I can't remember if we ever went there together. When I was younger than you the theory was that the best sunbonnets were made at Bosham, also that King Canute's daughter was buried in the church. Off Selsey there is a cathedral under the sea. It once stood on dry land but the sea claimed it. They say on rough nights you can hear the bells pealing.

A happy Easter, dear egg.

April 18th, 1941

I'm still delighting in the novelty of farming. The goats are still eluding me. They appear to be unobtainable, so I have settled to buy a cow. Then I spent a happy afternoon with Conrad, fertilising the field with ammonia phosphate so that it should grow richer and greener for my milk to be more plentiful for my cheeses. The whey will then fatten my four little pigs well. They are to be crammed into the goat house and have a little pen round them and never be allowed to take an unnecessary step for fear of losing an ounce of weight. Yesterday I went to Bosham for my bees, to be told by the beeman that they were almost unprocurable. Everyone is going in for bees and goats and I had been thinking how clever I was to cultivate stock that no one else would be likely to want. Then six more laying pullets arrived at the station in a crate, and I went to pick them and Papa up at 8 p.m. I packed them into the dickey and Papa into the seat and, looking at my gauge, was horrified to learn that the petrol tank was almost dry. I knew the only petrol station was shut and so we had to risk it, Papa in an agony of fret and fuss. Of course it gave out a little further away than Craigweil entrance from our house,[4] and I had to break it to Papa that it meant carrying a crate of pullets as well as walking home. He took it with a pretty

4 About a quarter of a mile.

good grace, and off we staggered; the crate was intolerably heavy and covered with sticking-out nails.

An army lorry came blustering towards us so I hailed it, which made Papa scream with shame and put the hens down, so I told him to leave it to me and to walk on which he was not at all loath to do. I asked the young soldiers to give me a drop of petrol to get me and my birds home. They said they were sorry they couldn't. I said I'd give them a coupon. They said no, it was strictly against the law. I said they couldn't leave a lady in distress and that I'd have to leave the car in the road with its lights on all night, and blocking the way if there was an invasion. They said they agreed, and that they'd break the law if I gave them a tin and had I got a rubber tube? I gave them the tin and told them I didn't happen to have a rubber tube on me. They backed their tank on to a side lane and fiddled for a few minutes and started to come back by the ditch like people ambushing. At that moment an officer passed leisurely on a push-bike. On seeing him they both lay flat on their stomachs, concealing the guilty red tin. He looked round but thank God did not stop, and they hurled the tin into my window and tore back to the lorry and were off in a flash. Still I was saved, and after putting the juice in and struggling to get the crate in, I arrived triumphant with car and fowls, so now we've got twelve birds laying eight or nine eggs a day and I sell them to the people who give me their scraps, which encourages them.

We had a pretty nasty raid here the night after the dreadful London one. I was all alone, Papa having stayed up that night. Conrad was in the house but not of course with me, and the house was shaking and the noise of planes and distant guns and occasional thumps was kept up all evening from nine onwards. At ten I went and looked out of the best bedroom window towards Portsmouth. It was light as day. What are called 'chandeliers' – clusters of bright incandescent lights that the Germans drop to light up the ground, and a steady light of a white-green colour that came from I couldn't make out where. I hated looking, but Wadey can't keep away from windows. We went down again and about an hour later there was a new succession of noises which we thought were incendiaries in the garden. We put the lights out and went out to see. As I opened the window-door an appalling crash, which was a land mine at Aldwick, tore the shutter out of my hands. The lights then were as violent at Bognor as they had been at Portsmouth. I couldn't manage to shut the shutter properly, and the blackout being then incomplete we had to sit on the hearthrug and go on with the *Times* crossword by the light of the fire and one candle. I did not fancy going to bed. There seemed at 12.30 to be a bit of a lull so up I went, and actually to sleep, only to wake again at 2.30 to a series of appalling crashes. That pretty well finished it and after a bit I got to sleep again.

The noise we took to be incendiaries turned out to be our soldiers firing at and bringing down a parachute flare. Hutchie is here, fat and greedy, and Hilary came for a night. He is frightfully decrepit, moves as slowly as a tortoise and is covered with gravy and ash and candle-grease and droppings from his drinks. His son has just died but it hasn't affected his spirits. He can't move or get up without some support and so always carries a very frayed umbrella about with him. It looks so strange indoors. Noël Coward too came down, fresh from America and lecturing for the Red Cross in Australia. He brought us some lovely nylon stockings from Kaetchen, but not a line from him. Last letter received five months ago. He knows how avid I am for news of you and him. What does he think it's like living here that he denies me any pleasure that he can give? I've cabled Bill to ask if the Cat has lost his powers or his reason or his life.

May 4th, 1941

I'm too busy to write. I've taken on more than I can manage and worse is to come. Yesterday I bought a seven-year-old cow for £27 and she is called the Princess. She is ugly and tame and heavily laden with milk. I was out collecting my swill when she arrived, but I met the men coming back who told me she would be sad and dejected for a day or two. Indeed she looked it, but I stroked her and gave her some dairy cubes, and was happy to find she didn't mind my handling her as I had imagined insuperable difficulties when I came to milk her. I put a big nail into the tree trunk near the little gate that leads into the field opposite the dining room and also a large hook at the height of my knee with a little pail hung on it full of meal. Then, armed with a halter to drag her by, and a sponge to mop her udder with, and my fine new pail that can't be knocked over because it weighs a ton and into which a hoof can't get because the opening is so peculiar, and my milking stool, I set off to milk. Nothing would move her from her disconsolate position by the fence near the lodge, so I gave in to her whim and milked her there with speed and success. She gave over a gallon and a half and it only took me twenty minutes. Hutchie watched and scoffed a bit, and Papa arrived and helped me feed the pigs, and we looked for eggs, and there were nine which is good (one day the birds laid twelve – a hundred per cent). Wadey is mad about them. All the farmer's daughter has come out in her and she is most keen and helpful and works hard too.

All that was yesterday. At night we put our clocks on so that today when we call it noon it's really only 10 a.m. This suited me with the Princess because as she's used to being milked at five, it became six and I gave her an extra hour till seven.[5] It was the most radiant morning imaginable – stainless sky, larks exulting above, a warm sun well up already and white hoar frost underfoot. Pail and stool under arm I marched into the field – to find no sign of the Princess. She had vanished. All the gates were shut and barbed wire all around the field. Mrs Barham[6] appeared and said she had *seen* her go out at 6.30 and Jones had gone to look for her. I did

5 During the war clocks were not put back an hour for the winter, but went forward an extra hour in summer.

6 Most families from the London slums had long since found the country uninhabitable ('all those trees!') and returned to their homes; but we still had one family, the Barhams, living in the tiny lodge by the drive gates.

not fuss but fed my pigs and pottered around knowing Jones would bring her back in a minute. Cows can't hide, poor things.

Getting impatient, I got my car and whizzed off to the dairy where I found my old Princess knee-deep in cow feed, gorging herself to the horns and I'm sorry to say cow-patting into precious rationed meal. I'd cleverly brought a halter and a pail of her favourite dairy cubes. I flung the rope over her silly head and to my surprise and relief she was not too glutted to follow the pail and me along the road. Every little while I'd give her a nibble to encourage her, and she came along famously better than me who had huge rubber boots on, unsuitable for a long walk, and my nightcap so that I dreaded meeting anyone. The Princess had of course no boots or cap.

When we got to the shops she saw through the pail hoax and stopped dead. Nothing, nothing would move her. I pulled from in front and kicked from behind and hullaballooed and shouted and threatened and cursed and even pretended to eat the meal myself to show how good it was, as one does to a fastidious child. No one was stirring. No sign of help. She was bursting with milk and I felt desperate, and after what seemed a year a Bay Estate[7] denizen in a motor came by and was brought to a stop by Her Highness. He got out and helped push while I dragged. No good. Then thank God three soldiers appeared and the five of us practically carried her the rest of the way to the stable gate, and there I milked her. It took me an hour. I was utterly exhausted. There were three gallons to be milked out – twenty-four pints or forty-eight tumblers. Then I had to get the Joneses to help me carry her into the field, which looks most appetising now the fertiliser has done its work and made the grass much more luxuriant and green, but it didn't tempt her and no sooner had I turned my back and gone to the dairy with Wade to measure the yield and take the cream off yesterday's to make into butter, than she was out again. Mrs. Barham actually saw her get over the barbed wire, but unfortunately Mrs. Barham from

7 The Aldwick Bay Housing Estate was immediately opposite our front gate.

London thinks cows are dragons and won't leave the house to raise the alarm till the idiot is out of sight and well away.

This time though she didn't get far. It's pathetic because it's due to loneliness and missing her old friends. I feel a brute. What shall I do when the goats arrive, which they will do this coming week? Mr. Simon Marks of Marks & Spencer found them for me at last – a pedigree one costing 25 guineas which he is giving me and a good one costing £6 which I am buying. I didn't dare take a peep into the gift-goat's mouth so didn't dare ask whether they were horned or unhorned. Between cow and goats I shall supply us and Jones and evacuees with milk and add a little to our butter ration, make a cheese three times a week off two days' milk and the seventh day use it for butter. All the whey and buttermilk go to the pigs, which have cost me £9.10.0 and which I shall sell again in three months for I hope about £40. The goats I shall keep and the Joneses can live on them during the winter, and the pedigree one can have a kid next spring. The cow will be keeping us in milk and butter and making sixty cheeses, for I hope about £20. The chickens will be eaten when they stop laying. It seems to me that if one doesn't pay labour and doesn't get swine fever or foot and mouth or white diarrhoea, one is bound to make.

May 13th, 1941

I write so seldom because my time is so filled. A goat arrived. Conrad and I went to the station to meet it. Emaciated and terrified it was, with a gnawed cord around its poor throat. We lifted it into the car. All our stock travel like the gentry in a limousine. When I got it out at the stables it gave a sudden spasmodic dash, backed by super-goatian strength, and freed itself from my nervous grasp. It ran like a satanic symbol across the garden, over the barricades and into the barbed wire.[8] I with the menace of mines in my mind

---

8 Part of the coastal defences.

pursued it into the wire and rescued it whole, but with its udder lacerated and bleeding.

I sent at once for the vet who pronounced it only superficial but agreed that milking was impossible. He produced a tiny bodkin – hollow – which he proceeded to put into the orifice through which the milk is squeezed, and let the milk flow through it into a jug. He told me I must do the same for a few days, which order paralysed me with fear of bungling the operation. However, I succeeded pretty well though an animal always recognises its doctor and is calm, but with me of course she was a frenzied demon and Jones used to hold her and I used to work away in the field, and the soldiers used to lean on the wall and roar with laughter when the goat giving a leap would upset Jones and me and the milk.

It's better now and the syringe is put away, but it's still a job that needs a lot of patience, and is not really worth the time Jones and I give to it. He has to hold her head and because it's so cold and I still wear a fur jacket and either she thinks I'm a billygoat or she just hates me anyway, she is always trying to give me a vicious bite over her shoulder. I only get four pints of milk daily and I ought to get six or eight. The milk is delicious, unrecognisable from the best cow's milk, and it's dreadful for Jones and the evacuees and Wadey to have to admit it's good – and admit they have to, for fear I shall give them two separate glasses of each kind and challenge them to say which is 'musty', which is what they want it to be. The Joneses have been awfully clever in saying that it's only when it's cooked that it's musty, but I'll fool them yet and one morning send them goat instead of their cow's milk. The Pig Family Hutchinson is in splendid fatness and should make me a nice profit and the country some fine bacon. I spend a lot of time asphyxiated by smell and bent double inside the old goat house, now the Hutchinson sleeping quarters, shovelling out the dung, and a lot more boiling up the swill which makes my mouth water.

The hens are Wadey's pride and her joy. One, our favourite, 'Sussex' by name, has gone broody which means that a mother's instinct for children quite overcomes a bird and no sooner does she lay an egg than we greedies take it, she gets to a stage of sitting on nothing, hoping to hatch out imaginary eggs and laying none. The thing to do then is to buy her thirteen fertile eggs and let her hatch them out. I did this and in three weeks hope to have a covey of yellow fluffy chicks. Meanwhile we get eight, nine or ten eggs a day from the other eleven. But the success of all successes is the old Princess. She has settled down and crops the buttercups and stands quietly to be milked, tied slackly to the garden gate. She gives me between four and five gallons a day, and with that I can supply our own house, the evacuees and the Joneses. I can make a pound of butter which more than covers our needs for a week, and also make about thirty pounds of cheese – good hard durable delicious cheese – a week, which really will help the country's food problem in a minute way. I tasted the first one yesterday, made in early April, and I do not think it could have been better or more professional. If all goes well I shall write to the papers and do a broadcast at the end of the season demonstrating what can be done with one acre and a bit of hard work by hundreds of old maids and little families who have got £50 to buy the initial outlay with.

 £28 cow – 7 years
 £11 pigs and pen
 £9 hens
 £1.10.0 – 2nd hand henhouse
 £1.10.0 pail and milking stool
 Total: £51

The food one can pay for as one goes along with profit from eggs and milk. But the English are set in their ways and if they've not done a thing before they don't fancy it now. They'll do anything dangerous. They'll fire-fight and become men and women of warlike action, but gentle agricultural arts they don't have any feeling about unless born or bred to it. To me it is full of glamour. The rotation is fascinating, drawing life out of the rich earth and that life returning its wealth to the earth by its manure, and the dovetailing of things. The pigs make the field yield more grass, the cow gives more milk in consequence, and therefore more whey, which the pigs lap up and fatten and manure the field again. I wish I knew more.

Today comes the super-sensational news of the arrival in Scotland by parachute of Rudolf Hess (great friend of Chips). We none of us know yet what it portends but it may be a most encouraging indication. Do you remember *The Flying Visit*, a book by Peter Fleming that I told you the story of? It's very reminiscent of it, isn't it? My hand aches. It's as broad as a navvy's from milking. It aches at night and keeps me awake when the bombs don't. They plastered Tangmere two nights ago, and I thought it was the garden they were plastering. Oggie was here last night and Venetia for the weekend. She still has forty children in her house and feeds them on parsnip jelly and reads Trollope aloud to them. Pam Berry came too. She laughed till her cheeks rained with tears when she saw me milking.

May 21st, 1941

Papa is ill and you can imagine the fuss I'm making. He has got a sort of flu-bronchial catarrh, green slush everywhere, and now the doctor here has put him on a drug called M & B which makes people want to be sick and commit suicide simultaneously. My usual tact deserted me when he said 'You mustn't catch it – who'll run the farm if you are ill?' and I said 'O I shan't be ill – people with something vitally important to do never are ill.' O poor Papa, it does worry me so and makes me hate the animals and the swill and the cheese and the whole bag of tricks. One of the Princess's teats has gone wrong and instead of a pure white spurt of milk appearing when squeezed, a nasty jet of *café-au-lait* comes out. So a friendly cowman is coming this morning to what he calls 'give her a drench', in other words purge her. I'm looking forward to that very much. Meanwhile he tells me to 'strip her', i.e. take what there is in that quarter away every hour, so I'm perpetually dashing over to the paddock and seizing the poor cow's udder for a minute's squeeze.

The bees are there and operating well, judging from the industrious appearance of their front door. Mr. Butler of Bosham arrived with them and his wife – a mute moron with a black veil over her hideous face. I wore a black veil too over Conrad's hat, quickly clapped on top of a white muslin headgear worn for cheese-making. You can imagine the sight. Conrad and Mr. Langmead, the intellectual farmer who happened to be calling, stood and watched the colonisation into the new hive, unveiled. Mr. Butler was unveiled also and ungloved, and he held the bees and smiled at them and talked to them and got stung repeatedly and thought as much or less of a bee-sting as we do of a midge-bite. Do you remember when you got stung on the Lake of Geneva, after an exceedingly dangerous crossing, lying under tarpaulins in a crazy boat? I think it was your birthday[9] and you were good and brave about it.

Everything went wrong the day Papa took to his bed. It was like a witch's spell on the farm, and cow and goat yielded less, the cheese all curdled and couldn't be vatted. The Hutchies squealed as though they had prevision of slaughter. Sussex the hen sitting on eleven eggs destroyed four of them with beak and claw. It's like when Titania and Oberon quarrel, everything goes wrong in the rustic world. I went over to Mrs. Rank's[10] to ask her about doctors and found her in a dressing gown suffering from too late a night. Her daughter Pat had broken her 'engagement' to a man they all hated two days before, and the day before she'd married an entrancing sailor who I'd taken a great liking to there last week while he was courting her. I asked for Johnny[11] and she told me he had a hangover from celebrating the wedding. Don't

---

9 It was – my ninth – and I wasn't.

10 A neighbour.

11 Her son, still a friend.

start hangovers yet for pity's sake. The battle rages in Crete. We are fighting without a right arm because of no R.A.F.

May 31st, 1941

Always your letters grow nicer. They speak more of coming home, which pleases me because, war or no war, as long as the hellish enemy is out of this green land, you must come back – I think when you are thirteen. Thirteen I feel to be an age of grown-upness when you can be no longer treated as a baby that must have bangs and alarms and disease and hunger kept from it. At thirteen you will feel perhaps that you must share in the struggles of other English boys who are here. By then, being more grown up, you will have something to say about what your movements are to be. So, although it's an odd year away, start thinking about it. Either we shall have won the war and everything will seem ecstatic, or we shall be still in a death grapple, in which case it will be intensely disagreeable. No fun, only want and stiff upper lips that never get licked, and heads held high in spite of dive-bombers and clothes scarce and no Long Island standards of pleasure and resources. Perhaps we'll all be dressed by then like Rob. Crusoe – alias Alexander Selkirk. I shan't be because I've always kept my fancy dress ball clothes, so can go on for years as a Velasquez, or Attila's bride, or Mrs. Siddons or Lady Macbeth, or for the rest of my life in my old nun's cloth.[12] It won't suit Papa to be shabby.

With Billy Welfare[13] we are practically self-sufficient here *qua* nourishment – eggs, butter, milk, honey, cheese. I don't take meat, sugar or tea anyway. Potatoes, vegetables, nettles and prawns and lobster and chickens for the table – no bread or fruit. I am

---

12 From her time as acting the nun in *The Miracle*.
13 An old sailor who sold lobsters and prawns on Bognor beach.

planting fruit trees this year but they won't help us till the fifth year of the war.

The news is always appalling but we still feel quite confident. Papa didn't see Hess. No one has except underlings. He seems very like me, quite ignorant and with the single thought 'Let me talk as man to man with the enemy, and he will see the folly of his ways and lay down his arms. We are bound to win and he is bound to lose. Why kill and destroy to prove a foregone conclusion?' Just what I want to say to Hitler, but I'd have a suspicion that I wouldn't be listened to whereas Hess thought we should listen, learn and inwardly digest and send him back with a godspeed and no flea in his ear. If he thought he was due for a bumping-off, he hasn't said so, but I think that probability must have come into his flight. He was being watched and known to be so-called idealistic because he didn't like general destruction.

I'm so much happier here at Bognor. I must have been more acutely unhappy at the Dorchester than I realised. The roses are on the verge of blooming, the irises and poppies in flower, buttercups and daisies mask the grass fields, the Spitfires and Hurricanes whizz by in the high empyrean – a misty silver formation – but from the garden do not look hell-bent.

The A.R.P. men stationed in one half of the stables have sent a complaint into Headquarters which was duly communicated to me. 'Could Lady Diana remove her goat from her stables as they had to sleep in the harness room and didn't like the smell?' I had a happy loss of temper, unfortunately only on the telephone. I said it was a funny thing, but the goat had been complaining to me only that morning of the A.R.P. workers and that nannies didn't smell but that I was going to get a couple of billies, if I could, and then they'd smell something, and that they ought to have a spell in London and smell burnt flesh or relieve men in Plymouth or Bristol instead of lying in a comfortable room for a few hours and smelling through their snores the smell that every farmer knows and loves because it's a smell that means produce and wealth and nourishment. Sick they make me. I've begged them to find other quarters, but I bet they won't as I charge no rent. They see me milking at 7.30 so they can't think it's a ladies' plaything. I did enjoy myself.

A fascinating weekend you seem to have spent among bush hogs and beaver-dams. If I could only get to Canada for a day or for one hug?

June 14th, 1941

So it's holidays again. They seem to be no sooner over than they begin. Is Upper Canada College a bit cissy, that they break up for a trifle like chickenpox? Why, good old Egerton House didn't disperse for measles, and would I think have held on united through the Black Death. I like to think of you with the Paleys and Kaetchen again, though I fear you'll be a fearful ignoramus later on. It will suit *me* because I shall still be able to drill unnecessary information into you, and you won't see me in my true dunce's clothes. I rather suspect that Cat of having got you back, using spots as a lever. If such is the case he is a bad cat and must teach you, not his tricks, but the things he knows about that you and I don't – figures, German, wisdom and worldly wisdom – very different things.

I'm sitting on a deal box in the middle of the garden path that opens on to that lush good bit of grass outside both sides of the stables. I have dragged the Princess along to give her a change of herbage, but I have to sit here to stop her getting back to her old favourite corner in her own field where she is fond of standing knee-deep in wet dung she has collected herself.

The khaki[14] ducks by my side are preening themselves and making Donald noises. They have no water to swim in, just a tank to submerge their heads in. It is out of farm fashion to give ducks swimming space, and yet they have to keep those awful feet. It seems dreadfully cruel, like taking us off the snows but leaving

14 Their full name was Khaki Campbells.

our skis on. It's the first summer day, the first without frost at night. Jones has brought the hammock out and Conrad and I will rock in it when he arrives this afternoon and look at the roses bursting into bloom hurriedly, and watch the bees making up for lost time. I have two hives now. Did I tell you of acting as assistant to the bee fancier at Bognor, Colonel Watson, when he came to open and examine my colonies? I had a veil over my face and elastic bands round my wrists, but I forgot my trouser legs like open chimneys. I thought I felt lots of bees crawling up them and attributed the sensation to my imagination, well known for its activity where horror is concerned. I didn't dare complain to the old Colonel, so I carried on till I was stung on the thigh. I didn't even mind that, but it made it clear that imagination was not all the trouble. So calmly and slowly, for one must do nothing spasmodic or hurried where bees are concerned, I took off my trousers and stood exposed in ridiculous pants, pink as flesh. Looking, I found the trousers lined with bees. It was a C. Chaplin scene.

I feel I've told you of this incident before. My memory is my worst failing these days. War bombings have quite confused it. Papa, recovered, has been fighting like a tiger with tooth and claw and fist, trying to reform his impotent Ministry, but how much he will succeed is another matter. Anyway he's enjoyed and is enjoying his *Kampf*.[15] Jeremy [Hutchinson] wasn't drowned, thank God, and has been made the father of a bouncing baby girl by his wife Peggy Ashcroft. Hutchie I see a lot of. He's here now, only gone up for the day. He's probably going to become a magistrate and sit in the courts and lecture the drunks and probably fine me for parking my car on his doorstep, and my! shan't I cheek that magistrate if I get half a chance.

My poor behind aches so from the deal box, however Her Highness is cropping away well now after standing for half an hour staring at me, with no comprehension of any kind in her

15 Struggle, as in Hitler's *Mein Kampf*.

eye. Your letters are my one big pleasure, though I have a lot of little ones in the farm. How to face the winter is what I try not to think about.

June 25th, 1941

How I neglect you. The truth is that I am never off my feet. Farming has got beyond me. The crisis of high summer gives me no time for lunch even. Every day more work crowds itself in. Someone gives me a cut field of grass if I will make it and that takes hours of time and pints of sweat. Then the Princess has been ill – rheumatic fever for three days which meant feeding her by hand and carrying pails to her. (She has recovered in consequence.) Cheese has to be made daily, as it's too hot to keep the milk for alternate days. A glut of *Dig for Victory* vegetables has to be marketed in Bognor. The pigs are as big as ponies and nothing fills them and they knock me and kick me around, but thank God I take them to market on Wednesday and bring six tiny naked piglets of eight weeks whom I can nurse like Alice in Wonderland. Then all the bee-fanciers in the vicinity cluster round me to encourage my rather faint enthusiasm. They are all pretty odd and have generally spent their lives out East; though they have a free-masonry and help each other all they can, they really despise each other's methods of handling bees and their ordering of the hives. My queen has done a bunk and a new virgin queen has been introduced with great application to tradition, pomp and etiquette by Colonel Watson, Mrs. Grey and me. I always get stung – last time on the tip of the nose – but I don't mind at all.

So the Russians are our allies,[16] and to me it alters the complexion of the war, maybe for the worse but in my mind to the good. People hate Russians because they are Communists and have done atrocious things to their own people and would like to convert us all

16 Hitler had invaded the Soviet Union on 22 June.

to their highly unsuccessful ways, but I prefer Russians so infinitely to Huns and fear their creed so much less than Nazism that I have no swallowing gulping trouble over fighting on their side. Communism has at least an idealist aim – men are equal, no nations, no money, all races are brothers, share your cow with your neighbour because it belongs to the state, etc. I hope America will take it all right. They have a big Communist bogey which they maybe have more cause to have than us. We have none. A handful of rich people think the Nazis respect the positioned rich and that the Communists don't, and they particularly want to hold on to their money. Never be caught by people who argue about Russia being worse than Germany – just consider if they are rich or poor.

Your letters are much better written than mine and clearer in writing, phrasing and meaning. I saw you last in a dim station – it seems a hundred years ago.

July 16th, 1941

I'm very *very* fond of you and today it seems a possibility that I may see you before I dared to hope to. The Ministry of Information has become well-nigh impossible. It has no powers at all and all the blame, and Papa, while thinking it wrong to resign on discontent or pride alone, is far from happy with his position. Today in the papers are rumours of the changes (1) Papa to be Postmaster General, (2) Brendan to succeed Papa, (3) Papa to be given a post abroad. The first two are absolutely groundless.[17] Papa couldn't even be offered the P.M.G. ship. It would be too *infra dig*. But the third report has some foundations, and it might mean adventure and travel and even seeing my own darling son again. We'll see. Meanwhile I try not to think about it but keep my mind rustic and turn my hay till 11 p.m.

17 The second wasn't. Brendan Bracken did indeed succeed my father at the Ministry of Information.

Last night Conrad and I stayed in the fields until 11.30, and in the almost dark tried to get the six pigs from the pen to the sty. Three we styed, three we let evade us. Once out these fat little white congested indolences became an energetic young wild boar and O the hunting and the stalking, the struggling and the sweating. It ended just before I passed out by grabbing them one by one by the back legs (the most difficult performance after getting them once more into the pen) and wheelbarrowing them into the sty, to the accompaniment of such blood-curdling yells and shrieks that I felt all Sussex must wake to the din and brand me as an animal torturer. The Princess has paid a visit to the bull and we shall hope for a calf next March. Meanwhile if I am transported to another continent who will tend my Princess? Where are my Moths and Mustardseeds and Cobwebs and fairy Monsieurs all? Who will stroke her ears and burnish her silken flanks and talk to her in her own voice (moovoice) as I do? The ducks are not laying so well, so I picked on one who looked as I thought uneggy and put her into a cramped coop and fed her on curds and whey. I told her that if she could eject an egg she would be reprieved, and this morning after the most determined straining and sitting and squawking Donaldwise, she produced a fine white egg, so her life is prolonged and I'm glad of it and in goes another poor tryer.

Spirits soar lately – the Russian fight – the waning of German confidence – the respite of bolts from our blue – the vigour of our bolts from their day and night blue. These things have buoyed us considerably but the longest day is past and the dread of winter is on your poor mother for one. Still who knows it may not be spent here, and who knows that I may not see my dearest dearest child if only *en passant*.

5

'Papa is a wreck'

SINGAPORE AND THE FAR EAST, AUGUST 1941–MAY 1942

Kiluna Farm
13th July, 1941

My darling Mummy and Papa,

Thank you so much for your last letter enclosing all the snaps.
Princess looks beautiful. I am also enclosing photos this time. I
am keeping an album of all the photographs taken worth having.
So far there are about sixty snaps in it. The one of your milking
the goat was awfully good, and I love the one of you and Papa
in the drawing room, whereas one of the pigs is priceless! I have
shown them to Dorothy, and she thought them all very good
indeed.

We have been having boiling hot weather lately, one day
about a week ago it was (this will make your blood run cold!)
120 degrees!!! Because of this, the swimming pool is a great
attraction, and we stay in about an hour every day. I can now
float and swim under water, and the swimming instructor is
teaching me to dive. I don't think I'm really terrible at it, although
I always face the problem of keeping my head down and my
legs together.

I suppose you can't swim at Bognor.

Lots and lots of love,
John Julius

In the summer of 1941 the situation in the Far East was giving increasing cause for alarm. War with Japan now seemed virtually inevitable; meanwhile the Prime Minister was receiving disturbing reports of the lamentable state of British defences, principally in the colony of Singapore itself but also in Malaya, Hong Kong, Australia and New Zealand. Time was almost certainly too short to allow for very much to be done; but my father was nevertheless despatched to Singapore with ministerial status. His orders were to travel as widely as possible through the whole area and to submit a report on the likelihood and probable consequences of a Japanese invasion.

It would never have occurred to my mother not to accompany him. Whatever dangers lay before him her place, she steadfastly believed, was always at his side. It need hardly be said that this view was not shared by the civil service or the military. Not only, it was pointed out, would the administrative and transport problems be greatly increased by her presence; there would also be bitter feelings of resentment on the part of many senior officers who had been obliged to leave *their* wives at home. My father, however, made no attempt to dissuade her. He knew, first of all, that it would be a waste of time; he was also aware that she would be considerably less trouble than the authorities feared; that she would always look after herself and expect – indeed, accept – no special treatment of any kind.

They flew off on the Yankee Clipper flying boat via Lisbon – where they were delayed for three days – the Azores and Bermuda, and arrived in New York a week or so later.[1] They spent a fortnight

1 It was a long journey; the Clipper's cruising speed was 188 mph.

in America – my father mostly in Washington, my mother all the time with me. She and I enjoyed ourselves enormously, flying one day to Washington (my first flight) and touring the FBI, just as she had done in 1939. All too soon, however, they left on the next stage of their journey.

Their four-month stay in the Far East was not a happy one. My father had looked forward to it, but he had cordially disliked Hawaii ('Give me Bognor any day') and from the day of his arrival in Singapore he felt his position to be impossible. The Governor Sir Shenton Thomas and the Commander-in-Chief Sir Robert Brooke-Popham considered him an ignorant mischief-maker; he believed them to be almost criminally negligent. His powers were enough to cause them suspicion and even alarm, but not such as to enable him to dismiss them as he longed to do. He knew, too, that all his labours would be in vain: his report and recommendations would reach London far too late to be acted upon.

For those of us who are nowadays accustomed to flying everywhere in the world at the drop of a hat, this chapter may come as a salutary reminder of just what wartime air travel could be. For my mother – who never overcame her fear of flying – every moment was an agony; but at least she was with my father. She could never have left him.

———

August 29th, 1941, Hawaii

My birthday[2] – and who remembered it? No one but you and Nanny. What a lovely belt! I love and need. I always said you were a darling boy whatever other people thought. The flight went well.

2 Her forty-ninth.

We had to fly due south to Los Angeles which added four hours (we need never have gone to San Francisco). The air was calm. I read and tried to forget and then came dinner and gin rummy for Papa and Tony Keswick and patience for me with Dorothy's cards and then to bed put back $2\frac{1}{2}$ hours. I woke in the small hours with my ears up to the explosion tricks, and the plane bumping a bit. Of course I thought it was a forced landing on to those bitter waves but nothing happened – it was just a change of level – so I went to sleep again to wake to a wonderful dawn glow at five and a steward's voice saying we should land in an hour. We did and there were all the expected colours and costumes, honey-coloured girls in dewy grass skirts and hair pinned with blossoms, handing us garlands for our necks and tumblers of pineapple juice. The heat is great but we pretend we don't feel it, knowing what is to come at Singapore.

The huge hotel of Waikiki Beach in which we live is all you imagine of palms and exotic flowers and minor-birds [sic] and surf bathing. We heard almost at once that instead of leaving 29th we should not be off till 31st, since then it has been postponed again till September 2nd and I expect more delays. Flying is certainly not a very express way of travelling, safe and slow perhaps instead of, as I thought, dangerous and fast.

Yesterday I went to a rich eccentric gentleman's house the other side of the Island. It was so beautiful – like *The Tempest* – magic, full of sounds and sweet airs that give delight and hurt not. The house was mountain built, lost in exotic ginger flowers and unknown waxen ones, and low sweeping trees made of ivory or rubber or something and imagine the surprise when under these freakish equatorial trees calmly chewing their Hawaiian cud I saw lovely Guernsey cows. My dear Princess came mooing into my heart. It's all very beautiful, but we are bored and want to get on. We left our great England to see a little scrubby boy, and to build up God knows what in Singapore, and not to ride with beach-boys on surf-boards or to watch a hula-hula girl start a heat wave by making her seat wave. The beauties of the Island will soon be swallowed up in defence developments, guns and airfields and training grounds and wireless depots and oil tanks. All the hideosities are ousting the umbrella trees and the butterflies and buds and ginger. It's a tremendously important U.S. base and will soon be armed cap-à-pie.

I think of you in a world of changing seasons, now plunging into a cool pool, soon seeing the trees turn into their gold and scarlet, then tumbling in snow and roasting chestnuts. With us it will be always the same – wet, hot and greenish.

Government House, Singapore
September 10th, 1941

The long flight is over. We arrived here at 4 p.m. yesterday after our only really horrible day in the Clipper. It was boiling hot, squally and leaden-skied, and we flew, not at 10,000 feet which keeps you cucumber cool and clean and kind, but at 100 feet. This means there is no air at all – windows don't open – and the whole beastly crowd of us were like live sardines in a tin on a stove, gasping, lying with no dignity and less shame in monstrous positions, smelling, speechless, loathsome to each other and to ourselves. The trip instead of taking ten hours from Manila took twelve but once we got near and the planes (now U.S. Buffalos) came out to escort us in, and Sing Sing at our feet looking full of character and charm, I felt better. There was the C.-in-C. Brooke-Popham to meet us on the dock, and impressive Government House motors, each with two Indians in gorgeous red and scarlet and white liveries, with queer scarlet hats (retained indoors). We are living in the gigantic Government House (I feel like a Lilliputian on a visit to Gulliver) until we find a house of our own – said to be an impossibility as nearly every general and almost all admirals from every quarter of our Far-Flung has turned up here and wants a house – but trust your brazen mother, we'll get one.

I wish I had you by the hand – we'd enjoy it so much together.

Belvoir Castle, Leicestershire, Diana's childhood home

Duff and Diana at their wedding, 2 June 1919

The Miracle – the Virgin comes to life, New York, 1924

Winston Churchill and Duff, Ditchley, 1940

Minister of Information, 1940

Pam Berry and Diana, c. 1938

Rex Whistler, c. 1943

Conrad Russell, in Home Guard
uniform, 1940

Raimund von Hofmannsthal,
c. 1936

Youthful voyager is John Julius,
son of Mr. Duff Cooper, Minister
of Information, photographed
aboard the liner Washington on
reaching New York. He's only
nine, but he's looking just a little
worried about things in general.

John Julius sitting on his trunk,
New York, July 1940

John Julius in New York, 1940

Kaetchen, c.1941

Kaetchen, John Julius
and Nanny Ayto,
New York, 1940

John Julius at Upper Canada College
Preparatory School, 1941

Kiluna Farm, August 1941
(Duff and Diana on their way to Singapore)

Lunch at Bognor,
c. 1937
(watercolour by
Rex Whistler)

The bees at
Bognor, 1942

Diana and Princess, 1941

Wadey and her hens, c. 1942

Diana making cheese, 1942

Bognor after lunch, 1943

Reading aloud at Bognor, c. 1942

John Julius
on his way
to Eton,
September
1942

Duff and Liz Paget at Bognor, c.1936

Maurice Baring and Dempsey,
c. 1940

I can't really get Papa to enthuse, he never looks round. They are all there, the hats like plates the Britishers won't wear,[3] the Malay peoples in skirts, so that until you meet them face to face it's hard to guess their sex. The living dolls with slit eye and yellow head protruding out of a sling on their mother's back, the smart boys who have gone into dress European clothes but still sit, so dressed, on their honkers, or straight on the roadway picking God knows what out of their toes. The streets plastered with advertisements, saying I suppose 'Buy Camels' or 'My goodness my Guinness' but being in Chinese characters looking ever so glamorous; it's all here.

Government House is as cool as a fishnet and although it is the size of Welbeck[4] we can all see and hear each other, which comes of having no doors or windows. My bed stands, mosquito-curtained, in the middle of a room thirty by thirty. For all that, I was woken in the night by a downpour of rain on the face, driven in from the Western Approaches, delicious and cooling.

September 23rd, 1941

Pencils don't show in this climate, it's too damp, so I'll try a pen and get spotted with ink like a Dalmatian dog. I'm still loving Singapore. The house is a dream – slightly Hollywood. I carry a jade-green parakeet, tame but ill-tempered, on my wrist or shoulder. Its name is Dickie Burong and it has vermilion cheek and nose. The Chinese cook is first class, but I have to look like a trussed chicken or pretend to be red mullet before he under-stands what we want for dinner.

Papa and I and Tony Keswick flew in a bomber to Batavia. I had a long struggle to get on the bomber – 'Women can't' – and a lot of bother but I won at midnight and we took off at 7 a.m.

3 From Noël Coward's 'Mad Dogs and Englishmen'.
4 Welbeck Abbey – huge country house of the Duke of Portland.

next morning. It was a two-engined Hudson and they'd screwed a wicker chair fast to the centre of the fuselage, but I couldn't see out of the window from it, so preferred to crouch on a wooden ledge. We were all trussed up in parachute harness, which robbed me of all feminine dignity. Nothing looks so shameful as straps between the legs in a skirt.

The flight took three and a half hours. We flew slap over Java, renowned for its jungles, swamps, crocodiles, cobras, rhinos, horrors of all kinds. I could hardly bear to look down and speculate on what would happen if we were forced to come down. No hope anywhere I felt – no space for landing. If by some miracle we all came down in our parachutes and stuck on the trees, and climbed down the cables through the monkeys and macaws to the surface of writhing snakes and bloodsuckers, what next? We light a fire maybe – a saviour in a search plane sees our column of smoke, and drops us a message of hope – then what, how could we be got at – no roads, no axes. It did not bear thinking of, so I looked away and read the life of the old Empress of China.

Batavia (capital of the Dutch East Indies and in Java) was never on our nursery list of capitals.[5] It was very ordinary compared with Singapore – modern town, spacious and sensible with wide streets and trams and no Chinese and many more white people. We drove for two hours upwards to see the Governor of the N.E.I. (Netherlands East Indies) and to spend a night with blankets over us. He is a great swell, corresponding to our Viceroy of India. Now of course, with Holland occupied by Huns and a homeless Dutch Government, he becomes the big noise with the eighty million inhabitants of what the Dutch call India (they call our India British India). A little Javanese, squat with big wooden face, stood behind each chair at dinner, attired handsomely in strange native liveries. They drop on their haunches when giving you anything on a salver,

---

5 Thanks entirely to her morning lessons, I knew the capitals of nearly all the countries of the world by the time I was five.

and if you give them an order, they clutch their private parts with both hands and bow from the waist.

The Governor was a true and good man without a ray of humour, but the country hates the Germans as much as we do, and will fight to the death if attacked by Japanese or anyone else. The destruction of Rotterdam after the collapse of Holland will keep their swords sharp for a long while.

October 3rd

In Rangoon there is a very famous temple-pagoda called the Shwe Dagon. It rises gold to the sky. Luncheon conversation was about it. To my surprise no one had ever been inside it. 'Footwear' was the explanation. 'You have to enter barefoot. An Englishman can't do that. People do everything there.' 'Full of lepers', 'the stink of the place' – out rolled the excuses. I said one's feet were washable, one did much worse with one's hands, leprosy wasn't thus caught, a temple *vaut bien* a whiff. They looked exaggeratedly shocked. I've got mixed. It was tea of course when this conversation took place, and when it was over we drove in closed cars to have a look round. When we came to the temple door I said 'I'm going in.' There was a bit of a scene. Captain Richmond looked revolted and Pilate-ish. Duff shook his cheeks at me, but I am blind and deaf when I list and in a flash I had my shoes and stockings off and was following the votaries into the great dark doorway.

It was one of the most repaying sights I have ever seen. I was quite breathless with excitement. In this high dark corridor that is always ascending are congregated sleepers, vendors, priests, water-carriers, every caste, every age, every race. Everything sold is beautiful – fantastically made miniature white pagoda-umbrellas to offer to Buddha, bunches of ginger-flowers, lotus and jasmine, cocks and hens like Chinese ornaments, shining gold Buddhas inset with jewels. On and on you mount, the stairs are very steep, faint with the smell of exotic flowers. Burma girls smoking always their 'whacking white cheroot and (actually) wasting Christian kisses on an 'eathen idol's foot',[6] their hair agate-smooth, though like the White Queen they carry a comb in it (so handy). They wear a flower in it too, and a clean muslin shirt (always clean) above their bright, tight sarong. At last you come out on to an open, circular court, in the centre of which rises the cloud-high gold-leaf pagoda, surrounded by hundreds of Buddha shrines.

The devotees vary from nakedish men who walk round and round, falling whistling-bomb flat between every two steps (progress is slow) and the pretty little maidens, smoking and playing with their babies under Buddha's nose. Orange and saffron priests lounge around, and little oil-saucers with floating wicks were everywhere being lit. I wished I could have stayed until dark to see the flickering, but Duff and Captain Richmond were weighing a ton on my conscience, so I hurried round. Even without pausing it took me over an hour. When I came out the atmosphere had improved a bit. My excited, radiant expression I think subdued Duff's irritation, but the Captain still looked nauseated and sulked.

Singapore
October 31st, 1941

Papa's Number 2, Tony Keswick, leaves us tomorrow by Clipper to England via Washington. He will bear this letter to you but you won't see him, poor swatting scholar, though I hope Kaetchen will. He takes the Mission's Report home to the War Cabinet and so part of our Far Eastern effort is over and finished. What next? The visit to Australia starting on November 3rd, a report on which follows the main report, which could not wait as events are so bellicose here. We shall be covering Australia and New Zealand

6 From Kipling's 'Mandalay'.

for a month, then back to Singapore and an Economic Conference, whatever that is.

Christmas will come this year in sweltering heat. The Sultan of Johore's wife says she will give us a party round her swimming pool. Heat will be in the very sod. I went to see her this morning. They have a zoo, a little elephant that I was ragging, only about six years old and six foot high caught my flimsy skirt in his trunk through the bars, gave it a sort of twist as he might have done to a banana on a tree and proceeded to try and get me and it into his mouth. I had to pull with all my strength to free myself. It would have been dreadful loss of face if he'd torn it off me from the waist downwards – I wear practically nothing underneath. In these countries face is of enormous importance. Riches, power, success, and getting away with something, good show, getting the better of anybody or thing, inducing respect or (better) fear, all give you face but you lose it by falling down in every sense, by lack of dignity or control, being caught out in a lie, beaten in a bargain, ridicule, no *savoir-faire*.

I miss you, and I miss friends. Papa is more homesick than I am. He wants his club and his books. I entertained General Brooke-Popham, Commander-in-Chief, Far East, last night. He can be relied on to go to sleep directly after dinner, but stupidly I let him talk, instead of talking to him, and he stayed and stayed. I also had a Chinese couple, Mr. and Mrs. Kau, both completely speechless – it was dreadful.

From the Stratosphere

This letter may read a little tight, because Papa has just given me a big dollop of whisky. I was trembling with cold and fear. Beneath us I assume are the mountains that divide Burma from Siam, but I can see nothing whatever but white dense cloud – above and below. I think of how planes lose their bearings and their height and I panic a bit, especially when the old boat gives a drop into an air pocket and I feel we shall be spiked by a mountain top. It's freezing cold however – we must be flying at a great height. We have been travelling round for a fortnight and covered so many countries, costumes, habits and languages that I often get very confused. Calcutta has been what I like least, the day shooting with the Viceroy what I like best. Sleeping in the splendour of the Viceregal tents I enjoyed. I felt as on a stage set for *Julius Caesar*, or the Field of the Cloth of Gold. I had a huge one, lined with printed linens, a large pole up the middle, as big as Kiluna's piano room and double the height. Real bed, carpeted floor, lamp-lit and romantic, a full-sized bath made of rubber in a little annexe, also a revolting Indian loo (that has to be cleaned by human hands – 'sweepers' belonging to the 'untouchable' caste of India). I roamed out by my tent's back door to try and avoid using this barbarity, but there were too many native policemen guarding the precarious life of the Viceroy for me to find the necessary privacy.

I loved too the 1,100 beaters bawling their lungs out as they tore down the hills, hurling rocks in front of them to arouse the game, and I adored the long ride home, three hours, half in a lovely sunset, then half in night's darkness on a very narrow path often precipiced to one side. Our only light was a flickering oil lamp carried by a vague Indian. Papa nearly died of it. I was sorry that he suffered so, but it gave him an idea of what I feel all the time in a plane. Calcutta is filthy and cringing, hot and ugly, a disgrace to the British and to the Indians. At night the pavements and gutters are like a battlefield, *covered* with what looks like corpses. They won't sleep anywhere but on the road. What saves the town in my eyes, though really it is too idiotic in a modern town, is the habit of allowing free range to holy bulls. Anybody can gain merit with their god if they acquire a bull, proclaim it sacred and put it completely unguarded and free on to the streets. So all over town you may see these beautiful beasts with humps on their backs, lying in the middle of the local Piccadilly, with all the traffic having to circle round their repose, or sitting like Ferdinand on the doorstep of the Bank or your own house, or helping themselves unrebuked from open stalls to the finest fruit and vegetables. India put a nasty taste in my mouth. Burma put a good one.

Hurrah! We're out of that blinding zone of cloud and looking down I can see occasional peeps of the plains of Siam, and looking up a peep at a Dutchman's pants.[7] Yesterday we left Calcutta as the sun rose, and came to Rangoon at noon. In the afternoon an American called Porley took us in his private plane to a place called Toungloo, where a hundred voluntary American flying boys, and of course many more groundsmen, are being trained to go and fight for China. I was deeply moved by it. All for a cause not actually their own. They put on a demonstration for us of eighteen pursuit Curtis planes getting up off a small runway with five-second intervals. The jungle has been cleared to make a field, and billets and hospital and messrooms, and they looked brave and young and purposeful. We're coming down now at Bangkok. We should get home to Singapore today. Maybe there will be a letter from you. I have not had one yet, but I've been away two weeks.

Melbourne
November 9th, 1941

I'm sitting in a deserted golf club, it's raining, the others are playing golf and walking round. I saw the little tree-bears, nursing their babies on a swinging branch. They only eat eucalyptus leaves, from about three varieties of that tree of which there are at least a hundred. It's very wise of them because no one can take them away as pets as they are too fastidious to eat anything else. There are also grotesque kangaroos hopping around, and emus that make a noise like a tin tom-tom, not with vocal cords but with some monstrous part of their stomachs. We flew from Singapore to Bali, coming down at Batavia (capital of Java) and Surabaya

---

7 Blue sky.

(naval port of Java). Bali is an island belonging to Holland of very famous unspoilt beauty. The natives are beautiful, tall and straight, with innocent radiant faces, and strong, well-built, well-covered bodies, naked (men and women) to the waist. Beautiful sarongs and head-dresses and flowers in their ears and hair and round their necks. We stayed in a perfect little collection of grass-made houses in a garden on the sea, half jungle and smelling of paradise.

After dinner a native dance was put on for us of such incomparable skill and sophistication of rhythm of utter beauty, danced to special Balinese instruments of wood and brass. I have never seen anything that ravished me more in the realms of travel, customs and art in dancing. Next morning we flew till dusk and reached our first foothold on Australian land – Darwin – a port on the north coast. The Antipodes perplex – all is reversed, sun, moon and stars, seasons and of course the south is cold and the north hot. There was not much to remember about Darwin except a lovely large very green frog *inside* the loo itself which meant that Papa and I dared not pull the plug for fear of meting it out a hideous fate. Luckily it jumped out in the night, which relieved us in more ways than one. Three thousand miles the next day, which brought us to Sydney after dark. During those fifteen hours I did not see one village, except the handful of houses round the two airfields we came down at to refuel. We were greeted by hundreds of flashlight cameras which completely blinded us, blindness added to that total deafness that so long a flight brings upon you, makes you feel not in the best form for selling yourself to the press.

November 21st, 1941
In the sky (as per) Australia to New Zealand

Papa and I have had a triumphal procession through Australia. They were crazy about us both, don't ask me why. Everybody claimed relationship. People are very isolated and they suffer from a desire to be part of the old country, and therefore work out genealogies to form a link with the living English. Every hospital nurse who ever had to make my bed or tend and treat me seems to have settled in Australia, and hundreds of Belvoir, Knipton[8] and Bognor men cropped up to talk about old times, which they remember very inaccurately. When you've done your relations and old times with nurses and old homes there aren't any more people, because the whole continent is inhabited by fewer people than London is. Canberra (capital), Melbourne and Sydney are really all we've seen of Australia and a little bit of what they called outback, meaning country and sheep farms, only they're called sheep stations. I wonder if one could bear to settle here. I think I could, given a bit of money so one could have a motor and a swimming pool and some ponies, and of course a farm, but I don't know – only those who go there young can adjust themselves. I'll stick I think to Europe or America, unless you come here and then I suppose I'll have to come hobbling behind.

I've just been sitting up in the 'conservatory'[9] with the charming and beautiful young pilot. No sign of the Tasman Sea 20,000 feet below. Another four days covering N.Z. at a terrific speed and then back to Sydney and Singapore. I wonder if we'll survive it. Papa is a wreck. He works dreadfully hard, speaking and broadcasting, and looking quite understandingly[10] at factories and works. I work equally hard, but no public speaking. I did a broadcast. It cost me a lot in nerves and composition but when I came to my own feeble passage addressed to the English children in Australia, a whopping great lump closed up my throat and I simply couldn't go on, wasn't it humiliating? I cry easy you know. Do you remember reading aloud in far away days *The Flying*

8 A village near Belvoir.
9 Cockpit.
10 I.e. while understanding absolutely nothing.

Classroom?[11] I always had to keep stopping to blub. The radio professional sitting with me covered it somehow and I came in for a finish. Meanwhile two of the most revolting English school-girls – huge, fat sixteen-year-olds – were produced for me to see as examples. I thought they'd be golden-haired toddlers. The monsters were chosen, I suppose, because they bore the splendid names of Sylvia and Joyce Duff.

Later. I'm writing now from Christchurch, a town of the South Island of N.Z. Such a day yesterday. Your mother, I am surprised to be able to tell you, was not frightened and behaved unconcern-edly. We left Auckland – in a bomber Hudson machine at about 9 a.m. for a three-hour flight to Christchurch. The weather was kind of ordinary – cloudy but calmish. At the end of three hours' flying over a blanket of cotton wool, we were told we should be in in about ten minutes. I didn't put faith in this information. The face and voice didn't seem true. After an hour the clouds parted a bit, and I could see we were over the sea with no land anywhere. We knew then, Papa and I, that we were lost all right. Occasionally a pilot would tell us 'we won't be long now', but with no convic-tion in his voice. After two hours of careering around very low on the water, they admitted that they had lost radio touch, and feared they would have to return to the N. Island (two hours back) – as landing without radio was impossible. I didn't much like the sound of this because I didn't dare to ask if the petrol would last. I looked surreptitiously round for a rubber boat, but saw none. After another half-hour of going northward we suddenly got in wireless touch and in another half-hour we had landed safe at Christchurch.

It is more English than the English here. Hedges, flowers the same, but the people think and dream and ask only of 'Home'. It's touching. A man called Sir Cyril Newall who was head of the R.A.F. in England during the Battle for Britain is Governor-General here. It must be cruelly dull in comparison, dull and

11 By Erich Kästner.

remote and far from the fray. Another two days here at Wellington and then back to Sydney for a night and then back home (Singapore) which will take four flying days by Qantas Line, sleeping Townsville, Darwin, Surabaya (Java), Singapore. Look them out on the map and try and take an interest in the old birds. I wish you'd discover, you could in New York, how many miles I will have flown. I'll put the names on the back of this.

＝＝

My parents returned to find Singapore at long last preparing for war, which was by now clearly imminent. On 7 December the Japanese had bombed Pearl Harbor; on the 10th their aircraft had sunk the two British warships *Prince of Wales* and *Repulse*; meanwhile they were advancing steadily southward down the Malay Peninsula, while Singapore suffered daily air raids.

It is far from certain that my father's report, which had left Singapore with Tony Keswick on 1 November, had as yet been even considered by the British Government; it had certainly not been acted upon. Churchill now appointed him Resident Minister, with authority to form and chair a war cabinet; but it was an empty gesture – there was nothing to be done.

Early in January 1942, having taken over some of the secret work from the female secretaries who had already been evacuated, my mother deciphered a telegram informing my father that Sir Archibald Wavell had been appointed Supreme Commander in the South-West Pacific. This effectively meant that my father's work in Singapore was at an end. It was confirmed on 7 January with a personal telegram from the Prime Minister: 'You should at your convenience by what-ever is the safest and most suitable route come home.'

They left Singapore on 13 January. Just one month later, on 15 February, Lieutenant-General Sir Arthur Percival handed over the colony to the Japanese. In all British history, there has been no more abject, no more humiliating, surrender.

———

January 14th, 1942
Above Sumatra

It was all settled in a few days. When Winston and the President fixed up the new headquarters of the Generalissimo[12] in Java, we were warned that Papa's office might automatically finish, and after three days of suspense during which Papa mooched around with nothing to do (for the Heads of the Services were leaving and the Civil Defence he had entrusted to an Engineering Brigadier called Simson) the telegram came saying 'Return home as soon as you can'. The Pacific Clipper route being finished, Manila, Guam, Wake (what a wonderful epic) having all gone we have to go back via goodness knows what to start with and then Calcutta, Karachi, Basra, Cairo. From Cairo it might be Malta, Gibraltar – or bang across the middle of Africa and up to Lisbon and so home. I'm dreadfully disappointed it is not to be by Canada. What can't be helped must be endured, and anyway I think it is too early in the year for you to come home. We must see how we all stand when your next holidays come round. The Germans don't look too healthy, and we don't worry about the Wops, but these slit-eyed dwarfs from Japan are a pest. They raided us every night in Singapore, but never seriously.

Our start yesterday was rather exciting. We were due to leave at ten and put off till eleven. Scarcely had we got to the airport

12 General Wavell.

when the siren wailed, the guns banged, the bombs fell and Papa and I, two soldiers, Mr. Kao and Mr. Yey (both Chinks), Martin and Alex Newboult were shoved down a lift shaft made completely of glass. It was a death trap but, as good luck would have it, during the hour's delay at home I said to the 'boy' — 'Bring me a last gin sling.' Of course he thought I'd said 'large' and he fixed me one the size for Gargantua so the whole raid seemed normal and pleasantly exciting to me. Hardly had the All Clear gone, and moves towards the flying boat were being made, when yell, moan, yell — over they came again. Back to the lift shaft for another half-hour. Then off as fast as we could get before the next wave. No time to discover what harm had been done. Rain and cloud enveloped us, which generally I hate but today we were all grateful to it, grateful even for the bumps and rolls that clouds enforce. We felt that they were veil and cover from the enemy.

For several days I had been feeling terribly at leaving Singapore and all our friends, just as things must worsen there. We had no choice — orders are orders — but Papa did an amazingly good job against obstructions from all sides to get the town and island on a better war footing, and as long as the C.-in-C. and the C.-in-C. of the Fleet were there, and as long as he was Resident Minister he had a certain power and authority, in fact quite a lot, being able at any time to wire home if the local government behaved too atrociously. Often it came to that, so they were frightened of him, but without those advantages he was powerless and we are dreadfully afraid it will slip back into the bad slothful hands of the Colonial Secretary, and the weak hands of the general in command and the sleepy griplessness of most of the civil servants. We have left a strong General Simmons as Commander of the Fortress who, since Papa forced martial law upon them, can, if he has the character, force his will over any civilian, and the Engineering Brigadier Simson to get on with shelters, rationing, better fire services and a million other things to protect civilians.

149

I don't know why I write you all these internal troubles of Malaya. They have been preoccupying me a lot, that's why – and much as I want to get home, it seems cowardly and will be thought cowardly by our enemies – the obstructing Victorian money-grabbing idlers – to leave at this moment. I mustn't think about it. To our surprise we flew due south to Batavia. There we thought the shelter preparations immensely superior to anything we have seen. We had dinner with Pownall and an air commander on his staff called Darvel. Wavell had gone back for the day to Singapore so that will hearten them I hope, though he's got a wall eye that droops and is dreadfully deaf. He is no doubt a fine fellow, and Pownall, his Chief of Staff, certainly is.

Batavia was blacked out of all recognition – out of finding one's way about one's room, or reading or washing, and we had to get up long before dawn (four actually) and grope about as best we could. We are now sneaking up the outside S.W. coast of Sumatra with a nice wall of rocky mountains between us and the yellow perils. We came down at a port called Penang – tropically beautiful. I bought two pairs of native trousers – I needn't tell you – and now we are up again and due to come down at a place called Sibolga, but no one knows if it has any accommodation or only grass huts, and coconuts for dinner. The next place would be a smart resort at the top northern end called Sabang, but our captain fears submarines and raiders once we turn the corner and head without protection up the Bay of Bengal to Calcutta. That gauntlet has to be run, Sabang or not.

In cities composed entirely of mixed populations – Chinese, Indians, Malays, Eurasians, etc., unless they feel that they are safer in town, in shelters, where food is and where masks can be got – they all desert their jobs at the first bomb and fly to the hills. It's so utterly different to England and civilised places. These poor natives have no traditions and not much understanding, have never had war anywhere near them and don't understand that they are cogs in a wheel which if it stops crushes them all. If in London the gas fitters, the electricians, the police, the firemen, the food sellers, the Post Office, the road repairers, the people who collect corpses and bury them, the drain experts, the transport people and what have you – all fled to the hills in Surrey, the Germans could have taken the place next day and taken with it disease and a demoralised, craven, defeated people. But these poor beasts here don't have a Nelson to turn in his grave, nor a flag that generations have died to hold high, nor anything to make them face up to fear and sacrifice. So imagine what a problem it is.

Jan 15th. Sibolga was quite a success and the most beautiful almost land-locked bay imaginable and unpolluted by man, as Captain Cook doubtless saw it. There was a hotel but it was thought better for us to stay on a trim little Dutch steamer that had put in that morning, so we did. It was clean, in fact luxurious, and we dined sumptuously with the two good grave dull Dutch captains, and talked of the Indies, and of hatred of Germany which they feel as fiercely about, or perhaps more fiercely, than we do, since Rotterdam's destruction can never be forgiven. They have done better than anyone in this Far Eastern war so far. Their organisation everywhere for defence and alternative trade and air routes is superlatively good. They have something of the Germans – an efficiency – but in every other way they are *not* like Huns.

We took off again this a.m. at the gentleman's hour of eight and are flying north to the Andaman Islands. Halfway we turned round – a half circle – and nobody noticed it but me. I'm all too perceptive on a plane. The sky had clouded over splendidly – from the enemy aircraft point of view – but visibility and cloud was very dense and I think our poor pioneering Captain was lost. Anyway he turned due south for an hour, found an island, and turned again, I suppose having got his bearings, and on we went in the direction desired.

Feb 1st. It's a long time later and we've got to Cairo. I wanted to send you a cable, but they won't put date or source of reception. It's not much good. I might have put 'Cleopatra sends kisses', or 'Too-ra-loo from Tut' but you might not have known what I meant and the enemy eavesdropper might have, and we don't want our destination and plans of flight advertised to Messerschmitts.

There is a route to U.S. from here so I'll send this off quick and start writing a new one. I long now to be home and plan ways and means to get you back as a farm hand.

January 16th

Never a dull minute.[13] We arrived at the penal settlement of Port Blair, Andaman Islands, at about three. I took a hearty dislike to it. No gentle Malays and intelligent Chinese, only surly filthy Indians and bad Burmen, criminals to a man though freed, and with their crimes written large on their faces. Another airliner came in from Rangoon and the west and disgorged three Australian officers. There seemed little plan and no action. At last we piled into two small motor-craft and spluttered off through high seas to Ross Island, some thirty minutes away. Ross is the select patch where the Chief Commissioner has a residency. There is a barracks, a post office, a club, a church and parsonage, a village institute and that's about all except for an old Circuit Home lately turned into a rest-house for air-travellers. On the quay of this little settlement, now evacuated on account of the war, stood the strangest old rickshaw-for-two that ever I saw, equivalent to the Irish bankrupt's buggy. It had six slutty-looking Indian jailbirds, with filthy torn white shorts and different shades of faded carmine tops and turbans, to draw it up a stiffish but very short hill. A quiet, unassuming gentleman in shabby European tropical get-up said 'My name is Waterfall. Do get into the buggy. I thought it better to lodge you in my house. I'm not

---

13 My mother is back-tracking here. She sent off her previous letter as soon as she arrived in Cairo, but she had not yet had time to write the saga of the Andamans. She takes this up now in the letter that follows, written from Cairo.

living there myself. I'm afraid the light is cut off and we'll see if we can't forage up some tea. I'm afraid we have no kitchen. I thought we'd dine on the other island with the Colonel and the Captain.'

The house was indescribable, very large and wandery and shapeless, with strange devil-carvings mixed with suburban taste. A huge haunted bedroom ('No mosquitoes on Ross', so un-netted beds), the inevitable plumbing horrors of India and an impossible trickle from a cold tap dripping into a pan-bath. We messed around and suggested looking at the flowerless garden, clinging to our hats and skirts that the wind was skittish with, while time *would* not pass. Dinner, he said, was on the other side at 8.30. One couldn't wash, one couldn't even go to the loo for very shame. I suggested dining at eight and we listened to a croaking portable wireless. I'm only interested in Singapore, and there was no news of it. We crossed over by launch. Daylight was fading. We listened to the radio again in the Colonel's melan-choly house, and a brilliant suggestion was made that we should move to the club and hear the radio there. This was welcomed as a time-killer, so we buggied over, the Chief Commissioner going as always on foot, and listened for the third time to the meatless programme of news. Still there was whisky at the club and some boys and even a woman not yet evacuated. There are only three left.

Then back to the Colonel's house and dinner and port, and a snub from the Chief Commissioner when I said that India was an unhappy country, and he said that I hadn't seen it and was talking about things I didn't know anything about. He was right, of course, but I was only describing my impression. That got the Colonel and the Captain winking and on my side, and cheered things up a little. The excuse of being woken at 5 a.m. allowed us to beat a difficult retreat across a troubled sea in a bit of a launch at about 9.30. The Chief Commissioner waved us off with relief, and we groped our way up in inky darkness to our inky house, empty but for ourselves, two witch's cats and

and three speechless Indian delinquents. After a struggle with washing and a stinking lamp we slept, but I was as usual eaten mercilessly by mosquitoes. No protection, no net, no artillery of Flit.[14] I chucked it at four and somehow lit and tended the lamp.

At 5.30, when I was dressed and packed, the three Indians padded into the room patting their stomachs and saying a lot. No means of understanding. I knew it couldn't mean breakfast and there was a tone of alarm. Duff slept, cheek on folded hands, through this babel. At last the word Circuit Home emerged from the gibberish, so seizing my torch I ran down to the Circuit Home, to find that our pilot was at death's door, 104 temperature,[15] swollen painful glands in the groin. The rough, tough, jolly lady-doctor Thornton who had joined our flying-boat at Batavia was well in charge and diagnosed it as something I had never heard of belonging to the malarial school. It was a body-blow. Praying that Duff would have got a move on and be shaving, but unable to explain my absence, I went with the eastbound (already late) Australians in the launch to their Clipper, and got all the low-down about our near future. News wasn't too bad. The First Officer of the eastbound aeroplane, in dual control with our First Officer, would pilot our ship, and a kind passenger R.A.F. boy would First-Officer the eastbound machine. Well, that's better than another day in prison, though two underlings at the joysticks is not my ideal. I got home at eight and found the Circuit Home people having a gorgeous sausage-and-egg breakfast after a lovely night in fresh rooms with netted beds. The Chief Commissioner, from long dealings with the punishable, must have thought up something to irk us, i.e. almost solitary confinement in the dark with three murderer-keepers and no breakfast.

14 The most popular insecticide of the day.
15 40° C.

A half-caste doctor, delighted to get a line from Dr. Thornton, proclaimed the Captain's disease to be the same as had the first diagnoser, so he is to be got on the aeroplane somehow and left in a Calcutta hospital. A wonderful procession formed itself of passengers, coolies and luggage. The lady doctor, quite a lot grimier than yesterday, me with my nightcap on to keep the hair from the hurricane, and in the middle the septic pink-coated bearers carrying shoulder-high the Captain on his bed. His mattress laid on the floor of the launch, he was tossed across the bay and somehow squeezed through the narrow aperture into the aeroplane. The lowest officer and I dragged and unscrewed and pulled at the chairs and tables in the smallest compartment until we wrenched them free, and he lies there now, a sort of dying Nelson in the hold. Devoted officers fan him and I mop him with eau de Cologne, for the heat is intense when we are at sea level. The shocking truth is that I'm frightened of infection, more for Duff than for myself, and I dare not say so. How lucky are those who don't think of every fatal eventuality.

February 28th, 1942

Well, my darling, we are back safe and sound and I am writing to you from Ditchley where to my surprise I found Jeremy Tree just arrived back from U.S., the size of an elephant but very charming. Our last bout of journey – Cairo to Malta, Malta – Lisbon and home – was very difficult. We stayed at the British Embassy in Cairo with Sir Miles and Lady Lampson who were sweet and hospitable and kind but thought to be our hosts for only a few days. In the end we were living on them and boring them and leaving them and returning to them for nearly three weeks. The first plane that left two days after we arrived departed without us thanks to a Priority Committee refusing to let me travel on it. Papa all but had a stroke and telegraphed home for an overruling of the nonsense.

This he got, but then no flying boat came in for a week and when it did, we were everlastingly told to stand down.

At last the fateful night came, the final goodbyes made, the luggage locked and stored in the hold, Papa and me strapped in our chairs and all aboard for Malta. I tried to compose myself – difficult since it was to be a night flight through gunfire and enemy planes. However I managed it somehow, thanks partly to us sitting in total darkness, which I took to be part of the blackout bosh. I had fallen into a half sleep when Papa shook me sharply and said it was all off, and we must get out and go home. The airlines hate to give you information of any kind, but we gathered that it was the engines that just wouldn't start, 'something electrical'. I didn't like the sound of all four engines depending on one thing.

The next night we were off again – the same goodbye, paraphernalia and the last drinks, the blue pill, the friends on the quay, the already familiar shipmates. Again I composed myself to sleep as soon as we had taken off the Niles's surface and everything seemed honkydonk. After about four hours (halfway in fact) I roused myself because I found a general unrest in the plane, too much vibration and passengers looking about them. A comfortable Scotch steward appeared next, looking a trifle green, and told us that orders were for everyone immediately to put on their lifebelts. These are part of your seat and have to be wrenched off the iron chair. We all obeyed, calm as cucumbers. I don't remember feeling frightened. It seemed certain that we were going to abandon ship, because the steward then went up the emergency ladder and opened the trap doors above, but I felt a sort of confidence that we should bob about in the sea in a rubber boat or a raft or something, and I didn't think of enemy submarines or ships picking us up and interning us for the duration, nor of the fact that a boat that size can't land on anything but very smooth water, and we had no idea whether we were high up or low down or if it was calm or storm – so we waited very calmly. I was shifting things I thought I'd need out of my bag into my pocket and in about twenty minutes the officer looked in to say that the 'situation has improved and we hope to get back to Alexandria'. So back we got, still in our life jackets, with the steward still at his post at the ladder's foot, though I could not see how in our huge cork belts we should ever get through the half-crown-sized trap door.

We got back to Alexandria and then back to Cairo at 5 a.m. to reappear like bad pennies at the Embassy. This time the engine had failed, and they had had to jettison, without much hope of getting the ship up again, all the petrol but enough to get her back to land. It worked, she rose again but it was a close thing. Then came two or three days' pause which brought us to Friday, 13th February. Again the same start, the same half sleep, the same everything except that your poor mother's apprehensions and nerves were not improving. All went well until 4 a.m. (we'd started at 9.30 p.m.) when we were told we'd be landing in a few minutes. 'So soon. How wonderful!' but no! it was old Cairo again. Despair. A few nights later we really did get off and crossed that nasty spot twixt Egypt and Malta where the Mediterranean is always, I feel, trying to drag me to its depths. It had tried to swallow the *Enchantress* and all but succeeded.

Dawn was breaking as we got to Malta. Peeping through the blackout curtains I had seen quite a lot of gunfire, and as we landed the familiar screech of the siren was going full blast. It is a very beautiful, old, romantic city – gashed and battered a bit but not comparable with our cities' ruin. The raid was on all day long but no one seemed to care much. We spent the day with Governor-General Dobbie, old, spartan, and in constant communion with God. No fuel therefore, no hot bath, a bitter shock to me as one descends pretty frozen from the upper air. Grace, before so-called meals, and TT [temperance] are house rules. The Governor Dobbie has the faith and heart of a saint and allows only rations on which no native can survive, Weevil-biscuits and Spam is the fare offered the high, though below stairs, said a visiting chauffeur, 'I had a whole duck to meself.' Dobbie's custom is to take the guests up to the roof whenever the gunfire grows particularly active. It's not the least dangerous, but cruelly cold and a long pull up of seventy steps, so I'm glad we were only in Malta for one day. We took off again as soon as dark – destination unknown.

It turned out to be Lisbon. We gave Gibraltar a miss but I saw it blacker than the black sky with three tremendous searchlights shooting upwards. No enemy could miss its position. At Lisbon we were lucky indeed and caught a Dutch plane within an hour of landing which got us to England by four that day. I could not believe that we were really home. I don't think I'd ever expected to be. The country looked black and freezing cold and the train to London was unheated and the town looked far more dilapidated than seven months ago – no paint, no railings, no glass, no maintenance but very moving and noble. Papa was like a child of ten, I a bit tearful. We are going to live in London till after Easter and then I shall be a farmer again, I hope. Mr. Mason has lent us his flat, 51 South Audley Street. Wadey and a char look after us. It's Christmas cold and not in my style. Artistically it gets me down but mustn't grumble, we are very lucky to live rent free.

Captain Frend of the *Enchantress* has gone to U.S. to fetch a fighting ship over. He said he could bring you back if I liked. What do you think? It would be a tremendous adventure. About April or May I think he hopes to get off.

The Fall of Singapore is one of the worst things – perhaps *the* worst that has befallen us. We'll overcome it – in time – as long as America and the British Empire are indissoluble.

6

'Locusts, thick as lightly fallen snow'

ALGIERS, JANUARY–AUGUST 1944

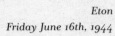

Eton
Friday June 16th, 1944

My darling Mummy and Papa,

People are all wonderfully optimistic about the war now, and Eton is raving, completely obsessed by the second front.[1] It seems to be going very well. What do you think about it, and what do the Free Frogs think, and what does Algiers think as a whole?

I only discovered about it by accident. I was walking along the passage, and m'dame[2] came up, and said 'Well, what do you think about the invasion?' I said, 'I'm getting bored with waiting now, and getting also slightly doubtful as to whether it'll come this month or not.' 'It's started, though' she said, in a voice of ecstasy, feeling, I suppose, overjoyed that here was someone to tell. My reaction to this was one of total disbelief. I said 'No kiddin' or slightly more sophisticated words to that effect. 'No,' she said, enjoying every moment of it, 'it's true'. I said 'whoopee' very sagely and severely, trying vainly not to start waltzing down the passage, then thanked her for the news, and tore off to tell everybody. To my great annoyance everybody seemed to know, but I had a little fun confirming it to people who came up and said 'Is it true . . . ?' Now I am trying desperately to get a map with flags to jab in. Dashwood has a beautiful one, but when I got to the shop they'd sold out.

Lots of love,
John Julius

---

1 The Allies had landed in Normandy on 6 June.
2 Eton patois for the house matron.

I did indeed return with Captain Frend, on HMS *Phoebe*, a cruiser. One April morning in 1942, at school in Toronto, I was summoned by Mr. Carson, the Senior Housemaster and told to pack. 'You're going home,' he said. 'But how?' I asked, excited but mystified. 'How should I know?' he said. 'There's a war on, and in wartime everything is secret. My job is to get you on to the New York train tonight. You'll be met tomorrow morning at Grand Central Station and told what to do.' Kaetchen was indeed there to meet me – as he always was – with a ticket in his hand to Norfolk, Virginia. I caught the next train, and was met by a sub-lieutenant who took me to the ship. The crossing, alone, without a convoy, took a fortnight – there was much zig-zagging to avoid U-boats – but I arrived in Plymouth in early May and took the train to Bognor, where my parents were waiting on the platform.

I spent that summer at Bognor. My mother ran her farm, my father commuted daily to London. He was now doing secret work, which included the planning of operations designed to mislead the enemy.[3] Every afternoon I took a bus, gas mask at the ready, to a tutor in Chichester, cramming for the Common Entrance examination to Eton. I got in, and my parents drove me down on 15 September, my thirteenth birthday. My mother, characteristically, had included in my suitcase a long rope with a hook on the end as a precaution against fire. It was – as I had warned her it would be – instantly confiscated. I, of course, wrote home

---

3 It was in this capacity that he became involved with the planting of faked documents on a corpse, the hugely successful Operation Mincemeat which gave rise to his only novel, *Operation Heartbreak*, as well as to the book and film *The Man Who Never Was*. Ben Macintyre has recently retold the story, with a wealth of new material, in *Operation Mincemeat*.

regularly; it would have been as much as my life was worth had I not. And so, I have absolutely no doubt, did she. But for the first fifteen months after my arrival, I am ashamed to report, there are no letters.

Curiously enough, she herself remembered little of the winter of 1942–3. Of course she would come down to see me every month or so. Eton is only twenty-odd miles from London; nowadays you can get there in well under an hour. But in wartime it was a very different story. Since my father never had the day off, she would come regularly, all that winter, alone, standing up in a crowded, unheated train. The cold was appalling. In my scrubby little room[4] I was allowed a tiny coal fire after 6 p.m. every other day, so there was no comfort of any kind. Still, lunch at a surprisingly good restaurant in Windsor was a bright spot, and the long afternoon we would spend mostly at the Art School because it had a minimum of heating. Her journey home again, once more standing up in an icy corridor, was blacked out (so no reading) and could take well over an hour. There was maternal devotion for you.

The summer visits, thank heaven, were not quite so taxing, and by this time my father was occasionally able to accompany her. For both of them, 1942 (after their return from the East) and 1943 were quiet years – she was once again engrossed in farming, while he actually had time enough to write his biography of King David at weekends. Meanwhile, my time at Eton passed pleasantly enough.

It was in September 1943 that Winston Churchill first suggested that my father should go to Algiers. With Algeria French but Paris still under German occupation, the city had been selected by General de Gaulle as the French capital-in-exile, headquarters of his newly formed French Committee of National Liberation. The Committee included all the various French resistance groups

---

4 It is one of the advantages of Eton that from the start every boy has his own room, even though for the younger ones it may be little bigger than the average sleeping-car.

opposed to the Nazis and the Vichy regime, with General de Gaulle as its President; my father's brief was to build it up as an effective body with which the Allies could deal, while doing his best – despite Churchill's deep mistrust of de Gaulle – to gain the General's confidence. The task would not be easy, and Algiers might be far from comfortable; but a great reward was promised: as soon as Paris was liberated – by now only a question of a few months – my father would go there as first post-war British Ambassador.

On 1 January 1944 I saw them off at Lyneham airfield.

———

Algiers
January 4th, 1944

I did so hate leaving you. I hope you had a nice time at the aero-drome and got back safe. The flight was uneventful if you can call 1) a noise that hurt and made sleep impossible for all, 2) boiling water but no towel and 3) a blaze of light on the ceiling to confuse and blind the top-bunkers and total darkness for the elite lower-bunkers (no reading one's fears away) uneventful. No masks or caps were used and we never flew high. I kept peeping out. The night was perfect – a silver earth and a sky brilliant with stars and a blazing dawn, then the Mediterranean, Africa and the Atlas. Algiers on time, deputations of French and English wading through a sea of mud, but the scene was sunlit and the dreadful flight behind me.

Now we are installed in our house, if you can call it installed when there is no cooking apparatus, heating arrangements for a bath, telephones, fires, heating of any kind, sofa, decent chairs, towels or anything else. Outside we have limitless acres of jade-green jungle but inside – Lor! If you were only here you would tell me not to be got down by such material things – I who have prided myself on accustoming the body to hardship. The streets are fantastic, but shops all shuttered because there is nothing to buy whatever. I spent some hours trying to buy lamps, as our house has only an occasional bald globe in the ceiling, and at last got a midget one (10 watts) painted all over with Scottie dogs. I miss you dreadfully. Nothing shall stop me from getting back to you for Easter.

Algiers
January 9th, 1944

My spirits are improving now that the hope of one day getting hot water or heating is past, and now that I discover that so many fine ladies are in the same boat. The only people who live like real ladies, in painted rooms and white satin featherbeds with heat pervading every niche and indirect lighting, are the higher ranks of the Allied Forces. They should be in their tents and their hammocks and their hangars and leave the soft delights to middle-aged soft diplomats.

Today we take to the sky again on a visit to the boss.[5] I shall peer down on the snowladen shoulders of the old man Atlas and pray not to add my burden to his. You wouldn't like it here, that I'm sure of, it's not like abroad. It's a dense mass of soldiers and sailors of all countries milling around without anything to do and nothing to buy and no transport – no buses or taxis or fiacres, only official cars and trams for the natives.

Bloggs is here and Randolph, not Bill Paley though I hear he's coming back from Italy next week.

5 Winston Churchill was recovering from a small stroke in his favourite hotel, the Mamounia in Marrakesh.

January 10th, 1944

Here I am on top of the deep romantic chasm, where Alph the sacred river runs. It's wonderfully hot: the sky is without blemish of cloud. We've just had a terrific lunch *al fresco* – stuffing, ham and chickabiddy smothered in mayonnaise, fruit and *gâteaux*, washed down with shandygaff. It's been a most wonderful *entr'acte* in the grim, cold misery of Algiers. We flew here in the Colonel's[6] fine plane. Four hours it took, and I weathered them. An ample champagne collation was served, and three charming young gentlemen were thrown in for good measure.

The party is a circus. It's lodged in a millionaire's pleasure dome, all marble and orange trees, fountains and tiles, in the richest Mahommedan style. We live in the hotel (two bed, two bath, one sitting room). We are guests of the United States Army, so a tray with gin, whisky, two sherries, Coca-Colas and a carafe of fruit juice, plus all the American *Life*s and *Time*s, are laid out for our delectation. At the villa there is a big set-up of decoders, W.A.A.F.s,[7] map-room, secretaries at two a penny, and your old Doctor of the Yeomanry, Lord Moran.[8] The Colonel's wife and W.A.A.F. daughter Sarah were on the airfield to meet us and buzzed us by U.S. car, complete with immense white star on its camouflaged side, to the pleasure dome. There was our old baby in his rompers,[9] ten-gallon cowboy hat and very ragged oriental dressing gown, health, vigour and excellent spirits. Never have I seen him spin more fantastic

---

6 Another alias for the Prime Minister.

7 Members of the Women's Auxiliary Air Force.

8 Churchill's personal physician.

9 The famous one-piece 'siren suit' of his own design. buttoning up the front, in which the Prime Minister dressed informally throughout the war. He had it made in various colours and materials, including velvet. On 21 September 1940 his Private Secretary Jock Colville described him in his diary as 'clad in his air-force blue, zip-fastened cloth overall which he straps tightly round his stomach and in which he looks like an Eskimo'.

stuff, the woof of English and the warp of slang. Max the Calvinist[10] is here, dressed in black and utterly uncontributive to the general pool of chatter . . .

In the evening we walk to the *souk* and buy what we can. I've bought the stuff for a dress, a pair of candlesticks, two pairs of shoes, a large straw hat of native design (of course), eleven metres of white linen, etc. Bumf unprocurable, sunglasses unprocurable, but the whole place offers a thousand times more than Algiers does . . .

January 13th. The last exciting day.[11] It began at nine with the review, beautifully staged in a little grandstand, the Caliph, El Glaoui,[12] the King of the Atlas, officials, wives, Duff and me. I cried from start to finish because of the yells and shouts of 'Vive!', the French's joy and pride in the token army that passed, their *avions* buzzing just over our heads, their own few guns, their own flags and courage. The sun blazed on this inspiring scene.

Wormwood[13] said a few words, exactly right, emphasising the honour and privilege of having so great a man beside him. Doesn't it all sound lovely? Thank God the *Vives!* were pretty evenly divided between them . . .

Later, after the review, which seemed gruelling enough on Winston in one day, we had our eighth and last picnic. The picnic consists of eight cars with white stars and U.S. drivers (the whole town is run by the U.S. exclusively) with two or three guests in each, some 'tecs[14] distributed around, and a van laden with viands, drinks, cushions, tables, chairs and pouffes. The advance party leads off an hour before the main body, reconnoitres and selects a valley miles away, windless, comparatively fertile and green, with water if possible.

10 Lord Beaverbrook.
11 By now the party had been joined by General de Gaulle.
12 Pacha of Marrakesh.
13 Nickname for de Gaulle ('wormwood and gall', *Lamentations*, iii, 19).
14 Detectives.

We, pioneers that day, chose Demnat. We drove some eighty miles through the country of the Dissidents, very beautiful, olive-green and fertile, with towns walled and fortressed by their *kasbahs*. We came climbing to a famous gorge, or rather to the lip of it, and there we decided to pitch our pleasure. There we laid out our delicatessen, the cocktail was shaken up, rugs and cushions distributed, tables and buffets appeared as by a genie's order, and as we finished our preparations the main party arrived.

The Colonel is immediately sat on a comfortable chair, rugs are swathed round his legs and a pillow put on his lap to act as table, book-rest, etc. A rather alarming succession of whiskies and brandies go down, with every time a facetious preliminary joke with Edward, an American ex-barman, or with Lord Moran in the shape of professional adviser. I have not heard the lord doctor answer; perhaps he knows it would make no difference.

I had just time to run down the dangerous steep mule-track to the cyclopean boulders, sprayed by gushing cascades that divided them. The pull up was a feat, and the sun turned the cold weather into a June day. All spirits rose to the beauty and the occasion — all, that is, except old Max Calvin, whose creased livid face is buried between a stuffy black hat and a book. A lot of whisky and brandy, good meat and salad, and 'little white-faced tarts' (to use Winston's expression) are consumed and then, of course, as I feared, nothing will quiet the Colonel (no assurances of the difficulties and the steepness) but he must himself venture down the gorge.

Old Moran once mumbled a bit about it being unwise. It carried as much weight as if it had been said by an Arab child in vulgar, rustic tongue. So down he goes and, once down, he next must get on top of the biggest boulder. There were a lot of tough 'tecs along, including the faithful Inspector Thompson, but even with people to drag you and heave you up it is a terrific strain and effort in a boiling sun when you have just had a heart attack.

Clemmie said nothing, but watched him with me like a lenient mother who does not wish to spoil her child's fun nor yet his daring – watched him levered up on to the biggest boulder, watched him spatchcocked out on top of it.

Shots were snapped, a little Arab boy was bribed to jump into the pool, and then this steep, heart-straining ascent began. I tore up for the second time, puffing like a grampus. It seemed to me that if a rope or strap could be found to pass behind his back, while two men walked in front pulling the ends, it would be better than dragging him by his arms. I could find nothing but a long tablecloth, but I wound that into a coil and stumbled down with it. Big success! He had no thought of being ridiculous (one of his qualities) so he leaned back upon the linen rope and the boys hauled our saviour up, while old man Moran tried his pulse at intervals. This was only permitted so as to prove that his heart was unaffected by the climb.

Algiers
February 25th, 1944

I'll try and be home for a day or two before the holidays. It's getting quite near – time to queue up for a place in the plane. I may have to return a few days before the end. Papa will be dreadfully lost here without me. He has no resources – no clubs, no sport, no cards, no books, no chums – poor, poor Papa.

It rains and rains and hails and lightens and freezes you in damp, but we mustn't grumble as January was a dream of sun and spring. Tomorrow we are to go chasing the wild boar, or *sanglier*. Papa has only got his dainty wedding boots and London trousers, a borrowed gun and limited cartridges. Snow will be on the mountainside where the drive takes place, and there is to be a lamb roasted whole by the local Sheikh or Kaid. Better perhaps to tell you about the boar hunt after and not before it takes place.

The Red Army celebrations were on a big scale on February 23rd. Splendid review – the Russians in four or five mammoth silver and glass cars. They had all been fitted out with dazzling gold-embroidered diplomatic uniforms. Madame Bogomolov[15] was in velvet and diamonds and sable, with an airy Parisian trifle on her humourless little head. We were all in a stand, or tribune, watching them salute the three Allied flags. First the central Russian banner to the new U.S.S.R. anthem (very reminiscent of the Czar's hymn) then Bogo moved automatically to the right and saluted the Stars and Stripes to the tune of *God Save the King*. He couldn't move over to the Union Jack for the *Star-Spangled Banner*, so the Yanks got two salutes to our blob. Then we had a reception at the Russian Embassy with all Algiers invited from Charlie Wormwood downwards, and there were enough cakes to feed Leningrad – literally thousands of them laid on tables in hundreds without plates, and laid on dadoes, and on the bases of statues in the passages – and vodka and caviar. A great joke.

I'm furious that the pig's wedding was delayed – now there's no hope of my seeing the thirteen results.

Rabat
April 1944

All went well and all goes well. When I left you[16] with such pain in my heart and such a matter-of-fact exterior, I took off to Paddington with Conrad. We were met at Swindon by a swagger R.A.F. car and officer and private, which deposited us nine miles away at Daisy Fellowes's Compton Beauchamp, a beautiful house. I wish you'd been with me to give me your opinion. It's for sale, but being an 'archigem' [old portmanteau word invented by Pa and Ma for architectural gem] would doubtless cost a fortune. Of

---

15　The wife of the Soviet Ambassador.
16　She had been in England for my Easter holidays and had now returned.

course it wasn't 8.30 that we were due to start but nearer midnight, so we had too long with Daisy but we were off at last, driving twenty miles in the loveliest spring evening – sickle moon and smells of new life and tender greens. As we neared Lyneham the clear sky filled with new constellations of aircraft.

We were three passengers, me, the A.V.M.[17] and Mrs. B. his personal assistant, who took his boots off and dressed him in his flying kit and soothed him and gave him his *Lilliput* magazine and treated him generally as Nanny used to treat you. I put on my boots and my padded combinations and laid me down, on a mattress this time, an improvement on a lilo. I went to sleep soon after we were up, my prayers said, and slept reasonably well till six. The other two were still logged so I got up stealthily and stood in an uncomfortable stance looking out of the mean little window. Dawn was there and sea beneath, not much else. The A.V.M. woke next and started his shaving operations with Barbasol, while I fixed my face. Mrs. B. slept on.

The A.V.M. must start yelling above the revs. 'If you want to make yourself comfortable, just go to the end of the aircraft.' It's no good shaking one's head, and yelling one can hold one's horses so I obeyed after a decent pause. It was light by now, and I moved gingerly down the fuselage (hold your breath now). Towards the end of the narrow body is a bit of glass flooring, out of which I imagine the bombs fall, and out of which the earth directly beneath you can be observed. I have often looked through it but seen little as the glass is too dirty and thick to give a clear view. Each side of the glass floor the aircraft starts to curve into sides, so it is natural, or at least I thought it was, to walk on the glass. I put my booted step upon it and my leg went *slap through* up to the fork. I was fortunately walking so delicately that my balance was instantaneously withdrawn to my safe foot and I dragged the culprit back to safety and got on with my business, and a strange business to be sure – a sanitary bin

17 Air Vice Marshal.

like a miniature pillarbox with a bit of sailcloth pinned up, all rags and tatters, which by holding with both hands one might achieve a bit of privacy. I felt I must admit to the breakage and told the A.V.M. who yelled 'We needn't tell anyone.'[18] I didn't know what that meant. Mrs. B. was awake by now and we drank some tepid coffee out of a Thermos and ate some chocolate and raisins.

Gibraltar whizzed past and at ten we were at Algiers itself, with Papa to greet me bursting with questions about you. The day was hot and sunny. A nice tame gazelle with Victory horns awaited my arrival in the courtyard and two boring chikors, a sort of duller partridge, were netted into a loggia. Freddie Fane[19] has invested in a lot of chickens and the cow, Fatima, is twice the girl and giving four gallons a day.

My orders were to be ready to leave next morning at eight by road for a three days' drive west – very long days. The first we covered 375 miles and got to a place called Tlemsin with a filthy hotel. Although there is no sign of war nothing is maintained – no hot water ever, no washing of sheets, no electric light bulbs and *filthy* food. Wonderful wild flowers in Algeria and sensational gold locusts, thick as lightly falling snow. They burst themselves on the windscreen and cover the road with their corpses, but they are beautiful. I thought at first they were butterflies.

Another long day's drive brought us to famous Fez, ancient capital of Morocco, a marvellous city untouched by modern hand, gushing with water and surrounded by green green hills studded with olive trees. We spent the following morning there, lunched with the French Consul M. Blanche, and came on a shorter drive to Rabat, the modern capital. We are two carloads – me and Papa

---

18 She apologised again on landing, expecting perhaps a word of apology or sympathy for the shock she had suffered. Instead, the AVM simply grinned and said, 'Oh don't worry, we can get that mended in no time.' Two years later, when he came to lunch at the Paris Embassy, my mother told the story to the assembled company. Still no sympathy: 'I promise you, Lady Diana, it was fixed in a couple of hours.'

19 The Comptroller.

and a chauffeur like Gary Cooper, in a new smart car full of my loose straw hats, loose coats and sordid basket of picnic food wrapped in eggy newspaper.

It's April 29th now and I'm in bed in the Consul's house at Rabat. It's 8 a.m. and I'm off soon to get this letter put on an airplane. Papa has already been recalled to Algiers so our plan of going on to Tangier doesn't look like materialising. He will have to take an airplane back and I shall thumb one somehow as I couldn't face that three days' dreary drive back again alone.

Algiers
May 15th, 1944

I have been listless and lazy yet busy this last week, hence a paucity of letters. You are all I love in England and for all that I haven't written for a long time. I sleep very badly – there's the rub. I wake at four, listening to an insane cock that starts his shrill clarion overnight and a rare nightingale and at last a deafening cacophony of early birds and late risers. I don't feel sleepy again till Mr Sweeny[20] in boiling hot battledress brings me some tepid coffee. I stagger into some hideous blue pyjamas (General Issue, 'G.I.', to the American Women's Forces) and meet an older but fatter lady on the loggia, and we are both made to breathe and count and bend and puff and sweat and groan by a younger, much fitter *culture physique* girl. The atmosphere is grey and oppressive. On such days as these Crippen killed Belle Elmore and Queen Elizabeth ordered lovers to be beheaded and armies surrender and children are fractious. The air is full of the golden snow of locusts.

I've just finished the *culture physique* and am off to pack parcels for French prisoners. It's exceedingly tedious, putting chocolate, butter, sugar, tobacco, soap, coffee and biscuits into

20 My father's batman.

little wooden boxes. There is no order and no overseeing. A wild cram-in, like you or me packing in a hurry Monday morning, and I feel sure it will be a brutal German who will open and gobble up the good things and leave the dehydrated carrots for the hungry Frogs.

The other day I took a car to the top of an Atlas mountain and walked and mule-back-rode for about twenty-six miles. I nearly died afterwards, but at the time it was wonderful and precipitous – a tiny mule path. One of our party, a sailor, had vertigo and didn't enjoy it so much. I adored it. We paused halfway in a strange oasis village by a gushing waterfall, ate our lunch, drank some wine from the Hoggar and composed ourselves to sleep, boots off and feet left in the stream to shrink and cool. Captain Wharton[21] (aged 65) dropped off with childish haste and snored shamelessly. Next came me who thought I hadn't slept at all till Vertigo Miller R.N. said 'Why do you sleep with one eye open?' so I suppose I did get forty winks. Next Minou de Montgomery, the other lady of the party and a Frog, tied a bandana over her face and slept like a baby, or rather like a nice dog with occasional whelps and whines, purporting to come out of dashing dreams. I'm not sure it wasn't all pretence.

Write what you have to learn in poetry, what your place is – the river – new boys – what you read in school and out and that you love me dearly. But for being deprived of you I'm really very happy and thrilled by the Resistance movement inside France, members of which we see a lot of – people who parachute in and out and people who travel always with their death dose. When danger is great they carry this dose in a minute box in their mouth as there would be no time to fumble in their pockets. It is swallowed when they fall into German hands for it is certain almost that under torture and an injection of that drug that deadens your resistance, they will betray their comrades. A man here the other day resorted to it.

21 Captain Eric Wharton, the Naval Attaché.

June 2nd, 1944

It is our Silver Wedding day – June 2 1944. If you had not come to me so late in time you might be twenty-three years old and fighting outside Rome. Thank you for being late. I wonder if you had any choice – if you chose us and the year – it's possible. I feel sadly happy – twenty-five years gone is the sad part. I'm crying a bit as I write, but they've been lovely years with no storms for Papa and me – not one – and I love him as much as ever I did. Some strange almost unknown Frog has sent me a silver necklace – very massive and chased with demon motifs. It's round my neck as I sit up in bed. Nightcap and common pink silk nightgown don't marry very well with its barbarity. You may see Papa before you see this. I hope you do, but I'll be miserable here without him. Encourage him to return soon, or he'll have less cause to return end of July and we do all want to be together. I've told Virginia Cowles[22] to go and see you. She is such fun. Ask her for Resistance stories. Tell her from me to take the most romantic of all the Pimpernels down to Eton – M. d'Astier.[23]

Algiers
June 1944

I am deeply worried about the situation of the de Gaulle Government being, or rather not being, recognised. Roosevelt is losing favour with me. Meanwhile we are losing it with the French daily. They will never forgive being kept entirely out of the liberation of their own country. They have united themselves under Wormwood. They have produced an army that fights to the death in Italy and would in France. They have organised a

---

22 A dashing young American journalist, author of *Looking for Trouble*. She later married Aidan Crawley MP.

23 Emmanuel d'Astier de la Vigerie, one of the leaders of the Resistance.

soul-stirring resistance inside their country. These advantages, hardly forged, are tempered and we use them, but when it comes to taking them into councils or taking their views on administration in their own land, or of letting them spill their own hot blood on their own earth – oh no, the President can't agree. I would hardly dare look them in the face if it wasn't that they all know Papa works all his flesh down to the bone (a long way) for them.

Algiers
July 28th, 1944

O I'm so hot. It's 90 in the room now at 9.30 a.m. really 7.30.

The house is overloaded. The boiler burst. Randolph has arrived fresh from a bad plane crash in Yugoslavia. He looks like death – emaciated, bent, caverns of black with two dead eyes lurking in them, water and bandages on his knees, a jolted spine, but spirits as ebullient as ever. He lies in a cupboard upstairs and is carried down to the sitting room by four Wop gorillas. Eve Curie fills another room with her khaki and medals and dreams of *échelons* and *mêlées* and *garde-à-vous*. Victor has the best room and is too big for it. I have to go to the docks now and collect a bag of bombs with him. Bloggs will-o-the-wisps around.

They all bring their breakfast trays on to my bed and smoke on it and lie on it and abuse each other across me, and only wear towels or underpants so show everything, and I get no moment to myself to write or to read or to think – perhaps as well for if I do I think sadly of not being with you or you with me because I do love you so, and hate to miss any part of your growth and affection and fun.

August 1944

Beloved, I'm so sad about Rex.[24] I hope you are. He was so fond of you and made fun for you. He was the soldier that I loved most in this vile war. He wasn't the kind that soldiers are made from – too sensitive and weak in body – too imaginative and delicate in every way – yet he dealt with the necessity as a soldier born and put more vigour and determination into the tedious life and grim fight than many a bloodthirsty tough, I'm sure.

I'm very weary and discouraged, though the war news is wonderful and should make up for all. It's too hot. I'm half glad you are not here. Everybody's nerves and livers are all over the shop. I can't keep my bedroom under 90 degrees. Appetites have gone and any zest for anything. One drips it away. Randolph doesn't really help me either. He's quite crippled and staggers into my bedroom at 9 a.m. followed by his breakfast. He is quite untrained and coughs and gurks like some dreadful dredger, bringing up repugnant things that have suffered a stomach–change, which he spews into his hand or into the vague. If I get up to turn on my bath he immediately takes my bed and puts his black dirt–encrusted feet on my sheets and sweats into them and covers them with ash and burns them with butts. He drinks all the gin and all the valuable fruit juice and is here, I think, for the duration as his legs don't improve. He is madly bored and leaves his mouth wide open to save opening it for perpetual yawns. Withal he's most affectionate and well meaning. Victor has gone home by ship. I had to motor his live bombs about the town and was thankful to get them on board the *Orion*. I'm dying to get a letter from you but quite understand trials[25] and journeys and excitements and alarms and excursions will have left no time for correspondence.

---

24 The painter Rex Whistler had been killed in action on 18 July.
25 Eton exams.

August 17th, 1944

Lovely letter received from you. I'm glad you did well in trials but you don't give me half enough detail. All my careful instructions seemed to have miscarried completely about your journeys etc. It looks really as though we'll all spend Christmas in Paris. What fun it sounds now. I suppose if we do we shall shiver in an ice-cold unfireplaced and unheated Embassy with neither light, gas nor water and dear old Spam and tinned milk again, probably with flying bombs as an accompaniment. Even that sounds nice from this country where we are baked and glutted with food and strong wines. I couldn't exist without the mountain chalet,[26] where it's cold and crystalline.

Last Monday I walked all the way down to the plain from the top, only about twelve kilometres, but every step of them jagged and perpendicular. I felt like a Mahometan Christian[27] plodding my stony way accompanied by Faithful – he too was an Arab – the city always in our view and never getting any nearer. I wore shoes from Morocco, all I've got. The kind of nails blacksmiths use hold them together and keep coming through the soles and into the flesh of heel and ball of foot. The Faithful guide (by profession the man who calls for *ordures*) would knock them in with a stone or drag them out with his teeth. I stumbled a lot and towards the end when pretty tired I hadn't the strength to save a stumble from a fall, and so went along collecting blood and future scabs on knees and hands and chin. I enjoyed it immensely.

August 27th, 1944

I've been to Rome. I said I would. I took Bloggs who got a few days leave. We hopped a Dawson[28] plane and arrived at 3 p.m. in

---

26 Which she had scrounged.
27 The hero of *The Pilgrim's Progress*.
28 Air Vice Marshal Dawson was, as I remember, head of RAF Transport Command.

Naples. The first thing I did was to go and see Tucker's brother[29] in hospital – quite a job, as there seem to be no sisters, nurses, orderlies or anything, so after reading and guessing and trying to deduce from signs and symbols what wing of this gigantic repair shop would be the thigh-mending department, I had to go round hundreds of beds looking for Timothy, like Edith Swan-Neck looking on the battlefield for the dead Harold. I found him at last, but he was unrecognisably thin and I was looking rather un-Bognor, so it took him a spell to recognise me. Squalor surrounded him – few pillowcases and lots of oldish stains, and six other suspended thighs all sweating and smelling, but he seemed very happy and uncomplaining and is due to return for convalescence.

I stayed a night with the Macmillans[30] – only Dorothy there – and was sharp enough to borrow a good car from a sailor I had got something on. Off we went next morning, a six-hour drive up all the battle route. Cassino is like some dreadful disease – unrecognisable as a town, more like suppurating leprous stalagmites. I went to the Grand Hotel in Rome. Randolph had got me a room. It's an old-fashioned sort of Ritz, translated for the nonce into a sort of Kremlin – men with tommy-guns at every door, because all the bigwigs with the exception of Duckling were staying there. Like the Kremlin too there seemed to be no charge for anything – rooms free, and if I signed bills for breakfast or Randolph or Mr. Wu's drinks – nothing more was heard of the item.

I had a banquet at the British Embassy for Duckling. I sat next to him, but every time he looks at me he remembers Wormwood and has apoplexy. I've written to him and said it must stop or he'd best not see me. I saw the Pope carried shoulder-high through two throngs of Allied soldiers, blackamoors and Poles and ordinaries, and he touched one per thousand of the

---

29 Timothy Jones had trodden on a bomb at Anzio and had had his leg amputated.

30 Harold Macmillan was at that time British Government Representative to the Allied Forces in the Mediterranean. Lady Dorothy Macmillan was his wife.

rosaries held up to him. I didn't enjoy any part of the lark. Now I'm back and am glad I did it. Back in a horrible U.S. Navy plane with no window. We stopped at Ajaccio but saw only the dust of the airfield.

So much has happened – Paris free and being bombed – we off any day.

August 28th – Freddie Fane and two Embassy people off today by ship. I'll do all I can to get a final week with you at Bognor or some place, failing that I'll be over to see you before the next holidays – anyway Christmas in Paris.

Too hot and too irritated with stickiness and flies.

7

'The giraffe shall lie down with the duck'

THE PARIS EMBASSY, SEPTEMBER 1944–APRIL 1947

My darling Mummy and Papa,

The Schmidt family have a very comfortable three-storey house in the residential quarter. Monsieur was out when I arrived, but I was greeted by Madame. I should put her age at about thirty. Unmade-up, but quite pretty, neat and tidy. She's charming and gives one the feeling that nothing is too much trouble. There are two children, boys. The younger one, Jean-Bernard, only two or three, and I have seen him but once. The other is four, with great charm and a faultless knowledge of French, German and Alsatian. He adores me, presumably because he made me read Babar while I was waiting for tea. It has now become rather a bore, though, because I can't ever shake him off.

The only other inhabitant of the house is a large Airedale, by far the most ferocious dog I have ever seen in my life, compared with which Cerberus would resemble a somewhat sickly pekinese. I live in perpetual danger of my life, because every time it sees me it makes a rush and has to be held back by Madame, snarling. My fear is extremely embarrassing, and is augmented by the fact that instead of saying 'It's all right; he won't hurt you' Madame looks rather worried, and says, 'I should keep away until he knows you better.' Hardly encouraging.

All my love,

John Julius

P aris had been liberated by the Allies on 26 August. My parents flew back from Algiers to London at the end of the month and left again for Paris a couple of weeks later. In mid-September I saw them off from (I think) Northolt, with an escort of forty-five Spitfires – the war was still very much in progress.

My father was of course thrilled. After a fairly unfortunate war – he had hated the Ministry of Information, while his Far Eastern mission, through no fault of his own, had been a failure, overtaken by events – here was the best job he could ever have asked for. He loved France, spoke beautiful French and could discuss its history and literature for hours; moreover he would be moving into one of the most magnificent houses in all Paris, bought by the Duke of Wellington from Napoleon's sister Pauline.

My mother was a good deal less keen. She was of course happy for my father, knowing as she did how much it meant to him; but the prospect of being British Ambassadress in Paris was daunting indeed. She had never enjoyed grandeur for its own sake; left to herself, she would infinitely have preferred to return to Bognor and her little farm. But she had no intention of letting my father down, and once installed in the Embassy she certainly made the best of it. At the end of the superb enfilade of drawing rooms on the first floor was Pauline's bedroom, with hangings of crimson silk and her *retour d'Egypte*[1] bed, with ancient Egyptian figures and sphinxes carved at the corners. It was perhaps a little short and narrow by modern standards, but my mother wasn't going to pass

---

1 Napoleon's return from his Egyptian expedition in 1799 had launched a craze in Paris for all things Egyptian.

up an opportunity like that; she and my father were to sleep happily in it for the next three years.

There was only one feature missing in this glorious house: it had no library – 'indeed,' my father wrote, 'hardly a bookshelf worthy of the name'. He therefore wrote to the Ministry of Works, proposing that if they would convert a suitable room into a library worthy of the building, he would fill it with books, nearly all leather-bound, on English and French history and literature. The Ministry replied, predictably, that the time was not ripe; he asked them how soon they were expecting the arrival of another ambassador who would be willing to present a thousand or more books. In the end the authorities caved in, and the result was the really lovely room, designed by three of Paris's top decorators, that we see today.

My own memories, from when I joined my parents there for my Christmas holidays, were first of the perishing cold. This was the most savage winter that Paris had experienced for fifty years, and the British Embassy was one of the few buildings to have any heating. We were also among the still fewer that could provide limitless gin and whisky, obtained at tax-free NAAFI prices – around sixpence a bottle. From the start, my mother established free-for-all drinks parties at six o'clock every night in the *salon vert*, open to all friends, French and English alike, who cared to drop in. For the French in particular, who had seen little enough of either drink for the past four years of occupation, these evenings were a godsend, attracting all the intellectual and literary elite of Paris – writers like Jean Cocteau, designers like Christian Bérard,[2] actors like Louis Jouvet. I would call them by their first names and mix them dry martinis and whisky-and-sodas; but alas, although my French was fluent enough, neither my conversational powers nor my understanding were up to the challenge. The fact

2 One evening Bébé Bérard, gloriously unkempt, with ash-covered beard and shoulder-length hair, brought his little pug dog, which instantly deposited a small turd on the carpet. Unhesitatingly he picked it up and put it in his pocket. My mother always said it was the best example of good manners she had ever seen.

was that I was just a bit too young: an awkward adolescent, superficially sophisticated perhaps for my age, but at bottom a rather
slow developer without any real appreciation or understanding of
what was going on around me. Had I been three or four years
older, I should have got a thousand times more out of it all and,
I like to think, acquitted myself rather better.

Among the British *illuminati* there were writers, actors, artists,
composers, conductors – all of whom had to be given their own
special party – musicians for Benjamin Britten, sculptors for Henry
Moore, the stage for the Oliviers, poets and men of letters for
T. S. Eliot. And, as always, fellow members of the Diplomatic
Corps to be kept sweet. Then there were congresses of world
scientists, football teams, the Salvation Army, SHAEF[3] – who had
their own clock and were always an hour late or early – whole
queues of voluntary services – the WVS,[4] the Mothers' Union, or
ENSA.[5] Finally there were the provincial tours, perhaps the most
exhausting of all, with endless lunches and receptions and dinners
given by Mayors and Prefects and Chancellors of universities
awarding my father honorary degrees. My mother always maintained that it was the most gruelling life she had ever led, far
harder and more exhausting than being a hospital nurse or an
actress or a farm worker.

What we all looked forward to was the Investitures, when my
father had to award decorations, usually the King's Medal for
Courage, to the heroes and heroines of the Resistance. Most were
humble men and women from the remotest areas of France,
quite often simple peasants who had never before been to Paris.
Some had sheltered escaped British prisoners of war for weeks
until they could be taken across the Spanish border; others had
slipped out at night to light landing strips for the tiny little
aircraft that flew from England with weapons, radio equipment

3 Supreme Headquarters, Allied Expeditionary Force, then based at Versailles.
4 Women's Voluntary Services.
5 Entertainment for the forces.

and undercover agents. Yet others had planted bombs under railway viaducts or blown up Nazi staff cars. Some had been arrested and tortured by the Gestapo, but had refused to speak and on release had instantly resumed their old activities. Eric Duncannon, my father's secretary, would read their citations, his voice choking with emotion; then a small, frightened figure would step forward and my father would pin on the medal, tears pouring down his cheeks.

Some months after our arrival at the Embassy, my mother found a country house. I have already noted her life-long inability to resist a drive with an open gate. It chanced that this weakness led her, one afternoon in 1945, to a perfectly exquisite small eighteenth-century house, with a garden running down to the artificial lake that extends eastward from the Château de Chantilly. There was no sign of life, so she rang the bell. It turned out that the house was leased from the Institut de France by Bill Bullitt, the prewar American Ambassador to Paris. Bullitt happened to be still in France, now attached to SHAEF at Versailles; my mother telephoned him, and he confirmed that he had no further use for it. The transfer of lease was soon arranged, and the Château de Saint Firmin was to be ours, first as a weekend retreat and then as a permanent home, for the next fifteen years.

———

Paris
September 15th, 1944

It's your birthday and we've sent a telegram but we don't know how or when it gets to you. From the beginning now – after many many happy returns to you (fifteen years old – *c'est formidable*).

We rose in a moment – a beautiful machine that Dakota – swift and silent. I could recognise nothing of England till we came to the coast, and a dazzling white Beachy Head lapped by emerald waves then proclaimed itself; like an artistic poster for Albion it was, and I was moved, more moved than on crossing into France. Here we all dropped our books and papers and skinned our eyes for flying-bomb sites and shell holes and devastated towns. I'm bound to say I didn't see a lot. The fields looked orderly and well cultivated, and the villages intact. I saw a lot of bomb craters concentrated in the centres of fields – lack of precision? Or something we are ignorant of? Soon we were circling over Paris itself – our fellow Dakota apparently motionless in the high air, and all around, dipping and diving and soaring like swallows, our forty-five escort Spitfires. Down we came to the little group of friends and diplomats knotted together on a completely bashed-up aerodrome. Victor was there.

We drove the twelve miles into Paris at a snail's pace with a dozen police on motorcycles. The people in the street hearing the clatter mostly stopped and waved or raised their hats, and workmen in groups would even raise a cheer. This was encouraging to my rather feeble spirits. The streets were quite empty of traffic in the suburbs, except for an occasional army vehicle or a confusing orderless merry-go-round of bicycles ridden by women and girls with panniers on their mudguard generally carrying a biggish poodle trimmed to kill on the rack, and their heads, if not sporting the highest, most shapeless and ridiculous hats fashion ever produced, then trimmed to kill like the poodles with bows and roses stuck in.

This held good for the heart of Paris, but here are added in the Champs-Elysées a lot of very old horse fiacres waiting for custom but too expensive to hire. The streets are hung and the windows are dressed with Allied flags, but there seems no ray of gladness or gaiety in the atmosphere. No cinemas, no theatres on account of electricity or cafés or restaurants because of food, except fabulously expensive black-market ones – accounts for it I suppose. We laid a wreath without hesitation on the Unknown Soldier's grave at the Arc de Triomphe. A good crowd had assembled in spite of it being the luncheon hour, and at two we got at last to our doss-down and where do you think it is? Our own old rooms at the Berkeley! Not a thing changed – the white-haired lady and all. It has been taken over by us for our staff and we have the first-floor rooms, nicer than before as there is no traffic noise and because you cannot get in for flowers – enormous millionaire baskets hanging over with enormous orchids (how do they grow them unless they have coal? I haven't seen any in England for years) and flowers from government officials and old friends and shops wanting custom and hotels and collaboration-ists working their passage home, and still they come. Mostly what we were told to expect was wrong – it always is. In this hotel there is electric light always, hot water since yesterday, and deli-cious food, though too much of it – always juicy raw chateau-briands and chocolate éclairs of your own dreams. After lunch we went to look the Embassy over – it's vast and makes my heart sink. I'll tell about it next letter as if I don't finish up with this one it will miss a bag.[6]

Paris
September 23rd, 1944

We moved into the Hotel Bristol in order to be grand and I'm not at all happy with the gloom and cold of Paris with no you, no Bognor, nothing much that I like except Papa. The pretty chestnut-windowed Berkeley was a solace and an old friend, only fifteen steps away from the street or the desk, and no passages, all compact and friendly. Now we have come to the vulgarest of two-storey flats seven floors up in an unreliable lift,[7] passages and isolation

6 The only post back to England was by diplomatic bag, personally escorted by a King's Messenger.

7 The very first evening, on their journey down to the dining room, they were much embarrassed to find themselves sharing the lift with Mr and Mrs P. G. Wodehouse, recently released from internment in Berlin.

and a ghastly expanse of hideosity, all so that we should have a private dining room and a bathroom each, with two basins in each, one for each hand and a third at chest height that can only be meant for vomiting. One is always warned of what isn't true. I was told there would be no heat or light or food but it would be most exciting and interesting. Well, there are masses of all the commodities and beyond that drab dullness and nothing more.

I'm trying to get to Algiers to recover at least half of my luggage and household equipment, but S.H.A.E.F. as usual is doing all it can to impede, so we don't get on at all – no linen, no china, no glass, no coal, no hope of getting into the Embassy. Papa goes and sees the torture chambers. They exist all over Paris – beyond belief horrible. The Huns put the men and women they thought could be made to talk in baths of iced water for hours, then in boxes made to sterilise clothes in that heat up to any temperature. They walled them up with their heads out, they hung them up by their arms and tied fifty kilos to their poor feet. They covered these rooms with the blood drawn from floggings and shootings. The walls of the cells are scrawled with messages, some warning newcomers who to mistrust among friends. One said 'C'est ma fiancée 12 rue de . . . qui est la cause de ma mort.'[8] Others wrote love doggerel verses. Very moving, isn't it? A German said in the Metro as a woman clopped in on high stilt shoes like mine but more elaborate 'to think that we meant them to go barefoot'. This explains the attitude of the Paris women in the occupation years – their grotesquely large hats hung with flowers and fruits and feathers and ribbons, and their high carved wooden shoes were a long nose to the Boches, or anyway that's what they say.

Raimund's been running round for three or four days accompanied by an enormous 100 per cent Hun couple whom he dug out of the Portuguese Embassy where they were cowering. He finds it quite impossible to get them locked up and he daren't let them go, so he'll have them till the peace like an albatross round his neck.

8 'It is my fiancée, 12 rue de . . . who is the cause of my death.'

Paris
November 14th, 1944

The great visit is over[9] – all the preparations, all the fears and the
excitements, but not the hangovers and not alas! the devastating
cold I took at the ice-cold ceremonies. At first I thought to have
the bunch lodged with us. O the scrubbing and repapering and
furbishing and garnishing and testing for security. Then I drove
down to Beaune with Bloggs to buy burgundy. The Hotel de la
Poste where you and I and Kaetchen lodged (and where I got in
a cross panic because you and K. disappeared in the morning's
starting-time and it was to buy *me* birthday presents. Dear dear
Kaetchen I miss him so[10]) was closed and we had time only to find
the wine merchant and be told that all was shut on Saturday and
if we wanted the wine we must get it out of the cellars ourselves.
Nothing nicer, so down to the depths we went armed with an iron
trolley with holes for bottles in it, and what fun it was pulling the
precious stuff out of its mould and penicillin and bringing it safely
into the sunlight. Five dozen we brought up unlabelled – '*très
mal habillé, hélas*' the seller said '*comme une belle femme avec
une mauvaise toilette*'.[11]

When I got home to Paris all plans had been altered. The party
were to be guests of the Frog Government and were to live at the
Quai d'Orsay. My disappointment was soon dissipated by relief
and the thought that murder would be unlikely to occur in our
house ('What, in our house?' said Macbeth hypocritically when
Duncan was murdered). I went round to see the rooms prepared
for them at the Palais. They had been blazed up for our King and
Queen six years ago – vast and ugly, with two very dated bathrooms of gold and silver mosaics – aglow with indirectly lit crystal
and pearls and fiddle-de-dees – Semiramis style and lovely I

9 Winston Churchill's first official visit to France after the Liberation of Paris.

10 He had died in New York in March 1943.

11 'Very badly dressed, alas, like a beautiful woman with a bad *toilette*.'

thought but much condemned by good-taste people. Goering had left his mark in the shape of a solid white china bathroom raying out infra-red and ultra-violet rays, everything in it too solid and massive for any bulk to break except the white American cloth (reinforced) on his rubbing table. He's burst that all right. Also a dressing room large and cupboarded for a thousand uniforms and mirrors in plenty and odd bits such as a stool you might see at Daniel Neal's[12] on which the unfortunates who have to try tight shoes on to hot feet squat and boot you.

Never was a greater success, from the frozen hour when we awaited the arrival on the airfield to the moment when he left this house with de Gaulle at midnight for the 'front' at Besançon. Much fear of assassination from German snipers on roofs and Vichy monsters. Still M. Luizet, the Préfet de Police, made a magnificent job of keeping the Duckling in safety, and in not letting the defences show. When the King and Queen went to Paris you couldn't see them for armoured men on armoured bicycles. This time the party looked unprotected, yet civilian guards armed to the teeth were in every window and sprinkled thickly into the crowds.

The first night we dined alone, meaning Edens, C.I.G.S.,[13] a few secretaries, Alex Cadogan[14] with the Duckling at the Quai d'Orsay. It was rather boring. Clemmie was sleepy and Winston, between Beatrice Eden and me, as difficult as he always is until the champagne has warmed him and until he has been able to draw the *whole* table into his influence. Two striving women, however beautiful or witty, are not enough, but after the feast, in the Napoleon III salon, with English whisky dropping on the exquisite Savonnerie carpet, his old magic took charge of us all as he weaved his slang and his pure English into a fantastic pattern.

Next morning your mother, dressed in a really fine suit of black

12 A shop for smart children's clothes in Portman Square, no longer in existence.
13 Chief of the Imperial General Staff.
14 Permanent Head of the Foreign Office.

cloth with monstrous collar of black fox and pockets of the same, took her place in the women's tribune alongside Mesdames Churchill, de Gaulle, Catroux,[15] Massigli,[16] etc., etc. We were segregated from the men which irritated me, more especially because being on a line with their tribune we couldn't see what was going on. The bands played, they all hoorayed, and the Great came up the Champs-Elysées in an open car – one so pink and benign, the other so sinister and elongated. Slowly they drove up to the Arc, did there whatever they had to do and then, the most dangerous moment, walked down again half a mile to their tribune from where, for an hour and a half, they watched the review of English, American and French troops, plus an endless detachment of *pompiers*[17] which had played a big part in the liberation of Paris. By this time I was blue with cold. I got home shuddering, with pneumonia seeds well sown. Dinner with Wormwood that night, following on long conversations that had rippled along most successfully all afternoon. Dinner very different to our last grisly evening under that roof. Smiles now in place of quinces and vinegar, and Duckling as happy as happy could be – all axes buried – a new Renaissance of Love Relations. The Giraffe shall lie down with the Duck.

Next day Sunday I was too ill with 'flu to make luncheon with the Big Shots at the local F.O. so stayed in bed drugging and sweating till dinner time, when we had our staff of eighty assembled downstairs at 7.45 and a de Gaulle dinner of seventeen assembled upstairs at 8.15. Of course Duckling was half an hour late and came to the staff party as the General was arriving so I had to miss the lower party and the P.M. giving out the news that the *Tirpitz* had been sunk.

The rooms all candle-lit looked as beautiful and classically pure as I looked bloated and blotched with cold and veganin, but I got

---

15 Wife of General Georges Catroux.

16 Wife of René Massigli, French Ambassador in London 1944–54.

17 The fire brigade.

through it and could appreciate that it was very successful. We had the Bogos[18] and Mr Caffrey, the U.S. Ambassador, and the Edens, and Vaniers[19] and Bidault.[20]

March 12th, 1945

The days are boringly full. They won't be when you come – only full of you. First we'll go up to the front and visit the regiment that I heap with favours. I don't know who we'll take – Teddie[21] perhaps. We shall have to do it grand and not in our own hobble-dehoy style. Then we'll see. The season is still cold and budless but there's three weeks to go before the awaited day. Papa has got to visit some provincial towns so it might be Toulouse and Marseilles. We might combine with him. All to be settled when you come except the visit to the front, which is more or less fixed.

On Sunday a very queer convocation took place. At 5 o'clock all the princes of the Christian Churches, the present Roman alone excepted, arrived in sombre black at the Embassy and retired into Rosemary's room, where beneath the smiling eye of a very young Queen Victoria they stripped and robed themselves into a true blazonry. There was the Bishop of Chichester, sober enough, and there were four or five dazzling gold Russians, and a few outrageous purple Archimandrakes [sic], all with beards and manes to their waists, and there was a distinguished Pasteur [sic] with clean Geneva bands, and uniformed Church and Salvation Army representatives. In our little Embassy church they preached and they prayed and they sang and they exhorted and they blessed in their several tongues and a choir of Russians warbled in the gallery,

18 Mr and Mrs Bogomolov, Soviet Ambassador.
19 General and Mrs Georges Vanier, Canadian Ambassador.
20 Georges Bidault, French Foreign Minister.
21 Teddie Phillips, the Embassy Comptroller. This proved to be an extraordinary adventure, but as my mother and I were there together there are no letters describing it. I have told the story in full in my memoirs, *Trying to Please*.

and our own dear choir of spinsters held their own in the chancel and then out they all filed again, unashamed of their startling feathers, these old clerical birds, down the Faubourg St. Honoré in broad daylight. The pedestrians were crossing themselves and gasping, the jeeps were crossing each other and gasping and gurking too. I never knew what occasion had called them together. We'd had the Bishop and Pasteur [of Huguenots] to lunch but the whole meal was too sticky and nervous for anything consecutive. I wasn't prepossessed by the Bishop of Chichester and much prefer the Dean.

Chantilly
June 25th, 1945

I enjoyed your long leave[22] very very much. Now you'll be having Papa down. He goes to England June 30th for a week or ten days, and he'll bring you all my love. We are installed now for weekends in our country home. It's what the fairies told of – without fault – six bedrooms, three salons, one dining room, five bathrooms, a royal park as your garden, cascades and lakes.

Think hard about your summer holidays and talk to Papa about them. I think the beauty of this place, since it isn't one's home, might not be enough to amuse you. I think about July a lot. I've thought of a walking tour over some mountains with a donkey, or into Brittany or Switzerland. I've thought of a flying visit to Harold Balfour in West Africa to buy material. He has a private plane, but he lives in the White Man's Grave and it will be the hottest time of the year. He passed through the other day and will be passing through again. I'll consult him. There's always Italy, if Bloggs is still there, or he may be here. We'll see, but I like thinking and talking about it.

We've had a horrible night of atrocity films – I meant to ask

22 Half-term.

all the collaborators, but only the English came who believe anyway. I went to bed sick and dejected and crippled with lumbago and feeling if only I could get to sleep I'd as soon not wake again. You mustn't let me feel that way. I want to live to see who you marry and what sort of children you have and if you know how to be happy, and what work you do, and if it interests you, and if your wife doesn't love you and help you, or if she deceives and bores and nags you and is generally the opposite of what you hoped from behind the bandage Love tied tightly across your eyes, I'll strangle her or get her exiled, I promise.

Another Paris torture was going to see a new French Academician received by his peers. The Academicians wear the most beautiful embroidered tail coat, like Papa's gold one but in different shades of green on a black cloth. A scarlet ribbon of the *Légion d'honneur* gives it an accent. Two old men made speeches of half an hour each in a suffocatingly hot atmosphere. The President was inaudible and everyone is over eighty.

———

At Christmas 1946 I left Eton. In those days of compulsory National Service I had been accepted into the Royal Navy, but my call-up could not occur before my eighteenth birthday the following September. It was agreed that I should put in six months or so at a French university. At this stage in my life I had a passion for foreign languages and had deluded myself that I was quite good at them. (Ten years later, when I tried to learn Arabic, I discovered how wrong I was.) In French, thanks to three hour-long lessons a week from the age of five, I had been fluent since childhood; Eton had taught me passable German; and at the age of twelve I had persuaded a godfather to give me a Linguaphone course in Russian. But in all three – and particularly the last two – there was plenty of room for improvement, so Strasbourg was clearly indicated. Alsace had been part of Germany between the Franco-Prussian and the First World War, and again during the second. Virtually every educated citizen was bilingual – or trilingual if you count Alsatian, which sounds like German spoken by a Welshman. Here, it seemed, was the perfect place in which to polish up my second foreign language, and the fact that the university boasted the best Russian faculty in the country gave me high hopes for progress in my third. Peter Storrs – nephew of the still-celebrated orientalist Sir Roger and Director of the local British Reading Room – was asked to find a suitable local family prepared to accept me as a lodger. His choice fell on a young lawyer, Paul Schmidt, and his wife Betty; it could hardly have been a happier one.

A word must now be said of Louise de Vilmorin who, to my great surprise, only now makes her first appearance in the story. Looking through these letters, I am astonished that my mother had not mentioned her before, since she had been part of all our lives. She was a poet, novelist, singer and *raconteuse* of genius, and my father had fallen seriously in love with her at first sight in November 1944, less than two months after his arrival in Paris; my mother, who never minded his affairs so long as the object of his affections met with her approval, loved her almost as much as he did – to the point where Parisian gossips were even speculating on a threefold relationship. This it was not; but Louise returned her love in a similar degree. At the beginning of 1945 my parents actually gave her a room of her own at the Embassy; she slept there for weeks at a time, and was there almost every day for lunch or dinner – frequently both.

I, at the age of fifteen the only member of the family not in love with Louise, was nonetheless knocked sideways by her charm. It happened quite often, when she was staying in the house, that my parents would be out at some official reception and she and I would lunch alone together. She would talk to me exactly as she would have talked to a grown-up, greatly improving my French and reducing me to howls of laughter with hilarious stories about her childhood and family. Afterwards she would pick up her guitar and teach me dozens – literally – of old French songs, a repertoire that would prove invaluable ten or fifteen years later at sticky diplomatic dinner parties in Belgrade and Beirut. I remember too the three of us – my mother, Louise and me – driving off on a week's holiday in the south-west, leaving my father working in the Embassy.

Gradually, after perhaps two years, my father grew restless. Louise was broken-hearted; but she recovered, taking up first with Orson Welles and later with André Malraux.[23] (During this last relationship she tended to call herself Marilyn Malraux.) She remained a close friend of my father until his death in 1954, and of my mother and me until she herself died on Boxing Day 1969.

═══

Paris
January 1947

I miss you terribly. Will you have enough to do? If no classes or lectures are obligatory and if there is no examination to work for? Should you not have some coaches who will take you privately two or three hours a day? I wonder how cold it is. Here one is curled and shrivelled by the temperature – roads icebound and very little heating. In London there is *no* heating at the Dorchester. They explained how it was lacking in order to be sure of keeping the hot water supply boiling. The next day there was no hot bath.[24]

I went to *An Inspector Calls* by J. B. Priestley and enjoyed it only fairly. I saw beloved Bloggs who asked often after you and of

23 French novelist, art theorist and politician.

24 This, be it noted, was nearly two years after the end of the war.

you. There were, of course, a few Emerald meals. The cold made her a bit testy. There was *Born Yesterday*, a new American comedy produced by L. Olivier – good enough. There was Victor[25] to give me lunch at Wilton's and to spoil that lunch by bringing Tess, so that I couldn't ask him if his marriage was doing well. Which reminds me – don't get engaged or married in Strasbourg. You must see a world of women before you pick one and *don't get picked yourself*, especially not in the street or bar. They'll contaminate and deceive you and most probably give you diseases of all kinds and so *méfiez-vous* now you're on your own and keep yourself and your love for something or somebody almost exactly like me, with a happier disposition.

? January 1947

L.L. and I and Juliet and Cecil and General Béthouart[26] came over by Newhaven and Dieppe on Sunday. England (East) already gripped in snow, we had to take the train to the port. Once aboard L.L. and I lay in our twin beds, boots, hats, veils and gloves all in place and slept on and off, while Cecil and Juliet tossed about in the visible next cabin. It was rough and pleasant. From deck to car at Dieppe (even the passport stamper came to the car with the equipment) so we were home again at 5.30. Miss Rosamond Lehmann is a beauty with a dense chunky cloud of grey hair (first quality) and Miss Vivien Leigh is also a beauty on a minute scale. She is so beautiful that all the hideous hats she tries on become beautiful on her impeccable little head and I see she finds it impossible to select the one that suits her best. She is as sincere and good as her face proclaims. We dined, just the house-load which made ten, and on Monday night we had a tremendous party – super-star 'Colette' 74-year-old genius of letters on the arm

25 Victor Rothschild had recently married Tess Meyer.
26 Former C.-in-C., French Army in Austria.

of her nanny-husband, bare feet, a quantity of shawls and everyone flat on their stomachs *en hommage*. Cocteau,[27] of course, and Marcel Thiébaut.[28] Nothing would move them until 2 a.m. and now I can't write any more but in future I'll take a carbon copy of my diary to Conrad and keep you up to date. All, all love. Write as often as you can.

Paris, Jan. 29th, 1947

So there was a cocktail for the British Hospital at the Officers' Club and another at Madame Faramont where Hoytie for reasons due to her sobriety took charge of the presenting of all the Americans to me. They were legion and she did not know their names – so it came to 'I want you to meet this very nice Colonel' or 'this distinguished veteran' and then there was the Marivaux play accompanied by the Laurence Oliviers – a deep sleep for all all of us, altho' I'm sure it's charming. This followed by a fantasy in mime where the great actor Barrault does Pierrot and his wife of fifty does Columbine with bare old legs – most *unappetitlich*[29] and this was followed by the back-stage visit. Champagne in the dressing room, bed at last. Golly it's cold, face, feet, hands and heart all shrivelled and stiff.

The mornings are very *mouvementés* these days says André the *huissier*.[30] This morning was Hogarth – here was Madame Porthault of the fabulous sheets, *luxe, moyen-luxe et grand-luxe*, the last category are paid with gold and loss of vision. Miss Lehmann was fingering them enviously, and has fallen for three nightgowns made for Queen Mab which will put her back at least £50. My description of Vivien Leigh's beauty had put them in a

27 Jean Cocteau, novelist, playwright, artist, designer and film-maker.
28 Writer.
29 Unappetising.
30 White-tie-and-tailed doorman.

twitter, so when she came down in a depressing little darkest red rest gown, her sweet face innocent of the slightest dust of powder or of a streak of pink on her beautiful ashen mouth my shock was almost as great as theirs. Louise looks like death and acting like the symbol of life, telephoning and weaving exaggerations. Cecil slouched in with Don Quixote grey hair in a short flannel plaid dressing gown. Larry Olivier in a smart brocade one kicked his way in, his hands holding a pair of Empire oil lamps in urn form – a present for a good hostess.

The *tapissier*[31] brought news of the hanging of George III and his Queen Charlotte in the anteroom. Jacques (*ici Londres*) Franck[32] came to look at the perfectly beautiful good repair tassels the Office of Works are trying to force me to send home in order that they may tear the silk off and replace with new because they cannot make new wooden moulds and cannot waste the silk put aside for the job. I can only quiet them by promising to get some wood moulds made here – hence Jacques's presence. Twenty press men with cameras were stampeding next door in their efforts to get Rosamond Lehmann who was eventually flung to them. A doubtful suspicious fellow, a friend called Momo Aveline called for orders and got the following: 1) Get made two gold forks, we hope at his own expense to replace the two lost out of my eighteenth-century picnic canteen that the Angleseys gave me at my wedding. 2) Sell a ring for Juliet. 3) Look at the wooden fringe on my bed and get some second-hand like it, as that too cannot be made in England. Teddie, the incubus, stands in the middle of all this, grinning while I fly at him. Why has he not got me footballs for my regiment, ordered two months before Christmas? Why are all the cars out of order with five men to repair them? Why has Roger, *valet de pied*, gone to Rome and Naples to see a *soi-disant*[33] godmother die,

---

31 Carpet fitter.

32 Interior decorator who had broadcast regularly from London to Occupied France during the war.

33 So-called.

at our expense with a living allowance and boasting that he is taking secret papers for the Ambassador and that he is to look out for a villa for *son Excellence*? When they'd all gone and I'd lied Juliet out to lunch I had a tray in bed with Rosamond by my side and I like her enormously, shy and affectionate, grateful, unspoilt, slightly devitalised, beautiful.

30th. The Lions' cocktail party was most brilliant. All the *éditeurs*,[34] Plon and Gallimard and Lafout, writers like Mauriac, Aragon, Malraux, Vilmorin and actors, beauties, odds and ends, all fans of Lehmann or Leigh. Jenny Nicholson, granddaughter of old William, daughter of Robert Graves and wife of Alexander Clifford said could she come and see me tomorrow a.m. as she wants to write an article, a very nice one about me for the *Mail*. I said anything she likes as long as she does not put it in interview form, so she'll come and what will she find, I dread to think, over and above the night-capped woman in the imperial bed.

31st. This morning – more sheets and chemises being shown, Momo coming with the wooden fringe already found, the house party *en déshabille*,[35] the press this time champing for Vivien, while Cecil was snapping Rosamond and Jenny Nicholson was appraising the scene kindly. When they'd all cleared out on their separate ways she remained and told me a lot to please me – how many embassies she has studied but none compare at all to this one – how she asks the French always what they think of me and the splendid replies she gets. How ambassadresses ought to be paid – for if they work the way I do they deserve it and if they are lazybones it might stimulate them.

Jacques Février has come back and been to lunch and tells me a lot of good about you. I love you and don't like that dog.[36]

---

34 Publishers.

35 Not yet dressed.

36 Cario, the Schmidts' Airedale, which had taken a violent dislike to me.

February 1st, 1947. Paris

Worst month of the year survived. The big trees I see through the window are snow-covered – there must be four inches on the balcony. It lends light to this gloomy hour of eight. Cecil B. is in bed (*fortement grippé*).[37] The Oliviers are still with us. Jubags is making far distant engagements, it looks like a lifer. The reigning Princes of Liechtenstein have returned refreshed to their principality, a relief to me as they haunt the bedroom floor. Hamilton Kerr, once an M.P., now nursing Cambridge, came to dinner – with nice accounts of J.J. in Strasbourg. 'Very good manners – he shakes hands with everyone.' Good old Embassy teaching, effective on the Continong, embarrassing in England. I remember Hutchie used to 'shake' on arrival and departure due I suppose to a childhood spent or half spent in Monte Carlo. Have you had whale steak yet on your menu? Pepys ate it. That we should come to this! It will be Jumbo next. Trunk soup.

Sunday. All so quiet not a mouse stirring. Cecil languishing in bed. The Oliviers are sleeping or working but not playing, Juliet doggo, L.L. gone to Verrières and Papa reading lessons in church. I am now going to write in innocence and silly assishness to Canon Bate of the Colonial Continental Church something and tell him that our Padre is good and well loved and that we don't want him to be snatched away and the Bishop of Tanganyika, who has not left his post for twenty-seven years, put in his place. The Padre sent me round two suitcases stuffed with clothes, lace and feathers, bequeathed him by a Greek princess. He wanted my advice on their disposal, thinking them to be of a certain value. 'There's one dress made entirely of brilliants, another beautiful black lace creation. The underclothes are marvellous and you should see the feathers.' Alas, alas, I had the sad advice of jumble sale when I opened the boxes and saw the saddest mess of tattiness imaginable. 1918–waist–round–knees numbers.

37 With severe flu.

Cheap and bad when new – of the underclothes Marguerite used a single effective word – *pourriture*.[38]

Del Giudice, the film magnate, once the independent producer of such films as *Henry V* and *In Which We Serve*, now sucked into the monopoly of the Rank combine, came to lunch and bored our pants off, and to dinner came Mr. Roger Furse who is doing the clothes for L. Olivier's film of *Hamlet* and M. Buchel the Oliviers' assistant, both nice boys – we played The Game[39] afterwards and the Oliviers acted worst.

Feb. 3rd. We are very fond of the Oliviers – I've seen all the sketches for the *Hamlet* film and they are wonderful. Vivien is to play Ophelia. Cecil still sneezing away. Duff read short stories (one good, two bad) by Elizabeth Bowen aloud to us while I stitched myself a gipsy skirt of silk – and for dinner the lot of us – six – went to Verrières where there was ice on the bathroom floor. The Game was played afterwards and Larry Olivier, rather too well oiled, was quite awful to Juliet – talking to her as one might to a disobedient dog, authoritative, very amusing for us I'm ashamed to say, but I hope she did not notice it too much. Our Oliviers leave us today and Lady Lascelles[40] takes their place, a disadvantageous exchange.

What news of the Airedale – it haunts me rather. Try and go in for an exam or is that not possible? I'm afraid you'll have no urge for work. I've found the German books and send them you as well as two 'Lifes'. Wadey has sent your watch. I'd better wait till somebody is travelling to Strasbourg. I think of you all the time.

February 4th, 1947. Paris

Lady Lascelles has arrived. I've had no talk with her – she is a very dull lady to me – no low-down on the King and Queen. I'd

38 Garbage.

39 An after-dinner acting game, not unlike charades.

40 Joan, wife of Sir Alan (Tommy) Lascelles, Private Secretary to George VI and, briefly, to Elizabeth II.

been out all day visiting a film studio where an English company is producing an English picture, because exchange and other difficulties makes it cheaper and easier than in England. I enjoy getting back for a few hours to that happy life – so sufficient to its unreal self, with no place for the true happenings. There was the gay lunch at 11.30 with the director Terence Young and L.L. and Eric Portman, the lead, and others in a canteen, and then getting out the sets and seeing again what I remember so well – yawns, yawns, yawns. Everyone waiting, yawning, the workman at the lights, the star waiting for the lights, the scenario people, the cameramen, one wonders always who it is that holds things up – cold excessive, which perhaps encourages the yawning.

I came back pretty frozen, and got into bed to warm and to avoid the droppers–in, and Joan Lascelles arrived to find me night-capped and in curling set, against a dinner party, with Laurence and Vivien Olivier and Cecil Beaton leaning over the bedstead sphinxes. I don't know what she thought – she is the symbol of England at its dullest and maybe its best. I'm sure she does not like the unusual. We gave quite a dinner for her, the Vaniers (her choice), and M. Delbos, Min. of State, L.L., Juliet, Cecil, M. Oberlé 'des 3 amis' (BBC 1940).[41] Canadian Ritchie[42] famous for having eaten the dog's dinner and got thro' it rather than offend his hostess, whose servitor had put it before him either in abstraction or a vengeful mood, Eric Duncannon, etc. M. Delbos my right-hand neighbour told me of his two years in solitary confinement at Orienburg. To start with he talked aloud to himself, but gave it up – he had no books for a year and later German ones. He taught himself the language but not to speak it. Never cold, always hungry. I turned gaily to General Vanier with 'imagine, imagine this man was without speech for two years' and he said 'Did Duff

---

41 A French-language programme (M.Oberlé was one of the *amis*) which was transmitted to occupied France during the war.

42 Charles Ritchie, No. 2 at the Canadian Embassy, later High Commissioner in London and celebrated diarist. The story of the dog's dinner was perfectly true – he told it to me himself.

tell you about our son?' I remembered full well that his son, six foot eight, strong and vigorous, exceedingly good-looking and exhilarating had newly taken Trappist vows. The General, saint that he is, thinks it's an honour and privilege that he should have been so chosen by God. 'He is a mystic you see, and I feel certain that in a few years he will be talking to God as I am talking to you. Besides how grand it is to embrace an order of that kind, no small easy order,' etc. etc. I asked what his mother thought, she is equally devout, and he said she was honoured too. I asked if the honour stopped her tears, mine were dribbling away as I spoke. He said, no. Juliet shows no sign of moving house. She talks so blithely of Friday week, she must do things on the day after that.

February 5th. Lady Lascelles goes today – three nights in slow trains to Klagenfurt, no such good news of Juliet. David Herbert and Michael, her son, are at the Ritz and she has said nothing to them of her probable *séjour.* Last night L.L., Jubags and I, dressed like empresses, went to the first dress collection of the season chez Molyneux. Band, buffet and champagne starting at 9 p.m. The other onlookers were chiefly belonging to the press in hats and snow boots. We looked unusual but I think it pleased Edward Mol[43] – with whom we had to sit. The collection was as usual, devoid of imagination or novelty or even taste. L.L. and I enjoyed giving the dresses names and writing these names on the programme, on the blank for comments, names such as *'Trop tard'*, *'le plus laid'*, *'cela pue'*, *'vingt ans après'*.[44] We then mislaid the programmes. Duff was meanwhile taking Lady Lascelles to a gala in honour of Marivaux at the *Comédie Française.* She admitted to me this morning that she'd hated it. Duff had slept deeply and enjoyed it in consequence. Joan had lunch on a tray in the *salon vert* cowering over the fire, and will have dinner before catching her train, equally alone in her bedroom. It's just too bad but *c'est comme ça* and I was always engaged. Delighted with your last letter and photograph you seem to like. In which you

43 Edward Molyneux, the fashion designer.
44 'Too late', 'the ugliest', 'it stinks', 'twenty years later'.

become a cynic of forty-eight. I won't lose it, then you can have it life-sized. Your life sounds beautiful, full of work and play. Miss Monique Schoen[45] calls on me tomorrow. I'll be sending jam and coffee and cigs. Great fun if you come for a Sunday – let me know number and hour and I'd call you. Love and kisses from us both. We do so love you and prize your sweetness.

February 6th, 1947. Paris

Another dress show last night chez Lanvin. Rather better clothes shown under far worse conditions. Small low rooms packed like Calcutta's hole – dense with smoke. Blazing light deforming one's face which was mirrored, for one's torture, from every wall. Really painful hard-arse chairs and lasting two hours. Michael Duff, David Herbert, L.L., Rufus Clarke, Jacques Franck, Jubags, none of us good for a buyer. One's eyes hurt too much to go to sleep fortunately. I'd had a wonderful and funny lunch with the two English playboys[46] and a Wop lady, a lunch of a memorable scallop dressed in cream and truffles washed down with a fresh Alsatian wine. I only like Alsatian or German wines in white, that's the truth. White burgundy stinks – Château Yquem is an exception, a freak, a favourite.

Duff and I have taken to clandestine meals in obscure restaurants. It's great fun and takes us back to walking-out days when I always had lunch with him secretly at one, and made my Arlington Street luncheon at a late 1.45.

7th. Nothing is going to budge Juliet – her son and David are so awful about her. I think they must have said something to her, which doesn't do any good for she asked me just now eating our salad and cheese in the *salon vert* (Duff was at a wine connoisseur's lunch at the Gyp Ambassador's) would I tell her when I wanted her to go, and I can only answer 'stay as long as you can'.

---

45 After the Schmidts, the Schoen family were my greatest friends in Strasbourg.
46 Sir Michael Duff and David Herbert.

I did add that the bedroom situation is a problem, that I have Gen. Morgan, S.A.C. Med.[47] and his aide and his mistress Clare Beck and Lady Rothermere and Peter Quennell and Auberon Herbert all to house next week, but she doesn't mean to take off till Sunday 16th. The whole staff has taken wings to London today for the Churchill wedding[48] – there is not one member of the Military Department left to deal with S.A.C. Med. Gen. Salisbury Jones, Rufus, Christopher, Eric Duncannon, etc. Teddie's gone too and Twinks[49] goes tomorrow leaving me with parties of twenty. Charlie Anglesey is gravely ill, may die. He had an operation on his prostate gland and has pleurisy and heart and blood transfusions. I should not mind if I was the family. I like the 'She first deceased, he for a little tried To live without her, liked it not so died' spirit for the long happily married. But, Raimund tells me, Liz, the others, all save Rose, who is probably going to get on with her projected holiday in Switzerland, are screaming and gnashing their teeth. What has he got to live for? Lonely evenings, unknown before, daughters dutifully taking turns to visit him. No more merriment – just winter.

André comes to my bed to tell me that he's not one to talk, in a household, but do I realise that Jean, *maître d'hôtel*, has set himself up in the room where the telephonists used to be and has had it done up '*en style princier – tout à fait comme s'il était chez lui*'.[50] I did not think it mattered much, but what does matter is that when I did mention it to that dolt Teddie he seemed quite disinterested and completely ignorant of it. The loafer Lucian, Teddie's No. 2, uses Raoul, chauffeur, to drive him about for his chores, so Raoul has struck I'm happy to say. The red Austin and blue Austin are liquidated, the truck is no more. It's serious.

---

47 Supreme Allied Commander, Mediterranean.
48 Mary Churchill was marrying Christopher Soames, former Assistant Military Attaché at the Embassy.
49 Twinks Baring, Social Secretary.
50 'In princely style – for all the world as if he owned it.'

February 10th

It was so lovely at Chantilly that Michael and David and I walked through the stilly ice-bound forests. A conference of swans from all around had assembled on a still liquid piece of the lake. Duff in tails had gone off to sign various peace treaties in the Quai d'Orsay. Ann Rothermere and Peter Quennell have arrived from a rainy Monte Carlo. I hope you are coming this Sunday. I shall have had a hard week – the house full and a lot of heavy entertaining.

February 11th. Last night Papa dined with the President and I joined him after like an Arab's wife. The ladies were brilliant, but the cock-birds *en smoking*[51] and no music detracted from the elegance. As usual a swarm round the buffet and the other rooms empty.

Two days ago Professor Bowra of New College,[52] identical with Isaiah and David Cecil, dined and told us New College had dreadful teachers and was pretty generally rotten, but that the undergrads themselves were the nicest in the world. A Frenchman of the Quai d'Orsay, Couve de Murville,[53] also dined and when we discussed a book in two volumes, each thicker than a telephone book, just produced by Paul Reynaud, I came close to a most embarrassing blob. I said 'The title is far the most sensational and amusing part. *Tordant.*'[54] 'What *is* the title?' Froggy asked. I saw it then, and seeing it I could feel my torso and feet flushing scarlet. Quickly I diverted the subject to a headline in a paper Papa was holding. The title was *La France a sauvé l'Europe.*[55]

Another day Simon Levi[56] took me to the early Flemish exhibition, one after my own heart. I believe sincerely that the

51 In black ties.

52 He was actually Warden of Wadham.

53 Maurice Couve de Murville, Prime Minister 1968–9.

54 Hilarious.

55 *France Saved Europe.*

56 French art critic.

European-American hand has lost its cunning. It is no longer capable of workmanship. That school of painting had it superlatively combined with genius. The Chinese I suppose still can use their slim hands and control them to their fancy's whim, but ours have pressed buttons for so long now, tapped type keys, used machinery whenever possible and got used to 'the pot of paint thrown in the public's face' because it is all we can do and otherwise must acknowledge defeat. These good French Impressionists have invented ingenious light and colour methods only to cover their deficiency, but as their colours come out of a synthetic tube and are synthetic too they'll fade (unlike the hand-ground pigments of the Flems) and then what will be left?[57]

Mr. Bevin came yesterday accompanied by his Ancient, Bob Dixon.[58] At the time of his arrival (Papa and Bidault waited an hour and a half at the airfield) we had a businessmen's club from Cardiff cocktailing below. They were on a goodwill mission to Prague, the whole depressing thirty of them. Jan Masaryk on a visit to Cardiff had visited the club and in his over-colloquial English had no doubt said 'You boys ought to come along to my place sometime – we'll show you a good time in Czechoslovakia' – little meaning it perhaps, but they took him at his word and were on their way. There were perhaps six French people in the crowd, but Ernie didn't know that when he went to have a drink with his Cardiff pals. They gave him a resounding hand. Of course it made their party. He made them a splendid h-less speech bidding them God speed and urging them on their return to Wales to do all in their power to encourage a higher coal production. 'We want to put this great country on its feet again, we want to feed it coal etc. etc.' The French listened ecstatically and left feeling warm and happy that all their factory wheels were spinning round.

---

57 My mother, it will be seen, was scarcely one of the *avant-garde*. One evening we were invited to the apartment of Gertrude Stein, to whom she confessed as much. Miss Stein explained that art had progressed in a dead straight line, and asked her at what point on that line her understanding stopped. 'Roughly Cimabue' was the reply.

58 Ernest Bevin, Foreign Secretary, and Sir Pierson Dixon.

Now we come to last night's dinner. Rosemary[59] came, a sober figure in black. 'John made me promise not to get tight – *you* don't think I'm tight, do you, Lady Diana?' I gave her a stiff whisky and she sat down in a dream and meditated alone. There were three South Africans and sweet Nancy Rodd[60] and Eve Curie and the Millards[61] and some strays. Bevin said goodnight at about 11.30. I looked desperately round for Bob Dixon to guide him into the lift. Bob had vanished *comme le camphor* so I piloted him myself. What was my nearly great surprise when he suddenly clasped me into his arms with the strength and immobility of a bear and buried his podgy face in my neck. So we stood for a full minute, or an eternity, then with a very slow utterly relentless gesture he shifted his mouth to mine. No struggles could have affected the situation. As well stand up against the mountain-weight of lava. I was agonised at the thought of Bob Dixon coming in and writing me down as an office-hunter seducing the boss, but as far as I know he did not see anything unless it was the lipstick that transformed poor Ernie into an end-of-the-evening old clown Joey. He asked me to stay the night. Could he have thought I would? Still there's life in the dear old dog and courage and character and humanity and a lot of other nice things, and if he likes to be foolish late at night, he should be indulged.

Not one word to a soul about Ernie. I have not even told Louise.

―――

I joined my parents for the Easter vacation in a villa that they had been lent near Monte Carlo. One day Mr and Mrs Herbert Morrison[62] came to lunch; soon after their departure my

---

59 My father's secretary (see Directory).

60 Nancy Mitford (see Directory).

61 Guy Millard, a member of the Embassy staff, and his wife Ann.

62 Then Deputy Prime Minister, later to succeed Ernest Bevin as Foreign Secretary.

father complained of feeling ill and was found to have a high fever. At first we attributed this to the Morrisons; alas, it proved to be the beginning of a long illness; he was to live nearly seven more years, but he never completely recovered.

———

Roc Fleuri, Monte Carlo
April 21st, 1947

When I left you tee-to-tumming round with a curly blonde, I stepped into the Rolls, rising above a faint call to go to the loo. Half an hour later however I was driven to saying to René Picot[63] *Je veux descendre un instant. J'ai horreur des toilettes des hôtels.*[64] Relieved, I went to sleep over the middle arm one pulls down in the car and was woken forty minutes later by René announcing our arrival. I missed you terribly. Papa asleep and calm. Next morning – yesterday – I thought of you a lot and wondered if John[65] had been sober and if the brakes had held and let a thousand fears beset me. I suppose Papa improves but it's very slow. His voice is still like a canary's and his eyes stare and his movements are as slow as growth in a plant and I have panics that penicillin alters people, but his energy is good for writing and reading and he does not stare into eternity so long.

I went over to Daisy's villa in the morning to exchange a bottle of whisky for two bottles of claret. Papa was to be allowed a glass for lunch. The day was unreliable in sky. Lady Katherine Lambton came to lunch. I have known her all my life – an aunt of Betty Cranborne (Salisbury) and mad like all the St. Albans family. Her eldest brother, the Duke, was in an asylum all his life. The present

---

63 The Embassy chauffeur.

64 'I must get out for a moment, I hate the facilities in hotels.'

65 de Bendern, my father's secretary.

Duke, her brother, thinks aloud and in consequence is frighteningly rude. Kitty's hair is rinsed Reckitt's Blue[66] but she looks good enough and entertained us with spite and sparkle at lunch. She shuffled off to spend her afternoon in the *cuisine* [casino] while Papa and I took a drive along the Upper Corniche and back by the Lower. This outing marks a stage of convalescence. Another stage was marked by his sitting up to dinner. I took a walk at 6.30 missing you more than ever. I walked up behind the house and came to many nice poor gardens, with running rills and olives and lemons and roses and stairs and crops and bridges. I looked my worst – trousers, scarlet shirt, milking coat and a straw hat and when I got into Rue des Moulins, I heard a group saying 'Lady Diana Manners' and I started round as one must at the sound of one's name and thereby gave away what I would gladly have denied.

Papa asked for a surprise and I found a little basket of strawberries that have this morning proved a big success. It's 9.30 a.m. and I wish I was expecting you in from tennis and that we had *Quicks*[67] to look forward to. This old diary will entirely change its character written to you and not to my poor still living Conrad.[68] Please, dull as it is, don't lose it for one day it may amuse me to read of the good old days.

April 22nd. My life is a bit dull but Papa's mending is the consolation. Dr. Grasset comes but once a day. We still have the tedious formula to get through – blood pressure contraption, temperature, listening with his whole head to Papa's chest, all three dimensions, heart, hearing, tapping with fingers on finger, *piqûre pour les reins*,[69] looking at *les urines*, *c'est très bien.* At 12.30, the day brilliant and warmer, we set off to La Réserve at Beaulieu – the type of place I particularly

---

66 A tiny cube of bright blue dye which, paradoxically, made white laundry look whiter.

67 Our favourite bar.

68 Conrad was on the point of death.

69 Injection for the kidneys.

dislike. Château de Madrid prices, but without the 'unusual' and without the market of new produce or the drop into the sea or the independent and furious waiter. Papa made me swear not to have a row about the bill, so I resolved not to see it. All the major-domos and waiters lay flat on their stom-achs as we arrived. I dressed as *l'Ambassadrice* in olive-drab, Papa with clothes hanging on his weakness as on a scarecrow. The beastly place spelt the wrong sort of *luxe*, yet everyone is taken in by appearance. I had *hors d'oeuvres*, (uneatable) square of beetroot as at a British Restaurant,[70] no onions, no sardines, a stale bit of tunny, while Papa had smoked salmon too salt to swallow. Half a bottle of claret was brought like a newborn baby in a Moses cradle, and newborn it was, and full of dregs and sediments. After fifty minutes, twenty of them storming, the boiled chicken and rice appeared – all right – what we've all had all our youth in the nursery and no better. That was all. An inferior pianist and violinist kept up a melancholy caterwaul and the bill was 3,000-odd. Even Papa was *décu*.[71] As a meal it couldn't compare with Le Puy or for that matter home here.

We drove on to Nice hoping to buy a Michelin '47 and failed and drove home by the Upper Corniche to the Sunday papers and some letters. I took a very long walk at six and bought enough of the unicorn material to make a shirt. I turned hair-pinwise back down a street that led me to *l'Escale*. The port was very noisy and gay, a lot of Froggy sailors newly arrived, teasing the girls and generally rollicking. I stopped to pass the time of day with Madame Quick and had a quick one at a little table by myself reading my letters in the sunset. How I missed you!

This morning the sun was radiantly hot at seven. I did not sleep too well so I thought I'd go and have a look at the market. Dear seven – I always love the different things people are doing that

---

70 Austerity restaurants introduced for wartime Britain.
71 Disappointed.

can only be seen at seven – ice-blocks melting at every door,[72] doorsteps being scrubbed, all the *commères* with their baskets, children going laughing and running to school. I bought a bunch of radishes (there was nothing much else except arum lilies) for Papa and have just gone to bed again to write you.

Monte Carlo
April 23rd

O dear, I've just finished with the most horrible night. I went to bed too early, because we old birds without duties or drink or possibility of playing games of chance against each other, since money is no object, can't keep awake after ten. Papa's leg is uncomfortable and his instep still hurts. We had rather a nice day. Pride swallowed and digested, we met Hugh Sherwood and Daisy as their guests at the Château de Madrid. I had a few nice little sharp yet conciliatory phrases to fire at the insulting *maître d'hôtel*, but he lay doggo and never showed his ugly face. We ate salmon and strawberries and afterwards Papa and I went on, in the Ford this time, to Opio.[73] All the olives looked alike and the terraces too. The gardens had more flowers, the branches more birds, but Polly was out. We had a rocky walk to a bench in her garden, where I flopped Papa down looking quite exhausted and in pain.

Last evening we talked about his having a pain in his foot, sometimes feet, for a long time, and sometimes a numbness in a nerve running down his thigh. Of course in the small hours awake I began to build a castle of Spanish horrors. What fell paralysing disease was he beginning? Was he to be another Reggie Fellowes or Maurice Baring or Lord Wimborne who had years of Parkinson's Disease, or Lord d'Abernon who was worse and couldn't be heard when he spoke. For years I've said 'Pick your feet up, Papa.' Now

72 Ice was delivered to the door before most people had refrigerators.
73 A nearby village, where Polly Cotton, an old friend, had a house.

I find his voice so weak, and you said his writing was feeble. Well you know what I can do to force fear into my veins and sweat and have diarrhoea. I'm told that when you are very frightened nature opens a floodgate in your system and adrenaline steeps your blood and gives you supernatural force with which to run or wrestle or climb or hit out and fight, but if you are wallowing in your adrenaline with no outlet of physical energy, the sensation – even pain – of the state is almost unendurable. That's my state very often, and O last night. Aspirins were unavailing, the loo saw a lot of me, my sheets were drenched in sweat.

This morning it's much hotter than previous days. The orange blossom outside our windows has broken its buds and let out all the sweetness. Papa has had a very good night. His foot has hardly any swell in it. I unbuild that demon's castle. Why shouldn't it just be chronic gout, fanned to inflammation by the toxic condition his disease has put him into? His voice is definitely stronger. I took a squint at his writing and that looked all right. He's a lot more *elastico*. It is only a fortnight ago that his temp. was 104.

Later. So encouraged, I went to the wig-fixer[74] who washed my hairs in oil and made them half as thin as they are. Then in the open Ford with Papa to lunch with Muriel Wade, once Muriel Wilson the daughter (now sixty-five) of the man whose house the great Tranby Croft scandal[75] belongs to (if you don't know the story remind me to tell it you). Willie [Somerset] Maugham was there and Monseigneur Pierre de Polignac[76] and the garden was known to be the loveliest on the Riviera, and so it is, for it is a garden in an olive grove. Then we came home and a lady came to see me, and at seven I took a long walk Roquebrune direction and up and along well above Roc Fleuri and came down upon it.

74 Slang. She never wore a wig in her life.

75 A country house in which, on 8 September 1890, Sir William Gordon-Cumming was accused of cheating at baccarat while playing with – among others – the Prince of Wales (the future Edward VII). Sir William sued his accusers, but lost his case. The Prince was called as a witness, and was forced to admit that he had been playing a game which was at that time illegal.

76 Father of Rainier, then reigning Prince of Monaco.

A new moon on her back, slim as a beam, nightingales (yes, nightingales) singing and a clash of smells. I did love it but deep in my heart was the dread of the night.

The night was not too good.

I got today two letters from Katherine. Conrad [Russell] is still alive but near his end. Listen to this. You could hardly believe what I read and I'd better quote:

> Last night a miracle happened. I went in to him at nine as I always do after he has been put ready for the night. And he called me and said 'I want you to send for a priest. I have made up my mind. I want to be received into the Church.' I nearly fainted with astonishment because − I don't know if you'll believe me, and if you don't nobody will − I had never said a word to him about it. I had said some prayers by his bed some-times which seemed to soothe him, but I had been much too afraid to say anything else, and it never occurred to me as a possibility now, though I knew in the past that he had thought about it from time to time. The day nurse said to me hastily 'He doesn't know what he is saying' but he repeated it and by another miracle [!!] a priest we know very well was staying with the Palairets in the cottage next door. I fetched him and he talked to Conrad and was satisfied that he was quite clear and he was received there and then and anointed. In the morning he talked of it again. I wondered if he might have forgotten but he hadn't at all. I am so happy about it. It seemed like a direct answer to prayer, perhaps Maurice's. Please be glad too. He is so safe now and his mind is so beautiful. I never realised the full beauty and storedness and wonder of it till I nursed him all this month, and this in spite of all the bad times.

Is this not extraordinary? Not so much to you but to me, to whom Conrad has talked so much about the Papists and never without contempt or jeers. When K. was converted thirty years ago he did study the Roman Church exhaustively. The more he read the less he believed. He and his whole family are born and raised as Liberal free thinkers. Was it a miracle? Is it the only true and living church?

Did he do it as thanks to Katherine, who has nursed him so tenderly and who wanted it so desperately? Was he unconscious and willed into it? I put (!!) after 'by another miracle' because there is always a priest at one house or another at Mells. We shall never know. I shall talk to the day nurse but if she is a violent atheist or anti-Rome woman she'll say he was coerced or unconscious. The two old sisters will be horrified and put the crime down to K. They always referred to her as 'that woman' anyway. Well, I hope in my heart that he knew what he was saying and doing and that it has brought him peace and resignation as true faith does – dear, dear Conrad. I can't help adding that conversions on death beds do not happen in non-Catholic houses.

24th or 25th. I don't know which. Another rather bad haunted night. Now I'm on the balcony waiting for Dr. Grasset, then we shall go off and lunch at Villefranche and then I must go to *Les petits Chanteurs de la Côte d'Azur* at Cannes and meet le Père Bienassis [one of the Sitwells?].

Today came two old trout to lunch – Corise, Marquise de Noailles and her half-sister the Duchesse de Clermont-Tonnerre, both highly intelligent and monstrous. The former looks eighty and is sixty-two about and doesn't try, and has travelled the world, a lot of West Africa, a lot of China, and dislikes her two rooms at the Hotel Balmoral, Monte Carlo, in which she sculpts, paints and writes. The Duchess was much older but still trying, painted to the eyes, with disfiguring dewlaps and still a very roving eye for her own sex.

April 27th. Yesterday on waking Papa decided to put off his departure for a few days. He is not fit for such a tiring journey, nor for Paris work. His foot does not improve much and when his doctor came for what he took to be his last visit, he sat me down in a chair and read to us both a programme of life and regime for the next four or five months. It was rather alarming and most depressing. He said Papa was in a poor state of health *before* the attack and that the attack was a blessing as it was an *alerte*, a red light. That his *foie* and his *reins*[77] were in an apathetic way, not eliminating poisons, and that this state would return *bien que ses urines soient impeccables*[78] and if he did not sleep with an open window, take a bath and a good rub daily and a big bath once a week with deep massages, be in bed eight hours in the twenty-four, play tennis and golf, eat sparsely of meat, no veal, mutton, pork, sweetbread, sausage, brains, pigs' trotters, kidneys, game, a little rabbit and chicken and sometimes a little beef, no mushrooms, truffles or pâtés, plenty of veg. excluding peas, beans, cabbage, beetroot, carrots. Fish yes, but not lobster, crab, langouste, oysters, no crustaceans. Only fresh cheese. Nothing to drink but a glass of claret for lunch. If by chance he had to be at a dinner party or long banquet an extra glass need do no harm, always provided that the next day should be devoted to water and fruit. He little knows Embassy life. Then when at last the longed-for holiday comes in August, spend it at Vichy or Contrexeville. That got us both down a bit. For Papa because although he clearly won't follow it, it must take the gilt off the gingerbread, and my future is to be one of worry and nagging and loss of a husband's love. But there it is, and O take warning and don't do yourself too well. Everything is paid for and, unfairly enough, punishment is more disagreeable than pleasure is ecstatic.

Monte Carlo
April 28th, 1947

My darling Conrad is dead. I cannot be too unhappy. He was longing to throw off his weary, disobedient body and the sooner his unconscious humiliation was over the better pleased we should be. He had a lovely serene life with no dramas, no ecstasies, no wife, no children,

---

77 Liver and kidneys.
78 Although his urine is impeccable.

no tragedies, and great love surrounded him. He had much too, to give. K. he had loved thirty years ago. She was there to hold his hand and guide him to her God, and me he loved and he knew that, though not there, he was secure in my devotion. Daphne [Bath], sweet, rollicking, drunken Daphne, was also one he loved most dearly, and she was there, and the sad old sisters found her most comforting and good. I'll miss the letters so desperately.

He has written almost every day since 1932. When first I took him to Cardiff 'Come to Cardiff', I said, 'and see me act *The Miracle*. We can stay at the Angel'. To my great astonishment he said 'Yes, I will.' My heart sank a little for although I'd always known him as another Russell's brother, I was quite an unfamiliar. I confided to Katherine my panic of having him on my hands alone. Should I be able to amuse, would he find the trip worth while? She encouraged me wholeheartedly and said that I must make him a friend, as she felt that when she took the veil (which she has not yet done, but doubtless will in time) she must be able to feel that someone would look after him. So we went together to Cardiff, and it was winter and very cold, and he loved *The Miracle* and afterwards we had a little supper, and in the morning we walked the town and looked at the great municipal buildings, and he held my hand in his pocket for it was so cold, and he told me he loved me and he told me the same every day until he lost consciousness in death.

The happiest time of our relationship was the Bognor small-holding days – after the Blitz, before Singapore, when we saw the seasons round, and he helped me to buy and rear first the hens, then the cow and goats and bees and pigs and ducks and geese – the haymaking, the quiet turning of it and gathering of it into the trailer, the singling of mangels, the hoeing, the milking, the cheese – yes, the cheese was the crux of it all. You remember the end, not the beginnings – the acidometer and the drops of the chemical Exlax is made of. He used to say 'I have never been so happy.' Are there any better words to say, or to hear from someone you love?

Then there were 'outings' – a journey to Elsinore to see *Hamlet*, the time Larry Olivier eloped after the play with Vivien Leigh. That was the time too when I bought the figurehead mermaid in Copenhagen – the nude, life-size, with impertinent breasts and arms held high above her head, and Conrad, for the first and last time, was so embarrassed by having to carry her through several Customs and stations – like one does an orang-outang that hangs low and heavy on your hands – that he got 'short' with me between Hamburg and I forget where. Then came the hideous moment when we almost *lost* the mermaid. She'd spent a safe two hours in the *consigne*[79] and at some junction got shifted off, as we feared, to Berlin, but we salvaged her and got her to Queensborough where the English steward said 'would she like a cabin to herself?' and I said she would and they didn't think it funny. They broke her finger stowing her into her berth and half the night in the adjoining cabin I heard hammering – the ship's carpenter, like a surgeon, had an emergency call to mend a mermaid – but it all brings Conrad back to me from the long years ago.

The crossword is Conrad too, and reading Trollope aloud during blitzy nights at Bognor when I'd sit on that low chair by the fire and knit you socks or sew a cheese up in muslin, while Conrad would read and sometimes have to pause for silent laughter, about Madame Neroni and other Barchestonians. He always said 'These are the happiest days of my life' in spite of it being wartime, and Portsmouth being illuminated with chandeliers in the sky, and though bombs were falling wildly. Once the shutter got loose and as I opened the drawing-room door on to the garden to attach it, a big explosion blasted off its hinge, and frightened us horribly. We had to sit then in the firelight as with the shutter had gone the blackout, and we were too shaken to go to bed. He was always wise and sound and uncensorious of morals and his own rare humour was better than any other

79 Left luggage office.

– angle, fancy and delivery. O dear, O dear – I don't think I'll write any more or think, with love, of the check suits, the turned-out toes, the stoop, the haircut by the ploughman with the help of a pudding basin, the deerstalker cap I gave him, the zip bag that brought his modest accessories and a pound of butter, eggs, the first primroses, the 'short-legged hen' and some 'pretty little tiny kickshaw'. He loved to give me expensive presents, but wanted them always to be great luxury – jewels and furs and the 'doing up' of a drawing room, and didn't really like paying for a cow or a Frigidaire.

April 29th. Papa really better and we're off tomorrow morning. The house, books, food, wages of three hired servants (all unnecessary), washing, mineral water not wine, unordered flowers and apéritifs which you drank like water, cost close on £400 for four weeks. Heating, gas, electricity, telephone still to come. Luckily Papa went into the Casino to cash a cheque and risk those old counters that had hung about his bedroom so long, and won £120, so that helped a bit. The chemist's bill was £10 and the doctor's may be anything between £50 and £100.

The weather is lovely. The Hoffs go the day after tomorrow and join us in Paris. I shall have less than a week to wait for you. All is packed in readiness. Antoinette shall have 2000 francs, the concierge a bottle of champagne, the concierge's wife a bottle of sherry, or *Chérie* as Leon[80] writes it, and the hirelings a nice shake-hand.

80 The Embassy footman.

8

'I feel as though I were getting married'

LONDON–PARIS–CHANTILLY, DECEMBER 1947–FEBRUARY 1948

J.J. Cooper, Writer CMX 847514
H.M.S. Royal Arthur
Corsham, Wiltshire
December 30th, 1947

Darling Mummy and Papa,

Here I am – on board at last, a sailor of the King's Navee, writing you instalment No. 1 of my log. I am writing it at 21.45 hrs (this is the best I can do as I don't understand about bells yet) in my bunk, with half an hour before we pipe down. Lights out at 10.15.

The food is not too bad. You queue up outside for about two minutes, then walk in, clasping your own mug, fork, knife and spoon which you keep for always, and take back to your hut afterwards to wash up. On your way in, your mug is filled with a thick soup (more profitably used as gravy) and a slice of bread is thrust into your hand, quickly followed by a steaming plate piled high with shepherd's pie or whatever it may be, mashed grey potatoes and a second veg. While you are trying to arrange all these in two hands in such a way as to fool yourself you're not going to drop them, another plate appears, covered in steam pudding or (today's choice) a slice of treacle tart. Not very good, but might be worse. You stagger in under your lunch, trying to balance the pat of margarine on the bread, and settle down at the first empty place at any of the six or seven big tables. Nothing to drink at lunch but the gravy-soup. At tea however (consisting of bread and margarine and jam) and at supper (same as lunch without the pudding) there are huge pots of steaming tea up and down the tables, already milked and sugared and tasting strongly of anti-aphrodisiac.

All the seamen's jobs are gone, I'm afraid, so I had to be a writer after all . . . Writers travel as much as the seamen, and I may be off to anywhere in the world in six months. Disadvantage of being a writer: no bell-bottoms, or blue collar, or round hat or anything. Just a dark blue woolly suit with shirt and collar, black tie and peaked cap. Like a Petty Officer, only not quite so grand. I look slightly more important but all the glamour has gone.

All love to you both,

John Julius

There are no letters in the second half of 1947, simply because I was with my parents for almost the entire time. I left Strasbourg at the end of the university term in June and expected my call-up on or about my eighteenth birthday in September. In fact it came only at the very end of the year, and almost simultaneously my parents left the Embassy.

We had been expecting the sack for a long time. The 1945 general election had brought in the socialist government of Clement Attlee; why should my father, a conservative politician who had resigned from the Foreign Service in 1919, have been kept on in Paris for another two and a half years? His staying power can I think be attributed only to Ernie Bevin's personal affection for us. Ernie must have had to withstand immense pressure from his Cabinet colleagues – and indeed from the Foreign Office itself, which took no pleasure in seeing its most desirable post in the hands of an outsider.

Expected our dismissal may have been; but it was still a major upheaval. Both my parents would have welcomed a couple more years; but my mother, I suspect, missed the Embassy life a good deal more than my father – perhaps only because he was far more reticent about showing his feelings. It was not that she particularly enjoyed being an ambassadress – though she turned out to be a perfectly brilliant one; but she loved hard work, and the Paris Embassy was very hard work indeed. Life at Chantilly, she feared, might leave her seriously underemployed.

On the other hand, it was Chantilly that made the whole thing bearable. By now we had no other home. Gower Street had been bombed, Chapel Street sold. Bognor was being sold too; it was perfect for summer weekends but impossible for anything more.

Chantilly on the other hand was ideal: just the right size, less than an hour's drive from Paris, with a perfect library for those of my father's books which he had not presented to the Embassy. It was also a remarkably beautiful house.

The Château de Saint Firmin, therefore, was to be my parents' permanent home, with a rather dark, depressing little flat at 69 rue de Lille as a Paris *pied-à-terre*. I certainly had no objection. The Navy and Oxford would take up a good deal of my time over the next five years, and then I should have to have a job; but a house in France would be fun for my friends.

Inevitably, the *déménagement* brought about a change in the letters. No longer did my mother have the whole Embassy life to describe and discuss; henceforth she writes above all of her friends. One of these, who seems to play a major role at this time, is Evelyn Waugh. He had been a regular visitor at Bognor before the war, and now the war was over he came back into our lives. He had always been a little bit in love with my mother; she had always been a little bit afraid of him. There was never anything remotely physical in the relationship; his devout Catholicism would have seen to that. What she feared was his manner, his prickliness and not least his intelligence, for which she felt herself to be no match. An additional complication was provided by my father, who went through periods of disliking Waugh intensely – the feeling being entirely mutual – though they made it up in the end.

There are two other features of these later letters that are, I think, worth mentioning. This first is my mother's (to me) rather surprising emphasis on her health. She was always a bit of a hypochondriac – though she never worried about her own well-being if she could worry about my father's – and now that she had relatively little else to occupy her she gave in to it more readily than she had been able to in former years. Physically, there was nothing wrong with her at all – now in her middle fifties, she was to live another forty-odd years – but she had always had a weakness for an annual retreat at a spa or health farm, in which now she had more time and leisure to indulge.

The second new feature is my parents' successors, Sir Oliver and Lady Harvey. She had, of course, every reason to envy them, but – apart from what they did to my father's beloved library – no real grounds for dislike. And, it has to be said, she did not behave well. In diplomatic circles it is not usually considered good form to remain in a country to which one has been recently accredited. My parents admittedly had little choice, but the Harveys surely had the right to expect a little more support from them, not to find my mother going round Paris telling everyone how awful they were. Finally the situation became such that it furnished Nancy Mitford with inspiration for one of her funniest novels, *Don't Tell Alfred*.

My joining the Navy came as no surprise. Compulsory service in the armed forces – occasionally commuted to work in the coal mines – continued for fifteen years after the end of the Second World War. Every public school had its training corps, and the hours I had spent crawling on my stomach through Windsor Great Park on sodden November afternoons had determined me to put myself down for the Navy – which, thank heaven, had accepted me. There were drawbacks. Unlike the Army, there was no question of my getting a commission; I should remain firmly on the lower deck. Nor was it guaranteed that I should go to sea. Still, I was pretty confident that it would be more fun, and on the last day of the year travelled down to HMS *Royal Arthur* at Corsham, Wiltshire, with a light heart.

———

Chez Antoine
December 31st, 1947

You poor mite! And it's snowing to boot. I'm cold for you and have got a night-club headache for you. I can see the skilly they are setting before you at this moment. My legs itch from the rough serge and my neck shortens its bareness with chill.

I rang up Droitwich and find that they are closed and reopening on the 11th so I shall go that day, Dr. Cohen permitting. He comes to look me over today week. What will he find? I should like to have those increasingly unattractive blisters taken out of my lids (Papa will oppose). The scars will mend at Droitwich behind black spectacles. I'll work out some halfway meeting place. There must be a Bath–Birmingham train with a town where I could go for the day so that I should see you.

Is there any hope of (1) reading a course on one subject that interests you and instructs (2) if you can practise Mr. Ruben's harmonies[1] (3) if there is any hope for a Linguaphone (4) any classes – educational – shorthand for a journalist's future?

Midnight. Papa and I went to a matinée – *Dark Summer* – a serious good play. He cried buckets to my dry eyes. Then I tried to sleep my night off from six to eight but was too nervous. So I'll say goodnight to my dearest boy. This hammock is horridly deceptive. Will it roll me out like a barrel before my leg has to be shown? Ugh, the cold and the smell. I feel for you but always remember it will get better. Drink less for your health and looks and charm's sake, beware of unclean whores, love your mother and sleep deep.

London
January 2nd, 1948

At last a postcard. I've been working myself into a fine fuss, you having promised to send me some kind of word immediately, and that's four days ago. So I couldn't send my first instalment, and my nerves drove me (I'd just found myself looking in the *Evening Standard* for Boy Murder) to shooting a telegram into the vasty deeps of the R.N. which may well embarrass you. I didn't sign it. I thought Honey Mummy would make things worse. Don't forget

---

1 No recollection.

Papa is now Sir Duff [2](kill Sir Alfred if you hear it said) and the Government true to form dims what lustre there was on the honour (an almost automatic one) by giving it simultaneously to the successor[3] who has not yet worked the day through. No matter – the worse and the more maladroit the better.

The 31st of last year I wrote you my dull little saga but I could only post it now because of hearing nothing. What happened the 31st? O yes, a day given to frantic hunts for disguise.[4] Evelyn Waugh paid me a morning call, portly as an alderman, dressed in loud and shapeless checks. He'd been obstreperous the night before and broken his host's decanters, so I had to dedicate an hour of my brief time to buying *amendes*[5] with him and a distinguished green cloth cloak to conceal Papa, topped by a tricorne. I found, later, enough at Nathan's[6] where there was a scrambling mass from the Smart Set, but a mask for his poor face I had to hunt for. 'We're not making any' (one sees why). At last having rootled out an unsuitable orange velvet dainty butterfly-shaped mask, I turned my mind on myself. I had sent to Paris for (1) my smart yellow satin full-skirted dress which at a pinch, with hat and mask, would have made a Venetian Carnival belle, (2) the old Russian tartan silk, an ally in a thousand balls, having already done duty as Lady Macbeth, Flora Macdonald, Prince Charlie and numerous Tchekov plays.

My object today was to find a Highlander's fantastic hat of ostrich – higher and better angled than a Guardsman's bearskin, with a long cascade of ostrich tails (if tails they have) falling over profile and shoulder. No luck – costumiers and Scotch shops laughed me to scorn. Evelyn bet I'd never get one. White's [Club] came to the rescue. Wu was sent to find me a Highland

2 He had been knighted in the New Year Honours.
3 Sir Oliver Harvey.
4 For the fancy-dress Chelsea Arts Ball, then held annually at the Albert Hall.
5 Literally a fine – here 'to make amends'.
6 London's main theatrical costumier.

bar-propper. He found me Andrew Scott who promised to do his best while promising nothing. So to lunch with Pam Berry in an ice-house together with Ann Rothermere and Lord Pakenham. He's a Catholic which makes a weird combination of faiths and he's a trifle unbalanced.

I got home at four. No parcel from Paris, no headwear. In despair I started ringing up all the barracks, adjutants, etc. no one naturally understanding what I was at. In the middle of the screaming a page brought into the room two cylinders or infernal machines with St Paulian domes, and these contained a choice of Scotch bonnets – not lousy and greasy from a private's head, but new as new and as becoming as haloes. My relief was a little dimmed by a call from Paris to say the dresses were to leave on the morrow – but the hat, I felt, could stand on its own. With an ordinary black dress and inspiration of details, it could steer me to Victory at the Albert Hall. So off again with the faithful David to a variety of Scotch shops where after usual frustrations I bought for 10 shillings and four coupons,[7] four mufflers which joined together by Wadey made the most ravishing of 'plaids' or shawl. Can you see it? Draped with my great skill (a piece flowing behind and the folds held in by my diamond roses), the hair lightly powdered, the ears ringed, a sprig of bay (stolen from the standard trees outside Mrs. Spry's shop, washed and oiled for the nonce) for Victory and Madame Bonnet's black gloves slashed with bottle green. O! I was good. I seldom say it. Belle of the ball and no mistake.

Dinner first – twenty strong at Warwick House (Esmond's), Laura,[8] an exceedingly common cow-girl, her lover Gerry,[9] a commoner chef (the last resource and humiliation of the dresser-upper). Ann hoped to be a sea nymph but became a classical Widow Twankey thanks to an unfortunate vermilion wig. Then there was Dick Wyndham, a realistic Arab, walnut-juice and all,

---

7 Clothes were still rationed in 1947, and continued to be till 1949.

8 Ann Rothermere's sister, later Duchess of Marlborough.

9 Koch de Gooreynd.

and Frank Owen, the pirate school. I sat next to him (he's an old friend and editor of the *Daily Mail*). He has not learnt to suppress *gros mots* – not the coolest sentence is said without a shock. There was the wraith Clarissa[10] and one or two pretty nondescripts in their mother-in-youth clothes – 1900.

The Albert Hall (when we got to the haven of our box that was sandwiched between friendly boxes) looked as it always did – too big and too exciting ever to plumb. Raimund, pretty tight and moustached, took me round and round the room – not dancing but staring at the ground-floor boxes and with the lack of inhibition that *travesti*[11] gives you, criticising the revellers to their faces. 'You're good', 'I don't think much of you', etc. In the old days these balls were dry, so that people had not only to take a box for secret drinking but also wear clothes – crinolines for example – that could smuggle in bottles in their folds. In these austere days all that has changed and there is champagne in the taps and the fire extinguishers, in the lily cups and loos. It's nicer because friends are welcome in every box and the drink seems to be pooled. I really enjoyed it very much.

I had two protestations of love – one from Christopher Sykes (another Arab) and one from Philip Jordan in civvies. I stood it till 3.30 and then started to wilt and when I tried to get Papa home he said he was staying. At the moment he had got on his lap a lady I'd christened 'Meat'. Her two gigantic though shapely legs seemed to cover him quite, so I gave him up and stumped off irritated, with Clarissa. No transport and determined drizzle made one's exit less dramatic, so Papa had time to stumble down and say 'You can't walk' but we started off and in a minute had been offered a lift with some strangers Hampstead-bound. I was put down at the Dorch. and Clarissa at her destination, and Papa went back to his meat for another half-hour or so and reeled home before I was asleep.

10 Churchill, later to marry Anthony Eden.
11 Fancy dress.

New Year's Day was general Hangover Day. Not for me, I felt bobbish enough and pleased with my success of the night before. I lunched with Mr. Wu at Wilton's because Wu's snobbery forces him to this place where there is only a choice of oysters and lobster (neither of which I wanted) and sherry at 9/- a thimble, and friends on one's lap and breathing and whispering all around one – no privacy and no focusing on your *vis-à-vis*. He took me (lunch over) to see a picture he was having framed. A1, half life size, a lady and gentleman engaged to be married, a priest they are calling on at his *bureau de travail* (1880). It is called *An Awkward Question*. Impossible to discover which character has asked what. We dined at the Hoffs – Isaiah and Venetia.

January 8th, 1948

Let's go back to Victor's party. It was a thumping success. I met Victor at the Savoy in the morning, there to sift out the *placement* and worse, to argue against the horseshoe table. We compromised on two tables and my *placement* (gold to Victor's copper). I asked tentatively if he knew anything about the conjuror. 'No,' he said, 'only that he's good.' Through it all we were stuffing down canapés of smoked salmon, cheese, blubber and what not, and munching olives and dropping their bothersome stones behind sofas and tables, and flinging back martinis and telling Pam Berry, who had barged in, not to interfere. So it was happy and funny and I felt secure about the candles and went off to lunch with two enormous women at your club, the Allies. Moura and Juliet were the giant-esses and we were cheerful enough.

The party started at 8.15. I'd taken an admirer called Mr. Philip Jordan for whom I felt responsible and Victor had Prof. Blunt[12] and a Mrs. David who were weighing on him. Mr. Wu is always a

---

12 Prof. Anthony Blunt, Surveyor of the King's Pictures, later to be unmasked as a Soviet spy.

souci but these disturbances were quickly quieted and we settled down in candlelight. The women were lovely. Judy, looking very pretty, was the plainest, Dolly Rothschild, Venetia and your poor mother the least fresh, but Pempie and Angie[13] and Freda[14] and Liz and Caroline and Pam and unknown Mrs. David were all dreams. Marietta Tree was the Widow Twankey but a pretty one. I sat between Vicky (he was sweating and mopping away with anxiety and with desire for success) and Mr. Wu in mellow mood. The conjurer was the worst ever – dropped all the cards, returned you your marked one without the mark, no livestock, kept one hand permanently in his pocket changing false for real, did the old sham-thumb-cigarette-extinguisher trick, but it didn't matter. The horror of his patter made up for weight of hand. No one attempted to move till 2.30 a.m. and then we all went to our separate homes blessing Victor for the elegant treat.

January 9th. Yesterday it was Brighton for the day, a jaunt for Papa and me, Mr. Wu, Daisy and Lord Sherwood. We piled into the Southern Belle at eleven. Lord S. travels with a large-size bottle of Worcester sauce in his pocket to lace his Bovril. The idea made my mouth water for so delicious a reviver and my disappointment was acute when the attendant said they'd run out this morning. With seven minutes still to go before eleven, my weak condition still allowed me to tear down the platform bluffing and thrusting to the Tea Buffet. 'A small pot of Bovril please, quick, quick.' 'Can't serve you until you are seated.' 'I've no time, no time to sit, just a little pot of Bovril please quick.' 'I'm sorry, you must sit down.' So I plumped on to a chair divorced from its table looking grotesque and again panted my request. No good, no Bovril. Off again to Lunch Buffet. 'Any Bovril?' 'Yes, if you sit down we'll give you a cup.' 'No, just a pot, small please, quick, quick.' 'I'm sorry we're not allowed to sell it that way.' Screaming

---

13 The Dudley Ward sisters, Penelope a film star, Angela married to Major-General Sir Robert Laycock.

14 Their mother, Freda Casa Maury, formerly mistress of the Duke of Windsor.

something about 'this country' and frustration and Labour Government I tore back and just hopped the moving train.

Brighton was flooded in sunshine and Mr. Wu and I took a Liberty Boat[15] while the others piled into a taxi. Meeting place to be the Albion. I had a *crise* of rage, as once before in the Venetian Piazza when, after waiting for the taxi riders, they drove up licking their chops and much brightened by an oyster and stout collation. Then Papa walked me halfway to our real destination, No. 1 Chichester Terrace – a flat owned once by Rufus's father and now the property of Lord Sherwood, dolled and daisied up into an aggressive Regency. Lovely too. I could spend a week happily in this large room, sun-flooded usually, warmed and luxurious, with Dr. Brighton treating me to health. Lunch was on the sticky side, but once swallowed Wu and I got away to give Rottingdean the once-over. Wu had never seen it and was interested not only as a Catholic to see Maurice Baring's home or as a short-story writer to see Kipling's home, or as a pre-Raphaelite to say 'There lived Burne-Jones' but because the village church is said to be the model for one of the churches at Forest Lawn, the crematorium at Hollywood that he has written a book about.[16] He was disappointed, as it bore no resemblance to its imitation, which carries not only a shrine for 'Recessional' ('God of our fathers' – Kipling) but also a copy of *National Velvet* treated with the reverence that might be used towards *The Imitation of Christ* MS.[17]

It appears that two people recently visited Rottingdean church and asked the verger if this was the church that had inspired Kipling to write 'Recessional'. 'Yes,' said the verger, 'and Enid Bagnold to write *National Velvet*.' Now we know that Kipling having scribbled down 'Lest we forget' threw it straight into the scrapbasket whence a niece retrieved it and saw merit,

15 On foot. Liberty Boats were the small craft which ferried sailors on leave between ship and shore. Since Navy shore stations were treated in every respect like ships, parties of men walking into town were always so described.

16 *The Loved One*.

17 By Thomas à Kempis (d.1471).

so Uncle Ruddy said she could keep it. This we know from Nephew Bloggs.[18]

I took Enid and Oggie out yesterday morning. We visited furriers, tailors and jewellers – quite the morning of the *femme du monde*. Alas we are none of us that. Enid fitted a smart coat of Black Watch tartan – shoulders padded to Atlas width. I made a criticism and mentioned the new look and bottle line, but Enid's a big girl and the narrower she builds her shoulders the vaster grows her bust. The furriers called me because of my design for a little evening wrap – Conrad's old silver foxes disintegrate ('*Madame porte ces foxes miteuses?*')[19] and I visualised a soft-as-soap chinchilla caress of a coatee lined with flesh-coloured satin (*seta pura*)[20] and a bunch of Parma violets nestling in its folds. Miss Pratt, furrier to Princess Elizabeth and friend to Oggie who loves towering over her, said she'd get me patterns of rabbit from Mr Goodchild,[21] and that's as far as I got.

My lunch was with Pope-Hennessy, James, writer and son to Dame Una, biographer of Dickens and others. I was a little shy, he's twenty years younger than me and nervous himself. It was all right and having talked so much of the Bloomsbury quarter and nos. 90, 92 and 94[22] we went to take a look at them exteriorly only. I did not feel deeply – it's all too long ago perhaps. I was very happy there – my first house. David Herbert and I had a rendezvous at three. I was dreadfully sleepy but determined to rouse myself and enjoy an outing. Chips was in the hall, so we got an invitation to the Maharajah of Baroda's cocktail party at 6.30. Papa reeled in

---

18 In fact, first cousin once removed. Stanley Baldwin's and Kipling's mothers were sisters.

19 'Madame *wears* these shabby fox furs?'

20 Pure silk.

21 Rabbit farmer at pre-airport Gatwick.

22 Gower Street. My parents bought No. 90 on their marriage, but were later able to add the first floors only of Nos. 92 and 94. By the time I knew it, the house therefore had a considerable *piano nobile*.

en route for Ditchley. He drew with pride from the cupboard his new Inverness coat – light-coloured, stiff with youth and from its pocket pulled a little roundabout Gorblimey[23] hat – a comedian's – Sid Field's. To this startling costume he added a pastel-shade muffler and a smart gold-headed stick – Edward VII. Papa thinks he is pretty correct in dress and deportment and conventional and would pass unnoticed anywhere. Once he wore pale flesh-pink shorts all one season at the Lido in Venice.

Sleep was gaining on me again and my yawns set David a-yawning, so we decided to lie ourselves down on the twin beds and take forty [winks]. Both afraid of snores, we both said that *occasionally* we snored. Both gave a grunt on dropping off, heard his or her own and changed position.

January 13th, 1948

Papa doesn't seem too well. He hasn't got up and says he has a headache. I do hope it's only last night's party. Last Saturday Mr. Wu came round (it's Wu week) with the illustrations for his new crematorium book. Excellent. He was in good spirits and friendly to the world, till the unfortunate James Pope-Hennessy called to take me to lunch with Maud Russell[24]. He then closed like a clam and in spite of my introducing him to a 'fellow author' only opened up enough to spit out some black poison. So rude was it that James admitted afterwards to great discomfiture. It was worth it for me for the pleasure I got at Wu's discomfiture on realising when I made him *une observation* that he was not only a respected writer but a dearly beloved Papist. For Wu there are no indifferent or inadmirable Papists. Raimund and Liz called for me in their car – lovely it was driving to Ditchley, with the radio blazing out the

---

23 The name originally given to a service dress cap in the First World War. The reference is to the Edwardian music-hall song 'My Old Man's a Dustman', re-popularised by Lonnie Donegan in the 1960s.

24 Mrs Gilbert Russell, sister-in-law of Conrad.

Third Symphony and the heater full on and the windows opening and shutting it seemed at desire's order. Liz took it all as natural. I'm still staggered by the magic of it. I hated your not being with me and saw us sitting in the Ford unable to leave a programme.

Ditchley as beautiful as ever and almost as comfortable (no, nothing like. Electric fires in the bedrooms instead of blazing logs and bells not answered and rooms of course shut up), but with the most disconcerting Rebeccaism[25] about it. Every object, picture, colour of flower, arrangement, design bought, placed and grown by the first Mrs. Tree is untouched and the poor second[26] fears to give an order to the servants, and Mr. Collins the butler who loved Nancy and shared her interests of garden and furniture, textiles and porcelain, keeps his eyes forever fixed on her uncertain ways. She is pure and good and beautiful and 'intellectual' and humourless. Poor girl, I wouldn't be in her haunted boots.

Early next morning off again as I was engaged to lunch with Mr. Wu and far too afraid of him to chuck. 'Where would you like to lunch? I thought the Ritz?' 'O no, Bo, not the Ritz.' 'Why don't you like the Ritz?' 'O because it's common, the wrong people still think it's smart, the food is uneatable. It's like being on the S.S. *Lusitania*, but still I'd rather lunch at the Ritz than choose a place that you'd criticise throughout the meal.' So at the Ritz we lunched, together with 200 *endimanché*[27] strangers. The waiter put us in the centre of the room, as sort of navel to this undistinguished body. The waiter in answer to Evelyn's demand for drink said 'Red or white?' 'What do you mean?' said Evelyn. 'Well, you can 'ave a carafe of either.' Before Bo had time for his stroke he added 'O, I see, you wants it bottled.' 'Is there no wine waiter or wine list?' gasped Evelyn. All this a great joy to me.

Afternoon siestas for both but under separate roofs. At six I bustled off to Victoria to meet Louise and Hubert de Chambure

---

25 *Rebecca*, by Daphne du Maurier, tells a similar story. Ronnie Tree and his wife Nancy had divorced, and he had married Marietta Fitzgerald.

26 Marietta.

27 In their Sunday best.

off the Golden Arrow. I was much too early and thought I'd fill time and exile sleep with a cup of tea in the buffet. There were only a handful of people wanting a cup, but I was told to stand in the queue. This I did, and resting my black handbag on the marble bar to delve for my purse which didn't happen to be there, I inadvertently broke a rather good big wineglass. I ran to the hotel of the station and producing credentials asked them to change me a cheque, explaining (too quickly) the difficulty of my situation. Of course he said no and of course I said what the hell. Louise arrived and Hubert de Chambure so I gave them a nice bite of dinner in my sitting room. Papa returned from Ditchley at midnight and bed was good and sleep profound.

The next day I was conscious all day how much *better* I am. I think another year of Paris would have brought me jittering to my grave. Sleep has improved a bit and despair more absent. It's you, O horror, who are as bad as ill-health. In three weeks I've had one letter. I know when it comes it's a bumper but I have to wait too long for news.

14th. Then it isn't three weeks only two and a bit. I dread the tedium of my letters once I get into my retreat. What shall I have to tell? I'm going to a home near Tunbridge Wells with diet sheet, resolves, Conrad's letters and mine. I'll tell you the address when I know it and I'm telling no one else. The English will think I'm curing in France, and vice versa.

Nothing much to say about yesterday – a lot of Louise and shops and a lunch at the Frog Embassy. Madame Massigli has left the Ambassador never to return. Food scrumptious. Massigli incomprehensible in either language.[28] I got Sachie Sitwell on the other side.

Papa's opening huge packages of new clothes from Leslie & Roberts[29] – suit after suit. I can't look.

---

28 His handwriting was also illegible, so there was little communication.
29 Extremely expensive Savile Row tailors.

January 17th, 1948
69 Rue de Lille

It's a long time, or so it seems, since I wrote. What has been done in the interim? I changed with a telephonic squeak and the flick of the fingers the whole of my business operations. 'Trousers', the figurehead of Trower, Still, Keeling, Mortmain, Dally & Dolittle I have sacked; Mr Allday the accountant also sacked; Drummond's still to be sacked and everything put into the subtle Jewish hands of Mr. Hart of Gilbert Samuel & Co. Trousers was like the conjuror (Victor's) – drops the cards, loses the certificates, a great exponent of the 'law's delay' in his own profession. New Broom Hart has filled us with hope as only the biased new can. There was, of course, another dinner with Emerald at which Papa did a talking marathon. Harold Macmillan was longing to place a word but could not. Louise never opened her mouth and the Treasury official, Mr. Ricketts, had no chance to justify his office, which was Papa's blitz target. Then dear Jenny Nicholson who's been ill came to lunch with me – sweet as ever, asking a lot about you and alas going to America to join her husband at once, so no help to me in my new life in Paris. I feel as though I were getting married. Always before when life has changed from England to America, Malaya and North Africa it's been temporary job movement. This time it's true change and I feel weak. It will get better.

On the 15th I went to Bognor. The sun made the new paper and paint glow and shine most welcomingly. Louise, Papa and I and Wadey picnicked. Papa went by car to call on Hilaire Belloc en route and we three went by train. He found Hilaire less to pieces in appearance than he expected – his beard was clipped, his flies buttoned, his movements controlled but his mind, while working perfectly for whole periods, even giving vent to witty remarks and song, would suddenly wander into voids. 'Don't you remember, Papa, that Mr. Duff Cooper was Ambassador in Paris?' said his Reganish daughter. 'Ah yes, let's see, you succeeded Lord

Lyons, didn't you?' Lord Lyons's tenure of office was in the last century. And then again he asked tenderly after you and was interested in every detail of your conditions and ten minutes after he had heard everything there was to tell, he enquired again with complete ignorance.

Bognor was in splendid shape. I should let it for a decent sum. Your pathetic school pennants still disfigure the walls of one room. Mr. McCaffrey I liked exceedingly – a man of hope who clearly loves work and prefers to *make* what we need. Wade's fowl alarmingly big and not laying at all. Edith[30] getting an old girl. Shall I replace her when the time comes? It's dreadfully uneconomic. If I'm not there to cut and carry people's lawns and odd corners of grass and plant the mangels and kale and single them and hoe and pull them up and fertilise the ground and lime it and carry dung to it from the other meadow, the farmer has to be paid to do it all and the hay must be bought at fantastic prices. In the end it supplies Wadey[31] and her few neighbours with milk and butter.[32] I ought to make the consumers of the produce pay the purchase and upkeep of the new cow, but who is to organise it? I don't see my way clear in any direction at the moment.

Our last dinner was at Coalbox's – a galaxy of stars – Vivien and Larry, Vita Sackville-West C.H.,[33] Harold Nicolson her husband, Thornton Wilder,[34] Rex Warner, etc., etc. I rather enjoyed myself. Louise and Papa loathed it. A row on coming home – Louise and I distracted by having to sort and address the *Echo de Fantaisies*[35] and do a hundred last chores and Papa with two business letters to write – he has not had much else to do – lost temper, head and good manners and said he couldn't do anything for the upset we caused and flounced to bed, red with

30 The cow, successor to the Princess.

31 Miss Wade couldn't manage Paris and was now living alone in the lodge at Bognor.

32 This arrangement had been in force throughout the Embassy years.

33 Companion of Honour, a distinction awarded personally by the monarch.

34 American author of *The Bridge of San Luis Rey*.

35 A new book of Louise's.

rage and refusing to wish L.L. goodnight. I, of course, was too angry to say anything and went to bed silent as a gaoler and deaf to his pathetic apologies. 'I know I'm spoilt', he said 'but I *am* sorry.' 'One can't cure hurts with apologies *always*', I said. So we slept cross. We had ordered our waking at 7.30 for the 9 o'clock Golden Arrow. Papa deliberately did not wake me till after eight. Was it fear? Was it tenderness? Was it just not thinking? Anyway when I awoke Wade had disappeared to a leisurely breakfast which kept her until 8.15, and 8.30 was zero hour. You've never seen such panic, porters all over the place sitting on trunks that were past all hope of shutting, me nakedish screaming, odd parcels to be tied, the guns, the cartridges, Papa's red box, things to be left for my return, things not to be left, get a taxi, get two, register what, leave this with Lady Cunard, my pipi to be sent to the doctor,[36] pandemonium. We made it, but Papa was more securely locked into the dog house. I let him out on the S.S. *Invicta* – we couldn't arrive in Paris like two sticks. We dined, *très Vilmorin*, at the Escargot – three brothers, Louise and others. So a new life begins tomorrow which I won't embark on now.

January 19th, 1948

We had a rollicking lunch with Eric and Donald[37] at Gafner's – *moules marinières et Camembert pour Maman, pour ne pas trop dépenser.*[38] Prices are worse. Eric has to be earlier at the grindstone. 9.15 is to be aimed at. Barley is paying no attention to the order. Donald thought out a queer little dig at the Harveys and stole from some film studio a hundred feet of film representing the Harvey arrival in Paris. The film was not processed, therefore negative instead of positive, and Donald had it run off

---

36 Nothing to worry about.

37 Donald Mallett, with Eric Duncannon and Barley Alison a member of the Embassy staff.

38 So as not to spend too much.

by mistake at the Embassy weekly film show. Funny – because as you know negative would show Sir Oliver as a black man in a white suit.

Lady Harvey took the Bishop of Tanganyika and two other divines and Barley to show the library after luncheon and said, so curiously I think, 'It's a beautiful room considering the difficulty of books.' To me, who have been brought up to the cliché of 'there is nothing that furnishes a room like books', it seems an extraordinary statement. She took her party through the bathroom, so carefully planned to be Napoleonic, saying 'My predecessor made this room since she was so fond of N. Africa.' That could have meant nothing. It was only the rug that had a black man on it, not an Arab or Berber, and the rug was no longer there. Still they all say Maudie is very nice – no candles and top lights and they don't like the grey of the dining room. Pauline's chamber[39] becomes a *musée*.

Gaston [Palewski] brought his blemishes[40] and there was a moment when to Gaston alone I said '*Je me sens un peu perdue*.'[41] '*Pauvre Diana*,' he said and a huge lump had to be swallowed or it would have fountained up to my face.

At eight Papa and I sallied out (Liberty Boat or shanks's). It was fairly fine and we thought Michaud would do as a bistro. Of course it was shut and on we staggered through what had become quite a formidable rain. No umbrellas, fineries getting spoilt, the fallen rich par excellence! On and on past gloomy ones, shut ones and at long last to the glowing beauty of Porquerolles with its 'all alive' oysters and lilac and mussels – I ate a cup of fish soup and we both had a coquille St. Jacques. We ordered some riesling and the man brought champagne. 'Take it away. We asked for moselle.' '*C'est Madame qui vous l'offre*'[42] – another lump but a happy

---

39 Where my parents slept in her bed.

40 He suffered from an unfortunate skin condition.

41 'I feel a bit lost.'

42 'It is with the compliments of Madame.'

warm lump. So we walked back home, orphans of the storm but the better for the champagne and the gesture. I cried a bit in bed. Papa was kind and comforting and didn't scold me for being silly – because it is silly as I was for the last two years always ill and often in despair in the Embassy – but there it is. I hate to have left the beauty of the house and the power to give pleasure.

Yesterday we went in Rufus's car to Chantilly. The light was brilliant – the snowdrops earlier and much bigger than other people's and the house was as hot as a conservatory but in dreadful chaos – discouraging chaos – much broken, too, by unowning hands. Old Man Regnier gloomier than ever. His sullen face showed so little interest when I asked him about the motor mowing machine that I thought it was a failure and didn't work. He will spoil all the pleasure in my garden. There seem to be a lot of musical instruments belonging to you.

Paris, January 19–20th, 1948

Not so much to tell you this morning. Arrival of Rufus with the dawn – hunter home from the hill at Baden Baden. He killed *des biches* which I think means does and I think of Louise on the *fête* of St. Hubert at Mortefontaine, crying over the cruelty of the chase and adding *Pensez que ce sont des herbivores.*[43] We ate at Michaud – omelettes and kidneys and red wine. We'd had a fancy, L.L., André,[44] Papa and I, to take a trip to Madeira by boat. One could get in they said at Havre or Cherbourg, stop a day at Bordeaux, another at Lisbon and Vigo and stay a week in Madeira among wild arums, huge straw hats, red and white hessian boots and wheelless vehicles on runners, and return to Lisbon and a motor that would take one home to Paris. So to Cook's I went. O, what a falling off. Nothing to be done, no ships go anywhere except a

43 'Remember, they are *herbivorous*.'
44 De Vilmorin, Louise's brother.

few occasionally to South America, overloaded with emigrants, cargo boats non-existent, one Portuguese ship a month from Lisbon to Madeira and back, but no bookings made. Ichabod, ichabod.[45] Too many cooks and not a drop of broth.

Wig fixing at the Bristol. I found the *Chef du Protocol* M. Dumaine peacocking up for his fine duties, hair and nails both being beautified. Quick home, me to meet Carl Burckhardt, only a minute with him but a pleasant one. He was neither fat nor thin. Sometimes he's as fat as Nestlé's chocolate and at others he is Greco-ed down and dragged ugly with empty flesh bags.

The Dorchester
January 24th, 1948

I haven't written for days because my life in London is flustered and unrhythmical. The ferryboat on Wednesday night wasn't bad. We boarded our *wagons-lits*[46] at 8.30, did the crossword and bedded down and slept like logs, to be woken by a crashing jolt proclaiming, it seemed to me, that the train had hurtled over a rock – due I imagine to an unexpected drop or rise between the line and the boat line. From then on a clanking of chains and the titanic hurling of iron bars on to other iron bars, Vulcan's million hammers and a metallic din kept us wakeful. Once on the sea it was rock-a-bye baby and a fresh, pretty breakfast to greet us in England at 8.30 a.m. Pale green everything – upholstery, paint, grapefruit, napkins, limitless butter and sugar. Then to Mr. Hart, our new business man, with Daphne [Wakefield] and to Dr. Something about my poor leg.[47]

Brilliant lunch at Box's and the great first night of *Anna* [Karenina]. I adored it but I don't think other people did and the

---

45 'She named the boy Ichabod, saying "The Glory has departed from Israel".' (1 Samuel 4:21.)

46 The night ferry to England. The train went on to the boat.

47 I remember the leg. It gave her a lot of pain, but mended itself over time.

papers did their worst. Vivien looked much older (always worrying to me) but I put it down to an ageing coiffure. Cecil's done a splendid job with the silhouettes and details. Some anachronisms I noticed – not Cecil's department – a cocktail table on rollers, a revolving door to the hotel, and twin beds. Raimund defends twin beds and says 'Central Europe' but I've never seen an old-fashioned house with twin beds. The lover[48] is a common stick, and the love scenes are bad, quite bad, but the others are all good and Vivien moved me so much that I couldn't stop crying and was still dripping when I got to Oggie's supper party. This naturally cheered the Oliviers up no end for they felt I think that the film wasn't the height of success.

There was Gladys Cooper[49] and Ali Forbes, the Moores[50] and Caroline and Clarissa and the Hoffs (gatecrashers) and Johnnie Mills[51] and lady and Chips and by degrees having eaten all the lobster (Oggie's) and the foie gras (mine) and drunk all the cham (mine) people drifted off to the very sordid ball at the Vic–Wells – fancy dress and a lot of ugly nudity, men dancing together and all smelling rather. I went because I could see that Oggie's song was half sung and she wanted to go and wouldn't without me, but I didn't enjoy it or admire it. Chips walked me round the throng and soon I got entangled in a new (or perhaps it's old) dance on the Spreading Chestnut Tree plan – 'Throw your left hip out' or something not very dignified.[52]

Next morning to the Middlesex Hospital to have diathermy on my poor leg. The receptionist had been so charming on the telephone that when I met her I had to tell her so. 'Michael', she answered, 'had such a dreadful crossing to America.' 'But Michael who? I don't know who you are.' 'I'm Juliet's granddaughter.'[53]

48 Kieron Moore.
49 Celebrated actress.
50 Garrett and Joan (later Lord and Lady Drogheda).
51 The actor, later Sir John Mills.
52 The hokey-cokey.
53 Sir Michael Duff was Juliet's son.

All the ladies are in jobs of this kind so the standard of civility is very high. The girl who applies the diathermy is an angel and used to be at the Regent's Park open-air school and left just as you came.[54] She must be very young to be in charge of those spluttering infernal machines. Too late I got a telegram from Enid saying 'Do catch 11 train to Oxford and see Timothy[55] married. Back at 5.' Imagine! Does this o'er-hasty marriage tell of seduction? We must not breathe it. The Cliffords would not go. The mother has relented, the father still too cross to say anything, the sisters not allowed to partake. Tucker[56] led the bride up the Catholic aisle and gave her away. At 6.30 Timmy rang me from downstairs and asked to bring Pandora up. So charming they looked and young, she wreathed in smiles with a white bunny hat and muff and gardenia spray, quite bridal and touching in her happiness. They were off to the Savoy for the night and then to Rottingdean for a day or two and then digs in Oxford. Very romantic. Enid delighted. Poor Laurian had had to go to the Clifford house and pick the bride up and snatch her, rather, from the family clutch, but although she was warned not to get out of the car, she was invited in and civilly received.

Now I'm going to dine with Emerald and a man at a restaurant. They will have been to a play while I have been writing to my dearest son and packing for my departure tomorrow. The retreat begins and will last three weeks. My luggage will cause laughter – one big white box of clothes, books, etc. etc., one huge black tin box of Conrad's letters, one large black box of mine, one Foreign Office 'bag' stuffed with letters and books and clutching hands [spring clips], one attaché case, one zip bag. Write to me here. I'm a bit nervous of being wretched but I can always go if I don't think it's doing any good to my body or soul.

---

54 'Miss Betty's' – my kindergarten.

55 Her son, Timothy Jones, married the sixteen-year-old Pandora Clifford (my future sister-in-law).

56 Dominie, her youngest brother.

Wednesday, January [27th], 1948
[Droitwich Spa Health Farm]

I've been here two days 'enclosed in a nutshell' for it's no bigger
– bright and flowery with hideous h. and c. and a very high hospital
bed. I'm really curiously calm and happy and I believe it's what
I need – absolute cessation from strain, food, faces, drink, fluster.
A pleasant, not dismal, lethargy has fallen upon me and I have
not got out of bed to open those bulging F.O. bags and weighty
deed boxes. I've lain in a coma and asked for a newspaper which
I can never get. My diet is of the most filthy – the boiled scrap of
fish, the scrape of marge on the lump of Ryvita, the tepid
Contrexeville, the English salad without oil by order, but I don't
mind at all. I go to my diathermy every day and I believe in it
because my knee is half the size, but is that due to rest? A pretty
woman massages me with dismally lethargic fingers. I, who am
used to my bright Parisian torturer, am contemptuous of this damp
thing and would like to be rid of her. Sister is Irish and ever so
robust.

I've been issued a radio from 'Welfare'. It only gets Home
Service and that through a deep hum like the French put on to
signal Hamlet's ghost. I've just listened to the New World[57] and
picture too clearly you and me drumming our duets out in the
salon vert and the pretty illustrated piano score you gave me. To
go back to the B.B.C., they spoke to me at lunchtime about fertil-
isation and the birth of young. If only I had had you or Papa or
David or Lulu to hear it with me. It was educational, not just
salacious and the tone was the tone of *The Children's Hour*. It
took off on starfish – easy enough – sperm floating and meeting
eggs. It dwelt on hens as a bridge and then took a deep decisive
plunge into the mire of mammals. 'Bears, dogs, cats, human
beings, rats and so forth' (humans were always a bit buried) 'found
it safer to have their eggs fertilised inside them' (I consider this

57 Dvořák's Symphony No. 9, *The New World*.

false, as a chick coming out of its carapace is far more advanced and perceptive than a puling babe). How is he going to get over this fence? I thought. No trouble whatsoever. 'The sperm', he said, 'must be passed by the male to the female from an opening in the male body into an opening in the female. The male passage is called the penis.' I never thought to hear that from Uncle Mac[58] or whoever it was.

I've read *England Made Me* by G. Greene – pretty good though not a patch, says Papa, on *Stamboul Train* – and I've read *Maurice Baring* by Laura Lovat, a book, I regret to say, less bad than I anticipated. Her little postscript, though too intimate in parts, I think well done for the unlearned and then there are so funny also exquisite poems – a few – and an unnecessary piece by Father Knox and another by Marthe Bibesco and Trenchard's wonderful obituary that was in *The Times*, and three very familiar Rottingdean photographs – the whole beautifully printed on good paper. Now I've started on the new Sinclair Lewis called *Kingsblood Royal* and I wish I hadn't because it doesn't interest me. I've guessed the surprise point and yet I am obliged to finish it to its last typed dreg. Anyway the point of the cure is to make no effort till energy claims one.

February 1st, 1948

I loved hearing your little squeak on the telephone. A Hindu patient, female, has wailed in prayer for two nights for the Mahatma.[59] When I think how all these big-wigs have cursed and ridiculed the old man, imprisoned him, considered him our great enemy and can now say the light has gone out. True, once India was handed back by the Old Queen's grandson,[60] Gandhi became

---

58 The host of BBC *Children's Hour*.

59 Gandhi had been assassinated on 30 January.

60 Lord Mountbatten of Burma, actually Queen Victoria's great-grandson.

a protecting power. Our Ali this morning quotes Bevin as saying that if the Labour Party had done nothing but give India to the Chutneys, that action would be enough to justify its existence. So don't let's have any talk of Tory misrule, they'll be responsible for what happens now.

The radio continues to occupy much of my time. I've tried hard with my pink eyes shut to appreciate Delius, Walton and Britten, our three musical glories, and I can't get it at all. It's slowness of ear, not because it's nonsense as I consider Picasso to be. I'm sure they are real, but I'd have to hear the same pieces thirty times running. I must have a good set in my smallest sitting room, relayed to my bedroom.

Most of the day I give to Conrad's letters. I don't think I can possibly do as Katherine asks and privately print a book of his letters and mine – mine are harmless enough, except that people would always get up from a browse minus their pants, but the wit of Conrad's letters is all directed against K., Trim,[61] the Catholic Church, all priests, his brother Claud, his sisters Diana and Flora. If I suppress all this plus tenderness to me there leaves nothing but farm news and money situation – wonderful bits about Daphne [Bath] but they would have to come straight out – far too indiscreet and bawdy.

I eat nothing but very good Jaffa oranges, apples and a bit of dry cold meat sometimes, but as the place is run with no direction that I can see, sometimes the patients' tray is brought to me and really! I wonder how it compares with yours. I've never tasted anything to compare with the vegetables and sauces – cloth and stale clothes the predominating flavour – and then the textures of the limp old fish and shredded bits of mince. I had an egg tonight. I always help the nurse to make my bed as it does help more than half, but she doesn't remember to time my egg's boiling and it was like a fives ball.

Oh dear, there's a terribly gloomy bit going on now about mine

61 Katherine's son, the Earl of Oxford and Asquith.

disasters and the noise of miners gurgling as they drown. I wish I knew whether it was more dangerous to fly or to mine. I bet flying kills more per capita.

Did you read Balzac? Are you interested in him? I've bought a great quantity of cheap volumes of his works, some in English, most in French. Shall I send them on to you? You mustn't whatever happens forget your croakings.[62]

February 2nd, 1948

I've got an appalling swelling on my eye – legacy of conjunctivitis. Is it a stye or an abcess? Half the white of the same eye is a lake of red – not like little veins but like blood in a stained-glass window. I'll be a dainty dish to set before a King and Queen when we go to lunch at the Palace in the middle of the month. I forgot to mention that owing to the stye the lower lid hangs down hammock-wise. As to the knee, it's sure to be arthritis, which cannot be cured. It may be fibritis [*sic*] which can be, but there doesn't seem to be any means of finding out. It's been X-rayed, but that's a gesture like signing the visitors' book. No report has come through yet. Ralph Richardson in *Anna Karenina*, you and I make the same noise with our joints, only my noises are involuntary. The place is odder and odder – no system at all. Last night I had four nightmares running, and took a sedative at 4.30. For the first time I'm woken at eight out of a precious though drugged sleep, with an enormous tray of breakfast – bread (not allowed), covered dish with stone-cold preserved egg lying on a chunk of grey sodden bread next to a pyramid of darker grey potatoes. 'Is this for me?' 'Well, don't you always have breakfast?' 'No, nurse, you know I don't, only tea.' 'I thought you did.' No apology and when I said it seemed absurd to drug with one hand and waken with another 'Well, I'm busy with my breakfasts now.'

62 The language of frogs.

I've been reading an account by me and Katherine Asquith of our tour camping in the Pyrenees. It isn't particularly well written or at all amusing but for endurance and dash and courage, resource, vigour and redoubtableness. They're not made like that any more, not even women. There's not a take-off without two mules having to be found to drag the car into position. The steering gear breaks twice, and through it all we were always cooking our meals, not sandwiches and hard boileds but pans and fires.

February 3rd. I'm going to speak to Papa in a minute. The ferry I hope to God has deposited him safe this morning on the white cliffs. I'm going to ask him to buy me a radio, portable. My mouth waters for the Third Programme and also for *Dick Barton* whom Evelyn (who condemns the discovery of sound waves and wouldn't listen if war was declared) has now fallen for and as he has no set in London has to take a taxi to the *Tablet* offices to listen in. It's an insanity.

It's 8.50 a.m. and I've just heard *Sheherazade* by Rimsky-Korsakov in its entirety. Now who but me would listen to that at this hour? Perfect it was. Now it's morning service, psalms being exquisitely sung. As soon as I hear that pure traditional music I'm transported to a particular vision and memory of childhood. There I am, kneeling in Rowsley[63] village church in the front pew of the left aisle, staring for a good hour and a half at a neo-Gothic stained-glass window, four crudely coloured scenes from the life of Christ. The light shone through it to us over the tomb of my father's mother – the Irish beauty Miss Marley, who died at about twenty-three. She lies there in marble on her elaborate Gothic base with a marble baby in her arms – the cause of her death – and a heavy wrought-iron gate between her and us. We could only see the top of her rose-crowned head and her baby's marble pate and her symmetrical toes a bit further on.

63 The village next to Haddon Hall, the second country house of the Rutlands, which dated back to the eleventh century. (It had last been added to in the sixteenth.) It had been virtually abandoned for some two hundred years until my mother's brother John took it in hand and gave it as sensitive a restoration as any house has ever received.

Mr. Parmenter took the service in a fresh surplice and a brilliant scarlet shot-silk hood hanging down his back. ('Oxford', they said.) There were wilting dahlias in little brass vases in the deep windowsills and at Harvest Thanksgiving the place was well stocked with rather poor fruit and meagre corn sheaves and always a pumpkin that one marvelled at. We had a scurry not to be late to start – endimanchés[64] with Father in a hired fly.[65] It stank of old wet stuffing; the windows pulled up and down, or didn't, with a strap; and we hated it – bored, bored. Noona never made it and it bored Father pretty well too, I think, though he liked the talk with the locals at the lych gate on leaving the church. I was dressed aged eleven(?) in a fawn coat with highwayman's capes to be like Martin Harvey in *The Only Way* and a wide-brimmed felt hat with silver galoon cockade (Franz Hals) and in the winter a beret, not Basque but big and pulled forward to be like Holbein.

I never remember applying myself to prayer or to listening. I was only wondering how much longer, O Lord, and also wondering if the wet negatives pinned on to a tape hung hammock-wise from our bedroom mantelshelf would be dry enough to print when we got home. All the Belvoir chapel hours are not evoked, from the fact I suppose that the choir composed of servants and husbands and wives of servants and the house guests was not a strong one or one to sing in harmony, unison or tune.

Balzac's life enthrals me and I'm reading *Eugénie Grandet*. Nothing to be nervous about, it's very agreeable. Did you read about Danny Kaye's hilarious success in London? I would have you know that hearing him for three minutes on the air – not a joke – I fell in love and wrote his name on a pad to remember to invite him when he comes to Paris.

I've been going through the old papers and have fallen on an envelope of congratulations on your birth – an amusing hotch-potch

---

64 In our Sunday best.
65 A light carriage.

of senders of the same words – Queen Mary, Chaliapin,[66] Marconi,[67] Willie Clarkson (famous theatrical costumier), Arnold Bennett.[68] 'Bravo Papa' comes from John Astor and 'Heartiest congrats, hope he will take his first piano lessons from me. Max Derewski'. Have you ever heard the name? It was one to conjure with.

I've put all Conrad's letters in order. They are alas not complete. There must be packets at Bognor or in Embassy corners. I have hardly touched my own, but I see no hope of making even a small collected volume for friends – too spiky, too intimate, too obscure because of catchwords and allusions, too sentimental. To expose that side would be a blast on my own trumpet.

I've just been asked by Sibyl, the girl who sweeps with her hands but has feathers on her feet (Miss Mercury, she does all the commissions to the village – stamps, change, *Radio Times* and shampoo) to buy a raffle ticket for some ignoble English unfashioned nylons. I naturally took two for two shillings and never thought to ask the 'good cause'. I hear now it's for the 'Garage Fund'. What could that mean? Day out for the chauffeur? Black market petrol? I must ask. I've got a very amusing packet of anonymous letters (love and hate) for you. I wish I'd kept more, I've had literally thousands. I found a cable offering me £15,000 for twelve weeks' cinema contract from D. W. Griffith, the man who made the first gigantic pictures, *Birth of a Nation* etc. Why did I not accept? I suppose it was war – or did my nerve fail, or was it family veto? No date on the cable. And I've read the correspondence of Gustav Hamel, the first man I loved, an airman, Swede by origin, who fell into the Channel in his cardboard monoplane and whom London society, England and quite a slice of the world mourned. He was missing for days and days and during the period of anxiety before resignation set in big balls were

---

66 Feodor Chaliapin, famous Russian singer, in love with my mother.
67 Guglielmo Marconi, radio pioneer.
68 Novelist.

postponed, friends wept in the street and Tommy Bouch[69] wrote me a poem to comfort (I don't know why I was felt to be the widow – I had very small cause). Also Papa wrote a beautiful poem published in *The Times*.

All this immediately preceded the war. Juliet in her very sweet and idiotic way I remember saying 'Nothing went right after Hamel was killed.' It is difficult to say why he took the public imagination with such force. He was golden-curled and exceedingly modest and flying was new. But there was a Lindbergh popularity about him – before Lindbergh went bad[70] – and Lindbergh wasn't killed. Papa often flew with him – open to the winds – no covered cockpit, one passenger snuggled up as in a toboggan, looping the loop. It was the desire of my heart to go up but not allowed – and then they say people don't change.[71]

Then I read the few poor letters of Basil Hallam, another famous star, a gent (Charterhouse) who danced and sang at the Palace Theatre in high-class revues. With him I had a passionate walk-out. It happened through a very suspect American called George Moore. For several years before the war he had financed Sir John French, for love and admiration's sake. He couldn't have guessed that French would become Commander-in-Chief; apart from that, there was no gain for George Moore in the relationship. It was French who gained. Moore took a big mansion in Lancaster Gate – 94 – since demolished, where French lived. There, at the beginning of the war, he started dances for me. His love for me was obsessive. I loathed him. I couldn't understand a word of his lingo. I was sickened by his physique, which was of a low, flat-footed Red Indian type. He had a wife whom he was divorcing in order to marry me. I was very young and couldn't cope at all. He covered me with presents, not one of which remains.

Sister here tells me that she was brought up never to accept a

---

69 Another ancient admirer of my mother.

70 By becoming America's leading isolationist.

71 In later years she was always terrified of the air.

present. O no, not even as a child were they allowed a box of chocolates from a visitor – bribery. And, worse, they might like the donor for that reason. Anyway Moore loaded me with gifts. He seemed immensely rich. There were white lilies twice a week (but a dozen bunches in wooden boxes to Belvoir) for about four years. There was a poodle, a gigantic sapphire said to have belonged to Catherine the Great, huge subscriptions to our Rutland Hospital[72] and a monkey with a diamond waistband and gold chain ('Armide', a brute). All this had to be accepted. (Not difficult to accept, you'll say, but I really did hate him.) He only once tried to kiss me, in a back room at one of his parties, and I made an earthquaking scene, left the house banging the door and complained to all my friends.

His parties were given entirely for my friends, and were called when they started 'Dances of Death' because at the beginning of the war no one dreamt of being anything but in despair. (After the first few months all London began to dance, as soon as 'leaves' began from the front; these, unlike this war, were automatic every four or five months.) Then they were called 'orgies' which in a way they were. G. Moore was about forty I suppose, and would leave the invitations entirely to me – no chaperones the only rule, or at least no one old – no parents. Young marrieds counted as chaperones. The war had made the scale of party – in which all the mothers kept watch on their daughters and their partners from the dowagers' benches – impossible, so if one could prove that young married people would be there it had to suffice the poor drearily staying at home mamas. So the riff-raff friends – a lot of bohemians (because Iris Tree and Nancy Cunard and I hunted in trios) used to roll up at nineish and dine at ten off fabulous exotics.

That was the note – American I think – always a novelty, never classical. Mangoes not grapes, absinthe not gin, presents in the oranges instead of pips. The very young friends back on leave were

72 The family house in Arlington Street had been converted into a hospital for the duration of the war.

mad with joy to taste and savour so much, so much. The girls always very pretty, the party never more than fifty strong, a wonderful jazz band, changed halfway through an evening in favour of Hawaiians or whatever the latest craze happened to be. Gallons too much to drink. How I loathed those evenings. No one could ever be bothered with Moore, and he only wanted to dance with me. I had to sit next him at dinner, hear him murmur love or chich-chich-chich hotly in my ear as we shuffled and bunny-hugged around. I knew that as I left he dismissed the band – 'the place becomes a morgue' – so with my kind and benevolent heart I'd stay and stay till I dropped.

Basil Hallam came into my life and therefore to these parties. He danced like a skater and with humour. After all, he was paid hundreds of pounds a week for letting people watch him, and I adored him. He used to drive me home at 4 or 5 a.m. and we'd spoon and be very serious and say we loved each other. I don't think I ever said so really – the words always stuck in my throat till I was much older. But we'd drive round and round Regent's Park in a taxi and hate to leave each other. The little room on wheels was a girl's only setting to be alone with a dear one. He had very little conversation but acknowledged charm. Moore didn't like him, as you can imagine. I called him (to Moore) my barley-sugar stick – note how disloyal. It sounds so trivial – it was rather.

It all ended. French fell from high command. Moore left for America owing. Basil was not accepted for the Army because of veins. It seemed extraordinary that he should dance and be unable to march, but so it was. He could of course have sat in an office in a railway station, but I suppose they really wanted him to carry on at the Palace and delight the boys on leave. Public opinion got too critical. I got anonymous letters saying I was a traitor to my country in holding young men like him away from their patriotic duty. He went into the Balloon Corps – what corresponded in those days to Blimps, not for defence but for observation, captive of course. Poor Basil was sick all the time. Then the enemy shot his balloon, he jumped in his parachute and it ended, because it didn't open.

February 10th, 1948

(1) Radio. I'm glad you're so interested. My new one – Papa's gift – is by my side. It's an Ecko and plugs in which is what I didn't want. Never tell Papa but I'm going to try and change it for that reason, except that in France and Chantilly and the Rue de Lille there is not likely to be the interference there is in a hospital with large electrical department. It gets the Third Programme but through a cackle of geese and burning timber, not quite good enough, though last night's *Electra* (Gilbert Murray's translation) could only be called top-hole. The Light Programme round the peak hours six to nine cannot be heard entirely free from a babel of distant tongues, like being in a closed room in the tower[73] while the building was in progress. Another thing which apoplexies me with rage is the non-relation of published numbers – 342.1m. (877 kcs) – to anything written on any set I've seen. On mine is written Medium, Short I, Short II. These words are never mentioned in the *Radio Times* (my hour book), so all reception comes from trial and error.

Dick Barton, Wu's tyrant, I can't get into – too much criss-cross of other programmes to fight. On the other hand I have listened once to *Mrs Dale's Diary* and have had to change the hour of my diathermy so as not to miss the next instalment – no story, just horrors of daily life. *Meistersinger* is being overdone, so is Delius, and O the horrors! One the other night of the story of the seven or eight men who were in an open boat on the Atlantic after torpedoing for seventy-odd days – only two survived – and the ghastly gurglings and chopping off of gangrenous legs with axes and the gasps and shrieks of parched throats, and men going mad

73 Of Babel.

and stepping off to drown. I didn't think it was fair on the people whose sons and lovers were actually the persons being depicted. I suppose they've only got to switch off before they hear their husband's death rattle, but some ghastly fascination may hold them.

(2) Knots. Bravo. Don't forget them – glamorous for me as are white tropical suits.

(3) I'm afraid I sent you a Balzac translation. I'll send you the others in French, though the one I'm just going to finish you won't care for as I did. I listened to Desmond [MacCarthy] on Arnold Bennett and Trollope – very good. Tonight I've got Elizabeth Bowen on Trollope to look forward to. For me he has enough humour, and a flavour as strong and delicate as fresh true bread. 'Trust Trollope', Max Beerbohm said.

9

'I must get up without coffee, that's all'

SETTLING IN, FEBRUARY–AUGUST 1948

It's turned out nice again – the sun beats down from cloudless skies in its most determined record-breaking way, trees are in bud, and Yorkshire is anything but what I expected of it in mid-March. The hounds of spring have really got cracking, and the Navy rejoices. The news comes through that the fleet goes out in force at the beginning of September; several battleships, lots of cruisers and destroyers innumerable are off to the West Indies and British possessions, to show the flag and tell the sordid little Central American states that if they try any funny business they'll be here today and Guatemala. The whole picnic represents about 230 writers like me. We have every hope, even, of going to South Africa on the way back. If, by some appalling oversight, I don't make it, there's always a hope for the Vanguard and the King and Queen, and Australia.[1]

Lots of love,

John Julius

---

1 The royal family were preparing to visit Australia and New Zealand in HMS *Vanguard* in early 1949. In the event it was cancelled owing to the King's health.

I t takes time to settle into a new house in a foreign country for the rest of your life. Both the Embassy and the Château de Saint-Firmin were furnished, but my parents still had many of their most loved possessions in store in London since the beginning of the war. They included my father's vast collection of books, largely of history and literature, some two thousand of which he had given to the beautiful library which he had established in an almost bookless Embassy. The first half of 1948 was, inevitably, a restless time for both of them. One of its high spots must have been my father's investiture as a Knight Grand Cross of the Order of St Michael and St George[2] and the lunch at Buckingham Palace that followed, memorably described in my mother's letter.

Quite apart from his decoration, my father was acquiring one or two new occupations in the hopes that they might improve his distinctly shaky finances. There was one mysterious one which he never properly understood and whose board meetings he almost invariably forgot; I cannot think it brought him in much. More important – and from his and my mother's point of view a good deal more enjoyable – was his directorship of the Compagnie Internationale des Wagons-Lits. In the immediate post-war years air travel was nowhere near as universal as it is today; the flights were less frequent and a good deal longer, the delays often considerably greater. Many people preferred to travel by train, and the Wagons-Lits company ensured that they did so in maximum comfort. Once a year the directors, representing the principal countries of western Europe, would hold their meeting in a

2 One of the several Orders of Knighthood bestowed in recognition of service. There are three grades: Commander (CMG – 'Call me God'), Knight Commander (KCMG – 'The King calls me God') and Knight Grand Cross (GCMG – 'God calls me God').

different capital – to which they would travel in their own private carriages, with bedrooms, drawing rooms and even bathrooms. I accompanied my parents once, to Madrid, but can remember virtually nothing about it.

I, meanwhile, was undergoing my professional training as a writer at a camp in Wetherby in Yorkshire, and playing the piano in the ship's dance band.

<hr>

69 Rue de Lille,
February 22nd, 1948

I write to you in spite of the fact that you might have left this universe for another one. I'm in bed in this rather sordid little two-room flat. It's *much* colder than charity and I miss, I can't tell you how much, my eagles and sphinxes and stars and my tent and my brass taps, and the general warmth and glow of returning to a house filled with welcoming servants. It's too cold to get out of bed, so I have to get help or talk to Papa downstairs by ringing up Loel's house opposite, but it rarely answers, so I'm cut off. I can't see to dress or to paint out this hideous cyst beneath my eye (they swear it will 'absorb' itself, but after three weeks it's not trying at all). So, by and large, I'm pretty miserable. Snow coming down in blankets today and I'd meant to drive to Chantilly where I hear the crocuses are up – the harvest of our sowing – but the weather is too inclement and Lapland-like. It will arrest the croci, I trust.

Now, London recital. High spots were *Tristan & Isolde* sung by Flagstad. She sings with as little difficulty as we breathe, and her notes are of 'red gauld', but physically it's a case of when's the balloon going up? She is to sing *The Walkyrie*, and I should like to go with you. For pity's sake tell me the *hour* when your leave begins and when it ends, and I will see if the opera is being given at one end or the other.

The second highlight was lunch with the King following on Papa's accolade. On arrival we were divorced by an R.A.F. equerry who shot Papa into the operational theatre and me into a waiting room where I was joined by Lady Spencer, a Queen's woman. She said wasn't it cold and I whined about sex segregation and my disappointment at not seeing the ceremony. It didn't take five minutes before Papa was out again – blushing, honours thick upon him – when Lady Spencer disappeared like camphor and the R.A.F. boy shot us into the drawing room and also did the vanishing act. The luncheon party was six strong – K., Q., two princesses and us. The Queen, another balloon about to take off, covered in two-way stretch dove-grey with very padded-shouldered box jacket, Princess Elizabeth pale blue and same box jacket, Princess Margaret lemon and same jacket. The King a sailor.

Conversation *très agréable* about the cold. The King's approach is of the whining variety. 'We can't get enough to heat the place.' 'I can't get them to cut the trees in the Mall – can't even see Big Ben now.' 'I dunno what it is – if one gets hold of a good book someone always takes it before one has finished it' – plaintive voice and suspicious rolled Rs. They don't listen to him much; it's *her* family and household. 'All right, Daddy', then a quick turn away and 'What did you say, Mummy darling?'

We moved into the dining room that gives out on to the hall – though it once gave out on to the gardens at Brighton, for it was lifted from the Pavilion and is remarkably eccentric in London – dragons and mandarins and palms and junks and phoenix. The pictures have been cleaned and glow with their pristine brightness, unlike those at Brighton which are mahogany-coloured from layers of discolouring varnish and smoke and breath.

There were a lot of well-grown footmen, looking more like workhouse warders than flunkeys. I hope it's only a hangover that causes them to be dressed in well-cut navy blue battledress tops, ordinary trousers and smart crowned G.R.s in scarlet on their hearts, but I fear they'll never go back to their red and gold. Kedgeree, with bigger and fresher salmon than we are used to, casserole of smaller and fatter chickens, sprouts and spuds and very common castle-moulded chocolate pudding, unbroached by me, selection of cheeses, sherry and moselle, and for Papa a slice of cold ham from the sideboard, he the only partaker. The conversation (when a word was to be placed through my particularly active barrage) of the most charming – gay, clever and amusing – criticisms of *Murder in the Cathedral*[3] that they'd been to the day before, talk of Osbert and Rex. Papa at one moment asked me if he should go on with a piece, already embarked upon, about T. S. Eliot. He said he was apt to become a bore on the subject of Tom à Becket. At another moment I asked him if I could enlarge on Laura Corrigan's[4] wig. This mutual appeal tickled them a lot. Then there was gossip about Cecil and Chips and Paris, and the whole meal scintillated – if not with wit, with fun and good humour and interest.

The Queen gets very pink in the face. They say she puts a lot back – port in lashings *before* lunch. Princess Margaret really the pin-up girl – petite, with faultless teeth disclosed by a radiant smile, wonderfully transparent skin tastefully made up, blue-green intriguing eyes, white arms and hands. P. Lillibet – they called her that – very pretty too and slim as a sapling if there only wasn't so much Queen Mary promise. A lot of talk there was about Granny – how she can't be kept out of theatres. She's amused by the least *convenable* of the songs in *Annie Get Your Gun*, and when she asked Princess Elizabeth about it her answer was 'Oh, Margaret sings it, Granny.' 'What a pity' said the old girl, and later 'that I didn't hear her.' Princess Margaret says she's refrained, fearing to shock.

Lunch over, we looked at pictures in the private rooms first, where are all the subjects I like best – Queen Victoria with a

3 By T. S. Eliot.

4 Mrs Laura Corrigan, American socialite determined to take English society by storm.

crinoline and lace bonnet nursing a baby against a background of blue sea and cactus – Nice, I thought, but it turned out to be Osborne, and Princess Alice 'aged nine days' painted from the foot of a lovely ormolu cradle by Landseer. Marriages and ceremonies of all kinds, the canvases massed with crowds, each individual a portrait by Tuxen, a Dane I think, of the 60s and 70s and 40s and 50s perhaps. Then into the big rooms and a squint at the Old Masters, less interesting and too cold. What I liked best of all was the Queen's own sitting room – enormous blazing coal fire, seemingly a lot of blue satin lavishly draped, white fur rugs, choicest pictures, the cream of the Royal Collection, a vitrine of Chelsea plates – flowers, veg. and insects, collected during the war – exquisite taste, a huge ormolu writing table in the great bay window that gives on to the garden and more flowers than a prima donna, beautifully arranged – only orchids, large sprays by the dozens of cymbidiums and one vase the size of a bath of that indecent flower – the name always escapes me – pink and flat with a male organ erected in the middle – at least two hundred of them in various shades. So it all ended and we left delighted, thrilled, amused and loyal, sharing the view that they had a delightful life and needn't have any more of the pity that I've lavished on them for years. I carried Papa's decorations in two big cases away with me and later put them all on – long mayoral chain, two stars, ribbons galore, and I went on appointment to call on Victor. He wasn't there, so the joke flopped.

I can't write any more. I must get back to crying my eyes out over my eyes. O I do hope I'll hear from you tomorrow. I'll send you the Wu story about morticians if it comes. I left it behind at the sanatorium but they'll send it on.

February 25th, 1948 [Chantilly]

At last a letter from you. I'm not awfully happy, but I will be when I get the hang of things. Aunt Norah [Lindsay], already in a death coma, is going to make a miraculous recovery. Aunt Madeleine, her sister, has asked me to write an obituary for *The Times*. Louise is away, which makes a Paris without trees. The snow is thick but after two blizzard days the pale pink misted sun glints faintly on the ice and the green copper roofs and gilded horses[5] – very beautiful. I pad around in unzipped snow boots and am forever losing one like Cinderella and not noticing it till too much later to recover it.[6]

Rufus has with determination landed a certain Mrs. Tiarks, a smoking useless lady, on to Papa as a secretary. I've got to ease her out. She can't do shorthand and hasn't a typewriter. Also she gets my goat from the lackadaisical chain smoking. Susan Mary is having a baby[7] and faints a good deal. The Embassy *salon vert* especially looks horrible – no piano, no screen to peep from and see if the going is good, nowhere to hide the gramophone, radio, broken games, etc.

I've at last been into the flat over the lodge that we are going to have from the 1st April. It's delightful – two bedrooms, two recep., kitchen and small room for you, very quiet, prettily panelled and corniced.

February 27th. My knee after this reducing rest has pumpkinned up again. It hurt so much that I bound it round with a little damp Thermogene. It had the effect of vitriol – purple inflammation and almost unbearable pain of fire. I groaned all night and this morning it's better, *mais hélas, je suis grippée*.[8] 100° temp. and aching badly and so much to do. O I do miss you so much.

The fashions have cheered me up. Molyneux at last has thrown away all the pads and uglinesses I fought so long, and now it's romantic and sob-stuffy and adventurous, but with my cyst I can't get away with even a semblance of faded beauty.

5 Of the château stables.

6 How can one not *notice* losing a snow boot?

7 As we now know, my father's.

8 But alas, I've got flu.

Eric threw a cocktail yesterday. I love seeing welcoming old friends. Norah Auric's[9] portrait of Eric is exceedingly embarrassing – a huge naked Adonis. He's delighted.

Paris
April 1st, 1948

So they rang Papa this morning and Odette[10] said she wanted a part in his new film about Lafayette, and Papa fell and was very polite to the pretty voice until they said '*Poisson d'Avril*',[11] and she also pretended to be an American official warning Bill [Patten] that Susan Mary had been caught changing a lot of Argentine pesos and Bill fell too. So much for April 1st. I forgot the date and played no games and no one worried to fool me.

Then, piling the car up with pig tubs, we went down to Chantilly, where I arrived in good spirits but was quickly dragged down by Felix the gardener, who told me nothing would ever grow and that I should have bought a property in Bretagne if I wanted 'returns'. I said California yielded still higher crops. He said the garden was too humid. I said it wasn't as humid as England, famed for its gardens. He said the motor mower was a toy and quite useless. I said he'd better go back to the hand one. He said the motor one saved time. I said in that case it fulfils its object. He said it had broken, and to demonstrate how wheeled it over all the big cobble-stones of the stable yard, which treatment would have broken any machine. So it went on – and in the house the pipes from the loos stick out like Leviathan's intestines. The one thing I mind, and the one thing they promised me would not be. So, down in the dumps we came home to find the Pattens and Odette, and now it's April 2nd and I shall get up and go to the market and buy a piece of

---

9 Fashionable portrait painter, wife of the composer Georges Auric.

10 Odette Pol Roger, of the champagne family, later greatly admired by Winston Churchill, who claimed to drink no other brand.

11 April Fool.

fish and a cheese for our weekend at Chantilly. I shall be thinking of you and hoping you are happy.

April 3rd. After scribbling to you yesterday, the bell rang once or twice and as I could not jump up to answer it, I left it. Soon it stopped. A little later a nicely dressed young gentleman walked in saying 'I am presenting myself as *maître d'hôtel.*' He wore a Newmarket style of mackintosh, brand new and a loosely tied white scarf à la Noël Coward. His trousers were pressed to a razor's edge and his boots shone like jet. He said he was thirty but he had been learning his trade for fifteen years. Grander and grander houses he mentioned as having employed him. I felt I was having a master and tyrant sold to me, and my resistance faded out. I could see the end would be my murder for the money he thinks I have but there was no resisting him – cook, valet, secretary and above all *débrouillard* and getting-order-out-of-chaoser. So I said would he go and be interviewed by Papa, whom I telephoned warning him of the magnetism of André, for such is his name. Of course he engaged him.

The eccentrics[12] have had a big go at the house and it looks cleaner and brighter and in much worse taste – all furniture is turned killy-corner and little mats have been dug out of the lingerie on tables and piano. Papa and I spent a couple of hours in the cellar laying the precious bottles in their niches. Teddy, who bought most of it, has surpassed himself in folly. There are dozens and dozens of cases of Neuilly Prat (it takes us ever so long to get through one bottle) and cases too of Cinzano which you will have to get outside somehow. In the evening we read *Phineas Redux* and did the crossword and I worked at my patches[13] and the wind roared like a lion.

April 4th. I had a useful day's work, chiefly spent in the cellar stacking champagne. You've never seen such a reservoir. I went to Chantilly and bought a fireproof dish in order that George should

---

12 The highly unsatisfactory couple whom my parents employed.

13 She often did patchwork of an evening.

try his untaught hand at a cottage pie. I bought the papers and stationery and a purple umbrella,[14] and then we took a walk and made the full round of our property, which extends as far as the eye can see and is grey with couch grass. I was dressed in scarlet tartan trousers, mobled[15] head, Rumpelstiltskin's hat and alas sockless feet in Moroccan shoes. The nettles are abundant but I rose above the stinging, forgetting that once before I had thought the moment's pain mattered little as I weeded with bare hands a whole bed at Bognor. Heavens, I paid for it in the night. Urticaria, for such I think it is called, has a retarded action and came into its flood of agony about 2 a.m. So the night was a brute. Papa read and I patched[16] and then to bed at 10.30. O I went to see M. Descamps[17] bearing gifts in gratitude – a bottle of gin only – but he was away from home and I'm to go this morning *après la messe*.[18] On the way I saw a little old tramp or perhaps workman of sixtyish fall flat on his face in the mud. I stopped the car and Good Samaritaned him on to his feet. He was babbling of the Foreign Legion in which he had served the world over, and of his sporting prowess. Alas, as I saw him walk away, very narrowly missing a fast motor, I realised he was both drunk and incapable.

Chantilly
April ?, 1948

Chantilly was looking most beautiful – cold as dawn but radiantly pure-skied. The graceful white swans[19] have four if not five eggs

---

14 The letters have so many mentions of the purchase of a purple umbrella that I think it must be a catchphrase – perhaps the last item listed in the game 'I went to market and I bought . . .' which we played endlessly when I was a child.

15 Wrapped up. A reference to the 'mobled queen' in *Hamlet*.

16 Did her patchwork.

17 Unknown.

18 After mass.

19 A quotation from 'Home on the Range', one of her favourite songs.

in the accustomed place between the banks. The house progresses not. The library, having galloped ahead for a bit is now static, mouldings and shelves missing and one thin coat of lilac paint only; downstairs bathroom a shambles still and Papa's future bedroom a scrap-heap. Water, boiling in every tap, was on – not boiled by mazout but by our precious coal as an essay. The mazout arrived in a tank during the weekend but has not been tried out. Papa and I lunched at the Tipperary[20] – badly – and walked to St. Firmin, buying a couple of whiting for dinner, some paraffin oil for salad and other oddments. We walked through the great park and admired the miracle of spring.

Next day Kitty and Frank Giles and a young All Souls man called Fisher, son of the Archbishop of Cantuar, came to lunch. Kitty cooked a fine dish of eggs and mushrooms and bacon and I produced a *foie gras* and Papa looked after the wine. We spend a lot of time laying bottles down in the two cellars (red and white). It all looks professionally laid and very impressive, but my opinion is that the brick and mortar shelves are not up to the weight, and we may have a disastrous collapse. The two young men were delightful – amusing, clever and agreeing with Papa. In the evening it's crossword,[21] patchwork and *Phineas Redux*.[22]

Sunday I had a hideous talk with old Regnier. He was crosser than ever, says he must have 6,000 a month more and that he'd like to go but can't find lodging, that the food I gave him poisoned his wife (she really had scarlet fever). I said that the milk in the tins that she took to be poison was drunk by us all exclusively at the Embassy. He said the servants picked out the bad boxes for his wife. There was talk about the unusability of the mower and the *auto-culto*, the advisability of an under-gardener being engaged and the aside that he was pretty certain to be useless too. Then there was a grievance that I had burnt all his dry firewood

---

20 A bar in Chantilly.

21 *The Times* crossword was a daily ritual.

22 So was reading aloud.

and not paid for it (the first time I'd heard of it) *ad nauseam*. He naturally doesn't understand the least what I'm talking about when I tell him that I dread visiting my own garden, that my hope is abandoned when I enter it, that the weight of my spirit after talking to him overcomes my small courage and extinguishes what rays I could give out. I ought to say '*Vous m'emmerdez*'[23] and threaten him with the sack, and then perhaps he'd perk up.

This morning we all came up – a sofa strapped on the *camionette* and both cars bulging with lamps and crockery and rugs and fish kettles for the new flat. I've now got two D-days – one Wednesday next when I must be out of this sty and into the opposite one (Thursday I go to London) and the 10th of May for Chantilly when Princess Elizabeth goes to Paris and might come to us. I have invited her. On 25th I go to St. Paul's, 27th Buckingham Palace (I told you that?), so I shan't have so many days to accomplish the Herculean labour.

Tuesday dawn. Papa's gone – took the ferry last night leaving me frozen and frightened and generally Gummidgy,[24] so I had an egg with Nancy Rodd and was in bed by 10.30, making lists and torturing myself. Now it's 8.45 a.m. and the eccentrics haven't arrived yet and I wanted to be earlier than usual to start the *déménagement*.[25]

I must get up without coffee, that's all.

April 23rd, 1948
London again

To think this is my first writing since I saw you. It's the fault, I fear, of Dr. Desmond McCarthy,[26] sent to me by Bertram to cure

---

23 'You drive me up the wall', only ruder.
24 Mrs Gummidge, a character from *David Copperfield*.
25 House-moving.
26 Not to be confused with Desmond MacCarthy, man of letters.

me of my melancholia. This he has been successful in doing by the primitive method of keeping me heavily drugged at night and lightly drugged by day. He has also cured me of all fine feelings, conscience, unselfishness, love of fellow-men, repentance, humility and mercy. So with new exhumed energy I applied myself to Chantilly and put you out of my mind.

The cure has also produced wild extravagance, so I sent for the very expensive paper shop to come to St. Firmin and more or less ordered the papering of the stairs, and of all the rooms of the flat as well. Louise was back from the south, still working like a furious beaver for Chanel without pay. We had an exhilaratingly rough crossing, coming back to England on the noble *Invicta*. The sea was green and crested with foam, the sun blazed on the white cliffs and, in spite of decks slippery with sick, spirits were gay.

Next morning betimes we were off to St. Paul's[27] the sun always shining on the scant flags and happy, happy crowds. I wore a new New-Looker[28] and picture hat to cover my cyst, and Papa, dressed to kill, got rattled at being frustrated by the traffic police. It ended well because we started late enough for every approach to be barred save the Royal Gate at Constitution Hill, through which we bowled as to the manner born and drove all the way to St. Paul's by the processional route. The crowds were all one could wish, packed the whole way, smiling and cheering, all and everybody. Outside the cathedral the sun doubled the glory of the Heralds, half gold, and the Palace Band, all gold, and the old Gentlemen at Arms, and a (to me new) posse of City Pikemen. Superb – straight from Covent Garden's *Faust*, yet real – with real steely armour in ribs on their torsos, lace collars on the armour, steel helmets brimming over with ostrich, and pikes three times their own height. I hated to leave the colour for the dark cathedral (where they left the Iron Duke), for after passing

27 For the Silver Wedding of the King and Queen.
28 Christian Dior's New Look had recently reached England.

the Beefeaters in their legion we of course sat in places from which I saw nothing. The choir had no strength, neither had the organ unless supported by the military. When I say I saw nothing I saw that ape Queen Mary burning bright in green gold, and a suggestion of blue which I took to be the Queen and her Princesses. There was the usual hopeless get-away, lost cars, flustered owners. All the men wore very ill-fitting tail coats, the younger ones made do with their fathers' and the older ones had shrunk or bulged into deforming theirs. George Gage[29] looked for all the world like a particularly grubby Eton boy – unpressed, unbrushed, unshined.

Dinner with Bertram and the Hoffs and Papa and after dinner off to the Palace for a spot of cheering. We didn't have to wait long before they were all out on the balcony, but it's too far away. They are such specks and the diamonds can't glitter at that distance.

> 69, Rue de Lille
> April 29th, 1948

The ball at the Palace was a splendour. We dined at Ann Rothermere's. She is big with child but not very big, and dressed in Jamaica muslin and *fichu*, looked like an attractive Creole. She should have had a pretty handkerchief tied round her black curls; instead she had a bit of a tiara. Betty Cranborne had a bit of a one too and Lady Eldon, ten foot high, had thought it wiser to tie a bolster round her hips and drape her dress over it, also to buy a 10/6d diamond crown, quite invisible at her height of head, at Harrods. The whole effect was deplorable, but she's so nice it didn't matter. Then there was that donkey Anthony Eden and monstrous good old Lady Rachel Davidson – 'in waiting' on the Duchess of Kent but rising above it. That was it, except

29 Viscount Gage, an old friend of the family.

for the very beautiful Duchess of Northumberland in a proper crown of diamonds that was torturing her forehead. I fixed her after dinner with strands of cotton that took the weight off.

There was no end to the prinking and preening and mouthing and combing, powdering and painting for the King, and the gentlemen in the dining room still were doing the same titivating downstairs. Lord Salisbury had his Garter in the form of a dickey buttoned on to his waistcoat and in my opinion much too horizontal, almost cummerbund. Papa's G.C.M.G. we had dressed him in, with book of directions to instruct, was said to be all wrong, so pins were found and he was redraped. He wore a Star too, and a fine show of medals and some blazing sapphire links – that day's gift from John de Bendern (J. de B., has taken, with view to purchase, a huge house in Ireland with salmon, snipe and neighbours, a Georgian house and all honkey-donk). To return to the ball: I enjoyed it very much and stayed till three. Beautifully dressed in a new Molyneux pleated pink tulle, semi-covered by pleated chocolate tulle and trailing a long garland of faded pink roses, I looked as well as I can these days. An aigrette hid my cyst and I had a lot of beaux and admiration – Antony Head, the Sitwells, Admirals Cunningham and Vian, George Lansdowne and a bit with the King. Papa had a sit-down with the Queen and lots of lovely women, Daphne Bath etc. Mr. Aneurin Bevan[30] came in a dirty lounge suit.

> *Chantilly*
> *May Day, 1948*

Things go from bad to worse. The new cook stinks and André's still a detrimental. I've never had domestic trouble before. Everybody else has it always, but I started with Wade and Holbrook

---

30 Welsh Labour MP, who as Minister of Health spearheaded the establishment of the National Health Service.

who had both started me and Papa before we had a house. Belvoir and Arlington Street were of course run by housekeepers and stewards and ultimately Father. I don't remember Noona ever giving the house a thought though she would think nothing of having two marble pillars, Forum size, sent by sea from Italy for the garden. Then came the war and there was still Wade to grouse but run it all. Then sweet Chinese lulled me in their competence and genius. Mrs. Kelly[31] and Wade for a bout, then four years of a Controller and secretaries, now no help nowhere. Henriette the cook looks a slayer and must have been an ogre's cook who likes raw food – fi-fo-fum not yum-yum.

All day we've been unpacking books, not that the shelves are dry. We put them in order on the floor and having not left paths through their density we can't walk to the back rows. All the books are buckled and wet and dog-eared and the damp has brought off the labels, and they smell and are foxed and torn and scratched, and naturally gaps in every set. I found Papa's first editions of Jane Austen and Fielding to my surprise in the Neuilly halfway house, carefully packed and labelled by me in a Molyneux box. Where O where are the other boxes of first editions? Where are the snows of yesteryear?

May 2nd. The Pattens came down to an uneatable lunch of doubtful fish, quite tasteless and garnished with giant grey potatoes. A *foie gras* helped and the *pots-de-crème* were swallowable just. The shame was unpleasant enough and rose to an unprecedented height when Bill went to the gents' to find it blocked and choked and stinking and unusable. Susan Mary, very broody, lay on the sofa looking into a future of cradles and nannies, while Bill and Papa and I played a bit of gin [rummy]. I won all the time, ding-dong-dell of ringers, but Papa evened out my gains with his losses. Papa on the wagon for May – a spot of claret at dinner.

May 3rd. I've seen M. Borniche the painter, who says it is quite impossible for him to put the loose shelves into their places while the books are on the ground. Of course it is, I quite see. I saw as

31 A Bognor cleaning lady.

we were doing it but couldn't stop. I've laid down Osbert's book,[32] which I'm adoring, in order to read the sequel to *Miss Blandish*[33] – *The Flesh of the Orchid*. It's horrible and I don't enjoy it nor does it affect me, but what's started has to be finished and there is so much to be read. David Cecil has a new book about Lady Dorothy Osborne, and there are some memoirs by Harold Acton and some more by Maurice Rostand.

Mazout is installed but is too thick for the pipe, so clogs daily and the water tepid in consequence.

Train to Paris (shaky)
May 11th, 1948

The domestic situation got worse and I got obsessed to madness. Jean, *maître d'hôtel* to the rescue. I rang his wife who told me he was in a place not greatly to his liking. I met him secretly at the Berkeley. He was looking exceedingly good and well dressed and I took him for a drive and was able to persuade him to chuck all and follow me. So he promised to find a cook, a valet and a maid for me. An immense load lifted from my aching mind.

I still had the horror of breaking the news to the sackees. Papa undertook to tell André and I had Henriette the redoubtable uneatable cook to tell. It is all to be realised in ten days, in fact next Monday, and Jean is to run the house completely

Miss Fry of 69 Rue de Lille informs me that the cow and four pigs will arrive at 10 p.m. on a certain evening. 'Oh no, Miss Fry' I moaned, 'that will mean midnight and how shall I cope with feeding and milking in the dark with a cross gardener?' She telephoned Normandy to tell them to start at dawn instead but they were already *en route*. Everyone went to bed except me, who

---

32 Probably *Great Morning*, the third of the five volumes of his autobiography, just published.

33 *No Orchids for Miss Blandish*, by James Hadley Chase.

stayed all night fully dressed in the drawing room, dozing lightly enough to hear a moo or a honk through the wide-open door. Of course they didn't come till nine next morning so that Papa and everyone else could say 'What did I tell you?'

The four pigs (one a hermaphrodite) squealed the place down as they were dragged by the ears and tails from the van to their poky little sty. The cow on the other hand, covered in her own dung in which she had been stewing for twenty hours, walked out with great dignity and, reaching her welcoming straw-laid stall, threw herself down to get the weight off her poor feet. She's very small, very thin and is as gentle as a sleepy baby – tiny undangerous horns, a very pale face with panda eyes. We tethered her out the next day and she gives quite a tidy drop of milk, but O the squalid filth of all equipment. I can't buy a three-legged stool, nor a cream skimmer, nor big bowls for the milk, nor a measuring jug, nor muslin to cover the pans if there were any, nor a churn. I give her nothing extra in the way of food. The pigs I feed with troops-repudiated porridge, 'processed peas' and what paltry swill we have.

Embassy news. Mrs Walker[34] came down for the afternoon to borrow all my flower vases for the Embassy royal visit and to grab three rolls of wallpaper (*mine*) because there has been an accident in Princess Elizabeth's room and it will take enough rolls of paper to repair it as will not leave enough to paper a room of mine. This grievance sank into insignificance when she told me that Harvey has had the dark green library curtains taken down and stored and the dark green carpet taken up and cut up for passage and bathrooms, and has replaced them with beige. I cannot tell you how this has shocked and hurt me. I am going to write a stinger to the Office of Works. I cannot think how they could have allowed it on expense, or how the Harveys could have done anything so dastardly. It seems to me as bad as if I had the Pauline Borghese chairs covered in navy blue. That room was made and designed by the best artist Bérard, the best entrepreneur Geffroi and the best dilettante Bestegui. It was passed by us to house the present of a library and that those ignorant Harveys can have had the nerve to touch it entirely passes forgiveness. He never uses the room himself and as the lending library book has been sent to us, I suppose no one goes into it or borrows from the shelves. I feel inclined to take an oath not to enter the Embassy during their tenure but I suppose at Papa's insistence I shall have to go as a *cure-dent*[35] next Saturday for the Princess Elizabeth reception.

General de Gaulle's brother Pierre, the Mayor of Paris, is asking a party of notabilities to a famously beautiful old palace in the *Cité* – Hôtel de Lauzun. Princess Elizabeth is the guest of honour. The host sent a list of guests to the Embassy, not for vetoing but as a polite gesture. Imagine his surprise and rage when, as a Gaullist, he is called upon by that ass Peter Hope[36] and told that several of those invited the Princess cannot meet, on account of their collabo[rationist] tendencies. I should have thought the de Gaulles would know which *collabos* they had forgiven.

May 17th, 1948

Things haven't got any better yet. The horrible staff took their dismissed departure on Saturday – Georges promising to return as soon as he had got his things out of Thérèse's flat, but I very much fear that when she realises that he has lied to her about leaving our employ she will terrify him into chucking us. Then I shall have those two cars on my hands again to remember to oil and to fill, to inflate and to garage. Jean is supposed to go to Chantilly with his *équipe* today so perhaps now is the tide's turn, but where is the enthusiasm and effort I used to summon? I can't find it anywhere – not on that lovely lake where the swan is

35 After-dinner guest (literally toothpick).

36 A member of the Embassy staff.

nesting, nor in this free and labour-saving flat. The dirt and the difficulties blot out the sun and the birds and the fresh forest and the interest of the streets.

So they cut the library carpet and the curtains up, since I heard of which I am making no more pretence about the Harveys. I wanted not to go to the ball.[37] Papa insisted, but the frights got the frozen mit – not a smile broke from me. The festivities are nil – a few perfunctory flags on Mappin & Webb and Molyneux and W. H. Smith and not much else. The English colony, from which list they omit any compatriots we know, i.e. Nancy, Alvilde, de Benderns, Violet Trefusis[38], etc., got together in the courtyard at 10 a.m. as she drove in from the ferry trip in a tightly closed car with Royal Standard on top. She brought the car and that ass Harvey never said 'Make it an open one' so nobody saw her at all except when she chug-chugged down the Seine to the Ile St. Louis. No one we knew was asked to the Elysée, which I'm told was well done in my tradition of candles and *mystère*, but the guests were pretty dull for them – Schumanns, Bidaults and the rest of them. No one we knew was asked to the Trianon lunch, so it's difficult to get much lowdown.

It was agreed by frogs and limeys that she opened the exhibition with grace and faultless French poise and charm of manner. The Duke is painfully bald, a few years will show him an egg. I could find no one asked to the reception but we rolled up to the Embassy at eleven. Old gatekeeper Christie tried to hustle our car on and got a barbed rocket from Papa. Into the Kings & Queens[39] where the gloomy hosts stood looking ghastly under the deforming light of a much brighter chandelier. The dining room had been used for dinner but was closed afterwards (the Borghese candelabra had been suppressed and no candles allowed). This left the ballroom as buffet and the smaller rooms and gallery in which to circulate.

37 For the visit of HRH Princess Elizabeth.

38 English *femme de lettres*, famous for her elopement in 1920–1 with Vita Sackville-West.

39 A reception room hung with pictures of assorted monarchs.

They had a band with a highbrow and no doubt beautiful programme but they'd thought it prudent to place it in the *cul-de-sac* of the dining-room side of the gallery. You saw the musicians sawing and bowing away but no sound came through the double glass wall and across the gravel garden piece (unfloodlit of course, in spite of the roof equipment I lent them). The flowers were rather reminiscent of the Dorchester because Major Lees[40] had sent for a Constance Spry hand from London. I did not think it a bad plan and she'd made a splendid, if a bit hackneyed, job of it, but the French reaction was 'You would never have done such a thing, now would you? Do they think the French have no art or craft?' In spite of all I enjoyed the party *enormously*. I liked not smiling at the Harveys, I had a sensational reception from the dear staff. So lovely the girls looked, so handsome the men – Virginia [Millard], Barley, Ann [Clarke], Mavis [Coulson], Hazel [Richards], Ashley, Brooks [Richards], Peter and Hellis Tennant, Sir Guy and Lady Salisbury Jones (Military Attaché), the beautiful Vaniers, all saying the thing to please me most. Lots to drink, rather nasty eats. The Princess looked really very pretty and acted gracefully and with charm. When I think in the last generation the difficulty of laughing Princess Mary (the King's sister) off!

May 26th, 1948

Eric's [Ducannon] party for the Princess was memorable for its horror. '*Qui sont tous ces vieux pompons?*[41] said Odette Pol Roger. The house in which the party was jammed had no garden outlet and belonged to his aunt, Madame de Neuflize. She had flung some withered blooms, sent up cheaply from the Nice market, in hideous colour combinations, and lit the dark room with a ray of electric light on corner tables. It was the hottest day of the year and there

---

40 Walter Lees, the Embassy Comptroller.

41 'Who are all those old fogeys?'

were three hundred guests. The Princess changed her dress and looked cucumber cool, the Duke, who had been poisoned at the Embassy, was like a rag. They had been lunching with the President's wife at Fontainebleau and had then sight-seen Vaux-le-Vicomte, a house so big that Louis XIV had the noble who built it disgraced for daring to vie with his king in splendour of palace. Her feet must have hurt. He spent his party in the loo.

The Twedes brought Baroness Blixen, Danish author of almost my favourite books, to lunch at Chantilly. I have no more servant complex. Jean has made all Sir Garnet for twice the price and well worth it. Maria and Angelo and Mireille sing at their work. The food is good. Cream naturally abounds. The place is as clean as it can be with workmen still neither in nor out. Pictures are going up. Gooseberries and salads from the garden are all that we can put on the table so far. I suffer shame of wardrobe with Maria. Donald [Mallett] is in severe trouble, in fact sacked by that arch-fiend Harvey, for going to look at the bedroom Princess Elizabeth was to occupy. It's an outrage – the Comptroller Lees had given permission. He hopes to get a better job with the 16 Nations or Marshall distribution and leave with a high head.

Sunday, French Derby Day
June 13th, 1948

I'm going to write to you now whatever happens. The only way of stealing the time to do so is by letting them all go to the races and staying leaning against a small haystack, made by Stephan, the Czech *aide-jardinier*. (Damn, I hear Melanie, the cow mooing – does it mean that I must rush her to the bull?) Back again after Operation Melanie – not bulling, I fear, but thirst. So now I'm sitting on another heap of hay from which she is eating. I've got the end of her very short rope gripped in my little finger and the tug and position and fear of pats and of her mounting over me is hell, so are flies, spiders and the cow's amorous lickings. They all, as I say, have gone to the races. I did it last Sunday and swore 'never again'. 'They all' were the Aga Khan and Begum (a big girl), Bill Patten and a pretty French *jeune fille* who curtseys to her seniors, Daphne Bath and Rufus, house guests. My hands are so swollen it's difficult to manipulate the pencil, just as the shoes were such a problem to my last year's feet. Is it milking? Sorting out swill? Tin opening? Heart? Dropsy? Or what? Impossible to say.

═══

In June or early July 1948 I passed out of HMS *Ceres* as a fully fledged Writer. I went first to my home base at Chatham, to kick my heels until the Navy found something for me to do. I longed, naturally, to be posted to a proper seagoing ship, or at least to some naval base abroad – Malta perhaps, or Trincomalee, or Hong Kong – but as a National Service man I suspected a year at Scapa Flow to be a good deal more likely. Meanwhile I took a room at a sailors' hostel – it cost a shilling a night, but at least it gave me a touch of privacy – and it was there, just a week or two later, that I received a posting better than anything I could have dreamt of: to join HMS *Cleopatra*, a light cruiser at present re-fitting in Portsmouth in preparation for the projected Home Fleet cruise to the Caribbean in the autumn.

═══

Chantilly
June 24th, 1948

You've gone to sea (I hope it will never be to seed) and I've thought a lot about you in your hammock, in peril – fierce raged the tempest – sea legs and your timbers shivering. I look forward with uncontrollable impatience for your first letter about life on the ocean wave.[42] I shopped unsuccessfully and lunched with Coalbox. Isaiah next me said Winston had woven a long piece after we had left and said (wishful thinking) that there would be war with Russia by August, calling the A Bomb 'A bomb Tom' or 'Tom' *tout court*. After lunch, at which my lack of confidence grew as I did not understand anything that was being said, I felt deaf and doltish. Papa and I went to *Gentlemen's Agreement* that was so highly praised by the reviews. We took turns to sleep and so saw it all between us, and a more boring, more humourless film I never did see. A nice journey on the ferry and at last back to Chantilly. The downstairs bathroom is stinking of stagnant drains and the carpet saturated and stained with leakage. The cow all but dry under the weak hands of Maria and Stefan. The lilies in full flower and breathtaking, delphiniums too.

Back to Paris to lunch, one wondered why. The weather (unexpectedly) was fine enough to lunch alfresco. For days we had been dreading the arrival of Lord Oxford and his mother, my oldest and once dearest friend.[43] I went to collect them that day at Le Bourget and had the good luck to witness the Duca di Verdura (known to friends as Fulco) coming out of the room where passengers are stripped to the skin and all orifices examined for contraband. He was screaming like a jay and swearing never to set foot on France's vile soil again. It's the second time in a few weeks that they've humiliated him and once they tore Natasha Wilson's clothes off because she was travelling with him. Katherine is very sweet and intelligent and funny.

Now I'm up to date. Pigs fine, duck fine, cow mooing; Jacques of the Embassy bringing a request from their second chauffeur that he might come to us. He has never valeted but Jean thinks

---

42 This was to be delayed another three months. *Cleopatra* remained in dry dock until September.

43 Katherine Asquith.

it's easily taught, and it's such a pleasure that they want to leave the Embassy for the Chantillians. True, I'd seen him yesterday when I went to collect some leavings and asked him if he knew of anyone about his own age who would like the job. True I elaborated on the charm of the situation, good food, foreign travel, smart car etc. etc., and the fish is nibbling. We've made a lot of hay but when I said, tottering under the weight of a stack I was lifting, 'Do you think the cow will eat this hay?' Stefan said '*Je ne le crois pas.*' I'm doomed to live among pessimists.

We buy butter in the black market and vegetables at insane prices and yet we have a cow and a huge *potager*.[44] It can't go on like this.

I looked in on Chips in London and found the Duchess of Kent, her sister Countess Toren, the reigning Prince and Princess of Liechtenstein, the Ranee of Kapurthala and the King of Egypt's sister. It was like a stamp album.

Chantilly
July 31st, 1948

It's near a week since you left me. Breccles[45] was sadder after you left – sinister sad. Poor vital Venetia brought to this little measure! It used to be a retreat of fun for me and Papa. He came back from the war for his first leave[46] and by letters to the trenches and from them we had settled to marry if he survived. He never went back to the battle (or on me) for while there in early November 1918 we heard the Kaiser had abdicated and the next day it was Peace. But the latter half of the war and for fifteen years after it was a habitual and favourite house – comfort, beauty, gaiety, friends, romance, fireworks, shoots, picnics, rest and this last visit was like

44 Vegetable garden.
45 Breccles Hall, Norfolk, home of Venetia Montagu.
46 This was in 1918.

an old woman looking in a glass and seeing her youth's radiance. Very agonising. In future (near future) I'm going to carbon paper my diary so that Vinny [Venetia] may hear a little of our lives.

July 26th. Unnecessary to tell you that I had a hideous day in London. Papa had fixed himself a lover's lunch with Caroline. I having ne'er a love got a nephew in the shape of Raimund to give me half his lunch interval on the terrace of the Dorchester and Chips welcomed me to coffee. It was too hot for my dark blue woollen dress and I felt sordid and unworthy of anything better than Mr. Hart of Liverpool Street. I got so hot and cross during the interview that I began to unbutton, in fact undress like the very mad. Mr. Hart mumbled something about strip teasing and that made me hotter and smellier (I have a theory that rage as well as fear makes your sweat glands *smell*). There was nothing I suggested that could be effected. I must let Bognor furnished for three years to cover rent, gardener, Wade, repairs and then you will be twenty-one and I can give it to you, and not dare to die for another five years, and when it's yours I'll have to settle money to bring you another £500 p.a. and that will mean that much off my income and we'll not be able to live in France and I and Papa will be driven home to your seaside shack and ask for shelter, and your beastly tart-wife will be like Goneril and Regan merged and bang the flimsy door in our noses, and we'll get a sheer hulk on Pagham or Bosham Marsh as Peggotty did before us, and Papa will make love to the paid help and I will be the real Mrs. Gummidge. So I said to Mr. Hart I never wanted to see his features again and I left buttoning my bodice and buckling on my belt and took myself to Mr. Mock the chiropodist who whittled my gnarled feet into pink feathers and restored equilibrium without chasing Melancholia. Then there was tea at Liz's and plans made to motor to Basle next week and claim my last year's thefts, and then on to Venice because Korda[47] is showing

---

47 My father's friend, Sir Alexander Korda, had made him official representative of the British Film Producers' Association at the Venice Film Festival.

three films in the Festival – *The Winslow Boy*, a Graham Greene
short story and *Spring in Park Lane*. Then we shall come back
with perhaps a day or two at Portofino for me and the same for
Papa at Opio. Doesn't it sound lovely, but all looks to me stale
and unprofitable and sad.

The ferry brought us over. We had a memorably nasty dinner
and walked up on deck to see the stars and the cranes and other
people laughing and now it's next day, the 27th, and I've done
the dentist and the rations and a modiste and gulped back a Pernod
alone at our station pub and uncombed my hair and come home.

Nancy Rodd is in residence, calm and cool and elegant. The
cow's a skeleton, the pigs far from thrifty, Colorado Beetle everywhere. Oklahoma[48] the only solace. Jean out of hand, Jacques
covered with blind boils and incapable of work, Mireille crossish,
Maria grovelling and talking such nonsense about a dying duckling
and about not having the right to kill it, i.e. take life.

28th. Today blew in Mr. Peter Coats[49] and Mr. Cornflakes,[50] the
editor of *Town & Country*. His main subject was 'the Duchess'
(not Kent – Windsor) but they made lunch quite gay and like mad
dogs we all swallowed quickly and all tore off to a most remarkable house called Raray about fifteen kms away – empty so that
I was able to salvage some scraps – and of a fantasy unparalleled
– two long and high walls forming a court in front of the magnificent house on the top of which is a stag hunt (formalised) in stone
silhouetted upon the sky, not bas relief. It was photographed in
La Belle et la Bête.[51] Then quickly in the opposite direction, to
Poissy – an appointment with Madame Galéa, the woman who
has the house of toys at Auteuil. She was the mistress of a famous
dead art dealer called Vollard and inherited among many hundred
canvases 300 Renoirs – three or four of herself. She always says

---

48 Then the fashionable card game.
49 Long-time companion of Chips Channon.
50 Kellogg, perhaps?
51 Film by Jean Cocteau.

'*Ils sont un peu partout*'[52] but I suspect her of keeping them in a cellar so as not to have to insure them which would give their number and worth away to the bloodsuckers. She'd come down to her hideous newly acquired riverside Edwardian residence to receive us with her *dame de compagnie*. She's quite old and is off to Geneva with an exhibition of toys and to Amsterdam with another of antique dresses, and a lot of her pictures have gone to the Edinburgh Festival. The house is full of hideosities and beauties. She is not a giver, except when it comes to a *goûter* and then she's profligate – tea, unending cakes, a porto flip, some chocolates, champagne and no 'nos' taken. Sick to the stomach, we left her and her hydrangeas and lobelias and her John Brown gardener and drove glutted back to Papa and a light dinner.

August 1st. Picnic day. It wasn't A PATCH on last year's when you were there. We put hats on the busts and the food was scrumptious – profiteroles stuffed with egg, rice and *foie gras*. The Pattens brought ham and Jerry Koch and then there was *crème-en-coeur* and fruit juice and *vin rosé* and Barley. Our own depressing crowd made our numbers nine. I had a wicked headache brought on by storm and by Jean who let out to me in the kitchen saying that he couldn't go on, that he was never off his legs, never had a day off, never had any money, never slept, couldn't eat. It destroyed, for ever, all my confidence in him. It was nonsense of course – he is not overworked a bit when Jacques isn't covered in carbuncles and if he is, he only has to hustle around and find the *valet-chauffeur* we are all hoping for. I'd told him the night before I had £60 in the house to pay the month's wages, and as to his days off he's perpetually having two or three when we go to London. I expect it was the heat and the thunder but it was a shock. Maria says he's always cross and so is Jacques and that since the war all men are unendurable, that the camps and the *travail forcé* and being soldiers or resisters, and the *marché noir* with all its temptations and the fact that women did everything, has entirely

52 'They're all over the place.'

demoralised them for ever. Even Jacques's carbuncles are part of the male break-up. She's not far wrong. Maria has been maddening about the deformed runtish little duckling. It died today after three days of lying unconscious on a hot water bottle. She is sobbing her silly heart out, while I rejoice. Jean has caught an ordinary rabbit and has set it up in a cage of wire and deal on the lovely grass slope. Maria's ducklings in another with their nappies and bottles and trays make the place like a smallholder's Peacehaven home.

Pam Berry came, scintillating and enthusiastic and gay and thick about the waist and very old-looking. Lots of dreadful stories about Randolph in America. He chose in his cups to go to bed upon a glass table in Herbert Swope's house and went through it. Now I'm off with the lesbian Madame Hubin to buy cow cake.

August 4th. Melanie wouldn't eat the cow cake. No letter from you.

10

'I told him to imagine I was Winston Churchill'

ON THE MOVE, AUGUST 1948–APRIL 1949

Our first entrance to the West Indies was one of the most beautiful things I've ever seen in my life. In the early morning of brilliant sunlight, we drifted quite slowly & noiselessly through a thousand tiny islands, rocky and wooded, set in a dark blue sea on which we could see four or five tiny white sailing boats. The sun and the blue and the total lack of any sign of human habitation on our first land for sixteen days made an absolutely staggering impression. There can have been no difference in the scene when Columbus saw it five hundred years ago.

We dropped anchor at about nine in San Fernando bay, which became in a flash covered with little rowing boats of curious locals. Then the Mayor and all the authorities came on board to greet us, all in immaculate white tropical suits. Trinidad is the most cosmopolitan of all the West Indies. As well as blacks and whites, they have browns, yellows, greens, reds and even an occasional and unaccountable orange. There are Chinese and Indians and Malays and people of nondescript Eurasian origin all jumbled together. The Mayor is Chinese, a double blue at Edinburgh University.

After half an hour or so the official programme of events and entertainments came on board. It staggered everyone. For the nine days we are here our proposed amusements, tours, dances, parties and entertainments fill about ten full-size foolscap sheets when listed. Every day there are about eight alternative projects. 'Tennis for thirty-eight ratings at Pointe-à-Pierre Club. Equipment provided. On to Waterloo Club for tea, cocktails, social evening and dance', or alternatively 'Tour of McBean Sugar Plantation for 150 ratings'.

And so it goes on, with invitations and proposals right and left. For officers and ratings, Trinidad has done better than any other island within memory. And this is San Fernando only. The mind baulks at the thought of what Port of Spain has got on for the rest of the Fleet, but it couldn't be better than here.

All love,

John Julius

When my father left the Embassy, his old friend Sir Alexander Korda invited him to be the official representative of the British Film Producers' Association at the annual Venice Film Festival. My father had never taken so much as a photograph in his life, but Korda reassured him: his job would be simply to show the flag, to preside at the occasional reception or dinner, and – naturally – to attend all the prestige showings of new British films. In return he and my mother would be accommodated, as guests of the BFPA, at the Gritti Palace Hotel for the duration of the festival, and would of course be provided with their own personal gondola.

My parents had always loved Venice – they had gone there every year before the war – and Korda's offer filled them with joy. The Gritti – which had only just opened – was determined to be Venice's best hotel; a private gondola was a rare luxury indeed; there were probably not more than half a dozen in the city. But now, as the letters make all too clear, depression struck my mother – as bad, I think, as she had ever suffered. 'Melancholia', as she called it, had always been the bane of her life. She worked hard to conceal it from the outside world but never made any secret of it to my father or to me. True, she had a reason; my father was obviously far from well, though whether he was half as ill as she imagined we shall never know.

In the second week of August, while I was still in Portsmouth impatiently waiting for my ship to get out of dry dock, they set off for Venice, stopping – as they always did – at their favourite hotel in the world, the Locanda di San Vigilio on the shore of Lake Garda. Kept by a permanently half-sozzled Irishman called 'Leonardo' Walsh (whom they loved), it was simple in the extreme:

the beds were rock-hard and there were no en suite bathrooms – not that this mattered very much, since the hot water was distinctly dodgy. But the little sixteenth-century arcaded building with its shaded terrace and its cypress trees breathed a quiet and peaceful perfection; and if your window looked out – as mine usually did – on the tiny little harbour to one side, you would wake up in the morning to find it almost blocked by a huge, flapping, tawny sail, belonging to the fishing boat which had come in with the dawn. Moreover Leonardo was a first-rate cook, and the food – mostly fish straight out of the lake – could hardly have been bettered.

Whether the melancholia overclouded even San Vigilio I have no means of telling; normally she was happier there than anywhere. But it certainly kicked in when they reached Venice, and was no better when they returned briefly to Lake Garda a few days later. It was not until they were back in France that the clouds finally lifted.

Another name that crops up with some frequency in this chapter is that of Nancy Rodd, née Mitford. She had settled in Paris after the war in order to be close to Gaston Palewski. He was General de Gaulle's right-hand man with an irreproachable war record, who was later to be the French Ambassador in Rome; but he was far from good-looking, and as a womaniser in a class by himself. Still, Nancy loved him, even though her affection was all too seldom rewarded. We used to see a lot of her; she would come round for lunch, dinner or a drink and was always wonderful company – as was her sister Debo Hartington,[1] a frequent visitor. (Another sister, Diana, married to the fascist leader Sir Oswald Mosley and imprisoned with him throughout the war, my father refused to have in the house.)

––––

[1] Later Duchess of Devonshire.

Chantilly
August 4th, 1948

I've just had a telegram from Judy saying our Venetia is dead –
died after four peaceful unconscious days. She was a good friend
and very fond of us and she had a lot to bear, so no grief. I think
we made her last years happier with Embassy jaunts. She liked
them better than anyone. I'm writing from Le Bourget sitting in
the *camionette* waiting for Cecil to arrive and incidentally the
King of Iran too. Papa and Pam have gone to dine with Susan
Mary and the Trees, and Cecil and Nancy and I are going to have
a girl's gossip at home, and tomorrow perhaps come the Hoffs
and Saturday or Sunday we're off to Switzerland. I shall miss you
a lot, if I don't get a word from you before I leave I shall cry.

The Trees spent last night with us. We were so encumbered
what with Pam and Nancy and Louise that I dossed down on the
drawing-room sofa. It struck me that Papa, the servants, etc. are
so unthoughtful of me that I don't think they knew or cared where
I slept. I'm a cipher and a drudge – it's my own fault, I know. I
cleared out the grate yesterday morning of all the cigarette ends
and scraps. The melancholy Jacques staggers down at nine,
clutching his carbuncled stomach, clad in a long filthy dirty white
coat to his ankles. He looks like a septic Pierrot. I hate him. Too
much about the servants and not enough about happiness or uplift.

Paris is dead except for the fashion buyers and 'collections'.
It's too hot to look at winter models. *Guêpières*[2] are said to be
going out and hobbles coming in.

August 10th, Geneva. Look what a time since I wrote. I'll have
to recapitulate quick. I let the house[3] to David Bruce[4] and
Evangeline, Virginia's sister. They'll only go weekends and pay
about £20 a week in dollars. Cecil came, rather bald and grey and

2 Wasp waists.
3 Chantilly.
4 U.S. Ambassador to France, subsequently to Britain.

low-spirited. The Hoffs came full of pep and Louise, Bébé, Cecil and I lunched at Porquerolles. Bébé's drug troubles are over thanks to enough strings being pulled round justice's throat. The *juge d'instruction* finally fell in love with him and is now seeking to lunch with him.

So we left it all on a grey day after lunch and motored to the bar near Bar where you and I are remembered. It turned out a peach of a place to be revisited. Next morning off again to lunch at Dole and there to leave my beautifying coat – damn. It was the official *patronne* who whisked it into the *vestiaire* out of hand. Over the Faucille with petrol failing – once we made the col I knew I could slide down but the last ascending kms were nerve-racking. Hôtel de la Paix, Mère Royaume, *crêpes suzette* etc. and bed, and yesterday morning into our wide windows broke a day of splendour and sparkle. There is nowhere like Geneva for an atmosphere of flag-fluttering holiday *sans souci*. My spirits put wings on at once. I shopped and bought Kitien[5] for my maids and nothing for you or Papa. I went to see my lawyer about the old legacy.[6] He was away, his stand-in told me the affair was wound up in Switzerland. We were waiting for English decisions. Doomsday next.

Raimund took us to a distant restaurant in a garden. Papa had a tummy upset and couldn't eat and spoilt my pleasure. At 5.30 we set off for Solothurn, a really lovely town – do you remember it? The drive through Swiss villages satisfied me well. They are really lovely and so secure and solid and sensible. Their wood was neatly cut and piled up for the winter, and their vine for their wine, their row of beans and loft of hay, their wise providence – until it comes to flowers, which they scatter extravagantly out of windows and doors and palings. You know that inside the bread is white and fresh and their butter rich and plentiful. I love it all.

---

5 Lipstick (*le rouge qui tient*).

6 A madman whom she had met only once had left her all his money: but she never got a penny.

This hotel, *Die Krone*, is first class. The beauty of yesterday is clouded and we are off now to collect my losses from Basle. Papa's tummy seems more settled. Splendid letter from you. God bless my dear little lubber – don't shiver your timbers. I'll try and get refills for our Kimberleys[7] but you'll get them in Jamaica along with rum and doubloons and don't forget to ask for Pina Fresca – in the streets of Cuba or any island where pineapples are grown. A huge tumbler of iced pineapple juice, well sugared with a head on it.

> *Pontresina, near St. Mortiz*
> *August 11th, 1948*

The Hoffs left us today. It's been a nice two or three days if only I did not irritate them and Papa at Oklahoma and if only he, Papa, wasn't a victim of a *crise de foie*.[8] I recovered a lot of stuff at Basle and in the course of it met Carl's niece at a *confiserie*. She was introduced to me by the Hoffs as 'Inez'. Back to me came a memory of 1939 when Carl loved me and was so frightened of this delightful situation being discovered by his protectors that he used to address his letters under cover to Phyllis and asked me to sign mine *ta nièce Inez*. I naturally thought it was an invention, but there she was, six foot high, stuffing down éclairs. I'm trying so hard to be good and high spirited on this trip, but somehow I'm difficult if you're not there. The hotels other people like I condemn before I've seen the rooms – too high class, too badly lit, and the rest of it.

We've bought a Swiss guide book. It has a lot of passes with accompanying letters: G – good, V.G – very good, E – easy, A – awkward, D – difficult. The pass we fancied on account of its position and direction was labelled G and A, but on the morning

7 A sort of pen.
8 A liver attack.

of the ascent the weather was so appalling that we hesitated over the 'awkward'. Luckily we chose a G and E instead because it was all but impassable. Bad petrol was causing the car to gurk and to falter. The windscreen wiper was hopelessly temperamental (this Kimberley is too). We stopped for an hour and a half at the foot to have the petrol drained out and the tubes blown through. It rained and hurricaned and snowed and fogged. The cars we met, and there were frighteningly few – were caked in snow and had their lights on at noon. However we did not meet darkness. We *did* meet over the frontier a river tearing across the road with a truck stuck in it and a queue of cars confronting each other. For a moment my old verve returned and taking on at full speed rocks and gullies and trenches and trees, got across the unfordable.

Exhausted, we found to our surprise at Trema a gigantic hotel looking like some lobby between Life and Death and there we lay till morning brought us the most radiant of days. A glorious road from Trento to Riva and there was our own dear lake rich with fruit and flowers and there was Mr. Walsh at San Vigilio, sitting in a melancholic probably tipsy heap, drinking his lunch of Chianti. There was no one staying there, for all his letters complaining of pressure. He's been too busy even to get to Garda for months, he told us, too busy tippling and spoiling the Locanda. I was cruelly frank and told him I disapproved of his having filled in with windows three of the first-floor loggia arches in order to make extra little rooms. He has also put up a melon-shaped sunblind like lido hotels and purposes to convert all the old flapping sail curtains into these horrors. He gave us a scrumptious lunch at a high price and we arranged to return for a weekend with Liz and Rai. On to Venice and the new hotel Gritti – very good. We have a lovely room and I'm not so cross as I was last year. Not so cross, but not very happy. I can't feel myself. Everything is stale and unprofitable. No friends. It's only really the English who buck things up abroad – the Randolphs, the Corrigans, the Chipses, the palaces and feasts. '*In questo palazzo c'e ogni sera festa*'[9] said the gondolier of a house a lot of us took together. Today there is John Gunther[10] with a slightly dreary bride, there are Mr. and Mrs. John Follet, the Ronnie Trees and an exciting Russo–American dressmaker called Valentina and that is all. No Korda, who I had hoped for, and so far no films. John Gunther is the only spot of fun and I tried to remember what it was pejorative that Kaetchen wrote to me during the war 'What, I should like to know, is inside John Gunther?'

August 18th, 1948
Venice

Venice is nothing if not quiet. Elsa Maxwell was signalled yesterday. Perhaps she'll be the pep. Charlie B.[11] has shown no kick. Sarah Churchill[12] fell from the sky and a lot of really very base film people. The great showings start tomorrow with *The Red Shoes* (Rank).

I got your letter yesterday – a great joy. My melancholia is so bad that it made me cry – don't ask me why because I don't know. I'm making Papa's life a misery.

I had a miserable day yesterday. A ridiculous August cold as a basis, promises that I didn't keep to take Sarah sight-seeing, a ghastly lunch in a beastly bistro watching Papa not eat. I working myself into the belief that he had a mortal disease. After a fitful siesta he went to play bridge while I walked miles going into every church to pray, then back to my bed and an effort to read a book about de Quincey and at eight Papa came back and said he felt better and I believed him almost. I had a slight suspicion that he was saying it to stay my fears, and we dined with the Trees and

9 'In this palace there are parties every night.'

10 American writer. Author of *Inside Europe, Inside Asia, Inside Africa*, etc.

11 Charlie Bestegui (or Beistegui) a Mexican multimillionaire, famous for the sumptuous fancy-dress ball he was to give in Venice in September 1951.

12 Winston and Clemmie's daughter.

Papa ate a bit and so I cheered up and we all four packed into the gondola and went to look at Colleoni riding against a stormy moon-flecked sky.

Now it's this morning again. I do hope I'll be gooder.

Much later – In fact it's the 22nd and I'm sitting at the familiar table on the upper loggia at San Vigilio. The sky gave us a fright till ten but has come up smiling now at twelve. Papa grows steadily worse. I have a feeling of a faint hope he is a little better this morning because although he still spends the greater part of the day on the loo, he was able at breakfast to chew a piece of bread and some *café latte*. O dear, O dear, I have been so panicky and naughty. He's as thin as a skelly and Mr. Walsh said 'looks ten years older' in his tactful way. His voice is the voice of the dying to which one bends one's ear to catch the last words. He shuffles more than usually and never registers my protest or my nagging cry of *elastico*. He is exceedingly docile which is so alarming, and plays kind little tricks to reassure me, like ordering a drink and pouring it away when he thinks I'm not looking. Apart from the anxiety and the cruel hells my apprehensions plunge me into, it's also so sad and boring to have holidays without the zest of meals and drinks. There'll be no journey into Garda this morning, and no looking forward to the excellent lunch. In Venice no Harry's Bars and no fun at all.

Enough of that. We got here last night and Liz and Raimund though they said they would meet us (Leonardo has kept the two best rooms and telegrams, three in all, have been sent to Salzburg to tell them of the importance) have *not* turned up. A telegram says they will arrive this afternoon. As we go tomorrow morning it's not much good. There are, staying in the Locanda, a couple of happy homosexuals whose dream of love is being shattered by a big bony Englishwoman who joins their table – a saga-teller without jokes and no pauses. I asked Mr. Walsh who she was. 'She's been here too long – like fish, she's beginning to smell', he said. Papa toyed with a grain of rice kicking it around the plate with his fork while I ate a curiously planned meal of *hors d'oeuvres* followed by a flaming rum-soused plum pudding. The other inmates I have not taken in yet. Meanwhile in Venice, where we return, the *Biennale* plods on. The English exhibition of pictures, Turner first, is excellent – the cream of the show for me. A mediocre collection of French Impressionists, a ghastly modern French room of *ordures*, another of Picasso, interesting Italian sculpture and some American turds. The film takes place afternoon and evening at the Lido in a mammoth airless cinema (hard arse). Dressed to kill, we went by launch to help inaugurate it. The English kicked off with one of the most embarrassing uncaptioned pictures I remember to have seen, *Eyes to See With*. It shows you pictures of the things you don't look at, i.e. Houses of Parliament, a cornfield, waves breaking on a rock, an apple tree in bloom, the stealthy eyes of a cat. No really I was ashamed. (Papa's chest is peeling – he pulls and pulls at long dead winding-sheets of it, then he feeds the minnows with our breakfast bread and now he's just tried the skin shreds on them and they've gobbled them up in a flash.)

We had the worst places in the house. The next picture was *The Red Shoes*, a picture to show that ballet can be filmed. Moira Shearer of Sadler's Wells is the star and there are lovely things in it including Massine and technicolour, but it's an hour too long. The story is puerile and it was uncaptioned. Now a ballet film can stagger through unexplained, but what are the Italians, who complained of this one, going to make of the *Winslow Boy*? Or the new Graham Greene involved story? When it was over we were all convoked to a party at the Excelsior – supper and dancing al fresco. I asked the head waiter 'Who is receiving?', as I wanted to make an *acte de présence*. 'Io',[13] he said, so I said 'We shan't need a table.' We hung about by arrangement to meet up with Sarah Churchill, the film actress who has never appeared on the screen (goodness, she must be bad if, as Winston's daughter, she has never yet got her name on the programme) and Captain and Mrs. Moore, a *very* common young couple who represent Korda in Italy, but they'd thought it simpler to go home and leave us looking. Film people as a whole are the

13 'I am.'

most ill-mannered people ever brought up. Why is it? Actors are not – Oliviers, Lunts, du Mauriers, Cochrans behave like gentlemen, while the film folk keep you waiting two hours and don't repent. The biters were bit the other day when Sarah and the Moores kept me, the President of the *Biennale*, a Senator to boot and Sir Arthur Jarret and mistress, the chief distributor of films in England, waiting for over an hour. Sir A. and his girl walked out after fifty-five minutes saying they were not office boys.

The next night I went to the American programme alone as Papa was too weak and loo-bound. I saw *Louisiana Story*, a backwoods almost actuality, worth seeing for the native backwood boy and his fight with a crocodile and his tame 'coon and his odd French language. This was followed by *A Double Life*, when Ronald Colman plays the strangling of Desdemona five times, otherwise not *too* bad. This film had captions and now I fear it may be only the English who have omitted them. The Swedes and Poles and Czechs and Mexicans who are all showing are bound to caption them.

23rd. I laid my hand on Papa's tummy yesterday on the off chance of having healing powers and the waters dried up and he ate a good lunch and at three the Hoffs arrived. San Vigilio was at its worst, a hundred cars blocking the yard, but they were delighted with it. Radiant weather, a bathe, a rollicking dinner, booze and laughter and clouds forgotten. Leonardo (steaming) introduced me to the Count and Countess who were dining here. I shrewdly suspected in order to see Liz, whose beauty I have talked of loudly, and now today is a sparkler and we are off to post this letter at the P.O. of Garda and throw back a few Cinzanos. They all ask tenderly about you.

Where we once lunched on Como
September 11th, 1948

With every fruit tumbling over me from a horn of plenty, unfailing sun, zephyr breezes, free rooms, gondolas and launches at Korda's expense, the perfect hotel, all the pleasures the film world can offer, I have been too suicidally wretched to write – to you I love best (coupled, naturally, with Papa). We bore each other quite dreadfully. I bore him because I study his every gesture, sigh, gurk or twitch, determined with dread to find him in bad health, which must be most horribly irritating, and he bores me because he is so spoilt that a kind word flung into the silences he thinks will suffice to interest me. He's never eaten or *drunk* a thing on these holidays, and is as thin as Augustus on the last day, i.e. a sugar plum.[14] It's obsessed me out of all proportion.

We left once-loved Venice thank God this morning and got to hated Como and this dear little inn. On the way we lunched with Isaiah and Ashley and Virginia, at San Vigilio. That place resists my depression and lunch was fun. Papa ate a couple of slices of salami and a sip of wine, and the sip was worth more to my spirits than a bottle of the same.

The films in Venice got more fast and furious. The last we saw was Puffin[15] Asquith's *Winslow Boy*, very very good. We had to see it alone with Puff in a private room and wait an hour for the projector man to finish his supper. We'd had none (not that that matters to Papa), so it was lucky it was good and we could say so sincerely to Puffin. Then there was a quite dreadful party at Torcello, an hour away from Venice. No incidents, no scandals, the nearest occurring at the last moment when I got into Elsa Maxwell's launch (on invitation), so did Orson Welles but he sulked with jealousy in the hold, a few others asked personally and a few unasked, namely a reputed artist called Leonora Fini and her two lovers. Elsa lost her head completely, and for no reason as the boat wasn't crowded. 'Get out of my launch!' she trumpeted. 'Get out, get out I say. I happen to like invited people and my friends. Get out!' I was deeply ashamed for her.

---

14 From the nineteenth-century German children's book *Struwwelpeter*.
15 Nickname of the film director Anthony Asquith.

Now a night has passed and I feel happier. Papa ate soup and ham and the place is sweet − modest to a degree but silent and cheap after the deafening expense of Venice. We are sitting on the terrace, Papa I néedn't say reading. The sun hasn't reached us, but the opposite over-populated hill is ablaze. We shall now make our way to Milan and lunch and buy some necessities, and this evening we hope to turn up at Portofino and find Jenny waiting with the *povero vecchio*[16] to carry our traps to the summit.

Chantilly
September 22nd, 1948

I never write, but from today I solemnly swear to scribe my day-book[17] without fail. My life has hobbled along hectically on a broken wing, commuting to Paris on account of Molyneux and *Hamlet* première committees, and I've had Nancy and Juliet and Jenny in the house. Juliet has encouraged and alarmed me. I'm really quite beastly to her, snapping her up and telling her to her face not to be so dense or stupid or irritating, but she has a greater sense of interior decoration and a better knowledge of gardens than I have (if only she wouldn't call cowslips *necatus anthroglotus* or the like) and I should be − and am − duly grateful for the help. Jenny has been screamingly funny. She's produced out of a hat lots of little catches. One goes:

> I was standing by the corner of the street
> As quiet as quiet could be,
> When a great big ugly man came up
> And tied his horse to me.

16 Indigent old man, of a kind then widespread in Italy, who did odd jobs for tips. The *Casteletto* was on the topmost peak above the village.

17 An Austrian neighbour at lunch once asked her whether she 'scribed her day-book'. She never forgot it.

Also

> The five o'clock whistle never blew,
> So poor old father never knew
> And went on working till half-past two.

She *is* a funny girl – one fault and one only. She cannot keep off the trunk[18] telephone. Paris from here forty times a day and about six Zurichs, Portofinos and Amsterdams daily.

Nancy has as good as finished her book. It's to be called *Diversions*[19] and she's pleased, but every line that she wrote at Chantilly – well fed, isolated and telephone-less – had to be rewritten. I'm thinking of writing my own memoirs at last. I was always determined not to and rather despised those who did, but Maurice's reread *Puppet Show of Memory* shows me how simply it can be done. It would be an interest and an absorption – delving into the past I shall forget the future.

Stephen, my lovely Czech labourer, has been seduced away from me by higher wages. Jacques is for the high jump. He refuses to work and puts the heaviest chores on grovelling Maria's back. Jean, noble and plausible as always, is a martyr to *crises de foie*, while Mireille is equally martyred by jealousy. Result is that Jean can never help us out in the Paris sty, because if he leaves Chantilly Mireille believes him to be sleeping with his wife.

Chantilly
September 25th, 1948

Now it's Saturday and weather to dream of – icy at dawn when I go out, blue fingers clutching milk pail, duck food, mangels and pig swill, the sun just up, sparkling on dewy spiderwebs and

18 Long-distance.
19 It wasn't. At this time she was engaged on *Love in a Cold Climate*.

not a breath of wind to disturb the icy splendour. By mid-day it's so hot – cut-down delphiniums are budding and blooming again. Animals fed and drained, I pick with paralysed fingers heavy-headed dahlias, golden rod, yellow daisies – everything in flower seems to be of gold and lasting, and I stick them in the vases in which they will so quickly wilt and then up I go and wake Jenny. She says I always wince when I look at her first – she wears a frilled linen nightcap, the opposite of mine, Hogarthian and unleashed.

Jenny, Papa and I went to Chantilly market. Everyone elated and stimulated by the weather made it gay and hopeful. I bought a block of paper, a red cord to tie my last pair of spectacles to my person, some white fringe, three figs and three small melons. I coquetted with the idea of buying some bunnies and I met my old *charcuterie* friend who bought the hermaphrodite pig. He knew (by tom-tom?) that I had a saleable pig and behaved a little too keenly for me to sell cheap. I made a date in the sty at 12.30 and after a pause at the *quincaillerie*[20] to buy a kettle, three enamel basins, two coffee cups and a purple umbrella, we went to see if the Golden Arrow was on time (and you know what that spells: Pernod).[21]

Melancholia still on leave. I've had a wonderful barter bit with the pig buyer. He and I leaning over the sty and Jean, with a face stained by tears of laughter, in the offing. He pretended that he had to throw the flesh of the hermaphrodite to the crows as it smelt so strongly of urine. He claimed that my promising sow, which he also wanted to buy, would be barren as a mule for anatomical and visible reasons that I really can't write about. I told him he was a fraud and an amateur. In the end he gave me 30,000 for the boy pig, and I was triumphant till that kind idiot

20 Ironmonger.

21 The *Buffet de la Gare* at Chantilly was a favourite watering hole of my father, who rather fancied the red-haired *patronne*. The Golden Arrow was the Paris–London express which hurtled through the station at full speed, so a visit to the bar was always described as watching the Golden Arrow go through, or checking that it was on time.

Maria told me it was worth double. We had a drink on the deal. *'Du porto, Monsieur?'* *'C'est mon préféré.'*[22] Great fun.

Yesterday was *les grèves*[23] in Paris. No autobus, no metro. The radiance of the weather quite spoilt its effect. No one minded walking. The taxi man who I spoke to was forced – to his own loss – to sit idly on his box for two hours. He hated it, he said, but *'il n'y a pas de choix'*.[24]

September 26th. Yesterday was a gallop of spirits and people and sun and fun. First to join the house guests was Wynne Godley (oboeist)[25] at 10.30. I met him at the station and frankly flinched when I saw his get-up, or rather the dirt of it – his trousers frayed, the seat much darker than the legs, and the deep khaki shirt looked smelly. He is said to wear his pyjamas under his suits, but I saw nothing peeping out. It was so hot that chairs had to be moved under the tree. Bill Patten, Papa and I went to see the Golden Arrow go through. Next arrived John Foster[26] and lastly Hector McNeil, the pick of the Labour Party. Luncheon was a rollick, John Foster and Hector talked well above my head – extraditions, foreign labour, economics. I was treading water and trying to smile and exclaim in the right places. After arrived a new couple, called Christopher Buckley, foreign correspondent of the *D. Telegraph.* He was a great success with Papa as he knew all the Belloc poems by heart, great chunks of the Wine Ode[27] and all the Ballades. They stayed to dinner and we spouted our pieces until all hours.

Jenny in a Guatemalan skirt and *décolleté* blouse and Wynne in his dirt and me in scarlet trousers and large straw hat and head in wimples, went over on invitation to Royaumont, the house of Max Fould Springer, and its adjoining abbey where intellectuals can live for 500 francs a day. Susan Mary, carrying great

---

22 'Some port, monsieur?' 'That's what I like best.'

23 Strikes.

24 'There's no choice.'

25 He was really a high-class economist.

26 A distinguished barrister, then working at SHAFF.

27 *Heroic Poem in Praise of Wine*, which Hilaire Belloc had dedicated to my father.

melancholy, came too, perfectly dressed in a light summer suiting and making us the more conspicuous. Wynne may go and live for a bit with the intellectuals, each in his not very narrow cell. As we walked down the vaulted corridors, wonderful part-singing came floating out of a rehearsal room. The cloisters were dripping with crimson creeper. The tobacco plant filled them with a drowsy smell. Break off for I forget what.

The faithful Collins drove us down to Wilton. Bobbety and Betty Salisbury are here and Tony, the Pembrokes' dull son, dined. The house is still occupied by the Army but why there should still be a partial blackout interiorly I don't know. It was very gloomy last night but the brilliant weather this morning exercises its despotic sway.[28] I'll get up and go and see Juliet. It's unpopular but I don't care. I had to ask the host for a glass of port last night and say he mustn't discriminate against sexes. All the women were parched.

Wilton
October 1st, 1948

The weather beams and grins and gilds this lovely country with heavenly alchemy. It is in a way unlucky that whenever I come back to my native land it is to the West Country on the rare days when sky and earth are radiant with purity and colour, and so always on the verge of regret I fall right into the pit of it and wish that we had not exiled ourselves. Papa is not so frail. Lady Pembroke – Bee – is sixty-fourish, straight as a bamboo stick and the same width and consistency. It's difficult to define how absurd, humourless, rather nasty and slightly pathetic she is. Your godmother Betty, one of our most mischievous fun-pokers and scoffers, stirs me up to her own boil of derision.

Reggie, the Earl, has at the age of sixty-five subsided into senility. He was one of those often-quoted crossword solvers

---

28 Phrase taken from an ancient Baedeker.

– quite ignorant, frivolous and dense, he could polish *The Times* off while his egg was cooking. O the change! Now, slumped in a chair, through rheum and phlegm he croaks questions at Papa and Bobbety – 'What's this? What's thirty-two across? What's three down – unpunctual Australian bird?'[29] At meals Betty and I can't get the poor old bird – he's like a jackdaw – to respond at all. The seven of us sit down to our meals on the stroke of the appointed hour. In front of the host and hostess, mid the fine napery and Georgian spoons and forks, are two jars of sugar and butter.[30] Betty was asked to bring hers and Bobbety's, so theirs are on the table too. It's ingenious if you're mean, because when Bee says 'Reggie, give Diana a little of your sugar' it's impossible to accept any.

Bee and Juliet can't be said to hit it off, and there's a struggle and a feeling of guilt if one goes from the big to the little house at Wilton. I had a date to go to Juliet the first morning. Bee smelt a rat and came to my bedroom, where I was putting on with satisfaction my new bottle-green corduroy skirt. 'I hear you're going over to Bulbridge – I'll walk you there.' So she did, through the lovely park, past lawns and cedars from Lebanon, past follies and over gushing rivers. 'We lunch at one. Don't be late' – always the sergeant-major. Bulbridge was prettier than ever, Juliet contented and full of sneers about Bee. We talked Latin names of flowers and studied out-of-date catalogues and when I left I also left my basket as an excuse to return. After lunch Betty and Bee and I took a long walk round the park and farm. She has a tone of conviction that makes you think she *knows*, but experience of an hour teaches you her abysmal ignorance of nature, animals, and common facts. I got guiltily back to Bulbridge for my basket and a drink.

October 2nd. Wonderful day, all glister and gold. Bee early to my room. I told her, mantling a bit, that I was going to Salisbury market with the Hoffs. I funked adding Juliet's name. 'O you're

29 Emulate.

30 Rationing – unbelievably, nearly three and a half years after the end of the war – was still in force.

going with Liz and Raimund, I might come with you.' 'Well, you know Liz isn't an early riser,' I said, indicating that I had a sort of lovers' tryst with Raimund. This she seemed to respect and told me not to be late for departure to shooters' lunch. Gay with guilty escape, we all had a lovely morning in the market and shops of Salisbury – the cathedral, the Close, the streets, the bustle and charm of it all! I bought a red Hungarian shawl for myself or Louise, a blue handbag, a pair of rubber boots for 12/– and I was back at 12.30. Bee saw the whole happy party arrive back from the fair and realised she had been duped. I felt sorry. Liz had told me that Bee knows she has no one's affection and no love from her children, and that she spoils everything, poor beast.

October 3rd. Sun just darting through the autumn mists. We are to visit Cecil this morning, then eat our lunch monotonously, then beat it perhaps secretly to Juliet's for dinner, and London after. There are sometimes as many as seven huge golden Labrador dogs in the sitting room, all well groomed and well trained, and subdued until someone moves to go out – then chaos falls and tables turn. Bee and Reggie can't get through a sentence to us without talking to the dogs at the same time – 'Sit', 'Basket, Bumble', 'Gently, Brandy', I don't seem to be able to finish with Wilton.

London later. Cecil was charming. Mrs. Beaton[31] very uppish indeed. '*I* laid the terrace down', '*My* house is wonderfully dry', etc. Bee had cheated Bobbety out of £2 on the books. God knows what she's done with me.

The weather has collapsed, and we drove back through drizzle and dense motor traffic in time to see a delightful Carol Reed/ Graham Greene film *The Fallen Idol.* Now we're in our narrow beds together laid.[32] I had a dreadful pang passing Emerald's corner.[33] I used to hate her ringing me in the night and talking without end. I wish she would tonight.

---

31 His mother.
32 Clearly a quotation, but where from?
33 In the corridor of the Dorchester, where she had her room.

Verrières[34]
October 1948

At Elsie Mendl's. Hot as July. Hostess in slim cool white crêpe-de-chine, hat shady and summery, big bow gripping it on under the chin. In a chair of course at ninety-four (but attributing weakness to the chilly summer), transparent skin, fresh and unlined and unbagged and free of make-up. She complains of having no mind or memory, but she can tell a very complicated story of crooks and mergers, involving names galore, without an effort. I got Mr. Bemelmans[35] and the King of Yugoslavia. His Queen, admired by many but not by me, was dressed in stuffy sage-green serge. I was dressed a bit stuffy myself in a new number made of red and black tartan, the black lines cleverly reduce the waist to a wasp's, on my head a beautiful little embroidered red cap of Louise's. My shoes let me down a bit and two left-hand gloves didn't help, but I was considered a bit of a *dernier cri* and the basket instead of a bag greatly admired. Bemelmans was exceedingly amusing about the visitation of Hollywood on Rome and the Pope. Zanuck (is that his name?) took His Holiness a newly designed collapsible streamlined staybright-shelled, plastic, portable altar. It was much appreciated by that monkey Pacelli[36] who could not resist playing with it throughout the interview. He, Zanuck or another character, when asked if he wished a medal blessed, drew from his pocket not a coin but the script of his new film ('Give it every chance' I suppose). Another man produced rosaries to be blessed – not beads or a chain as expected but a big ball of *knitted aves* and *paternosters* to be cut off by the yard.

Elsie disappeared for a rest after lunch and I returned to Verrières, stopping by the roadside to listen to *Orphée aux Enfers* on my radio. The sun baked down on me and I fell asleep. It would

---

34 The house of the Vilmorin family just outside Paris.

35 Ludwig Bemelmans, writer.

36 Pope Pius XII.

have surprised a policeman if he'd opened the car door and found it loud with music and red-and-black tartan and an unconscious woman slumped in her seat.

Everyone asks me if my husband is writing a book – I answer 'I don't know'. It sounds so silly, but Papa has always been super-stitiously secret about his literary projects. I know he has planned a book about Venice and one about Shakespeare and one about the Embassy in Paris, but has he carved out the initial chip?

[Paris]
October 12th, 1948

Last night I went out with the oboeist Godley. I had been deputed to speak to him about his dirt. He arrived *tiré à quatre épingles*[37] but I did it all the same, playing a double game and landing Nancy and Alvilde with his wrath from wounds. He took it well, however, and promises to do better. We had a horrible little dinner cooked by ourselves in the kitchen and went to a film *Dédé à Anvers* that is stark enough for the French to wonder why it passed censorship. I slept bang through it so received no corrupting flash out of it. Stumbling sleep-walking out of the theatre, we felt hungry, and it was 1.30 and a Monday, but we found a delightful Café de la Sorbonne in the Boulevard St. Michel (a place to be noted by night-starvers) and we ate eggs and *bananes flambées* and drank a *grog américain*. Next to me sat a romantic couple, arms and legs intertwined, and look of such ecstasy on the pretty blonde's face that I drew the oboe-ist's attention to her and my rasp rang out in appreciation of their love and the reflection of their love on their surroundings. I made a loud piece on this theme when the man turned to me saying 'I think I should tell you I'm English' and then 'Didn't I know you at Oxford?' to Wynne. We kept up fifteen minutes conversation about mutual friends. Wasn't it a curious foundation for acquaintanceship?

37 Beautifully dressed.

So no bed for me till 2 a.m. and I woke up at seven thinking I must have started meningitis, so appalling was the headache. It's gone now and I've done my chores for English friends – pink satin for Oggie's bosom, dark blue mascara for Enid's dear little lashes, net curtains for Wade, brandy for Chips, champagne for Henry.[38] I've tried on a yellow skirt and a pink–satin–checked–with–grey picture dress. Its bodice is made of roses only. I do my best but I'll always be a bum.

October 13th. 8 a.m. at Verrières. I buzzed down here at midnight after an amusing dinner at Nancy's. Her sister Hartington[39] has arrived. She's ever so pretty and funny – a lovelier Nancy – more frivolous and perhaps a little funnier and more exaggeratedly Mitford. She is quite worthy of the name which evokes the Whigs of Devonshire House, the beautiful Duchess of Devonshire, her daughter who married Granville and lived in my Embassy, and Harty Tarty the Hartington of the day and Lady Caroline Lamb, the niece of the house who married Lord Melbourne. It's a fascinating period of life and letter–writers which you will love to read about. The Duchess had some painful affliction of her eyes and one of the treatments she submitted to was a tight string round her throat which made the eyeballs bulge out. When sufficiently prominent they applied leeches to the jellies.

October 14th. On board the good ship *Arromanches*, Newhaven-bound and utterly empty. I've no passport – good, it's the second time I've left it at home. Papa has a theory that Magna Carta doesn't admit of them, so I'm trying it out – and what is bad I've no money. So magic is our name in France that neither discrepancy seems to matter a pin. I had a rather miserable drive in flooding rain and a broken windscreen wiper, but Beethoven, Bach, Gluck, Haydn and Mozart solaced me. The great excitement was the arrival (note the date) of your first letter. You wrote 28th and said it would

38 Anglesey, soon to be married.
39 Deborah, soon to be Duchess of Devonshire.

311

not start for eleven days so it only took three or four days. You were cold and wet and inundated and happy. It must be hot by now. I'm so jealous of you.

Yesterday I took Nancy and Debo to Dior's collection – a few wonderful things but a whole lot quite unwearable. The bulkiness of them is too uncomfortable. They seem to be made of felt, generously padded, yards and yards of umbrella-like pleats. The place was jam-packed – some clients sitting on the curve of the stairs, where no view was obtainable.

Back at Chantilly three or four days later. I never wrote in London – it was too hectic. I dumped my luggage on Oggie – no it's no use, I'll write in the train to Rome.

Train to Rome (for the Wagon-Lits)
October 20th, 1948

I left you plonking my luggage onto Oggie – her luxury flat a bower of beauty. By the bed a glass of water, a china slipper of cigarettes, pencils and paper, telephone, bell, books and candle, aspirins, cures and calmers for all ills, and herself a rose in satin padding – and eggs, brioches, cream and sugar. Then I packed alone into Sir William Rootes's motor and crept down to the wilds of Surrey to lunch with Flora and Diana Russell.[40] The day was shining and lighting the brightest autumn reds and golds that ever I have seen. One is always surprised at the glory and speed of the spring, but autumn does vary and this year it's a macaw.

To Flora's first. They both have broken hips causing them to drag and revolve in half circles as they walk. They both have lovely little houses (ten minutes in a car apart). Both houses are packed with memories, closely hung with pictures, every one of interest and association, nearly all relations painted by themselves, landscapes visited, old private theatrical programmes painted on satin

40 Conrad Russell's sisters.

from Woburn ('the Bedford place'). Then there are cactuses and seedlings on the windowsills, ambitious seedlings like tree peonies and oleanders and giant hemlocks and ledges, crumb-strewn at the open windows for braver birds. Something of Verrières, but much less sophisticated. The two of us bundled over to Diana's house. She is younger and had *endimanché*[41] herself and so had Flora. She offered me a glass of sherry. Flora had passed into another room. I accepted greedily. Pouring me out a half glass she called to her sister in a scarcely audible voice 'Do *you* want any, my dear?' 'She hasn't heard', I said, knowing she had not been meant to hear. 'She isn't likely to want any', said Diana, throwing up a prayer that she would not have to pour away another drop, but I was merciless and bawled 'Come and have some sherry, Flora.' I don't think she wanted any but we were secretly in the game together, so she poured herself out a bumper. Diana paled. There was nothing else to drink at lunch and a very meagre meal. It was all brought in together and plunked on to a dumb-waiter. The kitchen communicating, the 'sweet' might have waited for the first course to be eaten, but no. Luckily it was apple charlotte, which was able to burn our mouths after the very few minutes the preliminaries took to swallow. They didn't want to talk of Conrad – too embarrassed perhaps. I did, but didn't. They were loving of me for that reason.

That evening I went to a play with Cecil – two in one by Rattigan called *Playbill* – the first a very gloomy schoolmaster play,[42] good, sad and moving, with Eric Portman, the second the old rehearsal farce – this time *Romeo & Juliet* in a provincial theatre. You would have cracked your sides, being less *blasé*. The theatre was unheated, with the chill in it that freezes one's enthusiasm for the play. Kitty[43] was throwing a party in her new smart upper-part in

---

41 Put on her Sunday best.
42 *The Browning Version* and *Harlequinade*.
43 Paget (later Farrell), twin sister of Henry Anglesey, about to marry Shirley Morgan.

Eaton Place for the sisters of the bridegroom.[44] The wedding was started for me at this supper and went on from delight to delight to its last grain of sympathetic rice.

The wedding day broke bright. I shopped a bit and had to give a long time to dressing. It came off, I think – very dark, very thick silk – almost to the ground – minute waist, very open neck, a geranium between the breasts to perk them up and a red felt tricorne with veil. We lunched with Cecil. Papa wore a frock coat and top hat, grey and black buttoned boots, blazing white waist-coat. Caroline and Liz *endimanchées* out of all recognition – hats and feathers and artificial flowers, twice the make-up and all their colours chosen for violence.

The Thames had overflowed on Chiswick Mall, not badly, but it had caught about a dozen cars parked near the verge and they hunched there crookedly and funnily. The little Chiswick church had the gaiety of a village wedding. There seemed to be no London street, but only little shuttered houses brightly painted, all their windows packed with smiling faces. Queen Mary arrived in Cambridge blue, blue toque and dog-collar to match, umbrella and shoes like skis. Henry led her up to the front pew and then waited for his bride, supported by Laurence Whistler[45]. The McLaren little girl (Rose's), Arabella and Octavian von Hoff were the pearls in a pretty jewel of other children dressed in pale pink velvet – *scuola di* Tommaso Lawrence. The Bishop of Lichfield (full canonicals) left his newly-weds at the altar and advancing to the chancel addressed us to some tune, reminding us that we were not merely onlookers and sports spectators but partaking in a sacrament, and awfully like Christ at Cana. Coming out I saw poor little Coalbox bent double in silver fox. She can only see now a dreary circle of ground beneath her eyes. I told her to stay put and I'd find our car and drive her to Letty's Walpole house, half a mile away. I wasn't long about it

---

44 The wedding was that of my mother's nephew, Henry Anglesey, to Shirley Morgan, daughter of Charles Morgan the novelist. Kitty, Rose, Caroline and Liz were all his sisters.

45 Glass engraver, brother of Rex.

but she couldn't wait (enthusiasm not to miss departure and arrival too strong) and I picked her up almost at the goal. She bowls as fast as a hoop.

Mr. Charles Morgan had erected a marquee in the now rainy garden and filled it with twenty dozen champagne. The light of the tent was becoming, the eats superb. Ghosts that only weddings evoke were all there smiling and drinking. The bride I scarcely saw – a veil for the sacrifice (Papa had started to cry on arrival of Queen Mary – I held back for the bride). I saw her next behind paper rose leaves and waving hands but what I saw was good, *sympathique* and unshowy. The last cheers dying, Mr. Morgan and a few select still there to talk it over, Cary, Liz, Rai, Papa and I left for Bognor, which my next letter will tell you about.

Still train to Rome
October 21st, 1948

So we came to Bognor 8 o'clockish. On the Sunday night there was a memorable storm, deafening noise and rain flooding everything. The result was the ugliest of crossings from Newhaven to Dieppe. The sea bucketed us about and our lunch and glasses and bottles bucketed over the fiddles put up for security, and lots were broken while Papa and I ate our unattractive meal voraciously. There is no pride like the pride of not being sick when all around are catting and spewing. At Dieppe the real troubles began. The car had possibly been tinkered with. It didn't get us home till ten. Breakdowns of all kinds. Papa was splendid, running uselessly but willingly in search of help and finding none. Forges-les-Eaux was never lucky for me. It was near there that I got snowbound in '45. Tuesday there was lunch at Nancy's with David Herbert. No one got a word in on account of accounts from me of the wedding. There was Louise *en grande beauté*, dressed in her Hungarian model made of loud shepherd's tweed with black braids and frogs and fringes plus twenty huge gold and jewelled *trèfles*[46] and earrings and jewelled bracelets, radiant health and excitement over a new victim, David Bruce – Virginia's [Clarke] brother-in-law – O Law! Where will that end?

Early back to Chantilly to prepare the house against the party for Gaston's Gaullist meeting. It was – the evening I mean (not the preparation, which consisted of summer flowers, dahlias, delphiniums, daisies, roses, enough to fill four big vases from the garden) – not a success. Mireille surpassed herself with eggs in pastry and two poor Aylesbury ducklings brought up by hand and a pineapple baba sweet to set before a king. It was set before Gaston, Nancy, Alvilde, Ali Forbes and Jacqueline de Contade at 8.15 and Gaston started fussing at 8.45. Dinner was bolted. Papa wouldn't go on political grounds and we had to stand in a hall without a wall to lean on. A chairman spouted for half an hour, Gaston for *an hour and a half* – when I gave up and went, followed by all but loving faithful Nancy. Not that Gaston is not to the manner born an orator *par excellence*, adroit, trained, voice-produced, very-clear of very-clear, but after an hour my head span, my legs felt like wool and I thought there was danger of fainting or vomiting so we went out and sat on the cold wet step without the hall where Gaston's unrelenting voice rose and fell with the same penetration as from within.

Yesterday I gave some very millionairish orders – both wings of the house and half the wide path to be grassed and prepared for roses and lilies and again the whole flat to be licked with paint. I'll sell the diamond ring (your wife's) or the bold dressing-case (your wife's only if she had a huge house – there was never a table at the Embassy big enough) but it's no use with these treasures hidden, one in a jewel box, the other in a cellar, and groaning and grousing at the dirt and ugliness. Lunched yesterday with Susan Mary, did a dentist who wanted to extract a tooth as I was leaving for a thirty-hour journey, and boarded the train at eight.

46 Four-leaf clovers, her emblem.

5 p.m. We have now been an hour in a tunnel. Now, thirty miles from La Spezia, we are in the heart of a foul-aired single-line warren waiting for a train to telescope us from behind or from the front, or for another engine to arrive from Spezia and pull us out. It's very disconcerting and it's given me diarrhoea. We were almost two hours in that predicament. I discovered that the train was electric so we were lucky not to be in darkness too. *Ces messieurs les directeurs* kept wonderfully calm. The pleb Italians were a bit noisier. So we didn't roll into Rome till midnight but, day and night being one to the Wops, it might have been six on a winter's evening except that it was balmy and one wanted (at least I did) to exchange our limousine for a cloppety-clop fiacre. The colleagues all get down at the Excelsior Hotel, but we know something better and stay on the top of a Roman hill, one of the seven, overlooking Christian Rome.[47]

We are on the fifth floor with a little balcony and there beneath our feet bulges St. Peter's – domes and spires of a calendar of Saints – all with bells that summon sleepy faithfuls very early in the morning. We walked about in the forenoon, admiringly happy. *Aperitifs* on the Piazza del Popolo prepared Papa for his director's lunch and me for a well-deserved lunch with Signor Carandini, once Ambassador to St. James's. It was lucky I thought of him among the many 'angling' calls I made, for he had the Foreign Minister, Count Sforza, lunching and Mr. and Mrs. Crowther of *The Economist* so I felt from their point of view 'just the thing'. The afternoon was given to Joan[48] and me cloppeting round town and shops till dark. We had a very loquacious old driver and every time he turned to talk he laid his reins down and every time I picked them up and started off *au grand galop.*

Cocktails with the local English Military Attaché called MacNab. I made that invitation by explaining that I had lived in their house

---

47 The Hassler.
48 Lady Altrincham. The Altrinchams were the other British couple on the Wagon-Lits board.

in the Forum (it belonged to Gerald Berners). The programme for the proposed jaunt put the fear of death from exhaustion into all our hearts. This was the timetable for twelve middle-aged couples: 7.30 at station; *autorail* to Assisi arriving 10; three hours sight-seeing; 1, lunch; 3, motor to Perugia; three hours visiting the treasures and monuments; 7, dinner; 9, autorail to Rome arriving midnight. A plan to tire a Strength Through Joy group. It was decided against the night before. Half the day was amputated and we were promised a home-coming at six. That's for tomorrow.

Rome
October 24th, 1948

I'm reading the potted edition of *Mémoires d'Outre-Tombe* (Chateaubriand for babies). Very good. He goes to America in 1791 and takes an expedition across the Mohawk and into what he takes to be virgin forest. '*Je fus pris d'une sorte d'ivresse d'indépendance. Ici plus de chemins, plus de villes, plus de monarchie, plus de république, de présidents, de rois, d'hommes*'[49] but then he stumbles upon a 'hanger' (whatever that is) packed with Redskins, war-painted like sorcerers, half naked, *oreilles découpées*,[50] feathers and nose-rings. In their midst a little powdered Frenchman in an apple-green suit, *jabot* and cuffs of lace, sawing away at a miniature violin for the Iroquois to dance to. It was M. Violet, a dancing master paid with beaver skins and bear steaks to give them lessons in deportment and dance. He addressed them as Monsieur le Sauvage and Madame la Sauvagesse. He was proud of their lightness and Chateaubriand says '*en effet, je n'ai jamais vue de telles gambades. M. Violet, tenant son petit violon entre son menton et sa poitrine, accordait l'instrument fatal. Il criait*

---

49 'I was seized by a sort of drunkenness of independence. No more roads, no more towns, no more monarchy, no more republic, presidents, kings, people!'

50 Slitted ears.

aux Iroquois "A vos places, Messieurs" et toute la troupe sautait comme une bande de démons.'[51] He goes on to say how strange it was for a disciple of Rousseau to be introduced to the life of savages by a little myrmidon of General Rochambeau throwing an Iroquoian ball.

The great expedition took place yesterday and was proclaimed an unparalleled success. Perugia was scrapped like an old husk and that brisked us all up. 7.30 saw the twenty-odd depressing crowd of us, all middle-aged, a bit infirm but bright as buttons, fresh as daisies, right as trivets, keen as mustard (by the way it's the 27th and I'm *en route* to Genoa shaking like a jelly as we tear up Italy's shin-bone, the sunny sea lapping a grey-green deserted country on our left). We are all rather middle-class, the wives cling to their spouses like calves to cows, clutching their cuffs or coat-tails and anxious-faced if we lose touch. The countries too are apt to cling to themselves – Altrinchams and Coopers wink at each other across a crowd of Dutch, Italians and French and make a dash for the table for four. No tables on the 7.30 autorail however and no precautionary coffee to swallow before leaving, so I felt a bit faint and comaed during the three hours shaking in the thick mist that obliterated the lovely country of Umbria. We knew it must lift and were not afraid.

Out we all hobbled with our hand guides and better still our live professor-guide (an admirable man, brief, bull-voiced and discriminating) out and into an autobus that blinded us up to the sun on the heights of Assisi. I was there with Noona[52] as a child forty years ago and remember little. I think it's been improved since then – fewer modernities and no advertisements or petrol pumps, most lovely streets and churches. St. Francis – you know, the first to love nature and animals – a big modern-ish church, is built round his own Wendy-house-ish little

---

51 'Indeed, I never saw such caperings. M. Violet, holding his violin between his chin and his chest, tuned his fatal instrument. He then shouted to the Iroquois "Take your places, gentlemen!" and the whole party jumped around like a pack of demons.'

52 Her mother.

chapel and on the top of it is a whopping big gold Madonna that is said to move at twilight. We were not there at the moving time but Mrs. Dunn and her daughter (U.S. Ambassadress) and their sceptical Communist chauffeur saw it almost topple down, while Mr. Dunn didn't. In the cloisters of this same church is a bed of bramble roses into which many centuries ago St. Francis threw himself to overcome by pain some local temptation. Imagine St. Francis's surprise – not a thorn to draw his blood, and there they are alive and thornless still. It is claimed that no species of rose is without thorn and that these same roses transplanted regrow their spines.

On Sunday we had a date to visit St. Peter's and the Vatican. Thank God Papa resolved to stay home and get some reading done. He would meet us, he said, at the Trevi – a magnificent fountain into which you threw coins in order to be certain of return to Rome. St. Peter's was all that was expected. I kissed St. Peter's toe, or what faithful lips have left of it, and we turned our steps to the Vatican. *Shut on Sunday.* You can see why I was glad Papa hadn't come. It took a long time. It took the banging of the first door in our nose by a Swiss Guard with a halberd. He was dressed in working-blue and not the gay jester colouring and steel helmet worn when the Holy Father is in residence. At the next door it took a long conversation and a lot of lies to another Swiss Guard at a table. I said Count Sforza had given me a name to ask for in case of trouble and I'd forgotten it. No good. I asked them to telephone the Count. No, I could telephone if they'd get me the number. They handed me the book. They saved me by saying the Foreign Office would be shut. I told them to imagine I was Winston Churchill and what would they do then? They said '*Chiuso*'. It took the old trick of not moving and the three of us forming an obstacle in a bottle-neck, to get us moved on to the next barrier. Suddenly tedium is stronger than guardianship, the morale gives, the pass is sold.

The same story at the second gate, this time with a serious man in civvies. I got as far as a laughing '*Siamo molto, molto importanti.*'[53] This shook him into telephoning to some high power or principality which produced a tiny little priest carrying the key of the Sistine Chapel. He marched us off with stern instructions to return us. This was a triumph to be followed, after inspection of the chapel, by a far greater triumph. A grander, more canonical Father appeared carrying two massy keys. He was showing a rare little chapel to two teenagers. It was a chapel where H.H. goes on Easter Thursday and it has two frescoes that Michaelangelo painted to show what he could do. I knew it was not usually shown to the public and I asked if we too might not have a peek. The Monsignor, for that is what he turned out to be, beckoned us to follow. He was young and amused, had a bit of English and took a great liking to us. He took us everywhere – the purlieus, the board rooms and to see, from a window, his own quarters. Most desirable they looked, set in a cranny of the great façade of St. Peter's, a little flat rooftop, two little French windows opening out on to a terrace of geraniums in pots, canaries in cages, some socks being dried. He offered me a visit to the loo – I can only think to show off the plumbing. Then he started to 'dress' for lunch with an American diplomat. This meant putting on a fine red silk sash – '*obligatorio*' he said, "*ma molto antipatico*'.[54] One wondered why.

Off he bussed in a U.S. Army Ford and we in our car tore back to poor Papa. He'd been waiting hours. The Monsignor had warmed to his work and wouldn't let us off the remotest corners of the Vatican, and to make matters desperate there was no café in the Piazza del Trevi. Chianti on a hill outside Rome settled everything except lunch which arrived just as we had to start to make rendezvous with the colleagues. Back into the motorbus again, don't lose touch with Papa, hope they'll open the top, everyone in favour except a local Molotov who vetoes it on the

53 'We are very, very important.'
54 'Obligatory, but most unpleasant.'

courant d'air[55] ruling. That's the Campagna, there the Alban Hills, now harbouring old Pacelli[56] at Castel Gandolfo, there are the Sabines, Horace's Farm perhaps and there the Villa d'Este at Tivoli where we all bundle out and enjoy the fountains, take snapshots, get a bit splashed, general jinks and back exhausted at seven.

Now we come to yesterday – the last day of this very happy outing. The weather was not all that good. Jenny came through and I'm to stop at Portofino for two days. Betweenwhiles we had visited the U.S. Embassy and our own twice, once for dinner and once to see the garden. Ours is the ugliest house in Rome. It was the German Embassy before the war and poor pretty Lady Mallet is agonised as to how to get it better. I should have been appalled if I'd had to cope and as for the famous Palazzo Farnese where we lunched yesterday – it's the Frogs' Embassy – the gloom of it would have vanquished me. How it brings home the beauty of our Paris house, its light and gay atmosphere, its perfect size, its furniture, its bed and bath, its boudoir and *bibliothèque*. No other Embassy can touch it.

I must have missed a whole day because there was lunch with the No. 2 of the English Dips. – Ward by name and his nice wife and pretty villa and monstrous children. He took us along the Appian Way afterwards – just what I love best – all 'Love Among the Ruins'[57] – all the glades colonnades – all the bridges, courses, aqueducts. The vestige of the city guessed alone, stock and stone, so I cried a bit and Papa dropped off and Mr. Ward at the wheel didn't notice.

Yesterday we went to the Borghese Museum and saw Pauline in her nakedness lying marbly on her marble bed and we saw Bernini's idea of David throwing the giant-killing stone and gasped at its goodness. Bernini *is* St. Peter's and much of sixteenth- and seventeenth-century Rome, and there I learnt Caravaggio, hitherto

---

55 Draught.

56 Pius XII, then Pope.

57 Poem by Browning.

but a name, now a known master, and Danaë by Correggio whom I had forgot. Another new friend, once a diplomat to the Holy See, called Uttley, took us to Hadrian's Villa where one day I hope to wander with you.

Voghiera
October 31st, 1948

I'm sitting in a cold and comfortless waiting room in a ghastly junction called Voghiera not a hundred miles from Turin. Papa came into the *wagon-restaurant* after we'd left Rome with a face like Priam's when they told him Troy was lost, to break to me that there had been a landslide at La Spezia cutting off the line to Genoa, and therefore no hope of getting off at Rapallo. I took it well enough, in fact rather warmed to the adventure of detour and the unknown. Instead of a lovely welcome at 3 or 4 p.m. we limped on to this horrible place where Papa and I parted in silence and tears, he for the north, me for another limp to Genoa.

November 1st. Papa telegraphed me the following 'MISUSE WHEAT MILO VETO GENIAL EXIT SCOLD DOZEN MENUS'.[58] It quite worried me. I thought 'Can he have gone actually mad?' when an idea struck me, and sure enough after much thought I made sense of all but the last two words. Can you solve it? The unclued words may be corruptions (Got it! 'Do send me news').

The weather never cleared up, in fact it got worse and yesterday was a brute. I left this morning and they were leaving too by car and now I've got to the horrible Voghiera again and I'm sitting writing to you – pretty cold and miserable. I've got collywobbles and had a look at the loo – quite impossible – so vicious horses must be held, if they can be, till they're given their heads in the Wagon-Lit. There's another hour and a half to go. I've been here since two and it's four now. Occasionally I order an expresso laced

58 'Miss you sweet. My love to Jenny Alex. It's cold. Do send me news'

with a drop of Aurum, which is a liqueur made of oranges, about the best thing ever I struck.

I've got a book by Siegfried Sassoon about George Meredith because it's associated in no mean way with my early youth. Meredith is thought to be coming out of his eclipse after thirty years. I adopted him as a child because of having been called after *Diana of the Crossways*. At my age of fourteen to twenty he was 'the rage'. An exceedingly obscure writer, I pretended, I fear, to understand all he wrote. I clearly can't have done but I understood his two great poems, 'Modern Love' and 'Love in the Valley', and knew them both by heart. 'Modern Love' consists of fifty-one sixteen-line sonnets. Papa knew it too and does still, and all my *bande* of Oxford boys specialised in this genius, of whom Oscar Wilde said 'His style is chaos illumined by flashes of lightning.' I don't think you would ever swallow him, anyway not whole like I did. Noona had his volume of poems dedicacé-ed for my twelfth birthday 'But if she my Muse had been, Better verse she would have seen'. They must be the clearest lines he ever wrote. I remember with horror writing him a letter of thanks in what I took to be his own style. It must have been horribly embarrassing, but he answered it, writing 'Let the younger Diana know that her words came to me . . . *Cela m'échappe.*' I used to know it proudly by heart. It ended with something about 'if ever she falls upon Crossroads may she have a guide within', etc. etc. I saw him once, when perhaps only seven. He was already very old and crippled and supported by two servants. He'd come to Arlington Street, I think to be drawn by Mother's pencil. When he died I carried on just nohow – 'boo-hoo' and must go to the funeral (cremation rather) at Dorking and went with my governess Mrs. Page (Podgie) dressed out of Mother's wardrobe as a crow. Comic, why was I allowed? A figure of fun, arms full of purple iris which I flung dramatically into the grave along with a flood of tears. As we got into the train for home, eyes bunged out, scarlet blocked nose, J. M. Barrie, who I just knew, ran up and said 'Now you've got to be a good girl' – 'now' meaning after what you've seen and felt, I suppose. So naturally I'm enjoying the book.

Then I've got *Journey without Maps*, by Graham Greene, an unfinished book about John of the Cross, an unreadable book by Maugham and some flower catalogues. These ought to do the journey. I reach Paris in the morning, I hope, after a night with an unknown fellow traveller. What shall I find to greet me? A letter from you is my great hope. We are asked to Rothermeres for Christmas but Wadey has it that you want to stay with the Navy for the Feast and join us for New Year. So be it.

November 1st. The train was one hour late and the season got hourly colder. At last it puffed in and a surly attendant kicked me into my compartment with ne'er an *Ambassadrice* or a *Directrice.* I tried bribery with gold and tobacco to get the section to myself. I imagined, as I shivered in the unheated carriage, the shortcomings of my sleeping companion, old, fusty, smelling, an orange, a troublesome and fruity cough, train-sick, so it was a relief at Turin when the shadow of the coming event was the smartest of air luggage, a new plaid rug, a butler to see fair play. The event was no less than Spam[59] Churchill in the radiance of her success and beauty. I became the old, train-sick, coughing 'undainty' old 'un. Still the boot was easier on that leg. The cubicle now was drenched with expensive scent. The lovers from the darkness of the platform whispered anguished farewells. Spam's back, curved over the window door in coquettish kissing so-longs, was wagging its tail under the darkest sleekest of baby mink coats. My heart naturally sank a bit at the thought of conversation, but she was very friendly. Her new Italian jewellery had left marks under her ring and on her jaw her ear-rings had socked her one. A long saga of how Randolph had tried to remarry her filled up an hour. Poor Randy, he's so lonely and so lost, jobless and a disappointment to his father and his friends and himself, that Spam was touched and considered returning to her burden, if after a six month's trial she felt she could. The fool drags her out

---

59 Pamela (Mrs Randolph) Churchill. She had now taken up with the Fiat king Gianni Agnelli.

of a convalescent bed, drags her down to where we Christmassed last year starting at 7 a.m., drives all out, rather tight and talking ten to the dozen of what interests him, coughs and spits all night and is surprised to find her a wreck next day, though not sufficiently submerged to swear that never will she again be his wife.

A wonderful night. Slept from ten to eight, in spite of five visits from passport bores. Pam slept till ten and hearing that we should not be in Paris till one, turned over and slept till 12.30.

Home to Chantilly. Two glorious letters from Trinidad and Tobago. I do so wish I was there. O you dear little boy, keep safe and well and don't overpunish the rum.

11

'You really are a pig-child'

(FRANCE, MOROCCO, SPAIN, NOVEMBER 1948-APRIL 1949)

On Monday morning we sailed and we've been sailing ever since. Tomorrow morning we arrive and dock at 1 o'clock. Up until this evening, when the wind and sea got boisterous, it has been the calmest passage to Gibraltar anyone can remember. For four days there have been no clouds, and it has got steadily warmer – yesterday afternoon almost sunbatheable. The Captain's Office, however, has been all the time a hive of industry. First we completely repainted the office from the duck-egg blue we put on in August to a light cream. The office is in consequence brighter, though of unusual appearance owing to our having had time for only one coat, so that great patches of blue show through the thin bits. We like to think that this subtle blueness lends distinction to the office. It doesn't.

No sooner was the paint dry (yesterday morning) than we started an appalling job – the re-entering of every rating's Conduct Sheet. This is a paper showing all one's offences, recommendations, punishments, etc., and their Lordships have recently seen fit to redesign it. For two days now we have been copying from the old model to the new for 500-odd men – it's soul-destroying. Now nearly over, but if we don't finish it before we arrive and the mail gets in, heaven knows when the last offence will be recorded.

There has been no other news during the trip except an alarm two nights ago when a stoker was missing, believed overboard. From 2 a.m. till five frantic signals were being made, but then he was found, fast asleep in his hammock, unaware of any fuss, and everybody felt sheepish.

All love,

John Julius

This chapter divides itself up into three parts. The first is taken up with the usual news from London and Paris, further enlivened by the discovery by the press that my mother is 'in retreat' at St John and St Elizabeth's Hospital and its heavy implications that she was there for a face lift – which she might well have been but actually wasn't.

The story on page 334 of dinner guests leaving a house rather than shake hands with Jean Oberlé is a good illustration of the mood which still prevailed in Paris for several years after the end of the war. During our Embassy days, one of the most difficult problems my parents had to face was who had and who had not been a collaborator. Some were known to have been dyed–in–the–wool, others had been, equally undeniably, heroes of the resistance; but there was a broad penumbral zone to which, in all probability, the vast majority of French men and women belonged.

The last two parts are devoted to my mother's accounts of two memorable foreign jaunts, the first to Morocco, the second to Spain, to stay with the Duke of Alba in Seville for Holy Week. My father was not present on the first jaunt – I have no doubt to his intense relief; on the second he was, but, as we shall see, had good reason to regret it. My mother rather fancied herself as an expert on North Africa. She had after all lived for eight months in Algiers, and had returned there at least once with Bloggs Baldwin and me. Clearly, however, she could not compete with the distinctly tiresome former mistress of El Glaoui, Pasha of Marrakesh.

Chantilly
November 3rd, 1948

I'm back home, not particularly glad. I do so hate the *maîtresse de maison*[1] life. I like to be a queen or a tramp – the house books, the staff, the difficulties overwhelm me and keep me tossing at night. Khaki Campbells[2] are laying – I hear them quacking in triumph this early morning. Melanie[3] gives a gesture of milk. Piggy never comes on heat. Regnier has put most of his working time and all his greenhouse space into rearing wilted chrysanthemums – *la fleur des morts*.[4] They stuffed the house with them and then automatically whisked them off to the cemetery for the dead – and unknown dead at that. Yesterday we had the *jour des morts*,[5] and Maria won't wash sheets on that day as it becomes shroud-washing, she says.

Chantilly
November 5th, 1948

Please to remember, and a quiet one but a funny one. Caroline (French pronunciation) is what the staff have christened my pig. She has never shown any stirrings of love, no restlessness, no anxious honking for Hoggy – but, marriage bells in my ears, I got her with help and no trouble to enter her bridal trailer, and Enid and I dragged her in placid mood to M. Lamère, the other side of Lamorlaye. I'd made a kind of rendezvous with him a month ago, but today a furious daughter (the kind that will grow up into a *tricoteuse* of the Communists) shouted through the upper

1 Lady of the House.
2 Ducks.
3 Cow.
4 The flower of the dead.
5 Day of the dead.

window that the boar had been castrated. Nothing doing – get the hell out! We managed to get the address of another farmer out of her unfriendliness – and jolly unfriendly it was, for he lived a long way the other side of Champlatreux and his boar had been liquidated. So we bumped poor Caroline back.

Then she was bucketed off again, this time *du côté de chez* Senlis, where M. Bouchet was said to breed pigs. Not he but his brother had a big farm the other side of Ermenonville and there was a boar there. He'd seen it with his own eyes. The day was drawing most beautifully to its close – new moon and rosy flushes. M. Bouchet's brother was out – from the tone of his farm-hands, he was an ogre. We waited in fear. 'Fi fo fum' were his first words, his second were to the effect that he had a fine boar but he wasn't going to let it touch my sow. Diseases might be passed. I cajoled him into at least looking at her clean health. I assured him that she had never seen any other pigs but her brothers. He was obstinate in his negativism. But as soon as I gave it up remorse smote him and he said that if the pig was in condition to mate he'd allow a crack. 'Ah, I'm jolly sure she's not,' I said, 'I hope you will keep her till she is.' 'Not on my life.' He then softened and warmed to me in telling of how useless she would be as a mother, teats bang wrong and unformed and sterile. His advice was to fatten her up and sell her for Christmas, and that advice I shall follow. We got home in darkness having given poor Piggy a tiring, costly and abortive wedding trip of eighty kms.

November 6th. So I saw the Joneses off to Dieppe at nine. I did my chores, collected Jenny, paused at the *Marché aux Puces*.[6] buying a *coiffeuse*,[7] a piece of bottle-green velvet for shoes and a bag of hot chestnuts. Jenny bought a red silk umbrella and caught an unattractive cold. 'Five pounds wasn't much to give for the lampshade of a lifetime' is her latest overheard remark; but the briefest and most terrible I've ever heard is one waiter passing another and whispering 'He's eaten it.'

6 Flea market.
7 A small dressing table.

November 7th. Such a wonderful day too, leaves still glowing and cloudless skies. Papa and Jenny and I went to pick up young Oboe Godley and to see the *Golden Arrow* pass. I opened the car and thought 'I hope we don't have an accident – not in these clothes', for Jenny wore the loudest of scarlet jackets over a blinding orange tartan skirt. I was in a get-up rather different from the usual – violent green wool stockings, high platform soles, mid-length corduroy trousers and usual Kabile straw hat over wimple. Papa beat the band in a *white* jacket, lemon and white check waistcoat, pink carnation and little Gorblimey hat. Peter Rodd joined us for lunch in a waistcoat that had belonged to Harry Cust of red and gold thread, hand-embroidered.

November 8th. Misty rain. They want Papa to lecture in the U.S.A. for two months, October and November next year, and he's considering it. Wasn't it delightful about Truman?[8] I who only knew Dewey through Don Iddon,[9] who describes him as a robot, am delighted that cold and perfect machinery should break down, and plodding little flesh and blood shouldn't.

The Duchess of Windsor went to see Susan Mary and told her she had lost her *joie de vivre*, that buying clothes and jewels no longer interested her, all was stale and unprofitable, that all she had ever had was energy and without energy she'd lose the Duke, and then she fell a-crying and a-boo-hooing. Poor Wallis.

Chantilly
November 13th, 1948

I haven't written for several days. Paris isn't conducive with the painters in. I want to make the flat nice for your holidays and for Papa to live in while I do a retreat after your holidays. Juliet is

---

8 Harry S. Truman had just been elected President of the United States, beating Thomas E. Dewey.
9 *Daily Express* journalist.

here to help and to madden. Both bays of the gravel decorated with box and clipped privet are dug up, so is the immediate path in front. Lorries of earth are driven away and other lorries full of another kind of earth are due to arrive. By spring we shall have it all grass, with a much narrower path and beds round the house for flowers, rosemary, lilies, catmint, etc., and on the blanker walls an explosion of roses (I hope). M. Catelot undertakes it, a nursery-man from Chantilly, over-suave in cycling knickers and leather jacket. We are also tearing up all the barren shrubs – dead, diseased and mutilated by Felix. These are to be replaced by healthy, large, free-flowering specimens that will glow in summer and flush in autumn and asphyxiate us with their incense – at least that's the idea. It's when forming these plans that I would like to strangle Juliet for her outpourings of Latin-named sugges-tions. It impresses M. Catelot. He and she spouted for three and a half hours yesterday. It's made more tedious because the Latin is differently pronounced in French and English. Jenny left and Barley came, fresh and blooming from ten days of pneumonia. She's never looked better or prettier. She's to convalesce here for a fortnight.

Last night we dined with the Windsors – all right. My lost rank has its advantages – I don't have to sit next to the Duke. The party was pretty, in the Ritz's best suite, candles and the choicest flowers, caviar, vodka, Wallis looking her very best in off-the-ground white and gold lamé, clipped with two new gigantic yellow diamonds, the whole *surmonté*[10] and *panaché*[11] by the faithful Bahamian Negro in fine gold livery.

The night before that I dined at Paul-Louis Weiller's. Bébé and Denise Bourdet took me to the rue de la Faisanderie, where the front door opened on to P.L.W. regretfully saying goodbye to a lady I nearly recognised and a husband I did not. She quickly explained that she had been looking forward to dinner, but as

10 Topped off.
11 Given *panache*.

Jean Oberlé was among the guests she could not sit down. '*Mal élevée*,'[12] I thought, if you accept your host you must accept his guests. When we got upstairs Suzy Solidor[13] was being pacified in a corner of the room. She also had been on the way out for the same reason. Jean Oberlé was one of the '*Trois amis*' who broad-cast from London during the war, and he has certainly called almost every public figure a *collabo*.[14] They all were so, but natu-rally they don't like it set down and rubbed in.

Drinks and nuts arranged everything, and to my great surprise looking round I noticed that those I had seen the door close on were back, and punishing the vodka. You can guess the conversa-tion. 'We'll never get a taxi.' 'All the restaurants will be shut – it's so late and I've only got 500 francs.' All this said by the Dutch husband who hadn't been called a traitor, so he won and back they came to guzzle. The lady was the mistress of El Glaoui, King of the Atlas, and I've accepted an invitation to go with her (bringing David Herbert and you in my wake) to Morocco next year – Moors at their most lavish and fantastic, feasts and slaves, dancing and concubines, gazelles and *méchoui*.[15]

November 15th. Unto us a son is born.[16] I've just heard it from Alvilde on the buzzer. I'm sorry it's not a princess. You'll be firing your guns off, I suppose. The Windsors lunched yesterday. He told me the oldest possible chestnut as something new, i.e. 'If it's a boy they'll fire twenty-one guns, if it's a girl they'll fire ten, if it's a "miss" they'll fire the Duke of Edinburgh.' I heard the story first told when Lady Lampson was to have a baby, her Lord being twenty-five years older than her, but then it ended 'if it's twins they'll fire the A.D.C.'. We sat down fourteen – including a most amusing new friend called Leigh Fermor.

12 Badly brought up.
13 Famous nightclub *chanteuse*.
14 Collaborationist (with the Germans).
15 Lamb roasted on a spit.
16 The Prince of Wales was born on 14 November.

November 20th, 1948

Papa had left his guns in England last time we were there. He knew it was silly and I told him not to be lazy, but lazy he wanted to be. Every week I have suggested that someone should bring them over, and always he couldn't be bothered to organise the bringing although he knew the *chasse en Alsace*[17] was drawing near. So (O do take warning, my son) the last few days have been a frenzy of telephoning to Lord Sherwood where the guns lay, to Judy to collect them, to Purdey's[18] to help, to Bobby George[19] to fly them. The usual muddle and frustration ensuing the morning of departure – no guns, what's the good of going, chuck the whole thing. Purdey's had said that on Lord Sherwood's orders the guns were sent the day before to Cook's. Bobby George's minion called for them only to be told that they had been despatched by air to France. Every plane on the eve was met and searched. Not a gun – nor a line on the loss. Our train to Strasbourg was at 5.30. Rufus, Eric, Sammy Hood were all asked for the loan of their fowling pieces, and a pretty foul lot they were. I said to myself at 3.30 'I'm sure they are languishing in a customs shed at Le Bourget.' Quick, quick in the slow *camionette* to Air France's H.Q. in the Champs Elysées. A nice man telephoned O so slowly to Le Bourget, to discover in effect that they were there but couldn't be released without the requisite papers. That didn't worry me. In an hour and a half I could wrench them out myself, I thought.

As soon as I was at the wheel the *camionette* downed tools, so I had to run a hundred houses to the Travellers' Club. There I found Rufus, hired a car, minutes gone, tried to telephone Eric – out, Ashley – out, finally made an unknown secretary swear to ring up the Customs and say the Embassy guaranteed the red-tape-snipper. Tremendous sprint by outer boulevards

---

17 The shoot in Alsace.
18 London gunmakers.
19 Air Attaché at the Embassy.

to the airfield – no traffic lights respected – I arrived in hurricane vein and so rattled everyone, who thought I was due for a stroke, that I got the guns out with no message, I think, from the Embassy, in time to be back at the Gare de l'Est with ten minutes to spare. I was glowing with pride but I don't think anyone else was, least of all Papa.

Chantilly
January 26th, 1949

I've always been half hoping to hear from or of you. Now it's too late, I imagine you off timber-shivering today. I know Gibraltar. I don't suppose you make Gov. House – if you do look at the strange cartoons in the cloisters, look (naturally) for the monkeys and for nylons 9½, twenty if cheap. Loel turned up yesterday, recovered, bounding, full of schemes. He's got a new yacht which he's taking down now to the Mediterranean. I've told him to keep an eye open for *Cleopatra*.

The 22nd came Russell Page to stick sticks labelled lilac, syringa, etc. plus lots of roses in the garden, which forced me to neglect the Saturday guests, Lady Alexandra Howard-Johnson,[20] her brother Lord Haig and her ghastly husband, our Naval Attaché. Lord Haig had *fou-rire*[21] at lunch at his brother-in-law's account of how he marks down in a little book every ten franc tip he gives so that he knows that life costs him £7 a day. Poor Sandra, the wife – I see only the side Noémi tells me of – she cries and she cries and she cries and is quite unbalanced. Her mother, the F. M.'s wife, died barking.

In the evening came the Pattens and the charming Waldeners. She is young, English, Jewish, he won the Derby and they are

---

20 Later, after an acrimonious divorce, to marry the distinguished historian Hugh Trevor-Roper, later Lord Dacre.

21 Helpless giggles.

neighbours. I felt fine except for my poor knee and ate well. In the night I woke at three and groaned till morning with indescribable malaise and misery. I went to the loo with no hope of nausea explaining anything, leant over the basin and let out a noise that clearly woke everyone in the house, though the servants above were too delicate to admit it. A paper bag the size of a factory punched by a titan might have sounded the same. Greatly relieved, I went back to Papa's arms to feel as ill as ever in the morning. I had fever and aches and thought I cannot get up to face sixteen curiously assorted guests, but in the end my *noblesse obliged* me and of course once on the stage and its blaze and out of the shadow of the wings, I perked up and what a funny mixed salad they were – Madame Simone Berriau and a Dutch husband arrived long before anyone else. She is Queen of the Atlas on account of being El Glaoui, the Pasha de Marrakesh's mistress. She was an actress singer and he is a very successful so rich theatre owner. She it is who invites me to the Atlas. She swathes herself up worse than me, wraps fur and feather round her face and dare not take off her coat. Her husband's only use was as a recipient of a *Talleyrand* in Dutch.

Berriau, Drian[22] and P.L.W. all start on the great Atlas trip on the 15th inst. and are set on my going with them free in motors down France and Spain, but I can't be so long away nor under such a *compliment* to Paul-Louis. I shall suggest going ten days later by train and joining them in Africa – ten days in the Atlas and home – for the daffodils that take the winds of March with beauty.[23] I think slow motoring with curiosities might pall.

The answer from St. John's and St. Elizabeth's Hospital in St. John's Wood was so unusual for today that I read and reread. They say any day and so I've settled for Sunday. No one knows my destination but you and Papa and I suppose Cardinal Archbishop Griffin who I read is to be a fellow patient. White-winged nuns

22 Etienne Drian, portraitist and designer.
23 *The Winter's Tale.*

float around and I shall hear the bell that summons tired faithfuls to offices at all times. I look forward to it – Winston, Balzac, radio, patchwork, letters, diathermy, diet. Hope the result won't let us down.

London
St. John and St. Elizabeth
Monday, February 1st, 1949

You really are a pig-child not to have sent me any word of your departure. This morning I had the temerity to telephone Chatham only to be told *Cleopatra* sailed early last week. I shall ring up Liz tomorrow for news. I didn't want to telephone anyone but I am driven to it by the hardness of your heart or the tightness of your head or the hand of God.

Last night Papa landed his acceptance to dine with the Chambures on to me, and a cruel evening it was except for the *cuisine* which makes ours like a dog's dinner. I got the Governor of the Banque de France, Baumgartner, very nice, and a Mr. (Gentille) Alouette of the Quai d'Orsay – hell. Old Charles de Chambure, I suppose, saved it by never drawing a breath. He's been Ambassador in Russia of the Czars and in Rome under Musso. He knows me intimately and called me Lady Georgiana all evening, catching himself up and apologising and re-slipping, and he always tells me how his wife Marie will never forget my beauty hunting at Belvoir on a high horse. She'll be remembering the bells on my toes next, for she never saw me mounted. Marjorie and Letty used to hunt on very poor horses, lent or bought cheap as crocks. They wore brown riding habits – I don't believe other people did – billycocks, buns and thick veils and were said to go 'like smoke'. So the old man talked through dinner, through the move and on to the end, to me and the other lady bores while Louise was having a better (though not good) time with the men in another salon. My escort and I lost the Ambassador between the porch and the car. We were to drop him. We found him doing pi-pi against a plane tree at the gate.

28th. I gave up to fussing about my London retreat and what to take. Books, nightgowns, caps, shawls, a fine white embroidered wool bed cover (much admired), writing materials, pills, clock, the china Algerian, Browning, etc. It's all in, including the rotten radio that doesn't work. There was time for meals, so we lunched with the Charles de Polignacs where to my pleasure was Colette, the famous old writer. She flatters me and I flatter her a lot. She's seventy-fiveish with a younger servant-husband, a Dutchman. I wished I had brought a copy of *Talleyrand* to give him.[24] She is dreadfully crippled with I imagine arthritis in the hips – two sticks and a mass of shawls and rugs and coats and scarves of sombre colours, and protruding at bottom two very flat white naked feet, brightly pedicured. The other end (on top I mean) is in a cloud of smoke – hair – but to my eyes indistinguishable from a halo of true smoke – lovely. Then there are painted cat's eyes, the same top and bottom. I think we are both fascinated by each other's eyes. She pulled up her sleeve and showed me a little thread of pearls I recognised as mine but I had no recollection of ever giving them to her, neither had I missed them. I betrayed no surprise, only pleasure that she should wear it. She said the old Prince of Monaco (the fishy one) used to hold little octopi in the hollow of his hand and she thought it so charming, so did I. The others all screamed.

Papa hasn't been sober for two days. He dined at the Travellers' with those dreary old gentlemen. I believe he's the youngest of the gang. It's the Committee.[25] They dine very well, play a bit of bridge, enjoy it so much that at 12.30 they go off for a spree. This time at 2.30 they made for their homes, old Somebody Something at the wheel, and bless me if the car wouldn't start. See them all push-pushing till they got it to the river (risking strokes) from where there is no downhill. A passing car shoved them with its

24 My father was plagued by copies of *Talleyrand* in Dutch.
25 Of the Travellers', presumably.

bumpers – *resulta nada*. Another passing taxi was traitorously hailed by Papa who hired it and rolled in at four, very wobbly but so delighted with the fun he'd had that I lacked the heart to scold,[26] or to kick him out of snores to wake the dead and the Seven Sleepers and all adders with a jolt.

Yesterday I arrived. A very bad get-off from Rue de Lille. Passport, put carefully in basket, not to be found. Everything ransacked, books shaken, ashpan sifted, everyone blamed, Embassy warned to warn the authorities, found by Jean under the car seat in the nick of time. Wadey would have gone down on her own idea, fished it out and shoved it under one's nose without comment. These servants think of nothing. Journey uneventful, calm and expensive, except for no cabin and no lunch, glassy sea, no pick-ups, taxi easily found. 'St. John & St. Elizabeth, please, Grove End Road.' 'O.K. lady' and I arrived.

St. John & St. Elizabeth
February 2nd, 1949

This hospital is out of the National Health racket and Cardinal Griffin of Westminster is upstairs. The porter showed me to my room at seven when I arrived. It looked pretty small and gloomy and thread-bare, but then I couldn't see the outlook which next morning was revealed to me in all its splendour of wide gardens and trees pressing through large modern style windows each side of an angle and outside a spacious balcony. The walls are bare and dirty, an austere crucifix the only concession, meagerish bed, fairish linen and sordid bed-table, cupboard with no hanger, well-placed light, h. and c. I'll be all right. There's an armchair too, and a table that pulls up astride the bed. A kind and common nurse came and checked me in. Next of kin? Age? 21 guineas a week! Any false teeth? Any drugs? Temperature and pulse – Bovril – Sister will be round. She came

26 Browning again, 'A Toccata of Galuppi's'

round – an unsmiling ramrod of the old Guy's school. I felt a
probationer again, trembling before 'Strings' – trained nurses, so
called because their caps were tied on. Strings were called by the
name of their wards i.e. Sister Charity, Sister Eyes, Sister Isolation,
unaccountable Sister Theatre. They weren't old though they seemed
so to me, and some were sympathetic, even kind, without smiles
of course. Matron was naturally old and breathed sulphur and flame.

So Sister left me an old blue pill as a treat. I slept well after a
long and lovely read of *Madame Bovary*. I finished her off to be
ready for Winston in the morning, which unfortunately started at
seven, a nurse jolting me out of a deep sleep. You never see the
same nurse twice running, so they never learn your ways or care
about you, and you can't care about them in consequence. All the
young ones are the class of ward-maids, and remember absolutely
nothing. I wonder if it's the war or atoms, or the radio waves
harnessed through our bodies into our sets. I have to tell them to
give me my medicine, to tidy the bed or room, to take the tray
away – just like the servants. If I put Jenny to bed I look round,
open the windows, see the water and glass are near, matches in
case, no light in her eyes, etc. That used to be the joy of having a
nurse with a shiny white starched belt and cuffs and gleaming
apron. These ill-spoken half-baked sluts have no heart and no
head. Matron is a nice old Irish peasant, a Sister of Mercy, hooded
and draped in cleanish white, under-Matron the same. The rest
are 50 per cent nuns – one a dream of beauty, quite young, as
tall as Louise with her starched hood pinned up for action into
an elaborate *moyen-âge* coif. I must learn why she is a nun. She
looks radiant, so does little Sister Celestine though she's too shy
to speak. My beauty is Agnes, meaning lamb.

I've read Winston nearly to the end (it's my third day) and
lived in it panting and having to put it down from emotion. His
style delights me – always the child's word in serious sentences
'His Majesty's Fleet *lolling* around in the Mediterranean' and in
purest prose he tells the reader of his good fortune of being able
to sleep by his own will – however grave the situation, however

taut and terrifying the crisis 'I can always *flop* into bed and sleep and wake refreshed'. He was First Lord in 1914 and mobilised the Fleet (as Papa did in '38, thereby giving Chamberlain another chance to avoid war at Munich, for the mobilisation shook Hitler and depth-charged the General Staff). On the declaration of *this* war he was given the Admiralty after eleven years out of office. 'On this the Board were kind enough to signal to the Fleet "Winston is Back"' (Floods of tears). You'll have to read it.

I brought the broken radio back. It's obviously had a heavy fall which those varlets never admitted. They said a valve had got broken, but omitted to mention that even the carapace is in pieces. However two men-menders arrived after threats and bribes and took it away and brought it back. It's good enough. I scarcely hear the Third Programme but they said they never met anyone wanting it. I said 'Can I get foreign stations?' 'Nobody listens to them', they said, so I'm left with *Much-Binding-in-the-Marsh* and *Mrs Dale's Diary*.

One really feels in *The Gathering Storm* that Winston was born and trained and forced fallow and released for the great moment. No one in the Cabinet during those eleven years seems to have been preparing and learning and making contacts and assembling information, figures, technical detail, following the infancy of radar, magnetic mines, even atom potentialities, as he was and it was to *him* that the world figures came and wrote for his views – and beside all this he was writing *Marlborough*, building walls and a cottage with his delicately pretty hands, painting and travelling. What a paragon!

The juke box is playing the *Siegfried Idyll*. We once tried it as a duet. Like many another it wasn't a great success. Talked to Rai this morning. He was laughing madly. Liz is not going to Africa, so I don't suppose I will. Kitty and Charles Farrell go to Singapore. Papa comes over today. I hope he brings me a line from you. If you get a day off, go to Tangier. David will be there probably. Ask at the chief hotel (a Moroccan name like Mamounia only not) for Miss Jessie Green – a well-known

Englishwoman. Say you are mine and she will do everything to help and put you in touch with David. Papa arrived having left his attaché case behind with all my mail, but nothing from you he said.

John & Lizzie[27]
February 3rd, 1949

Winston says of us English that we hate drill and we have not been invaded for a thousand years but that as danger comes nearer and grows we become progressively less nervous; 'When it is imminent they are fierce, when it is mortal they are fearless.' I hope it's true of you – I don't altogether think it's true of me. He adds 'These habits have led them into some very narrow escapes.'

Papa's come, but I won't see him and only talk on the telephone. No word from or of you. What can it mean – you've never been as naughty. I've finished Winston this evening and feel lonely without him. I've plunged into another Flaubert, *L'Education Sentimentale*, but am sticking as in a bog. I'll have a course of Maurice Baring in between. There is an enormous apathetic pigeon on the bare tree at my window wondering if it's going to have quads. Pigeons in London used to be entirely dung fed, now with only iridescent oil to peck at I wonder they stay. Pigeons are always in towns – *rara avis* in the country – curious now that horses, their stable food, have been outlawed from the streets. Nancy writes from Paris – she has been to tea at the Embassy and writes before the story fades, but there wasn't much to it. Lady Harvey had rung up to say she had a cousin staying. An excuse to ask *her own* friends. There were only about five guests, but for all that tickets were issued for cloaks. There was only the cousin and two rawish new attachés and Barley and Cecilia and Kitty [Giles] wearing contact lenses. Nancy it seems

27 Hospital of St John and St Elizabeth.

had never heard of them and nearly fainted with horror. 'Under the lids, darling. It's the sort of thing that as a child made me not want to live.' Then there was a letter from Rosemary (send her a p.c.) rapturous about the New World and Truman and the inauguration parade, cowboys and girls, teenagers throwing cart-wheels, all the fun of the fair, but no letter from my only son, so no fun.

Feb. 4th. I'm disappointed about Cardinal Mindszenty.[28] I'm afraid he's even frailer than he feared he would be (to save his skin?). He seems to have recanted, wishes to support Church and State in future, pleads guilty, admits to having asked the U.S. Embassy in the person of little Seldon Chapin (Algiers colleague) to get him away by aeroplane – 4000 dollars offered. All the evidence is based on letters written and received by him, found buried in a canister in his garden. How were they found? Why were they kept? Is it a frame-up? U.S. and England have been officially refused their requests to send an 'observer'. That's this morning's news. I talked to Noémi the moronic about Jenny's castello. She said '*Il paraît qu'en Italie il y a de jolis petits coins.*'[29]

February, 1949

Your longed-for letter arrived this morning. Papa told me the day before yesterday it had come and was *en route*. O I did enjoy it and laughed aloud, a thing I rarely do (unlike you and Papa).

Sugar Daddy Weiller rang up. The N. African party is still on. He suggests my travelling with *la belle* Madame Teissier,[30] meeting them at Marrakesh and from there a week into the Atlas. I ought to do it. They are not quite my kind – if David Herbert came I'd

---

28 Of Hungary. The Communist government had put him on trial on 3 Feb., and he had pleaded guilty to all the crimes of which he was accused.

29 'It seems that there are some pretty little corners in Italy.'

30 Mary Teissier, married to the industrialist Lucien Teissier.

not hesitate, but will he leave his boys? I can't invite a bunch of them – if only they were normal and I could arrive with three swains all my own while Madame Teissier had to make do with Paul-Louis and Madame Berriau's Dutch husband.

To go back to Morocco. My inner eyes see this Atlas expedition as Chréa[31] and mules and cedars and long treks – the pack mules, a desperately long day of sweat and loss of direction and suddenly when thoughts of death by exhaustion and exposure weighed on one, the silhouette of a high Kasbah, trumpets signalling arrival of strangers, slaves, torches and all the splendour and beauty of barbaric luxury within, baths of rosewater, gazelles and fountains in my bedroom. Instead it will be American limousines whizzing one up canted roads to the doors of an Edwardian stone house, from which blares a radio, a blaze of light from the ceilings and all the discomforts of a second-class hotel. There's the rub, but I'd better go.

A lot has happened here since I wrote. I told you – or I didn't – that the *Evening Standard* was on the warpath. We'd scotched them with a lie, I thought, but three days later they had two paragraphs in the *Londoner's Diary*. I nearly had a stroke. 'Lady Diana resting', my whereabouts, 'Sir Alfred [!] tells me she's only resting', the price of the room, 'She visited a plastic surgeon before going in', 'She wears dark spectacles and her face is swathed in light bandages', then *my age*,[32] which I resent (stupidly) and a bit about my rheumatic legs – altogether too horrible and malicious. No one knew but Papa, who is no blabber. It must have come from the hospital itself, and we suspect the mother of a girl appendix opposite. She's a Mrs. McCorquodale and I knew her twenty-five-odd years ago and never could like her. The nurses knew she saw me going to the Diathermy Dep. and recognised me. My spectacles are put on to hide some acid I was given to put on my cyst that drags the lower lid down (it's done no good) and

31 A mountain village to which my parents used to go to escape the heat of Algiers.
32 She was fifty-six.

chiefly so that people like her should not recognise me, and also out of a kind of vanity that forces me to hide myself when all the aids are not there, even from the nuns and maids. 'Can *that* be her? That funny old thing', my inner ear hears them saying. The 'bandages' is my poor little bald-pate nightcap which I forget (its being so familiar) arrests attention.

Well, the poor nuns were dreadfully upset and felt the leak reflected on the hospital. Raimund wanted me to consult John Foster of S.H.A.E.F. and bring a libel action. I was for ringing up the editor and insisting on a *démenti*. There was no one in the office till next morning, by which time my poor pillow had counselled me to do nothing. Don't suppose it's libellous to be said to have had a face lift (I wish I'd had one), besides it was only an inference. If I'd got them to promise to put in any kind of *démenti* (which I couldn't have) they would have twisted it into another poisoned arrow, for their orders from their chief is never to spare me or Papa. What earthly interest is it for them to know where I am? Or to spend days snooping for so dull a piece? Why, three-quarters of the readers no longer know who 'Lady Diana' is. It's a lesson never to do things in secret. The result of it all is that the telephone never stops ringing and all the old mad fans like Ellen Terry's nephew, Bobby Craig, and Norma Terry the maniac who has troubled me for twenty years, ring and ring and take up my nerves and the nuns' time. Huge floral tributes arrive which I send straight to the chapel or wards. They are not in my picture of this week.

St. John's
February 12th?, 1949

Tomorrow I leave this charming establishment. There will be tears all round, chiefly from Nurse Jones who would die for me. She's a good, bubbling, warm, enthusiastic young woman that I too am fond of. The nuns will take it calmly. I'm told there is a ward here in which all the patients are nuns. I must try and look as I go out. They are all in their white coifs with white sheets pulled up to their chins, not reading, but chatting incessantly like budgerigars.

Here is some most sad and shocking news. Our Bébé B. dropped down dead but yesterday. He'd had a few warning little strokes but he looked so well and pink, *pimpant* and glowing, that it was difficult to think him unsound. He was at a rehearsal of J. L. Barrault's, fell suddenly and did not move again. Looking round in my mind, I can think of no *Frenchman* I liked as much as Bébé, and in Paris I am now only fond of Swiss Carl. With Bébé I was flattered and comfortable and entertained and really fond of him. One has to remember for comfort that it was the perfect death, not of course from a Catholic point of view, nor a true Protestant's who prays against such an eventuality in his Litany. He was a great hypochondriac and afraid of death, unable or too weak to postpone the event by avoiding temptations. The drink and the drugs were never put away in spite of the clinic weeks of detoxication and – sad to relate – these frailties had sapped his inspiration and effectiveness. The stage he could still dominate, but not his canvases, and every artistic money-spinner had copied to perfection his little facile drawings. O but he was lovable. I see him most vividly coming for the first time to the Embassy, hair streaking over his scurfy collar, shining little face as clean as a shower in the middle of the old nests of birds and beaten eggs and ash and scent that his beard was stuffed with, septic trousers, always their flies ajar. '*D'où as-tu ce noir pour tes ongles, mon chéri?*'[33] Jean Cocteau asked him. '*De Londres,*' he answered glibly. Once at a picnic in the forest of Fontainebleau he danced like an inspired Nibelung, lightfoot and *sans souci*. Think what the *bande* will be like today. I've written a sob to Boris.[34] I could never bear Boris but I had to

33 'Where did you get that blacking for your fingernails, darling?'
34 Boris Kochno, Bébé's partner, formerly secretary to Diaghilev.

write to someone for my own sake, and I suppose the poor sod will be distraught.

It's so difficult to think of nuns without their uniform – 'habit' one should say. I can't picture these old girls – or young ones – without their mobled trappings – hair cut to the root, otherwise like other women – me – so strangely different they are from us when dressed, so strangely different from us within – and just the flashy surface the same. This does not apply to monks and priests.

Feb 13th. Listen, beauty boy. I've almost settled to go to the Atlas. Now that I have your dates I would try to meet you in Tangier. What rollicking larks if we could accomplish this meeting, almost worth missing the crocuses that I broke my back and health to plant.

Chantilly. I had a moving farewell and left the hospital with Nurse Jones in tears. I distributed six jars of my own dear bees' honey, bought a pair of bedroom slippers, green, a pair of smart black shoes, a pair of dark green trousers, *un pullo vert rouge*,[35] a funny kind of cap. In the afternoon after a bite with Chips, who looked blotched and crooked as though he'd had a stroke, I went off shopping again. At four, whacked into drowned fury, I hurled myself into the restful luxury of the Leicester Square cinema, where I giggled over *Mr. Polly*, then to Liz's and Rai's, then to *The Heiress* with Liz and Peter Q. Then to the station and Brighton and an ideal taxi-man of sixty-five who talked about his clothes. He had a suit of good blue moulded to him for his wedding – it cost a guinea, and his daily drink at the old Bell used to be a pint of coffee (black) and a big rum mixed 'that kept the cold out'. 'The others they like 2 to 1s (2 gins to 1 whiskey).' Listen, I arrive Gib. on 24th or 25th and go to Tangier – can you work for the same dates for I could put you up in an Arabian Nights house belonging to Barbara Hutton.[36] Try your best.

---

35 Her French maid thought that a pullover, pronounced in the French way, meant a green 'pullo'.

36 American Woolworth millionairess.

Marrakesh
March ?3rd, 1949

The great thing is not so much new blood for refreshment but *being* new blood to others. I keep the table in roars. I'm considered the wittiest, funniest, most original angel that ever visited this dull earth. It's put the morale up splendidly, though it does no good to the knee. I'm a bit behind on my day-book so let me tell you briefly that we got off at mid-day on a certain Monday, that we were hours at the two frontiers of Spanish Morocco, that we ate ham in fresh breads and Rumpelmeyer cakes while the fools filled forms, that we drove through the clear radiant air, through fields of wild blue iris, past camels and poor donks and that we came to Fez at about sunset or 6.30. They made rooms somehow. The men slept together. We walked in the souks. The goods have sadly degenerated even since '44. When I think of the cheap fascinations of the '30s, the shoes and djibbahs and silks and leathers and dyes and corals – now it's really the refuse of European village shops, not a yard of real silk anywhere. It's a national unknown. Gleaming rayon is substituted, plastics, membraneous belts and bags in place of leather, cotton jumpers instead of djibbahs. Too, too sad.

Spices they can't change, and flowers and fruit. There are still the artisans too, hammering copper and planing sandalwood, the beggars and the filthy water-seller with a bell and tepid water in a bloody goatskin, but there's no temptation to buy. P.L. gave me an inferior dressing gown and Mary bought one that suits her fairness, otherwise no purchases. Next morning we did some mosqueing and souking and left at noon for the south by a mountain road. Lovely it was and not frightening, but slow enough to give us lunch at 4.30. What a strange place it was – *l'Auberge d'Henri IV* – no town, no clients, delicious food eaten on a stoop in the sun, washed down with good red wine. We sang straight through lunch, when Drian remembered that he'd a friend called Dampierre, a resident Colonel *en poste* nearby, so he was telephoned to and off we rollicked to Kasba Talla where the little outpost was preparing for a *Bal Musette*. The sweet fat Colonel in his cumbersome native cloak and his wife in her smart gent's grey flannels with jewellery, lots of female understrappers cutting bread and hanging up festoons. An accordionist was at once sent for. Mary and some understrappers executed a sensational Russian dance. A lot of brandy was drunk − I think it was brandy − and we whirlwinded ourselves away and drove till midnight brought us to the old Mamounia and the charming balconied rooms that look on palms and eternal snows.

I imagine it's the 3rd of March. Yesterday was a lark. Brilliant weather, very hot by day and cold by night. Simone was round by eleven to take us protocolairly to the Pasha. I've rather come round to him − dressed and swathed as an Arab, he looks very distinguished. The beggars at the gate, the splendour inside I like. The house we paid our first call upon seemed to be some kind of pavilion and not the biggest palace. He is almost speechless and one eye is now much lower than the other, but he walks too fast for me and, like all his tribe, likes the walk to be hand in hand or little finger in little finger. He showed us round his house, all built by himself but quite traditionally − the usual collections of chiming clocks, a bust of Winston and very pretty individual little bookcases for *Marlborough*, *The World Crisis*, etc. We left him promising to return for dinner at nine and repaired to the European guest house where I should be staying, but even Simone who lives there must see that the change from sunny Mamounia among my friends to the cold hideous dirtyish bedroom she can offer me, would be too much. Anyway I've laughed it off. So we sat on her sunny terrace and Drian said he'd like to smoke a pipe but that he'd forgotten his tobacco, so Simone clapped her hands for a slave to ask the Pasha for some pipes for me. A selection of all kinds were brought in a trice and other funnier ones continued to arrive along with a packet of tobacco with a picture of 'Prince Albert' (Ed.VII)[37] on the wrapper. We wandered across to another

37 Can this be right? There was, I think, a 'Prince Edward' tobacco.

pavilion – a stately pleasure dome empty of anyone – velvets, brocades, carvings, dense carpets, four windows open to the four winds, full sunlight, flushed faces and good humour. They are all pretty nasty about the one whose back is turned.

I've learnt all about Simone. Peasant background. At the age of fifteen and a half the heir of the château seduced her, and his family, furious and fearful for their son, did all they could to separate the lovers. She, *légèrement enceinte*,[38] eloped with him to Morocco, where they were apprehended by the police (orders from home) for *détournation de mineur*.[39] He was sent home guilty, while she cried and moaned and was pathetic and deserted. The right hand of Lyautey,[40] General Berriau, then married her. He was some forty years her senior. Not unnaturally it was the death blow for him and, dying, he put his child wife's hand into El Glaoui's and said 'Don't let poor Simone starve.' She went back sorrowing to Paris. The Pasha, also in France, called with renewed condolences '*et tout de suite il m'a violée*'.[41] That was all to the good, for since then, so she tells us, she is a free wife to him. '*Souvent quand il fait l'amour et c'est l'heure de la prière, il se lève, il dit ses prières puis il recommence.*'[42] She's pretty awful. Papa would die of it, but it's a great amusement to me. She reads us her morning's courier – one from Colette. One can't imagine the old man still being a love, though the lickety-split walk showed vigour. In the afternoon there was sightseeing and the great reservoirs and the tombs and the *souks* and always the snowy background. The private golf course too, unlike any other, green as Ireland in this tawny bareness – Coca-Cola in a 'Stop Me' at the door. He has seven sons – all *types épatants* according to Simone, and all loathing one another.

38 'Lightly pregnant.'

39 Child abuse.

40 Marshal Hubert Lyautey, first Resident-General in Morocco, father of French colonialism in North Africa.

41 'And there and then he raped me.'

42 'Often, when he's making love and it's time for prayer, he gets up, says his prayers, and then goes on with it.'

At nine we dined in the main palace – a lot of ceremony and groups of great fat Nubians draped round doorways. He greeted us at the door, rather dingily dressed in greys and brown. Davies makes his burnouses, djelebiahs or whatever they are called, but he makes them of lounge suiting and it's all wrong; Moors should be dressed in spotless white. He's got a splendid little bar – mobile, I think – like an illuminated miniature Alhambra. There were nuts and chips and kickshaws and little glutinous squares of hashish to sex you up a bit. Dinner very good, followed by '*diversions*' – eight fattish, pretty ugly women jiggled around with brass cymbals on their fingers and a man with the most primitive of stringed instruments. Then a chorus of boys jiggling too. I think the Glaoui must suffer dreadfully from the tedium of watching such shows for seventy years. The dance and the jiggle and the tune have not been changed for centuries and were never inspiring, but I liked it all right as you can well believe. I go on boring everyone with the word Tellawet, which is the name of his *château féodal* in the Atlas but I don't know if we'll make it.

Marrakesh, N. Africa
March 4th, 1949

It's the Moorish meals that get me down. Fortunately the nauseating taste of the oil saves me from eating some of the dishes, but some of the twenty courses are excellent. The *tortilla*, always delicious, and a certain chicken, soaked in tomatoes cooked with onions and honey, were handed or helped, European fashion. One estimates vaguely what one is likely to eat and restraint is easy but with the great dish in front of you, one picks on and on till one sinks under the excess. This happened yesterday – the second lunch at the guest house. We did some sightseeing and souking, but my knee and my fatigued digestion brought me to rest at six and I settled to stay abed and miss dinner. P.L. was anxious to see boys or girls dance in the *quartier réservé*, but the concierge here was so discouraging that the plan was renounced, so while he wrote some letters we ordered dinner for three at my bedside. I dressed up as a yashmaked odalisque on my bed, the lovely Mary padded the bosom and hips out with my sachets and jersey, veiled her face, kohled her eyes and played castanets (*à la danse du ventre*) with two bedroom keys. Drian put on a fez and a mackintosh and a carpet rug over his shoulder, so when P.L. came back the *quartier réservé* had come to him. This story has very little interest but it serves to show what infantile high spirits still obtain in our *parti carré*.

This morning was a London fog and got me properly down as it didn't try and lift till noon, when *la reine de l'Atlas* came round with a dashing son of Glaoui to take us to lunch with another son about thirty miles away. It was a very pretty *bled* (i.e. ranch or farm) with a severe house like a tawny unornate Doge's Palace. This son, less glamorous and gigolo-looking than the two others I have taken in, I thought delightful. The house was the simplest and in a way most Europeanised with bookcases as a background to the divans. It made me long for a bed next a wall of books. The hosts always start you off with a neat whisky as an *apéritif* – a thing I can't gulp. Champagne for lunch itself and twenty-two courses. Drian played the entertainer this time – really very amusing he and S. Berriau were with their stories. The Arabs laughed immoderately and genuinely. They have all been educated in France, so I suppose are *au fait*.

After our glutting and singing of highly indecent songs, full of *gros mots*[43] that I don't understand but have to pretend I do, we watched the lazy women picking up oranges to put in baskets that they carried away on their heads. The fruit trees are in blossom and the oranges heavy on the branches. Then there is the background of snow and through it all my poor knee. We were home in time to call on Madame de Janay who used to come to the Embassy. She lives in a minute house in the Arab quarter

43 Rude words.

and is never returning to France. We had the treat of a European sit-down dinner at a restaurant in the town – I ate a sliver of ham, Mary nothing, P.L. some salad and asparagus and Drian tucked into meat. Next a fiacre and a guide and two cloppety-clops took us to a small clean Arab room in some hidden part where three little boys of twelveish and their musician danced and their master led. Unnecessary to tell you that the bare beauty of it all, the extraordinary charm of the immaculately clean little boys who, I imagine, are taught like geishas the art of affectionate demonstrations and general charm (they had been part of the Pasha's troupe the other night and their old master pretended that they were allowed to dance for no one else) was made ugly by the 1000-watt bulb hanging from the ceiling – unnecessary also to tell you that I got it out and six candles substituted. Really it was very very pretty. The little boys' gay smiling faces, their kissing of our hands and burying their smiles in our laps, delighted me.

Tangier No idea of the date – it's Monday
[March 7th, 1949]

We are still chiming in harmony and unison (a paradox) and all goes as well as I have power to tell except for my poor leg which robs me of all lightness and makes me tired in a quarter of the time. We had a second Arabian meal with Menebi, son of my old darling, in the house I have often been to. The successor is more sophisticated and has suppressed the myriad timeless clocks and undecked brass bedsteads. He has laid two of the most beautiful carpets in the big hall – they look like desirable Aubussons and were made at Wilton. Jessie Green was of the party, which had been arranged by David and her for me and my friends. This of course did not suit Simone Berriau, the Protector of Pashas. It was exceedingly amusing. Jessie speaks Arabic as her first language and has dandled all the Menebis on her lap. Her first remark to

Simone breaking into French was '*Vous ne parlez donc pas la langue arabe, Madame?*'[44] Sim got the place of honour at the divaned low table pulling me down on her right. Jess said '*J'aimerais mieux attendre l'invitation de mon hôte.*'[45] S. won on this one because the host wouldn't even come into the room, though a group of brothers and cousins ate at the other end. S. went on handing titbits to Jessie to show patronage but Jessie held her own and got in some wounding back-handers. My *bande* said '*C'est tout de même joli de voir quelqu'un de vraiment bien élevé.*'[46]

Before the blow-out we'd visited first a crumbling villa lost in flowers and we'd called on an extraordinary couple half Belgian half American – crazy Hell's-a-Poppin sort of house. The bedroom boasted of a bed of silver clouds and cherubs, a big piece of verdure tapestry, one outsized macaw, one big white cockatoo, two grey pretty polls all uncaged, five or six dog baskets untenanted, and in the small bathroom opening off this menagerie at least fourteen tiny Mexican animals called dogs yapping from their communal box. Crucifixes, Buddhas, emperors' heads, *antiquaire*'s junk of all countries and epochs filled in the gaps. The garden was jammed with dangerous dogs and cats enclosed in an agreeable den to keep them safe from the Alsatians. There were a million pedigree fowls and there were unbuilt stables where the horses were due to arrive and be installed the next day. Sleeping Arabs strewn everywhere – very unusual, as all the Tangier residents are.

Paul-Louis is next to Papa in childish enthusiasm and high spirits and a great extemporiser of verse. He sings his snatches when he's not jabbering. He'll take all the teasing you can give him, which is irresistible. Mary's beauty is incomparable – the princess and the pea type.

44 'So you do not speak Arabic, madame?'
45 'I prefer to wait for my host to place me.'
46 'Still, it's lovely to see someone who has been really well brought up.'

Aboard the good ship DJENNE off Spain
March 14th, 1949

It's hardly worthwhile dating my letters, if what Papa writes me is true. 'You left Paris on February 23rd. Your first letter, written in the train, was dated Feb. 16th. Your second letter, still travelling, was dated March 25th. The third letter (you had obviously given more care to the question of dating) bore the superscription March 27th or 28th, 1949. You got the year right anyway. In No. 4 you are less meticulous, heading it "No idea of the date. It's Monday" which internal evidence leads me to suppose was Feb. 28th. In No. 5 you temporarily abandon the problem of time, but in No. 6 I gather from the heading that you are in Africa and that it is March 4th and still 1949.'

I'm told I'm to go to London with him on March 21st (I can't – too much planting to be done) and have some knee treatment there (quite useless for a few days) until you come back on the 25th. 'We'll all have a jolly weekend (where?) and go to *School for Scandal* on 28th. Return France next day and keep J.J. with us until he has to return which I suppose will be about 6th, on which day we leave for Madrid for a meeting of the *Wagon-Lits*. We stay there until Sunday 10th on which night I have reserved sleepers for Seville (!). We must stay there until Easter Day for the biggest bullfight of the year and we must leave there on Monday night 18th (sleepers reserved) going straight through to Paris where we arrive the 20th.'

Meanwhile I set the Duke of Alba a snare into which he has plopped. I asked him if he had a pull with a hotel in Seville, as rooms can't be got. Result: he's asked us to stay in his palace. They say that staying with Alba you drive to the bullfight in semi-royal state, like the King at Ascot.

Papa says the brave crocuses, daffodils and primroses are pushing their way through the snow, many more than last year. Good.

I was disappointed about not getting to Gibraltar. I got a seat on the first plane but could get nothing to bring me back. Don't imagine I didn't ring up the Air Com. Spencer (?) Gib. and ask him to send me back, but he said he wasn't allowed to take civilians (moments like those make one regret the dashing days of the war). I couldn't wait for a following day's return, as this good ship was due to leave at 7 a.m.

The trip to the south of the Atlas excelled all hopes. Let's see what happened since I wrote. There was a nice picnic arranged by me to Asni – a village and kasbah in the foothills. We had our delicious lunch of chicken and asparagus stuffed into light rolls, and then we sprang on to mules and rode up through the glistening air and shimmering olive leaves to the Kasbah. From there you look down, a few metres only, to the flat mud roofs of the village, with occasional groups of squatters picturesquely distributed. An old man invited us to tea and down we went through a warren of clean mud streets into a Christian *crèche* – mangers, kine and humans in draperies. Out of the *crèche* we climbed – a pole instead of a ladder – to get to the flat roof. Here we squatted on straw mats while the hosts brought us delicious mint tea. From the different roof levels came little puffs of aromatic smoke, and one of these chimneys blew us out a pretty little giggling shy girl of twelve. She was a bit frightened of being stolen and soon disappeared down her chimney again.

The great trip started at 8 a.m. next day at the Pasha's. Here we formed a *cortège* of four cars and drove slap into the Atlas. By 9.30 we came to an earthly paradise, a château Kasbah buried in blossoming fruit trees, olives, gushing mountain streams, green-yellow willows, buds and flowers. The little dependant Caïd was there to receive the Pasha and his followers and guests. His retainers, fifty strong, were lined up to salute their feudal lordship. We were led on to the sunlit court carpeted with rugs and took our places for *le petit déjeuner*. Same as *le grand*, plus porridge and drop scones and honey. I said it was not so unlike the English breakfast I remembered as a child at Belvoir, i.e. porridge, with sugar and thick cream (these last we were spared at the Caïds), next a choice of at least six hot dishes – kidneys, fish, grilled chicken, kedgeree, scrambled eggs, rissoles. These were often rounded off by a boiled egg for the robust. The permanent sideboard of cold ham and chicken, pork pie, cold game, a galantine and potted meat, was always there for the taking. Stratas of starch shaped into scones, buns, Belvoir fingers, toast and new bread filled gaps, and jam and honey smoothed it all down. (Of course I never heard the end of my thinking everything like England.)

We came to another son's, Mahomet's, country seat at 11.30 where we were immediately handed a bowl of fresh milk and dates – country manners. I forgot to say that through the little breakfast there was Berber music off-stage, and that emerging on to the big court after the meal there were a hundred women standing in a square clapping and singing and jiggling. The thought of lunch at 12.30 paralysed me into ill humour, made worse by Simone goading me 'to be nice' to the Pasha. The lined-up servitors outside numbered a hundred or so, the house was built high over a ravine, well watered and rich in fruit and oil and corn – most beautiful, though inside it had been Turkish-Bathed and Wagon-Lited up at fabulous expense. The poor Mahomet, having greeted his dad, faded out to deal with the twenty-four dishes. We had to look at the lot cooling in the corridor – no *apéritif*, I can tell you. Even El Glaoui I think was bothered by the glut of food and waved a few dishes away untasted. The second roast sheep, for instance, was repudiated and the *petits pois* (Paul-Louis's passion) were whisked away from him before he could finish the common dishful with a spoon, which shocked us at most meals.

Poor Paul-Louis made a frightful *gaffe*. You remember how I often laugh at the inevitable reference to the sheep's eye when Arab *mechouis* are mentioned. That somebody has to inform you how the guest of honour has to eat it is a certainty. I claim that in N. Africa at any rate it is not the custom. (I'm not drunk, but in the train on March 15th and it shakes.) So Paul-Louis to prove me wrong arranged with Mahomet behind the scenes that eyes should be on the menu. The unfortunate host, probably unable to tell his guest that the joke was in doubtful taste, ordered that a plate should be handed to me individually, on which rolled one eyeball, pupil down, and another static one in a bed of bleeding fur. I tried to smile through my disgust but the Pasha was clearly outraged and the offending squint was swept away with a gesture and his temper remained unhappy till our departure.

At 3.30 we shook all feudal dust from our feet and soared over the Atlas in the smooth Cadillac – P.L., Mary, Drian and me. The road was not frightening, very high, a bit of snow here and there. The foolish chauffeur Achille drives like a snail and to my liking. At nightfall we came to Ouazarzat and to a *gîte d'étape* (French equivalent to the resthouse of our colonies). I stayed in one of ours in Malacca once. There's a great difference. We had the cleanest simplest rooms, each with a shower and boiling water, delicious dinner and *accueil*, deft service, fresh smooth linen. From Ouazarzat on there is not one thing, house or person that is not part of the Berber picture – not an ad, not a pump, not a 'How could they'. A kasbah which forms a village was first marvelled at but the drive through the Valley of the Dades surpassed almost anything I've ever seen in surprising beauty. Of course 'surprise' had something to do with the gasps of Ohs and Ahs, and the time of the year too, for feathering and flattering and bedizening these clotted hundreds of pink and yellow rugged mud fortresses, crenellated and ornamented, were clouds of almond and cherry blossom mixed with the silver of unleafed fig trees. All the French administrative buildings and *gîtes d'étapes* are built like kasbahs, the barracks and the prisons too. The Berbers are generally on horseback, the men heavily veiled, against the dust I suppose, and women wear all their jewellery and silver and amber *parures*.

We lunched at a place called Tinertin and made some little excursions up valleys and back again as snow made detours impossible. That night we dined with a Resident-General at a place called Ksares-Souk. They could not put us up so we had to stay at a private enterprise inn called *Roi de la Bierne* – pretty bad, better say no more about it – no bedbugs but O dear, the drains. The next day took us over the Atlas again through Azrou to Fez. The day before had been too lovely and this second day was rather anti-climatical. Paul-Louis would drive very fast on mountain unparapeted roads and only yielded his place to the chauffeur when I cried. Lunch was gay. Mary and P.L. climbed trees after it and while we rested before dinner, this tireless man went out to the souks and bought five carpets and God knows how much embroidery junk. The bargaining, not the goods, is what he's after. His success in beating his fellow down to less than half the price asked stimulates him like strong wine. I bought a nice white fur rug for one of my bedroom floors, but nothing else.

We arrived the next evening at Tangier. We kissed Drian goodbye at Fez. Mary came with us to see a property of agricultural interest to P.L. but not to me. From there she went back by Arab train to Marrakesh and we finished our journey through the Spanish Morocco frontier. They take roughly two hours to get you through. We got to Tangier too tired and too late to do more than peck unanimatedly at a bit of hotel dinner. David was around and he had put freesias in my room. P.L. and I shared a suite, sitting room dividing and single bath. Completely compromising, but I'm too old and too tired for it to matter, and I do not think Paul-Louis has a shadow of *sentiment* (sentimental sentiment) for me any more than I could ever have had for him. I've been a splendid travelling companion, always mellow and smoothing of French susceptibilities. I've opened a few doors for him, but not more than he's opened for me; I've cost him a pretty penny and he can afford it, and think he's *very* fond of me. I've fought fatigue and boredom at times and won, that fortunately he does not know.

I'm attached to Tangier – it's a capital and not a tourist town. We took a cocktail in Jay Hazlewood's[47] minute Arab house – the prettiest thing that ever I saw. The tiny courtyard and different layers of roof all pricked with candles, the rooms and windows, the sills, the birdcages and witchballs all carried their burning candles. Nothing like the 'living flame' for lightening my spirits. It's like a hard bargain

47 One of the Tangier set.

to Paul-Louis. An *antiquaire* had given me a little pipe like a reed and a packet of some curious weed. It may have been hemp or hashish or marwarah or what have you. Two puffs from the doll's bowl of it and it's out – the pipe and the candles dissolved my glooms and gaily we took ourselves to the *Parade*, a funny restaurant run by Hazlewood. Flamenco singers had been ordered for the nonce and by good luck a famous Spanish dancer with her English lover was dining at another table and, in her coat and skirt, danced like only Spanish gypsies can. There was a lot of clapping and *Olés*. The party waxed furiously. There were bouts of Lambeth Walk and Reels. Hunt the Slipper was too difficult on account of my arthritical knee (not better but much worse), David's and Bat's[48] slipped disc and Janie Bowles's[49] tubercular hip, but we had a fine Sir Roger de Coverley.

Next came the Saturday Gibraltar disappointment. David and Tony Porson and I, only a little the worse for wear, lunched at a funny garden joint on the hilltop outside the town, and there was Jessie to take leave of at 6.30. Charming distinguished Jessie Green. She lives on £280 per annum and has a fat Fatima dressed in pink brocade to wait on her, a dachshund, a motor car, a garden of lilies and fruit trees and the grace of a queen.

=====

So, as she had hoped, my mother had wangled an invitation out of the Duke of Alba – the grandest grandee of Spain. The visit was only moderately successful, not least because my father's health was once again giving her cause for anxiety.

=====

48 Bat Touge, a friend of David.

49 Jane and Paul Bowles were distinguished American writers – he was also a successful composer – both basically homosexual, who spent much of their lives in Tangier.

Palacio de las Dueñas
Seville
April 13th, 1949

There's a little boy here of six months, a descendant of the great and loathsome Duke of Alba who tortured the poor in the Low Countries and descendant too of an impure love between James II and Arabella Churchill. He's called Carlos or Carletto, and Jimmy Alba loves him more than parents as a rule love children, because the tiny pink cherub represents true (as he thinks) blue blood, and that blood his own. We've had ten hours on end in his company yesterday in a cumbersome Cadillac from Madrid to Seville, so there isn't much I don't know about the Duke of Alba.

I sat between him and Papa. When Jimmy wasn't looking at his watch Papa, who kept his in his closed hand, was opening it to look at the time. When Jimmy wasn't picking at his face, Papa was picking his poor nose. Papa had coughed all night and been doctored with Argyrophedrine. I'd not slept a wink for sweating (with fear of his death) and consequently diarrhoea, so the long ten hours through the country of Cervantes – Castile – through narrow mountains and deeply down into Andalusia; the pause for a good lunch at a government-run inn, the mosque/cathedral at Cordova, the courts of the mosque smelling so strongly of orange blossom that one wanted to swoon and become part of the ecstasy – all these things were stained by apprehensions and listening for Papa's breathing and expressions. 'Why is his mouth slightly open? Isn't one eye more closed than another? Are his veins, those in his hands, rather swollen? I mustn't pull up his trousers to see if his ankles are coarse or refined.' Too silly. The night before had been as good as sleepless because of a new reason for my ill humour, fatigue and leg *défaillance*, namely Parkinson's Disease – progressive and paralytic, endured for eight years by Maurice Baring, who had an *agitans* added. It also brought slow death to Lord Wimborne.

How I run on. I like Jimmy. He's of another age, a long past age. He talks like I suppose Spanish grandees spoke in the time of the Catholic Kings — husbands and wives are put into male plurals, thus 'the Duke and Duchess of . . .' are called 'the Dukes of . . .'. For instance I liked him saying as we passed some municipal buildings plastered with '*Patria, Pro Patria, Gloria Patria*' etc. *ad nauseam* 'I disapprove of all that. One's life belongs to the King and one's honour to God only.' Rot in a way, for one might say 'King' means *patria*, but it didn't in the middle centuries — nationalism wasn't invented and Jimmy is still in Christendom. We arrived here at seven. What does one see of a town, looking wearily out of car windows? Nothing, but there seemed to be flowers and the overpowering smell of orange flower and in the centre of a maze of tiny streets we drove into the interior of this lovely palace, lost in roses the size of peonies and bougainvillea breaking over walls like great billows, lemons and lilies and court after court with fountains and flowers — really beautiful it is.

The servitors were at the door, the baby awaiting the granddad's arrival, the English nanny, respectful up to a point only, was at the door to present the chubby charge. The gracious Duchess daughter was also in attendance and we were shown to our rooms, each big enough and high enough to house a forest tree. Tiled floors, baroque wall decoration, Franco–Spanish beds and furniture, h. & c., uncompromising porcelain lavabos, cupboards in plenty that one only saw in servants' bedrooms in my childhood, stained mahogany deal with no pretensions, on the other side of the passage and anteroom, both hung with the period of prints and lithographs and daguerreotypes that I can look at for hours, are a row of Victorian well–plumbed bathrooms. All Sir Garnet.

Dinner at the unearthly earliness of 9.30 meant only Jimmy, his daughter and us two. His darling old sister can't eat at these early hours and so dines and lunches out and jeers at Jimmy. We picked her up at 11.30 on some street corner. It's hard to know what we are actually doing. Although one may have had the plans explained in English, one can't hope for the incessant changes that occur in an *improviste* evening to be translated. Anyway we left in a station wagon, owner-driven, and made our way with Jimmy's sister (not Jimmy) and the darkness and some friends, through the full-moon-lit street to the outer wall of the Alcazar where last night a certain Virgin was being processed. The crowd was very gay, no suspicion of religious respect or knees coming into it, but 'Stop-Me's,. of sweets and toys and general relaxation.

The procession was a revelation. It takes an endless time to pass as the huge catafalque which carries the Virgin, dressed in gold and jewels and hardly visible for candles in silver candelabra and silver canopies and treasure of all sorts, has to be carried by forty or fifty men who cannot see or breathe as they are underneath and covered by the valance. The human tread gives the holy figure a dancing progress, quite different to the effect of wheels. Before her goes in the same fashion Christ carrying his Cross, or before Pilate, or some other scene of His life, and hundreds of men all carrying candles in very high white sugarloaf hats that turn into masks with slits for eyes, all carrying real candles. There is fortunately no electric light to outshine the mystery. The Virgin's candles are so numerous and bright and big that one's eyes dazzle. Sometimes a 'spontaneous' starts a song in crudest praise of the Virgin, then all must stop till he has finished his Te Deum. Of course I wished you had been there, but Papa was quite good, and Doña Sol, Jimmy's sister, has a passion for the processions and goes on all night from one to the other. The next one we picked up at the door of her church where those gigantic processional chairs have to be manoeuvred into the narrow entrance. Sometimes it's impossible, so a man with a ladder runs up and takes off the Crown of Thorns and all haloes and then without an inch to spare it scrapes in and the crowd applauds. I enjoyed it very very much but I don't know that five days of the same will continue to satisfy. Today we have done some gentle sightseeing with the host – the museum and two Virgins in their church preparing for their outing. The rich lend their diamonds for her bedizenment, so soldiers with carabines guard not her wooden person but her treasure.

Palacio de las Dueñas,
Easter Sunday, April 17th, 1949

Easter Sunday, and bells pealing, cocks crowing, cats yawling, Spaniards kissing and kissing, the Duke's aunt bawling away into the telephone and Papa, poor Papa, snoring to drown all these noises combined. I don't like to rouse him although it's near eleven, because poor Papa's in a poor way, but it's best to start the saga where it was left off.

The processions of the Virgin continued day and night. In the hours of sunlight the candles are eclipsed. The secondary carried catafalque of Christ (either before Pilate or carrying the Cross or the Descent, always a many-figured group) looked a bit Lord Mayor's Show, but at night they are mystical and beautiful. Papa and I freed ourselves from the kind pomp of the Albas and sneaked into an open fiacre from which one can see the charm and character of the town, the narrow beflowered and freshly whitened trafficless streets round the Alcazar and Royal Palace. It's a little district where once we lived so long, so long ago.[50] The houses look into the miraculous orange-laden gardens of the Moorish-Christian kings and here the fountains still play although because of the drought it is forbidden. The Duke who has every colloquialism and usually gets them pretty right i.e. getting a move on, getting into hot water, narrow shave, etc. will call fountains 'squirts' and yesterday describing an orgy he said 'the champagne flew', not unnatural but funny to think of bottles whizzing through the air.

It's more than three days later and there is too much to

---

50 Perhaps a quotation. My parents never lived in Spain.

remember and put on the record. I'm in the train now in the Claret[51] district, the grilling sun is I hope ripening the blood of kings. Processions succeeded one another day and night. These gigantic gold and silver altars, much bigger than billiard tables, have to be carried by invisible carriers through needle's eye doors, so by these doors of their own church, outgoing – the Cathedral their target (ingoing and outgoing) and their own temple (incoming) leaves plenty of dangerous corners. The lower-class districts boast of unrestrained crowds, the applause is deafening. The Blessed Virgin might be Hitler or Sinatra. The extempore singers who bawl a call to prayer song are unheard. With the crack figures from noble churches, the crowds show tenue, total silence and all lights of the street extinguished.

So we found ourselves in a little private room, street level, hired for the nonce. It was Maundy Thursday and even the Duque had come to admire the million candles burning upwards to the jewelled figure. Papa sat on a chair placed on a little platform about three or four foot high, erected to allow a view to those not in the first two rows. Imagine my horror and his pain when to allow of someone pulling his chair further forward, his chair, pushed an inch too far, toppled off with Papa. Darkness, silence – except of course for my groans. I naturally thought him dead. We gathered him up off the stone floor. I could not see his colour or his shape. I did not think of his spine, but his poor nut I felt sure was cracked. He could not speak for a full minute. A doctor, or rather the greatest oculist in the world, the one who puts dead men's eyes into sockets of the living, was of the party, and by touching pulse and heart and looking to see with a torch if his ears were dribbling proclaimed him alive. Dribbling ears means cracked skull. Breathlessly he said he was all right. Shock had robbed him of speech, and sure enough he recovered enough to stand and even to walk to another passing of the most famous of the Virgins – la Macareña – she goes in at 2.30 p.m. (It was

51 Spanish, presumably.

366

of her that the Spaniard said that he had no faith in God but he believed in the Macareña.) When we at last got in at 3.45 I found Papa's elbow bleeding superficially, and his side very painful. We half suspected a broken rib and the next morning found him in really acute pain and totally immovable. A doctor was sent for. The *Señor Duque* was not to be called till eleven, but the young Duque found physicians, father and son. It was horrible to see them turn him over gently, turning him over on the right side[52]. . . They found two ribs broken and insisted on an X-ray coming to the house. I, thinking of the pesetas, said 'porque'. They explained in 'The Game' language that they must know by a photograph how to strap the patient. A few hours later the operators came with their immense and magical apparatus, but they strapped him in yards of adhesive plaster *before* the plates were developed. So it was a racket as I had feared. O he did suffer, did Papa, getting up and sitting down and he does still, though less. We went out again that night to see the Virgin of the Gypsies come over the bridge. I went for a nice potter in the afternoon and ate ice creams and sat (by hiring a chair as one used to in the park) in the cool Cathedral.

The four pretty young things who don't go to bed − Colin Tennant, Mark Chinnery, Caroline Scott[53] and Christian Carnegy[54] turned up, together with two other very pretty young things − Julian Pitt-Rivers and Pauline, Hermione Baddeley's daughter by David Tennant. We saw them at the bullfight on Easter Sunday and they, being English and tourists, had naturally found a place for Spanish dancers, so there we repaired from seven to nine and drank sherry and watched not super performers but quite good enough for our unsophisticated eyes, and one girl of such incomparable beauty that I had to take broken Papa there the next day and he was blinded by it. I should tell you too that on one of the

---

52 Quotation from *Frankie and Johnny*.

53 Later to marry Sir Ian Gilmour MP.

54 Later to marry Sir John Smith MP, founder of the Landmark Trust.

procession days I went to a smart enclosure built out before a Government building of sorts. In these boxes, hung with red brocade, all the ladies were in mantillas. The little daughter Duchess could never say the word 'mantilla'. She called it 'it'. When would you like to put it on? I shall put it on at six. My aunt is not putting it on. When the moment of putting it on came, two kind black women came, as though to lay me out, with combs and clips and brooches and they plaited strands of my back hair into tiny little snakes and made an intricate fortification that was guaranteed to hold a towering tortoiseshell comb and heavy black mantilla. No flowers they said because Christ hadn't yet risen, but all the other girls had flowers and bows too. I put it on again with a carnation for the bullfight but it was almost raining and umbrellas were going up and down nervously and I was practically the only one with it on.

In the enclosure where we took Laurian who came to Seville with the Infanta on a jaunt, the lady next to her asked if I was the Queen of Spain. Laurian like a silly said I wasn't – if only she'd said 'I think so' she might have started something. This story put my shares up a lot – others got the wrong ambassadress and told others that Lady Harvey staying with the Duke of Alba and was unexpectedly gay – no end of fun, beflowered and walking the streets, so gay, so sensational (so unlike Lady Harvey). I got very fond of Alba and left him Monday night with regret and resolves to go next year for the fair, if possible with you as I don't enjoy anything so much without you. Papa had weathered the night pretty well though he looks to be in acute pain. Then it was train time, and a dinner that you couldn't keep on your plate, so uneven is the permanent way, and a night and a whole day in which I got through a month's correspondence, and at 11.30 we got to Paris.

Paris was all that can be expected of it in April – sudden wealth, like a woman who wins the *grand lot* and runs amok. Chestnuts and fountains, splendours of all ages, the river, the shining bridges, the dense greenness of the *Bois*. There we lunched, in company with Jenny and a new protégé photographer. It wasn't a great success as Papa had a meeting at three the other side of Paris and *looked* like it the short fussy time we were there. The food wouldn't come and it was not happy. Jenny thinner, spottier alas! and going that night to Portofino. I went to see Nancy who had no news, though I gave her a mouthful. I had a bit with Louise. She has been having love dramas in Austrian mountains and with no less a man than Tony Marreco – Ursula's shake-off.[55] She seemed happy and well though starving as per. Another's love, even if not returned, has its charm to the ageing, as well I know, and she had quite the look of youth renewed that should be part of the lover's gift to you.

Here comes the disagreeable bit. I have torn up your cheque to Papa. I want please a cheque for £44.

20 original cheque
 6 journey to Paris
 3 losses at cards
 5 general pilfering
10 lent by Papa

£44

---

[55] My cousin Ursula Manners had been briefly married to him some years before.

12

'I saw some cripples this morning, which
makes me think I'm in the right place'

(CHANTILLY-PARIS-LONDON, APRIL-JULY 1949)

Three evenings ago the officers were invited to a party given by Lady Ross, who lives only a mile or two away. The secretary describes her as American, fiftyish, still very attractive. She was apparently secretary to Lord Ross and married him on his deathbed, thereby becoming the third biggest landowner in the British Isles. All the officers got plastered (one was escorted upstairs less than an hour after arrival) and many didn't stagger back till the next morning. Our dipsomaniac medical officer, who looks and talks like a dilapidated and debauched Noël Coward, has started a passionate romance with her, and gone off to Ross Castle (?) for the weekend without telling anyone. The Commander is furious . . .

Lots of love,

John Julius

In the early summer of 1949, it seems that we were all, in our different ways, whooping it up. Not that – for the lower deck anyway – there's much whooping to be done at Invergordon; but we had Denmark and Norway to look forward to, and both were to come fully up to expectations.

Meanwhile life in Paris – in marked contrast to that in London – had shaken off all traces of wartime austerity. It was as if the Parisians, all up and down the social scale, were determined to make up for the miseries that they had suffered during more than four years of Nazi occupation. There were no shortages, of food, clothes or anything else, while in England we were all still queuing up, ration books in hand. In Paris the season reached its climax with *La Grande Semaine* – the Great Week – in which every day, or every night, saw some fabulous festivity. For my mother, her family and friends, this culminated in the surprise ball that was given by her friends – not quite, as Nancy Mitford wrote to Pamela Berry, 'by all Duff's mistresses' – in her honour. Her letter does not make it altogether clear whether she enjoyed it or not. I hope she did, but I doubt it. She mentions her blushes. People who ask me about her always find it hard to believe that she was plagued by shyness; even entering a roomful of strangers was a sore tax on her courage. The ball as she describes it must have been an agony to her.

Chantilly
April 24th, 1949

I've got too much to do here – my bones ache with hosing the new planted grass four hours a day. This morning thanks to God it rains and works for me. There are workmen in the house papering my new bedroom. They've been there ten days instead of the four I anticipated. They've irrevocably stained two carpets with shifting radiators and letting them trickle. They spoilt two last year too. The room is a shambles and they sit in the window embrasure sunbathing and munching and sipping while I push that mowing machine round with my stomach as my arms are too feeble. Only Noémi and I do any work at all and the poor little *femme de ménage* Georgette, who was supposed to come on hectic days. She has now to come all days and has been given all the animals to feed because Daniel *a laissé crever une lapine*[1] and he's always going to a wedding. Mireille visits the gynaecologist tomorrow – goody-goody.

We had a fairly boring lunch party, off cold fish drenched in garlic mayonnaise, and took the Sunday walk to the *hameau*[2] where the deep-drinking *gardien* was sitting – a sodden Cerberus. Since the regretted death of M. Mallo[3] the houses are irrevocably locked. They all went home but Nancy and at 6.30 Sir Noel and Lady Charles appeared en route for Ankara, their new post. He looked *pimpant* but his poor wife is a figure of fun in daylight. Her face is so crowded with dabs of misplaced colours – perhaps I should not throw stones from my glasshouse – she looks like an old good-sort actress and her producer has told her to be careful of her vowel sounds, but she doesn't know *how*, so she puts three vowels for one: 'biearnisters' (sliding down the) was her best yesterday.

Barley came to dinner. Nancy told stories of early married life with Prod through shouts of laughter. It must have been

1 Let a doe-rabbit die.
2 A little cluster of eighteenth-century single-storey painted pavilions, on the lines of Marie-Antoinette's *hameau* at Versailles.
3 The previous park keeper.

nightmarish. They stayed once on the royal yacht of the Duc d'Aosta, correct and grand. Prod, plastered, came in at 6 a.m. and threw all the bottles of rare liqueurs from the cellaret in the ship's saloon over the gunwale to witty worm friends[4] on the quay.

Chantilly, April 27th, 1949

Very little to report. This morning I did a bit of hoeing but what I hoped would be an orderly patch with neat rows of Hungry Gap Kale is an Augean stable as big as a hamlet – thistles and nettles and roots of saplings and rocks. O dear, discouraged and frustrated again! Mireille visited a doctor yesterday to be reassured about her female organs. The report was excellent – clean bill – result a bad *crise* today – migraine, *douleurs atroces* and the rest of it. So instead of a Pernod we had lunch *chez* Madame de la Gare, watching the trains go out. Next I was fortunate enough to meet M. Blanchard, the *tapissier* – a rare chance as I was able to snatch from him the curtain material he has harboured untouched for six months. He was nice about it and said he quite understood. Life had become intolerable. No one learnt any trade, no apprenticeship – impossible to find workers – he'd become a *fonctionnaire*, working for the Government. Now I'm struggling to make the curtains myself.

The day before we went to Paris to the hospital to get Papa unstrapped. Most of his skin came off with the plaster. 'It won't take any more', said the doc. So it's just the bandage now and fewer clicking sounds (i.e. pain-saving groans).

The cow situation is acute. At a month overdue, I insisted on a vet listening for an accompanying heartbeat at the mother's side. Yes, he heard it but vowed that the cow could not have been to the bull till *late* last July, although Jean and Mireille (now less sure) swore it was July 1st. Then Jean, although twice ordered by

---

4 From 'Sitting on the Fence', by Nathaniel Gubbins, a weekly column in the wartime *Sunday Express* which we all thought hilarious.

me *not* to send her to the farmer's for her lying in, did so. Now to us a calf is born – today – and instead of having it to human view displayed among buttercups on the sloping meadow, it's in a sort of maternity home.

You have just telephoned – a lovely surprise. You sounded alert and gay. The weekend is a teaser. Papa's partners (he never knows what of) called Debroux came to lunch. The Walter Elliots are here, also came Prod and his sister and brother-in-law Golly and Simon Elwes. The Elliots I love in spite of such frightful ugliness, they're like accidents and like accidents one has to look at them. I'd asked the Admiral Lacaze, the 85-year-old *new* Member of the Academy who has stepped into Germain Martin's cold shoes. He refused but said he'd call in the afternoon. Four old, old gentlemen (one couldn't have been real) arrived at 2.15 (pudding time). I had to leave the gay table and sit myself on the *canapé bleu* surrounded by a classical semi-circle of frock-coated caricatures. Coffee, liqueurs, smokes all refused. Shouts of merriment kept leaking out of the dining room. My wimples and sombreros, trousers and pearls, paint and bare heels were not the thing. Hardly had they gone than very worldly Alvilde turned up with English escort and talked mundanities with Christian names to the uninformed, so I took K. [Elliot] and Walter away to the farm and introduced Walter as *Ministre de l'Agriculture* and we wondered at the calf and then took a bit of a walk to look at the swan on her nest, and at 8.30 arrived the Millards (Ann in unusual beauty). Then a tall man called Fenwick, a horsy neighbour, then the dear Hervé Alphands.[5] At 9.30 I could wait no longer for the final three – Mrs. Fenwick and Mr. and Mrs. (Czech) Walter Farr (*Daily Mail*) so dinner was all set. At 10.15 they arrived, straight from the hunt, three-corner-hatted, gold braid, muddy boots, very delightful, I thought. The dinner became hilariously gay, but Jean and Georges looked daggers and Mireille hasn't been up this morning – sulking no doubt.

Monday 2nd. The Harveys came to lunch, bringing Ava Anderson.

---

5 From the Quai d'Orsay. He a highly amusing diplomat, she a professional singer to the guitar.

Duff in his new library at the
British Embassy, 1947

Diana on the Embassy staircase

Diana on Pauline Borghese's bed,
the Embassy, 1945

Diana and Paul-Louis Weiller (centre) with Gerald van der Kemp (curator of Versailles, extreme left) and Serge Lifar (dancer, second from right), c. 1947

After dinner at the Embassy, 1946. Léon Blum, Vincent Auriol, Winston Churchill and Georges Bidault

Children's tea party, the Embassy, c. 1945

Château de
Saint-Firmin,
Chantilly

The drawing room (with Bijou)
at Chantilly

Louise de Vilmorin and Duff
at Chantilly, c. 1950

Louise de Vilmorin

Evelyn Waugh at Chantilly,
c. 1955

Diana and
Paddy Leigh Ferm◄
Delos, 1955

San Vigilio

Duff at San Vigilio

Diana and John Julius,
London, c.1944

John Julius (left) H.M.S. *Royal A*
Corsham, Wilts, January, 194

John Julius and Diana,
Chantilly, c.1949

Duff with Willow, c. 1953

John Julius
looks back on
his childhood

Duff and Diana at John Julius's wedding,
Sutton Place, Guildford, 5 August 1952

A wow it was, Oliver as bad as hoped for, Lady Harvey beautiful – but only I thought so – a faded impressionist, boater worn as a halo. Lady Anderson wearing the same headpiece, but tilted over her *intriguante*'s little eyes, looked really frightful, a thing for children to run shrieking back to Nanny. A very good smell came from one of them. I asked from which? Ava said 'Well I did put some *Mon Péché* in my hair' – her hair being a dead mat of dye. But she was exceedingly funny about Sir John Anderson showing his bull-dogs off in the Cruft's dog ring. There is a technique – you go at a trot holding high your exhibits' leads that their heads may be proud and upheld. Sir J. had his chance and missed it, so no prizes.

Chantilly
May 8th, 1949

I've been remiss – forgive – and here goes. Papa is going to have his poems privately printed by some precious press, organised by Ian Fleming and Lord Kemsley – no pay but fifty copies given which should cover all Christmas presents and many weddings. I tremble that they will be considered too unmodern (all the better for that in my view) but I don't like a breath of criticism where Papa is concerned. Half will be actual translations and the other half *called* translations like E. B. Browning entitles her original verses *Sonnets from the Portuguese*. I opened the old black tin box of Papa's letters to find forgotten fragments and got lost in the past and dreadfully depressed. You will perhaps read them one day. They are wonderfully happy letters – never a groan, the antithesis of mine. This week's bag is my dearest treasure of a glass and red morocco miniature library of classics – the gift of Maurice Baring. Papa took all the little books out to fill an upper shelf (quite unpardonably) and I suppose frankly scrapped the exquisite container. Another dear treasure – Major[6] himself, in

6 An Airedale dog, which I just remember as a child in the early 1930s.

grey Danish porcelain. It used to stand under a glass globe in that 'reserve' room. The globe is there unbroken and the dog's gone.

We go hand in hand to an osteopath, said to be a genius, Papa for his ribs and the bruised nerve in his leg, and me for my various racking pains. He's like every other osteopath, just a drain to throw money down. He cracks my vertebrae and glows with satisfaction as though a crack was a cure. Osteopaths have a single punishment and crimes have to be found to fit it, other-wise *resulta nada*. Papa has to lie on his back to sleep and the snoring has driven me to filling my ears with bright pink wax. This preparation is called Quies and was used successfully by the wakeful during the bombing of London, but don't imagine it drowns this noise.

Melanie has had her calf. It's a boy! (not that sex matters as I get rid of it at once) and we are inundated with milk – at least four gallons, and that's a lot of milking. There's no gardener till next week. We have Daniel, the baby Indochink parachutist, and a clod called Quarmi, a farmhand. The paths are all overgrown and covered with branches and twigs, *par contre* the grass round the façade is grown enough to look green if you lie on the gravel and look along it, and the pansies and forget-me-nots make it a corner of a foreign land that is for ever England.

The new gardener comes in a week. He's merry but there isn't one neighbour or *commerçant* who hasn't told Jean that he's a *vaurien* – good-for-nothing – and a robber of churches. I talked to his patron's wife this morning. She thinks he's first class and what I saw of his present garden looked most ship-shape so I suppose it's the beastly French hating to see a man get a good place. Madame Regnier came round squalling like a jay asking for money for her hens and wood. I have said she shall never get a centime from me till Felix divulges the name of the man he sold my motor pump to. He won't, so it's a deadlock. He fears I shall find out what he got paid for it. Jean thinks perhaps £100.

May 9th. I'm all alone. Papa's gone to Brussels for his *Wagons-Lits*; the more they meet the worse the *Lits* are. My dinner has been a cup of hot chocolate, my entertainment the Xword, the radio and writing to you. I was in Paris this afternoon and saw Louise back from a love affair in England with Tony Marreco. My old pal Prince Paul of Serbia, the Regent that was, I lunched with – wonderfully unchanged – liberated from first Kenya, then the Cape. He is so happy now and going to live in Portugal or Switzerland like the rest of the kings; and Louis II, Prince of Monaco, has fallen for the last time and that boring Rainier reigns in his stead.

On the boat to Folkestone
Friday, May 13th, 1949

I'm sitting in the Captain's cabin between Calais and Folkestone. I'll be in London by four, trying out a new route. It enables me to get to Salisbury tonight. David will meet me at Victoria and whizz me down in his car.

Last night Raimund and Papa and I dined with the Windsors in Paul-Louis's house rented by them. The feast was for Harry Luce.[7] The company was far from distinguished but the appoint= ments – my dear, the appointments! She's dolled the gloomy house up wonderfully. On entering one is conscious of the freshest, most elusive scent of flowers (an artificial product) that doesn't stale or die during the course of the evening, a cold perfume that seems to wake the spirits to innocence and joy. Wallis herself in fine repair, dressed in what might be the stiffest Persian black and gold kaftan with springing skirt off the floor and plain oriental neckline, more ravishing when the stand-by-itself material turned out to be transparent against the light and featherweight, and some very fine diamonds worn negligently. The Duke looked his withered self and never made head or tail of anything I said. The stairs were flower-lined, rather commonly as for a wedding. The dining room entirely

---

7 Proprietor and editor of *Time* and *Life* magazines.

candle-lit, footmen in royal scarlet, the faithful black Caribbean in the same livery. Paul-Louis's magnificent 'orse's 'ead of the Greek period carefully concealed for reasons known only to Wallis.

Eve Curie had changed her type – tender she looked and berry-brown, with no Abyssinian hairdo or austere army expression, instead glamour, coils and gentle eyes and smiles. Everyone else there seemed to be called Allen, except Geoffrey Parsons and wife and some other *Time* and *Life* or *Fortune* and Mr. Tony Biddle. The table had so much upon it that I got bewildered – Saxe Negro slaves and monkeys and fruits falling from Nymphenburg cornucopias and flowers and candles and boxes for toothpicks and cruets of course, and matches individual and cigarettes in gold boxes and five equal-sized knives, ditto forks in white Dresden china (I had to ask which to take for what and further blotted my copybook by using my side plate as an ashtray instead of a gold dish). The Duchess had to reprove me. Raimund made it all possible. I saw Papa doing a turkeycock with Murphy, the *Life* man who wrote the Duke's memoirs for him. Raimund excelled himself in funniness. He had a splendid piece about a *tête-à-tête* dinner with Luce. It is the object of the staff to make it clear to the boss how high is the price of living in Paris, and R.'s account of his dodges to get the bill up, the ordering of what looks cheap and is expensive, the simple compote in which he got half a bottle of liqueur poured, I can't remember the multi-dodges. When he told it, Teddie said 'Why didn't you tell the waiter to stick the price up?' It was very characteristic, I thought – of course Raimund couldn't have got it across his lips. Teddie maybe always does, or takes a rake-off.

The farmhand named Quarmi, who helps while we have no gardener, talks in a quite unintelligible way. Enunciation and accent and technical-of-the-land words allow me to understand very little of his message. The only piece I got *in toto* was when he told me that his daughter of twenty-five was in hospital with a fibroid in her womb. I told him not to be unduly anxious, it was most common to women and that I used to carry one myself. He replied '*Oui, mais Madame n'a jamais uriné noir. On peut uriner jaune, rouge et même bleu, mais Madame n'urine jamais noir.*[8]

I'll post you this and write from Wilton. Papa goes to Opio today. There's a man who's being tried by law for curing people of everything except cancer and V.D. with footbaths. All the doctors admit it's miraculous so I've wired Papa to bring me back some *Tisane Mégère*. To fit in any gap between footbaths and osteopaths I've consulted Dr. Salvanoff, Professor of the Universities of Moscow, Pavia and Berlin. He's near a hundred and guarantees me a total cure. It's a whole-time job – seven different pills always to be taken half an hour before a meal that I don't take, baths with a secret fluid added, private parts to be thickly vaselined before immersion, so many drops c.c. in such a degree of heat increased every second day. Tuesdays and Thursdays are sort of overtime days, with twice as complicated a regime. There are compresses too and a hot water bottle laid on my liver for forty-five minutes morning, evening and after lunch – rather nice that. I need hardly tell you that he attributes everything to liver. Jean's is in fearful shape – yesterday I think really because he feared to go to Paris on account of the socks Mireille would give him if she thought he'd slept with his wife. He told me that he was vomiting all the while, in the train, in the car, or if he walked twenty yards.

Chantilly
May 24th, 1949

Back again in Chantilly with new gardener (idiotically wifed) installed.

My luggage into France far excelled any baggage I've risked before. It seemed so formidable for the ferry train that, tired and with a heart faint from exhaustion, I got a man from the Dorchester to take me and my paraphernalia to the station. As he was not

---

8 'Yes, but Madame has never peed black. You can pee yellow, black, even blue, but Madame has never peed black.'

allowed past the Customs he wasn't worth his hire. The line-up consisted of a suitable suitcase, a butler's tray to which were tied two prints (very large) of nabobs, three baskets of plants for 'bedding out', a lot of earth attached to avoid wilting and consequently unliftable by me, the old basket very full of Winston's life and flower catalogues and last minute parcels, a basket with stick and wheels made only in England full of old shoes and strange pieces known in old Bognor days as 'improvised utensils' for the dairy, a hat, two large size skimming dishes (unprocurable in France), stray coats, a pair of new rubber boots and twelve quacking Khaki Campbells. It's nice to be able to tell you that the whole 'lot' went through the frontiers like a dose of salts and that the ducks kept all the passengers awake. They are only four weeks old but their lungs can drown the ferry noises. This trip, had the ducks drawn a quiet breath, one might have thought oneself in 1940 again. There were alerts, All Clears and tremendous artillery fire. Alvilde in the next cabin and I both thought we'd been, like the governesses at Trianon, translated back to D-Day. In Paris Jean was waiting with no bad news. It comes out as one discovers it.

Chantilly
May 25th

Mr. Wu was expecting me to lunch with Nancy and Christopher Sykes, whom he has engaged as a courier for his continental trip. 'Make a note of that, Sykes', he says when the Petit Palais or a remarkable glove shop is mentioned. Wu's books have made him so rich in every country that money is not thought or talked of. Everything has to be done in the tourist spirit of 1910. So in that vein we met them at Fouquet's bar and drove (to their disgust in my *camionette*) to Maxim's, where we had a rather inferior lunch in orange artificial light, with a lot of chi-chi and a whacking bill. I had chores to do and they had a Turkish bath ahead to sweat out their last night's debauchery. Christopher can't eject one word now.[9] It's not nerves for he's very happy as a courier, spending another's money with no questions asked. Nancy thinks it's his wife's fault.

O I forgot, we didn't make straight for our chores and baths but took in Père Lachaise on the way. We wanted to have a look at Nancy's narrow bed – the gift of Tony Gandarillas[10] one day when drugs and drink got him without resistance. So there she will lie in a little stone sepulchre between Tony in corpse and a two-month old son,[11] till the Last Trump. I'd heard for years of this famous cemetery, where great names are as common as unknown ones, but as we couldn't find a porter to give us a plan (there are ninety acres) we found neither Nancy's hole, nor Oscar Wilde's nor the miracle-working one, nor Chopin nor my darling Bébé, scarce cold. It must be one of our next outings. That night I dined with the same party at Rue Monsieur, plus the Colonel, but as I've started my whole-time regime I wasn't the life and soul, and thought in consequence the evening was a sad failure for all. Quite surprised I was when Wu said afterwards how much he'd enjoyed it.

Next morning I met Papa at 9 a.m. from Opio. On a lead he led not a miniature black poodle as expected, but the prettiest eight-month-old golden slip of a cocker, more sentimental and maudlin and silkily ingratiating than you can hope. 'Willow' is her name and she's totally untrained and Papa is so in love that he thinks of putting off his business trip to London next week. His trip had not been as happy as hoped. It had rained incessantly, but Loel had given him this well-bred puppy so the trip was worth the disappointments and the hundreds of pounds all the meals cost him.

David's House at Wilton. The next morning I was stirred out of my insomnia by the chorus of English birds and blazing sun. One of the pleasures of David's house is that you need not raise

---

9   He had a very bad stammer.

10   Erstwhile Chilean diplomat, now living in Paris. Much addicted to opium.

11   Tony's. (Not Nancy's, certainly.)

the voice to speak to those in other rooms, like a dormitory. All morning we marketed and I bought dozens of common plants (all easily got in France) weighing a ton because of quantities of soil to protect them through the time of the journey. I bought too a cumbersome butler's tray as a table and two fluttering prints too big for the suitcase, and some rubber boots and everything that was unpackable and unhandy. We called on Lady Essex, the great breeder of Maran hens, six of which Lady Pembroke had sold me as 'pullets just coming on the lay'. Devil an egg did they eject and Lady Essex wasn't surprised because she said Lady P. had no pullets to sell. When I unpacked them I was surprised at their outsize and Madame Regnier said 'Elles sont des vieilles',[12] but I explained that the English didn't cheat. It now appears they do.

Chantilly
[Dated May 24th, 1949 but probably May 27th or 28th]

Willow's charms have quite undone Papa – unmanned him. Acute diarrhoea mixed with blood is praised and she sleeps in a basket by his bed within touch and he gets up with eager energy twice a night to take her out though she does it on the stairs coming back. Imagine then the horror of seeing with his adoring eyes the little dog flash downward across his vision as she sprang from my bedroom window and thumped onto the gravel at his feet. She moaned and howled the howls of pain, while the Sunday guests Cora Caetani, an unidentified Russian, Hugo and Virginia Charteris grouped themselves round her like the dying Nelson picture. My throat closed with fear as I hobbled off (I can hardly walk) in search of brandy. When I came back, glass in hand, the moans had stopped and she was lying as flat as a wet autumn leaf. 'Is she dying?' I asked. 'Afraid so', they said, but she struggled force-fully as I forced the nasty stuff down her gullet, and in a minute

12 'They're old ones.'

she made a complete recovery, plastered of course and later drowsy, but really none the worse. The *premier picqueur* (not an injectionist but like 'picador') came and dieted her diarrhoea and all's well but the carpets. *Willow willow waley.*

Hugo and Virginia Charteris are all that one can desire in beauty and wit. They are deeply and gladly in love. On Thursday evening Nancy arrived in a hired car with Wu and Christopher.[13] I took great pains to fete Evelyn – best room, best wines, selected books and flowers. He is something left from the wreckage of my admirers. He used to tour with me in English *Miracle* days, read *The Wind in the Willows* to me, motor through Scottish glens, carouse with Nationalists (including Linklater *Private Angelo*[14] – later) in Edinburgh bars and soothe and flatter me. His coming here was an excitement. Dinner went all right – he's never easy – and Christopher stammers dreadfully, but we went to bed with unhurt feelings and I for one looked forward to the adumbrated morning plan of Senlis or Ermenonville or the Museum[15] itself.

At 7.30 a.m. it was drizzling and leading old Melanie back to her field who should I meet but Mr. Wu beneath his umbrella. 'I suppose you wouldn't like to lunch with me in Paris', said he, instead of 'Where are you going to, my pretty maid?' 'No, no,' I said, 'I've ordered a *cordon bleu* lunch, the rain is pouring. No, no.' We had our individual breakfast trays in Nancy's bedroom. The sun broke through loyally, but I could feel a desire on his part to be off and something was said about an exhibition at the Louvre that could only be seen on Fridays. I was able to deny this and add that it was shut anyway at twelve and we could have lunch at 12.30. A little later he said he did not know if he could keep his hired car till after lunch. At this I said that I would counter-order the meal and that he'd best be off as soon as he could, which he was. When I was out of the room he'd had the decency to ask

13 Sykes.

14 Eric Linklater, author of *Private Angelo.*

15 Of the Château de Chantilly.

Nancy what she would like. She'd cravenly answered that she didn't mind, knowing it was ill-mannered and most wounding to me. Christopher the same, but he had the excuse of acting courier and taking orders, so they left.

I told Wu a bit of what I felt. I told him with all his efforts to be a *grand seigneur* he's never been a man of manners etc., and when I heard their car roll away I cried; I cried with disappointment and a wounded heart, but Papa was so sympathetic and loving that it was worth it. I don't understand why it is that I always have a row with Wu, and with no one else do I behave so spoiltly. Perhaps my exceedingly painful leg contributed to my irritableness. It's worse than it's ever been. True, the Russian professor said the treatment would induce suffering, but I think he said it by way of insurance. I can't sleep my pathetic four or five hours for the outrageous slings and arrows. To be still hurts more than movement.

Chantilly
June 2nd, 1949

Today *thirty* years ago at this hour I sat under my wedding veil in the sombre morning room that gave on to the cobbled courtyard at 16 Arlington Street. All the family had gone to St. Margaret's and I sat like an *objet d'art* under a glass globe that was my modesty and waited for my father. I was dressed (too soon) in palest gold tissue, covered with lace picturing tall Madonna lilies. Later it became your christening robes, but during intervening years I used to put it on before going to bed on June the 2nd and run up a flight of Gower Street stairs to surprise Papa in your night-nursery, then his dressing room. On my head I wore a crown of orange blossom made of seed pearls, the work and gift of your earliest old friend Louise Piers. When Father at last fetched me his temper was short and his gills were white and his top hat had no jauntiness. We drove behind Mr. Price the chauffeur in a powder-blue

Renault car, and the crowds being enormous and slightly out of
the control of mounted police, Father lost his head and put it and
his trunk right out of the window and bawled the crowd out. Under
the church's awning a man dashed out of the populace with a
missive. 'Read this, read this before you proceed' he said. It was
the Ides of March over again and I read, fearing obstructing news,
only good wishes from a lunatic.

Thirty years later I lie at Chantilly feeling most hideously ill.
Fourteen pills a day after three weeks of totally innocuous absorption have at last caused a *crise de foie*.[16] Was this their object? *On
se demande*.[17] Last night was five years of purgatory. Papa snored,
the dog snored and panted and scratched. I took the maximum
sleeping dose, just not overdose, but it was powerless against the
noise and knee pain and bogeys. So this morning I let Melanie
stew in her own milk and sent for the neighbour milker. She never
turned up and at ten they told me so I had to tear down to the
field, and in a fine stew the poor girl was.

Chantilly, June 8th, 1949

Princess Margaret Saga. I'm sure she came to show the Harveys
her disapproval of their attitude towards us. She'd no other
reason. We don't know her, we'd nothing to offer her. At the
hospital[18] in white-gloved Matron's gloomy little den, unenliv-
ened by a bottle of pop and some sponge fingers, she asked me
if I lived in France. She was not looking as pretty as I remember
her at Buckingham Palace when we lunched after Papa's accolade. Molyneux had done his worst with a cinnamon silk suit,
some milliner had weighed in with a common little hat with
white pompoms. The inevitable white shoes were worn and I felt

16 Liver attack.
17 One wonders.
18 She had visited the Hertford British Hospital.

387

disappointed. The eyes and smile give her all she needs, if you are lucky enough to be the one talking to her. 'I wish you could have seen where we live. I did leave word at the Embassy how welcome you would be but I don't suppose you heard of the invitation.' This last was not said naughtily – I meant, in the general brouhaha it is natural. 'Is it too late?' she said in the Queen's innocent child's voice. 'Of course not, but there is only tomorrow and it takes almost an hour each way.' 'May I let you know in the morning?'

So little did I think that she meant anything but politeness that the next day I let Papa and Jean go to Paris for lunch, so by eleven when the lady-in-waiting telephoned to say they were coming at teatime, I was calling up every young man and girl I knew to help and tracking Papa and Jean all over town. Those I caught up with but no one else was I able to rope in, not even Susan Mary who would have helped, just Nancy, Papa and me, the Princess and Lady Mary[19] were all that mustered round a board in the picture room groaning under strawberries and cream, éclairs, kickshaws and hot and iced tea for twelve. There was the trousers trouble with Papa[20] – not bad though and I won. I argued she must have some fun for the *déplacement*. She was commonly but most becomingly dressed as an edible little tart. She'd been dipped into a light shocking pink dye pot, her shoes were black and dainty, her eyes and smile quite breathtaking. Lady M. not unlike Princess Eliz. in a beret embroidered with pearls (!) seems a perfect light-in-hand sister for her.

She might have been one of our own daughters – gay and talkative, funny and as attractive as a mother could wish. We made her talk and tell us her journey stories and good she was about the Pope. 'O he was ever so sweet. I was told I must curtsey to him three times. I imagined I should have room but when the

19 Lady Mary Strachey, her lady-in-waiting.
20 The battle of the trousers – whether she should or should not wear them – was a *leitmotif* in their married life.

door opened he was right there and I went – donk – donk – donk into his lap' (I expect 'donk' is the family word for a curtsey, don't you?). I thought it wiser to hurry things on so that she should want to stay so after tea I hustled her into the open Ford and took her through the grille next door to ours as far as the *hameau*.[21] I'd telephoned in the morning to have it opened but M. Fossier not being at home it was locked and barred, but she thought it fairy-like and romantic and the birdsong of 'God Save' and the sun, already low, spotlit her.

From the little mill we drove on to the Castle Cap, whose gates opened to her (not a soul about) and from there we drove into the courtyard of the Great Stables. We went inside and O she loved it. I pointed out those four high round tunnelled windows. I don't know if you remember them. They are deep as deep and strange oval. 'It's as though a horse had put his hoof through', she said. Louise might have been praised for the just-ness of the simile. Off home she drove, gay and I'm sure delighted with the outing. It had the tang of the forbidden. She had clearly been genuinely appreciated by disinterested people – there was fun and the three hosts were in a sense famous. Eric told someone reluctantly that she had said it was what she had most enjoyed in Paris. Next morning the French were telephoning to say '*Quel triomphe*'. The English did not telephone. The ball, they say, was disastrous, all husbands and wives clung together, never a good sign. Sammy's hop was gayer and they had Colette Mars.[22] End of Princess Margaret saga – she wrote thanking me for a handkerchief from Hermès which I gave her, a very hand-some little letter summing up the Chantilly delights. Nancy stayed the night and played canasta.

I never knew the date of the visit but the next date to tell of is June 3rd, the day after I wrote to you. *La belle* Madame Teissier

---

21 A little group of cottages with painted murals – probably inspired by Marie Antoinette's *hameau* at Versailles.

22 A popular cabaret singer.

asked me to dine chez Maxim's to celebrate a fiftieth anniversary of fat old Albert, the *maître d'hôtel*. Everyone dressed 1899 and general gala. It's my black hole is Maxim's, but having an actual dress of the period given me by Mrs. Patrick Campbell and worn by her, I suppose I couldn't resist the temptation to show off its ivory satin embroidered with gold baskets overflowing with forget-me-nots and spangled worked intertwining bows and ribands. Mary Teissier got me a period hat from Reboux to shade my shy face from the hideosity of Maxim's illuminated skylight. Paul-Louis was to be of the party and the Alphands and poor Lucien her husband and Papa who ran out. Looking in on Dolly to pick up newly arrived Olga, I asked her to send me a hairdresser at 9.30 p.m. as I felt I'd never make my childish hair stand up with assurance and assertion. The dressing was no end of fun. First the hat, tho' promised by word of mouth that afternoon, never turned up, but the coiffeur did (*le champion du monde*[23] he was – last year he made it in Paris and hopes to retain the title this year in Rome). With him came a *maquilleur*,[24] whose care I did not require, but I turned him loose in the hat and feather and flower and tulle boxes and told him to assemble everything into a hat. The champion really made a beauty of me and as correct as my perfectionism desired.

Alas! all the fun was in the preparation. You'd have enjoyed it so much. God knows what one paid to dine there but in return one got away with a porcelain plate commemorating the occasion, specially printed magazines, sweets, scent, favours of all kinds. There were very few really dressed up – Mary and I and about six others – but by the time the favours were given, consisting of first-class paper hats, boas, moustaches, toppers, eye-glasses – the room looked grotesque enough for us to appear the uncomic *femmes du monde*. The climax of the elegance was the *défilé*[25] of courtesans of the date. Introduced by Jean Cocteau in romantic and abundant

23 World champion.
24 Make-up man.
25 Parade.

words, they walked under spotlights to their tables. Beautiful young women dressed as dear dead women whose names you've never heard of and I never saw – La Belle Otéro, Liane de Pougy, Cléo de Mérode, etc. etc. The grisliest moment was when the *actual* Mistinguett,[26] aged seventy, as fat and deformed as an old sow, joined in the procession (was it luck or an arrangement – we never knew) and took a place at a table near us. The moment for deep laughter was when Paul–Louis donned his favours and looked like four Marx brothers in one and executed a kind of sitting dance on his chair at table – smiles gleaming through the moustache. The mirror in front of him seemed to please him, for he kept it jiggling for a long time without a vestige of self–consciousness. I was home by two – the faithful Noémi got up unasked to unhook and unpin me.

Chantilly
June 26th, 1949

There's a lot to tell you of *La Grande Semaine*. It's never been more hectic or more crowded into one glorious hour. For us it meant the Marie Blanche party for Yvonne Printemps.[27] Next night the Hospital Ball, a huge success. I don't know what it brought into the coffers but it certainly brought by tombola a signed copy of *David*[28] and the *pièce de résistance*, a diamond ring plus hand–some pearl, to the strong box of our Padre Dunbar. It also brought to the Duchess of Kent an evening of mad whirling pleasure till 5 a.m. To me it brought a moment of tortured embarrassment, seeing the organiser being bawled out by Lord Kemsley, who having paid for the performance and transport of Ambrose's band, found himself tableless. I returned immediately to the task of mollifying the Baron. No one had tables except the egregious Harvey, but we

26 Actress, dancer and singer, at one time the best paid female entertainer in the world. She was actually seventy-four.

27 Actress and singer.

28 My father's biography of the biblical King David.

fixed one up and I succeeded in making him forget. Paul–Louis, my sugar detrimental, escorted me from fireworks to cabaret. All the stock–in–trade, Suzy Solidor and Colette Mars. The night was superb, if freezing, and permitted of the garden in short doses. David and Rachel Cecil, our guests, were last out at 6 a.m. for lack of transport. They are not night birds. The modest Rachel was handicapped by not having brought any jewellery ('Really not a thing'). I lent her the trembling spray which improved her morale.

We came back next day to rest at Chantilly and to gather force for the surprise ball in my honour on the following evening. Not much rest, for the Duchess of Kent, fired by Princess Margaret, had proposed herself (with a view to irritate the Harveys) to tea. I got some White Russians, detrimental Sugar–Daddy, Fulco the Sicilian Duke, Charlie Bestegui and many others. The day was the answer to a prayer. Leila Ralli, a Greek and best friend of the Duchess, makes everything easy and charming. The Harveys have not once asked her. So the servants were pleased because we had Prince Paul the ex–Regent of Jugoslavia as well – and we were *ravis* and Paul–Louis was in another world, but in one of which he dreams.

A blazing sun rose on the 24th, Midsummer Day, and dazzled us to Paris, increasing my nerves with its beams. I can't remember how I got through the day. I had a bad fall two days before, damaging the damaged knee. I went to Elizabeth Arden to get ironed out and having no car had to walk from the Vendôme to the Rue de Lille, thereby undoing what good was done. In the flat I found Barbara Rothschild with her husband–to–be Rex Warner. (If you see his book *The Aerodrome* buy it for me, and buy any other you see by this writer, read them if you see them in libraries and tell me about them – we must know.) I've read *The Aerodrome* three years ago, I thought, as little as I remember, that it was diabolic, but I must have got it wrong – he's the gentlest of men. Will he be true? Barbara is so passionately happy. She is to be married next week, but his unscrupulous behaviour towards his wife and three children – his wife who is beautiful, Barbara's age and adoring, he has thrown away like an old glove – will he do as much for his new wife? 'The Colonel would never do a thing like that', says Nancy with pride. I wouldn't put it past the Colonel. I asked them to my party but they declined – too happy alone.

Then I dressed in my satin, the colour of the eyes of *les filles de St Malo*.[29] Frightened still, we tooled over to Tony Pawson's apartment. There the candles were lit, the buffet spread, the garden lit. A suspicious-looking chair, dais and rug in back centre lawn, and friends and strangers in profusion. Many English over for the nonce.

At twelveish I was invited into the green room. A lovely lovely spectacle was showing – twenty white-robed diaphanous girls of great beauty were spread on the sofa cushions *en parterre*. Some carried their unicorn's head[30] on a stick, others had grouped their emblems in corners. The heads appeared to be living, with faintly tinted pinkness of nose and blueness of temples, their manes were feather-blown and their horns wreathed in roses. Two sinister beasts were stamping around with stallion behinds and impatient hoofs, one as black as night, the other red as blood. Leonora Fini, the designer, wore one head and Ann Millard the other; weaving through all this heraldry and romaunt were two nudish dancers – one from the deep south – dressed in a few roses. I was crowned with a huge white head that hid my nervous face and gave me the confidence of the Obsolete. They led me to the chair on the lawn, now under the projectors. The virgins processed in, Maxine[31] lay prone at my feet, the great unicorns were my supporters, mantling my blushes. The dancers tripped, Jacques February[32] playing two rooms away was unfortunately unheard by guests or *figurantes*.[33] For me the moment was in the green room, once on the stage the projectors blotted out the effect. Maxine alone knew the story and

---

29 *Les filles de Saint-Malo / Ont les yeux couleur de l'eau.* A popular song at the time.
30 The unicorn was my mother's self-appointed emblem.
31 Maxine de la Falaise.
32 Jacques Février, pianist.
33 Performers.

knew what it all meant because she it was who had thought it up. No one else knew. She will tell me next weekend when she comes for the Chantilly Stable Ball.

Papa and I motored back through the pink dawn to Chantilly – Orson Welles mist, clear roads, no lights necessary. It was glorious and strange. The first chorus of birds greeted us at 4.15 when we got home.

London
? July 10th, 1949

I lunched alone with Pam who wanted me to warn Nancy that Gaston is in love and she in danger of loss. My instinct is not to interfere. One is more likely to do harm than good. Why cannot Pam write herself if she believes in meddling? There is nothing poor Nancy can do except to come bustling back, leaving her trip with Sir Oswald and Lady Mosley on their yacht, and to no avail. Gaston doesn't love her enough to be drawn back from fresh adventurous arms and from a potential bride and mother. One can only hope the young lady is nauseated by him, or loves another, or is divorced and not annulled.

For the Buckingham Palace party I wore the water-coloured dress worn for the unicorn ball and looked horrid in spite of the sparkle. We dined with the Heads[34] and four virtual strangers alone in a huge reception room at the Ritz, all too shy for the open restaurant. We had the fun of dressing Papa up after dinner – safety pins galore – and there the fun ended. The party like last year takes place in what appears to be a house of the dead. At 10.45 there were no cars in the big court, no lights, no interest. We drove round to the *entrée* (a smart door) – the same that side, no one coming or going; a footman opening the door puts the fear (or hope) of it

---

34 Sir Anthony (later Lord) Head and Lady Dorothea (Dot). He had been Minister of Defence, and was subsequently high commissioner in Lagos and ambassador in Beijing. Dear friends of my parents.

being the wrong night out of one's mind. You walk on down the endless passages, no sound, no sign of life, no smell of scent or cigarette, no ash, and at the last turn the hub and noise of a thousand guests covered in jewels and decorations, pacing leisurely the red-carpeted saloons and galleries under disfiguring lights.

The Queen[35] was radiantly beautiful in a straw-coloured tulle crinoline sewn with diamonds and hung with them and crowned with them. The blue Garter married the amber happily. She told us how kind we'd been to Margaret. O no, it was she who had delighted us. How sweet of you to say so. O Ma'am how pretty she is. O how nice of you to think so, etc., etc. The King very robust and Princess Elizabeth so lovely I thought she was Princess Margaret and wondered at her not saying something. She's as slim as a mannequin and has a look of Caroline. The Duke of Edinburgh gay and suitable. Quite early on I began to pester Papa to be allowed to go home. 'Stay and let me go', was the line. I couldn't find any of the people I can bear, i.e. David [Cecil] or Antony Head or Andrew Scott or Douglas Fairbanks because they all go to the ballroom and I won't because I don't want to be asked to dance, and if one won't dance one must sit on the tiered red brocade benches with dowagers and the Chinese. The Queen dances a lot and then she sits with her partner on a very wide though low dais which makes them gloriously conspicuous. They glow and bridle and preen and mantle. I watched Antony and Douglas Fairbanks put through this hoop and I sat with George Gage in the offing, waiting his chance. Just when he saw it they all moved on to supper.

Just like the Pagets[36], the family sit together with not more than two or three outsiders. The Duchess of Portland moved off alone. She's my godmother so I followed her, with my eyes only. To my surprise she walked deliberately into a corner like a punished child. Then she started to tread the ground. She's eighty-four and never smoked so it couldn't be the extinguishing gesture. The movement

35 Mother of Queen Elizabeth II.
36 The Anglesey family (see Directory).

then became that of a dog covering the traces of its nuisance and at last I saw the drawers appear on the pile carpet and the poor old six-footed Duchess had to bend down to gather them into her bag.[37] It used often to happen, but now I suppose they are not worn. Nothing – or the 'camiknickers' – have taken their place. Poor Kakoo looked too terrible and kept spectacles on. I had a nice bit (only one) with Admiral Troubridge and Guy Salisbury-Jones, now retired. It was 1.30 by now and Papa, enjoying himself, agreed to my going. We started to walk down an interminable gallery lined with people of the Services we had not seen for twenty years, all anxious to introduce their hideous children. It was there I spied a second table, not the buffet but a real table for ten in one of the drawing rooms. 'I will be good', I said, 'and try once more.' I proposed that we should pick up some pals and make our own party. I sat down while Papa went to collect. There were plenty scattered in that large salon. Alas! before he'd a chance Dick Molyneux, Lord Sefton's uncle and heir, at least eighty-five and stone deaf, plopped down beside me. The chums came leaving a gap round us two. O it was hell. It went on for half an hour and at last my trials were over and away we went.

Champneys, Tring[38]
July 18th, 1949

We got here sixish to be greeted with a message from Papa that he had landed at Deauville. I was 'signed in' and shown the ropes. It's a ghastly place is Champneys – red brick mansion suitable for asylum or institution. The patients mooch about *en déshabille*. They are neither fat nor crippled, so look like Bedlamites. One middle-aged man in a Jaeger dressing gown was playing with an outsize toy Spitfire in the fruit juice bar, another limber little patient ran jet-propelled through histories which couldn't be said

---

37 Quite simply, the elastic had broken.
38 Then known as a health farm, now as a spa.

to have interested him. After that I went supperless to bed. I couldn't read on account of the words swimming and coma. A tall fair girl, half nurse half maid, poked her head in and stared when I rang my bell at 8.30 next morning to know what happened. With no meals of course nothing happens. One hasn't to be ready for anything. She stared in an insane way and said she didn't know to everything. 'You won't get afternoon tea', she suddenly informed me. 'I don't mind.' 'No, but you won't get it.' 'I never have any.' 'That's to say you won't if you don't ask for it' then 'Are you a patient?' 'Well of course, what else could I be?' 'Could you tell me your name?' 'Diana Cooper!!' 'Oh!' And she left the room covering her face with her hand as one does to an accident.

At 8.30 a doctor called and said nothing. It was the chief, the Dreamer – Dr. Lief, poor man's Lionel Barrymore, respected like the Mahatma at Champneys, Tring. He left me a chit of paper telling me to report in the treatment room at ten for massage. Rather dull, I thought. The Charles Addams atmosphere increases as you get among the nudes and irrigations. They put me under a hot shower after the massage and rubbed salt into me – rather nice that was, and back I steamed in Yuma's[39] black satin dressing gown and my bald pate cap and Algerian slipslops, bath towel, rubber cap, book, specs and drawers in arm. The day looks long when you are back in bed at eleven and my head still ached too much to read but the radio was loyal and later I got better and read a Simenon book of short stories – all I'm good for – and the papers.

My room's all right, looking on to burnt lawns and cedars, no comforts but all essentials, radio and telephone plugs, light over bed, hangers. I shall not leave it until I leave for good. I graduated to Osbert's book, from which I shall rise to Winston's. Today is Monday (third day) and it's been colonic irrigation – beyond description horrid and humiliating. Twelve gallons pass through your guts, while a lady stares fascinated at the outflow. Next I had a sitz bath – equally humiliating but funny – two little baths in

39 Dress designer.

which you sit knees to chin, one very hot and one ice cold. You bear one for three minutes, the other (the freezer) for one. It's a struggle to jump from one to the other and you do both twice. It must be nonsense.

I saw some cripples this morning which makes me think I'm in the right place. My knee is practically well – unfortunately before I came here and we shall never know if it's the hot weather or if it's the diabolic Russian professor in Paris with his magic baths and his sixteen liver pills a day.

13

'I wonder if Dolly's up to her tricks again'

New College, Oxford
October 6th, 1949

This morning I paid a courtesy call on Isaiah, my moral tutor.
He advises me to spend these first few weeks going to every
politics or philosophy lecture I can, so as to see what I'm up
against. Then I must select one or two courses of lectures and
follow them seriously. But if you could see the list of lectures
– not a single title fails to strike terror in my heart. I quote three
examples at random: Selected Problems in Scientific Method,
Naturalism and Non-naturalism in Ethics, The Theory of Ideas
in Descartes, Arnaud and Malebranche. 'All right,' I said, 'and
what books should I read?' 'They'll give you a list later on,' he
said, 'but I'll give you a few titles now, if you like.' I took two
of the books recommended out of the library. Of the first,
Whitehead's Science and the Modern World, I have read the first
chapter, twenty-two pages long, and understood not one syllable.
It's very discouraging and robs one of all self-confidence.

All love,

John Julius

I had arrived at New College, Oxford, to find that my Moral Tutor was the celebrated Isaiah Berlin. I never quite understood what a Moral Tutor was, and I don't think Isaiah was any too clear himself; he was intended, I suspect, simply to be a rather vague guardian angel who would keep a fatherly eye on the undergraduate's well-being. Over the next three years I was to see him a lot and grew to love him dearly, but of moral tutorship I saw not a trace.

I had agreed, rather reluctantly and on my father's advice, to read PPE – Politics, Philosophy and Economics – but after a fortnight I changed to Modern Languages, choosing French (why? I already spoke it fluently) and Russian, which I did not, but had been studying on and off since the age of twelve. It was the greatest mistake of my life. My father had implored me not to. A foreign language, he argued, could not possibly be taught at an English university: the only way to learn it was to go to the appropriate country, stay with a local family and immerse yourself in it night and day. As to the literature side, that was positively dangerous; literature was designed to give pleasure, not to be the object of analysis and study. How right he was. While I was at Oxford I must have read some two hundred French and Russian classic novels; I have hardly ever picked one up since.

My parents, meanwhile, continued to live at Chantilly, shuttling backwards and forwards to London and holidaying in Italy in the summer; they also took the cure together, this time at Aix-en-Provence. In the past my mother had done this alone; it was only now that the state of my father's health persuaded him to accompany her. When he could bear it no longer they returned home, she to her continual domestic problems while he worked on his first and only novel *Operation Heartbreak*, and, later, on his autobiography *Old Men Forget*. The Venice Film Festival continued as a hardy perennial.

=====

Chantilly, Thursday
October, 1949

O undergraduate, I think about you and your Serbian prince.[1] How did you get on – how cold were you that first strange night and how generally apprehensive? I'm very cold today. It was summer heat at noon yesterday in Paris but today here it's bitter. Our journey was pleasant and uneventful. I found myself curiously exhilarated. The sun and Dover Castle never gleamed more beautifully – the cliffs at their misty whitest put a lump in my throat. A lovely new ship, *The Maid of Orleans*, was understudying the *Invicta*. I felt it was last merriment before winter.

Nothing new in Paris. Cecil waiting to be picked up by me, uncomfortably packed with crinoline in my dirty Ford. Off we bowled to the U.S. Bruces – Elsa Maxwell, Elsie Mendl and the Walter Lipmanns, Helen Kirkpatrick, Robert de Billy. I had a pleasant enough dinner of memorable food. Evangeline looked like a ravishing Sir Joshua in dead blue draperies of taffeta, Elsie was next prettiest. Next morning the horrible restless mess of our new life in France – Noémi's idiocy, the telephone ringing perpetually but not functioning, Papa swearing he must have a secretary, no orders carried out, dirt and chaos in charge. Barley, Papa, Cecil and I lunched at *Le Doyen* (badly) out in the sun. Papa sent his *oeuf cocotte* away as it was rock-hard, his cold partridge was also

---

1 Prince Nicholas of Yugoslavia, son of Prince Paul, had just gone up to Christ Church. With English as his first language and a superb sense of humour, he was one of my closest friends. He was killed in a motoring accident at the age of twenty-six.

dismissed as dry and tasteless, even the protest plate of ham and chicken ordered in *pique* found no better success and a mouthful of mediocre cheese was all that got down.

So we went to bed, and dear Willow was put in a very creaky basket by Papa's side and she scratched unintermittedly all the long night through. I was awake again at 3 a.m. and got no more sleep, so I know. Then the duck started waking France. I've never heard such duck-a-wauling. Mireille says it's because there is only one drake to satisfy the many – absolutely untrue. Then we walked through the park to Chantilly. It was grey and sad and I thought how much I missed you and I hoped you missed me, but you won't have time. John Russell,[2] Miss Europe's husband extremely amusing – lots of long messages from Aliki (who I've seen but once in a crowd). I must, she says, be sure to dine with her next time we are in London. She wants her side of the story[3] heard, I opine.

Now they've all gone and the dread moment has come when I must face up to life at Chantilly. The garden is an unrecoverable jungle. The gardeners must be sacked. Madame hasn't produced with all my resources one rabbit, one egg, one litre of milk, except when drawn by the Communist at the railway crossing.

Chantilly
October 8th, 1949

So we waited hours at Le Bourget, your godmother Essie,[4] Noël Coward and I and Papa. The delay was because the Heads' new baby was what is known as a 'blue baby' and no good, dying and bound for insanity, and it took on to die this very day, and the

---

2 Sir John Russell, our ambassador at various times to Ethiopia, Brazil and Spain, whose wife Aliki had been Miss Greece (never Europe) and was formerly married to Paul-Louis Weiller.

3 Of their divorce.

4 Ethel Russell, an old American friend of my mother's.

Heads, torn between sense and sensibility, could not come. The Scotts missed the aeroplane and chartered another. It's a nice party – Noël volunteered to do his new stuff. Within six months he will release a review *Hoi Polloi*, a play *Home & Colonial* and a film heartrendingly emotional – another *Brief Encounter*, played by Celia Johnson and himself.[5]

The songs were not good enough – one about Josephine had the commonest of all jokes about historical figures. 'Du Barry was a lady', 'Good Queen Bess', etc. Another about cats wasn't too bad. The best one is told of the Three Dames – supposedly Dames Sybil Thorndike, May Whitty and another – and why they were made Dames, but when he broke into *I've been to a* Marvellous *Party* and *London Pride* they were of a far far better calibre. He amused us till 1 a.m. blowing his own trumpet and hoping that he was concealing the fact, but he'd forgotten it when I was told that he was sitting next Virginia Clarke at lunch and that she was uniquely interested about the stage and its celebrities. No go to him, said he, he never talked theatre.

October 9th. Yesterday shone gloriously from the start. The sweet and tender Willow who makes my few sleeping hours more fugitive by scratch, scratch, scratching in a creaky osier basket, gave every sign of wanting to be put out at 2 a.m. so down to the kitchen I groped, finding no switches. She shot out into the moonlit fog and no calling and cajoling would bring her back. I waited, eating all the bits of cheese I could find and at last, barefoot and frozen, gave it up; leaving the back door wide to the burglars, I regained my bed. Not worth telling. She was there in the morning when solicitous Papa went to look for her at six.

The day was beautiful enough to forget the night and after marketing with the house party we were set to receive an enormous group for lunch. All the dahlia heads had dropped off and the last zinnias had wilted on account of Noémi forgetting to put water in

5 *The Astonished Heart.*

the vases. Prince Dimitri[6] brought a small flourishing medlar tree reared by himself, the which was planted ceremoniously and a bottle of champagne cracked on its pot, breaking the pot not the bottle, and Hugh Fraser came bringing a Miss Kennedy with whom he is in love, and little Greek Leila Ralli came bringing her own sleep that immobilised her on the stone steps for two hours in the midst of the hurly burly.

Chantilly
October, 1949

I dined with Mary and Lucien and Drian and Felix Youssopoff, murderer of Rasputin. Very old[7] and once I loved him, so near forty years ago. He was at Oxford and often wore, it seemed to me, cloth of gold, pearls and aigrettes. Those were the days before the bloody assault and before the revolution and before Aunt Marjorie chose Charlie and not him to marry, and he sang his Russian songs on his guitar. The other night, once we got the top lights off and the candles flickering, he looked his twenty-year-old self again and the voice and verve were what I remembered in the days of my infatuation.

Chantilly
November 4th, 1949

That ass Judy went on saying 'It can't be a cold, I've got "Tschuu-u-uu, snort, snort, snuffle, sobs, schlosh" because I've never had a sore throat or tickle.' She outspanned or spewed or outpuked on me all right, and has laid me low too when I wanted to be brisk and brilliant for David Herbert whom I found in

---

6 Romanov, nephew of Tsar Nicholas II, then secretary of the Travellers Club in Paris.
7 He was actually sixty-two.

Paris on my arrival Tuesday morning. London's single day I put to a lot of good with Oggie's help. Papa had a room at the Dorch. and it still is a bit of a sentimental emotion to return to the old defence. I can visualise the 'lounge' as it was in 1940 with half-painted women lying in horrible heaps in chairs with their dirtyish linen pillows under their tired cheeks. I wondered always *who* they were – not residents surely, for they would have had a bed in the basement or cots in the passages. Perhaps they came for dinner and claimed they could not be put out till the 'All Clear'. Then on any floor as I turn the bend to the left of the lift my throat fills for Emerald – her voice, her welcome, her little treats and curious presents, her utter lovableness. O dear I miss her so.

I made a perfect journey alone with my cold. Aspirin-calmed, I slept through most of the ferry clanking, my luggage, as usual, a bit bizarre – one small zip bag full of honey and coffee, two huge cardboard boxes of plants from Bulbridge and double armful of camelia tree branches, quite unnegotiable into any entrance or exit and filling a *wagon-lit*. I lunched at the best of the Chinese restaurants. *Superb*, with David, Alvilde, Janey Bowles and an eccentric American *née* Hungarian tzigane. I'd met her and liked her a lot in Tangier. And then Truman Capote. They never warned me so as to watch me flinch, but I didn't. A sturdy little pink girl of fourteen, with her blonde straight hair plastered neatly down all round, short for her age in rather light grey trousers and turtle-necked sweater with feminine curves suggesting through, and lovely little white hands and delicate chain ring and bangles. There you have Truman.

That night I had him again. I got quite fond of him – my love of freaks perhaps – and he's anxious to be liked and warm. I'll have to have another go at his incomprehensible book.

Remember the 5th of November is for us over here the *Saint-Hubert*, so with my cold smothered and smothered myself in a fur coat the property of Molyneux I go with Papa to Rambouillet and watch the hounds bay and hear the blessed mutter of the Mass through the strains of horns blown in harmony. A hound with leafy collar will be held by a Louis XIV-liveried hunt servant in front of the altar. The priest will tell us how God loves the herbivores to be hunted. The pack will be blessed, chocolate and brioches will be eaten. The Duc de Brissac will blow a solo on his horn, the riders will be off. We'll follow up in cars till we're bored and then we'll have a big fork tuck-in and so home to go dancing with horns on at a venerial ball at Royaumont.

Papa deep in writing a scenario which we developed one night when the Ford broke down on us in Paris. We tried to go to *The Snake Pit* on the Boulevard. We couldn't as the time was wrong and we dropped into a large luxurious café (one to be remembered for its comfort, ladies, first-class orchestra and its *consommations* in rooms where the orchestra is relayed – quite our place for a snack) and then got lost in working out the plot, based on *Operation Mincemeat* the true war op. of dressing a corpse up as a Colonel carrying documents re the proposed landings (naturally deceptive) and having the poor thing with its private pocketfuls, the picture of its girl, its decorations, washed up on some Portuguese beach. We make the corpse one who was a patriot and incapable, miserable by being useless in the battle, but in death vital to the war's winning. I think he'll write it as a short story first.[8]

Later. Papa came back a crowned victor, shot the record for the fourth Republic – 494 in pheasant, 150 to his gun. Carl was outclassed. Kitty [Giles] five months gone, sweet as pie, great losses to us when they go to Rome.

8 He did, though more as a novella, under the title *Operation Heartbreak*.

January, 1950, Chantilly

Papa's little surprise Sunday lunch for me was an old American sculptor called Jo Davidson who sculpted half of me as the Madonna (the wax mask which you are familiar with) and his monstrous though nice wife, and Mr. Bill Stoneman, U.S. journalist, christened by me 'Lava' *tout court* in the Blitz days because he over-insisted that London would of necessity become lava before the year was out. He had a monstrous and not so nice wife. Papa shook his cheeks[9] at Jo who was being admiring about Tito who he'd been sculpting and who had turned the charm on – also the successful corners of his country were shown to the poor sucker. Jo is a fine old figure, vital and lovable, and didn't mind the cheek-shaking and anyway was screaming so loud that he heard nothing. Most of lunch we talked about Helen Keller – did you ever hear of her? Blind, deaf and dumb. She now at the age of seventy speaks five languages that she can't hear, writes books, lectures and gives twenty hours of each day to working for the blind. Polly sits beside her (a lady) and taps out shorthand on her palm of what people are saying. Helen always says to Polly when they leave 'Don't forget your spectacles.'

Love from Papa who's just broken surface.

Chantilly
January 22nd, 1950

Dolly's hippopotamus daughter la Duchesse de Maille (the only issue of Dolly's minute loins and the collaboration of two huge Polish husbands, one *costaud*[10] Dane and a queue of lovers) gave 2,000,000 francs to an American lover, in whose trousers they

9 Lost his temper with.
10 Beefy, strapping.

were found (in cheque form, and that cheque not valid – in France a crime) at the Swiss frontier. So hippo is in trouble and Mogens telephoned to Nancy about it under his breath 'So Dolly can't hear me', he said.

Nancy is with us for the weekend. We came down Saturday and I've been hard at it. A new lease of life has been granted me by His giving his beloved sleep (which is it? I never know – is the sleep or the receiver beloved?).[11] So I've ordered a long wall of new planted peaches, to say nothing of an orchard. I've moved the furniture about like chess pieces in the effort to make Norah Fahie's room the Home Beautiful. The stairs are not very happily decorated and the corridor not at all successful and unrelated to the stairs in colour and style, and the carpet's liverish filthiness aggravates the mess. Stop everything – hold your hat on – Noémi has just announced the birth of nine piglets – two dead make seven. The fowls are laying too in the bitter white ice-painted *paysage* and poor Melanie is the size of a cowstall. Both goats are in pod.

I offered Mireille a motor ride to her home town in Arles near Aix. With tears she declined the invitation – couldn't desert Jean. '*Je dois me sacrifier, je le sais*'[12] and a lot more nonsense. Why can't Jean take a ticket and go too? Because it bores him no doubt and he hates to divest himself of the kingly robes he flaunts at Chantilly.

Papa's story progresses and Aix's peace should see it finished. Meanwhile exciting news from U.S. – offers, obviously Cecil de Mille from his Bible-inspired studio – for *David*. Now Korda bought the rights of *David* when it first appeared. You might have thought the Psalmist's life was clear enough in the Book for anyone running to read but no, for the second time the film magnates think it's an original story – or at least a pepped-up one – by Papa. Korda has agreed to relinquish his right and share the proceeds. We've asked 50,000 dollars. We might get 10,000 and if they give 20,000 that would mean a new car and some nylon shirts and bills paid off.

11 The Sleep (Psalm 127).
12 'I must sacrifice myself, I know.'

January 27th, 1950
Hotel Riviera
Aix-en-Provence

I've just written you a filthy postcard. I won't say any more because I've just seen the postman through the window wobbling on his bag wheel with the weight of his load – perhaps part of it is from you to me. We got the out-of-the-blue telegram from Graham Greene and his fine Sin personified[13] asking us to lunch at the Ritz which we did prior to starting south to be decarbonised. It was agreeable enough. Papa was *épris* by Sin and I by Graham's sympathetic approach, not by his appearance. That grows increasingly embarrassing to look at. The colour and the patina seem to belong to something guilty that has been *seared*, perhaps by contrition but I think not. They talk glibly about buying a house in France. He speaks of his wife and she of her children. I wonder why they cling to us? Perhaps they feel lost in France – no friends and cut off by language from the big literary guns who can't bark in English. Nancy was in a stew about her Bobby Hennessy film.[14] They've read it and say they gave her most of the story so they'll pay her £250 instead of £500, but they had promised her that when they told her the bare outline. She's fighting it.

30th. Hotel *Roi Réné*, Aix-en Provence. Where we stay until 15th February. Oh dear, such a dreaded announcement I had to make to M. Swellin, the proprietor of the *Riviera* – namely that our projected stay of three weeks in his hotel would be beyond our endurance. *Navrés, navrés*, was all I could say, and *trop animé*.[15] There's no word for privacy, which is the clue of our departure. After a memorably terrible journey down from Saulieu to Chalon in darkness, fog and skating conditions, and from Chalon next morning to Vienne actually skating on the *verglas* at

---

13 His mistress, Mrs Walston.

14 Could she have meant Bobby Henry from *The Fallen Idol*? He would have been a natural for *The Blessing*.

15 'Terribly sorry, too much going on.'

15 kms an hour and twice getting drifted ourselves and having to cajole and bribe men to push us out, instead of lolling and staring and having the fun of seeing nine *camions* cast on their backs, we got to our destination, so happily remembered in August and so cruelly austere now – a clean cool room, no curtains, a little heating, no armchair, no writing table, no lamp. We were driven to the lounge, where a lovely fire was surrounded with drinkers, card players, bloods of the neighbourhood all so gay and loud and happy and loudest of all the radio. How could Papa work? And if he doesn't work there is no point in his coming here, for he more or less ignores the cure.

Now we're in the royal suite in a hotel with revolving doors and *vitrines*. There's not a lot of heat as the rooms are Embassy height and the chandeliers and sconces give tallow-dip lights. The chairs are spindle and the water *un peu juste*,[16] but we're much happier because of the *privacy* and possibility of work. If it would only warm up it would be pleasant and just as I hoped – reading *Little Dorrit* in the evening and stitching the patchwork at meals and during the reading. I'm on to my fifth Gandhi day.[17] The doctor can't believe it naturally and Papa thinks he's a splendid doctor because he's told him quite alarming things such as tension seventeen when it should be fourteen, *le coeur un peu mou*,[18] and traces of sugar in the urine and the rest of it, he advocated drinking. Now I wrote to the fool before we arrived saying the patient drank too much – far too much – but being a fan of Papa's and having probably read *Talleyrand* he says he's perfect for his age and not to stop the booze on any account. A bottle of wine a meal he considers O.K. As for whisky, it never did any harm.

Of course the poor mutt has no conception of how the Anglo-Saxon drinks whisky. He imagines what is called 'a whisky' actually under two teaspoons in a beaker of water, not quarter of a tumbler

16 Dodgy.
17 One of her periodical fasts – no food at all, effectively a hunger strike.
18 Heart a bit sluggish.

of Scotch with a splash. So now he drinks wine at lunch which he doesn't at Chantilly and lies, poor fish, in a tepid bath for quarter of an hour and drinks the famous water in tiny sips and gets a flabby massage under a tepid drip-drip and is put to bed for an hour. I do only the massage and the tiny sips. The town is too beautiful. The great Cour Mirabeau[19] in winter trim, with men standing lightly on the topmost branches of the huge ghost-coloured planes to amputate them, is a surprise when one has always seen it coolly dark beneath the dense summery branches.

Nancy writes that Honks Mosley (all Dianas are Honks – I'm Honks Cooper) is bringing out an Xmas book called *Are you an Hon?* With questions like 'Would you rather be strong and healthy or witty and clever?' Nancy suggests 'Would you rather be canonised or mediatised?'[20] Dolly she says is in despair because a Perhapsburg has married into the unmediatised family of Ligne. A journalist came to see Nancy to ask her to write an article on English writers in Paris. She said 'Well, who are they?' 'You, Peter de Polnay and Koestler' was the answer. 'My screams rather annoyed him.'

Aix-en-Provence
February 10th, 1950
(and my tenth day foodless)

The cure progresses. My empty stomach has been made more difficult to live with on account of Papa's cold passed on to me in a more virulent form. For days it's lasted and it's still rumbling. Never again will I Gandhi except at Tring where we are all in the same boat and all the electrical and plumbing devices are there to function on the curing parts. Here in the land of *bonnes tables* and with this ridiculous old lady who strokes instead of be-labouring me, it's not worth it and makes it boring for Papa too.

19 The main street of Aix-en-Provence.
20 Don't ask.

I take a vicarious interest in the menu and choose the dishes most appropriate to his liver, kidneys and other parts, but he's eating more than ever before – spirits off and only a small ration of wine makes Jack a happy boy.

The skies have been rather beastly. The cold isn't piercing but has no spring in it. The town is preparing with zest for the Carnival. All the *forains*[21] in the mechanised caravans are here in their thousands. There is an arena of seats round the big fountain and there are switchbacks and the Star and the Caterpillar and a hundred booths for fat women and skeleton men – all the fun of the fair and I can't play alone and Papa is not a swing or a round-about. The shop windows are full of Pierrot costumes in yellow satin and masks and dominoes. We've done nothing. I've lain in bed most of the time reading *La Chartreuse de Parme*. I've only digested one volume out of four so perhaps haven't given it a fair chance but the summing up is *dull* so far. Yesterday I had the great treat of Louise's second instalment of *Juliette* – wonderful. It's a short book (three long instalments) written to be filmed. You'll eat it. I won't send it, but I'll keep it carefully for you. She should have gone by now to Paul-Louis's house in Strasbourg, for a year, so she thinks. I'd put it at two or three months but she never writes.

There's a nice market here made nicer by the niceness of the Frogs (the pets). They really are pets. If they were so disposed in the north I should be much happier. It's smiles and little *politesses* and winks and self-last all the way. I dropped my red pocketbook, stuffed with sterling, in the market. It was returned before I got home. There's a bit of *foire aux puces*[22] where I've bought for fr.100 a present for Auberon more useful than the one he gave me – a compact leather snuffbox prettily labelled *Lanterne à poche* and inside a collapsible contraption and candle beyond compare. I've also bought a sachet of faded pink satin and lace with green embroidered 'D' for fr.100 and a lot of strips of chintz

21 Fairground people.
22 Flea fair.

for my patches and a strong electric lamp that focuses down on to one's employment leaving the room in inky gloom, and a kilo of kapok to make a new pillow for Willow. It's the twelfth day now and I've had a cup of nourishing yoghourt.

My mind is full of election.[23] Speak whenever you can.[24] It's splendid practice and say the wrong word rather than 'Ah . . . or . . . er'. Elections gave me at thirty-odd an interest in politics and a vague comprehension.

Aix-en-Provence
February 10th, 1950

It's all nearly over. I broke the great fast and that makes luncheon expeditions possible, so we've been to Marseilles twice and to Cassis and today we go and look at a double-starred Abbey of St. Maxime near the Abbaye de Celles, where once we went with Papa and found an Englishman who opened that day and hadn't an egg or a sprout in the house. Since then he's earned a star in Michelin so I suppose we'll eat there and not in the Abbey bistro as intended. We've learnt to love two new dishes – *quennelles de brochet* and *loup flambé à la fenouil*. We read and read *Little Dorrit* aloud. Papa is tireless out of kind considera- tion but we never get even halfway. Then I read a book by drunken Polnay[25] called *Into an Old Room* (a line from Fitzgerald's poem ''Tis a sad thing to see the year dying'. Polnay lived and wrote the book in Fitzgerald's house, and we are never allowed to forget it.

Fitzgerald's *Omar Khayyam* was refused by the publisher and privately printed (250 copies) by the translator (or author we can say – it has only a very vague relationship to the *Rubaiyat*),

23 A general election had been called for 23 February. It was won by Labour, under Clement Attlee.

24 I never spoke at all. Politics still left me cold.

25 Peter de Polnay, Anglo-Hungarian writer.

quatrains (for that is the meaning of the word) being considered of no account in Persia, and a few given to his friends and the rest sent to Quaritch to sell. He sold them for a penny, and as soon as Swinburne and others discovered its genius, it was selling at a guinea a copy. Now that edition, as you can imagine, is price-less and fingered at Cambridge by the privileged as the Grail might have been by Galahad.

Every day the town waxes faster and more furiously *forain*.[26] If only you were with me I could enjoy it. The fireworks are going to be stupendous, but we shall miss them and be satisfied with the *défilé* and the hurly-burly. I shall buy a mask to surprise Papa. Susan Mary writes that Kakoo and Moucher Devonshire,[27] our most self-effacing duchesses, failed on their appearance alone to get into Dior's. Susan Mary put it right. She also tells me that Bill's efficient, modern-moralled girl-secretary can't dry her tears over Ingrid Bergman's baby.[28] The first day she had to be sent home, and she'll never suffer a disillusion so severe.

Nancy writes that Dolly's chauffeur told her *que Monsieur est à la mort*.[29] Mogens went into Dolly's bedroom and had a heart attack at 2 a.m. (Tony says because he found Kinsky in bed with her). He's dying of fear and terror like in *The Speckled Band* and the reason is that his brothers in Denmark have both got cancer and he thinks he'll be the next. Anyway at vast expense they lugged in the kind of telescope you see Mars through and gazed at his heart. Nothing wrong at all, so he's got up again and is painting the Duc de Doudeauville.

Same evening. We did go to St. Maxime Abbey and got actually into the bistro which looked inviting exteriorly, and Papa went so

26 Bucolic-festive.
27 The Duchesses of Rutland and Devonshire respectively.
28 She had had a baby by Roberto Rosselini.
29 That Monsieur is at the point of death.

far as to say *nous voulons déjeuner*,[30] but once into the dining room we were put off by the single gloomy men at separate tables and by a handful of gloomy whiny children, so with courage I said Papa was mad and he knew perfectly well we had friends at Brignoles and that when he says *déjeuner* he always means *apéritif*, and out we skedaddled without a backward glance. Papa's become a most dreadful moral funk. He'd sooner face really any disappointment, discomfort or misery than face up to a fellow man and cut his loss. We'd still be at the *Riviera* or back in Paris if it had been left to him to escape to the *Roi Réné*.

So we came to the Abbey of Celle and were greeted by Mr. Morris as though we were the only begetters of his success. The place, bathed in the first real spring sunshine, looked enchanting and the food was A1. The visitors book in which Papa had written a verse had been stolen, so he wrote another Rubaiyat and Morris gave us a big *parfait de foie gras* (he's sold £2,500 worth to Fortnum's) and a hideous hand-woven scarf which a palateless old spinster weaves so as to be monkish, and I think he's just the man to advise about the English restaurant which is always gnawing me. I think the opportunity of a lifetime presents itself at the next French International Exhibition (1952?). There is sure to be an English Pavilion and eating-house and that's the moment, with the Government's backing, to be allowed the running of it. Then if it were all the rage we might carry it on *en ville* afterwards.

Mr. Morris profoundly remarked that why Frogs pay so highly for their food is that to them a good meal is an entertainment as the opera is to us, so that £2 or £3 for a big dinner isn't much. I can't see it like that funnily enough, unless it's a picnic or cooked by the party with laughter and 'What did you do with the lard?' Besides I never eat but the tail end of a fish or a pig or an orange, so can't see two quid go out on that.

P.S. I wonder if Dolly's up to her tricks again. She's buried two

30 'We want lunch.'

husbands – one tied in knots of arsenic agony. She *is* naughty – poor Mogens does so enjoy life.

Aix en Provence
Monday, February 13th, 1950

Dear! What we have been through. Let me, though, before I make your blood congeal say that we think all's well. We had to go, protected by the *conservateur*, last Saturday morning to see the picture gallery – delightful, and nice examples of many schools and a full-face portrait of Sir Thomas More (saint and ours) first class, Flemish. Ingres, a lot of desirable stuff, and no Cézanne who'd lived and painted at Aix. The keen little M. Malbos had a room set aside of works of Cézanne's friends and the frock he wiped his brushes on and etchings from his hand and extraordinarily academic detailed student's drawings, as impeccable as Ingres. He had three watercolours, one I was proud to note given by our Ivor Churchill,[31] but no canvas. He knew it was silly, but stronger than himself was his desire to let us into his secret. That very morning he thought he had bought one from a man who had paid 250 francs. So he smuggled us into his den to have a peek. You never saw such an enormity, or rather such a *mesquinerie*; he feels sure it is Cézanne's wife and well it may be, like a picture of one's head coming through a hole in the backcloth on which is a bicycle or a kilt. The face is three sizes too big. He's going to give the seller 50,000 if it's genuine. Why, one asks oneself, did the purchaser give 250 for the daub? One might easily give £250 for the gamble but why 5/- to disfigure a wall? How funnily this letter may read in a hundred years, like writers who listened to the first performance of *Tannhäuser* and rioted with rage.

Papa and I and Willow piled into the Ford to make a bolt for Toulon and lunch. Halfway to Marseilles we stopped to open the

31 Lord Ivor Spencer-Churchill, a distant cousin of Sir Winston Churchill.

car, and as Papa (believe it or not) helped me on with my horrible new fur coat, we saw Willow had jumped out and already was the other side of the arterial road. I knew at once what must happen. I heard the 80 k.p.h. *camion* tearing round the slight bend, and was so certain that the silly thing would start across in her road-senseless way. Nothing to be done. I buried my face in my hands. I heard the grinding of the brakes and the rush of the engines already dying in the distance and then I looked and saw this pathetic yellow rag turning over and over then lying still and the yelling and screaming. We tore to pick up what we thought must be dead or dying and laid her still wailing on the roadside. A very little blood was dribbling from her mouth. Of course her general state was one of dementia, though she soon calmed down and reduced the yells to little moans. It was a miracle, for the car had gone right over her − between the four wheels − and she was not dead.

We carried on to Toulon rocking her, and she even managed some lunch, but the next day she was so completely exhausted and in pain that the vet was consulted. He thinks she's cracked her shoulder bone. That's the only place that hurts her badly, so she can't walk and won't try on three legs and really she is still too exhausted. Today she's what Nanny calls brighter in herself, but still she won't move nor will she drink, nor will she go placey, big or small. O what a miracle! She had endeared herself to us quite disproportionately during these two weeks, and we'd trained her into such obedient deportment and habits. She'll be as good as new I think, and much better by the time we get to Chantilly.

The great Carnival opened on Sunday. Really the Cour Mirabeau was so beautiful in the glistening sun − stalls of vivid colours, hats and masks and confetti and sweets made a chain each side under the huge skeleton trees hung with lanterns. Cold and brisk it was − not *Mediterranée* at all. We had seats in the tribune and I really think I enjoyed the procession as much as anyone. The Ohs and the Ahs all around us amused, so little was necessary to please them. '*Ah, regarde les jolis bouquets! Oh, le vieux soûl, comme il est drôle! Ah, les bébés – bravo les bébés!*[32] There were the huge chariots with mammoth figures – one's eye, quickly learning the huge proportions, saw the real living people as pinhead Lilliputians. Confetti thrown by all and if possible stuffed into laughing mouths. I got a throat full. Nicely dressed in green tartan and a red tartan scarf and red tricorne which carried a black velvet and lace mask in case, and new gloves, I was in gay spirits and keen to join Maria de Grammont who had invited us to meet the *toute toute petite noblesse de Provence.*

Le Baron St. Marc lives *au premier* in the Cour Mirabeau and there at four we found them and the Aix *gratin*,[33] sitting in a circle drinking badly made tea and eating delicious brioches. The Baron, whose moustaches of a white and orange mixture grew almost the width of his narrow shoulders, was soured by them not being half as big as his father's. He was deeply shocked at my having the confetti thrown at me, and that I should have got a mouthful outraged him to the point of trying, in vain, to make the promise to hie to the *Préfecture* and lodge a complaint supported by the name of Baron St. Marc. A coy English widow resident of Aix said to Papa 'There's a book I've read three times and I shall read it another three. Do you know what it is? It's called (pause) *David*.'

Today we went to Marseilles again to fill up with petrol against the big trek north after tomorrow. We had a spiffing lunch at a restaurant we're very attached to now, *Canupa Vieux Port*. I had a glass of hot wine because my fingers had unfortunately died, which warranted the indulgence. The best liver ever, garlicked and *fines-herbed* in a sizzle of butter, followed by a compote of orange in kirsch. Papa wolfed half a dozen oysters and a tasty piece of duck and orange too, and coffee for one.

---

32 'Oh, look at the lovely bouquets! Oh, that old drunk, isn't he a scream? Oh, the babies – bravo the babies!'

33 Aristocracy.

14

'Like the unsettled colour of newborn things'

SEPTEMBER 1950–JUNE 1952

I'm delighted with my rooms — two splendid little second floor ones looking out on to Holywell. They are perhaps a little noisy, but that's the only disadvantage. Do come and see them as soon as you possibly can, and make some helpful suggestions re decoration. I've got a piano, and I've bought myself with some of the £50 birthday present a wonderful portable gramophone, equally amenable to short or long playing records. I'm delighted with it and a hundred yards away is the University Record Library with five or six different interpretations of anything you want — and the score thrown in. The only pal here has been Nicky and, more recently, John Parker, who finished his trip with a hike through Austria and Germany. He spent £40 in six weeks. Now the pals are arriving thick and fast, all trying to make up for lost working time.

All my love,
John Julius

This final chapter covers more than two years. Apart from the death of King George VI there are no major events. My parents' life settled into the pattern in which it was to remain until my father died on New Year's Day 1954 and, although we kept constantly in touch, there was frankly rather less of interest for my mother to write about.

One subject of perennial interest, however, crops up more than once in the course of the chapter, and indeed provides the final anecdote: the Windsors. We saw them quite often during the 1950s – and every time we did so I thanked heaven yet again for his abdication. It was the best thing that could have happened. As King Edward VIII he would have been a disaster. In October 1937, less than a year after their marriage, he and the Duchess visited Germany; they called on Hitler at Berchtesgaden and they expressed fervent interest and admiration for everything they saw. Had he remained on the throne, and had England been invaded three years later – as everybody expected – there can be little doubt that he would have been reinstated as Hitler's puppet. It was a narrow escape indeed, and – let us make no mistake – we owe it in large measure to the Duchess. Poor woman, she was always reviled in England; but had she never appeared on the scene I hate to think what might have happened to the country. She may well have saved it, and the Empire too. Could she, perhaps, be the answer to the empty plinth in Trafalgar Square?

Whenever I met the Duke he seemed to me to be almost unbearably sad, and bored out of his mind. He never bothered to conceal the fact that he hated living in France. He would have been much happier in Germany, where he spoke the language; his French was execrable, and he made no attempt to improve it.

Even in English, apart from golf and gardening he had lamentably few topics of conversation. The Duchess was a good deal more fun, with a *penchant* for rather good wisecracks. (She is said to have said to him, at the height of the crisis, 'Darling, you must understand – you can't abdicate and eat it.') Late one night, on a nightclub banquette, she told me her whole story from beginning to end. I sat there transfixed, conscious that I was actually hearing it at first hand and determined to remember every word the following morning. As it turned out I remembered precisely nothing, but I don't suppose it mattered; I soon realised that she must have told it hundreds of times, and it was all in her memoirs anyway.

Ajaccio, Corsica
May 14th, 1950

My tulips were a wonder and a staggering surprise – large purple and pink and yellow birds on the wing, hugely feathered and strong. Now there's a lull and the syringa will be opening and Norah will be getting her seedlings going, I hope. She has no green fingers I fear, but Mireille's are as green as spring. Maud Nelson and an artist called Battersby arrived one night at Le Bourget. We fetched them to Chantilly and supped them and slept them so that next lovely morning the artist did sketches of the house preparatory to making a picture for the writing paper and taking measurements of the panels in the drink room. I have an idea of genius, if he can carry it out – in each panel a still life *trompe l'oeil* or trophies signifying different phases of our lives – Admiralty (dolphins, anchors, tridents, shells, wreathed horns), War (cannons, grenades, ruins, bombs), Algiers (camels, straw hats, flowers, roofs, gazelles), Miracle (skeletons, rosaries, gothicisms, bells and books, Death's scythe, wig paste and prompt books), Embassy (my Vendôme column,[1] gold plate of Pauline's, *Légion d'Honneur*, books, France–England alliance document), garden (rakes, trowels, flowers and baskets). Good idea?[2]

Papa and I rolled into our free *Wagon-Lits* and woke up at Antibes, Mistress Gloria[3] on the same train looking a picture and an obvious tart. The yacht *Sea Huntress* is really delightful – *silent* and spacious, and a steward suitably called Trim and good old Loel only wanting others to be happy. He succeeds and I am very happy. I do not think he'd succeed so well if I hadn't thought of bringing Ed Stanley along. Ed laughed at Prod for having been a hospital nurse and a banker and everything that is mentioned but he's no better himself. He's always seen, heard, smelt, felt and tasted everything and if he really can't think of an answer he says 'I *used* to know.' Still I love him. Loel is his own captain which adds charm and keeps him on the bridge in spite of the fact that there is a robot pilot that can be trusted. Ed said goodbye to his three blonde girls and off we steamed at five on the eleventh.

A breeze freshening quickly livened up the boat rather too much, and Gloria quickly swallowed the new miracle seasick drug dramamine. I refused, but during dinner I felt none too dapper, so swallowed the pill and in ten minutes was right as a trivet. Canasta fills dull moments. The twelfth we woke in Calvi – most beautiful, sun and snow mountains, really picturesque little town and a citadel smothered in wild flowers. What early May can do to any place, Glasgow even! And what it does to the harsh high

---

1 A wonderfully dotty model of the column in the Place Vendôme; the statue of Napoleon on the top could be dressed in three different sets of clothes. It was a present from Louise; I longed for it and was furious when my mother left it to Paul-Louis Weiller.

2 Martin Battersby's panels were a great success, not only at Chantilly but later when my mother moved to London. Alas, after her death none of the family had room for them. They are now in storage at Belvoir Castle.

3 Gloria Rubio, former mistress of my father and now married to Loel Guinness.

bastions and crumbling higgledy-piggledy houses soaring up in disorder is miraculous. I held my breath for the blue and yellow wealth of flowers. The beauty was surpassed next day when we sailed into a deep gulf called Porto. There at the mouth of the romantic river was a scene that must have made Captain Cook open his eyes wider – so beautiful – huge eucalyptus trees and junglish virginity – no sign of man until a little dancing dug-out boat came laughing alongside holding Tarzan and a young half-naked girl. They didn't stay to speak and I wondered if I had really seen them.

We walked up the river. I shall remember it always – myrtle and cistus in bloom (called interestingly enough *maquis*[4]), asphodel and flowers without a name and wild thyme underfoot. In the afternoon we took leave of lovely Porto and by evening reached Ajaccio, founded by Ajax (I wore asphodel in my black shirt for his memory). Dinner ashore – quite a lark – and this morning we have done all we can about Napoleon – *maison natale* and tomb of Madame Mère and and now I'm sitting, my *pastis* to hand, writing to my dearest son and wish, O so much, he was here. Just bought some whitebait in the market to relieve the monotony of ship's tins. I'll go and look for some red pepper.

Chantilly
May 29th, 1950

I made a funny joke – a rarity for me – on the yacht. We were discussing the name for Loel's new ship – *Diana? Gloria? Gloria Mundi?* 'Better', said I, 'call it *Sick Transit.*' We listened, Daphne Bath and Xan Fielding her boyfriend (a parachuting Adonis alas half her age), to the Derby on the radio. They backed eight horses both ways – twenty-four chances – and not one of their selections was

---

4 The word *maquis*, literally 'scrub', took on a new meaning during the war when it was applied to the French Resistance.

mentioned by the commentator after the 'They're off'. Joe Alsop[5] yesterday told me of larks at Breccles – you and Isaiah and the singing and the brilliant fun. Does Isaiah like you? I hope so. I think he's like diamond Dr Dolittle, so brilliant and so tenderly good.

Sachie and Georgia[6] and Moira Shearer, accompanied by the Hamish Hamiltons, were here the other day for lunch. Moira, one of Sachie's loves now alas for him married, is most exotically beautiful – real scarlet hair and ashen colouring and huge murky blue eyes like the unsettled colour of newborn things and of a slenderness to break and to snap like a tulip, and she a Scotch lassie. Sachie said of a most hideous bore who had been killed and when asked how 'Well, you'd hardly believe it, but he was shot *accidentally.*'

Chantilly
September 1950

Papa returned late from shooting. I'd been happily in bed and had just begun to imagine him shot and no one with the nerve to tell me when in he puffed having met with his usual mischance. On their way to the meet some 100 kms away a stone, invisible to man, had struck with pistolic report the *camionette*'s windscreen. Complete blackout for the driver, glass in crazy pavement and clouded at that. They backed down to a village using the door as windscreen and the glass was cut out to allow the hurricane of 60 m.p.h. in to bite into their flesh. Nice two days' sport. On the return the usual. Pierino gets out to wipe the substituting mica and '*Papa pense pipi*'. Pierino leaps in again in the night darkness and buzzes off oblivious and blind to Papa's vacuum at his side. Papa left screaming and half crying. Poor Pierino. He can't get over it. In a kilometre he had realised and returned to the desperate '*Excellenza!*' but O his hysterical

---

5 American journalist. Second husband of Susan Mary Patten.
6 Sacheverell Sitwell and his wife.

description of it 'Ze croyai aller fou and croyait mort'[7] with gestures.

Moura came today accompanied by Tom Cadett,[8] by train too, very devoted of them. Moura twice the size and particularly nice. She'd had a good time coming home from a French holiday alone, stopping at a fair and riding a pig and shooting at the range till she won a bottle of white wine and drinking it on the spot, and shooting again till she'd won two flower vases. When I first knew Moura she came to Bognor with H.G. Wells and we went to the fair and H.G. played hoopla till he won, but instead of getting a double-lifesized pink velvet rabbit that he'd flung his hoop to win, the prize given him was a packet of a cheap cigarettes. He made a serious row in his falsetto squeak and fought and lost.[9]

We are reading *The Outcast of the Islands* aloud. It makes the whole difference to me in this uncongenial country life to have a book that two can get back to. The walks are to be more systematic – exploratory ones lasting an hour and a half and taking winding mossy ways.[10] Then there's the 'sticking in'[11] and then the letters to get in better order and then the book. I'm writing believe it or not from a Chinese restaurant by the Sorbonne – a few Europeans struggling and giggling with chopsticks. I have ordered a Cantonese sausage. We'll see what it gives.

Chantilly
September 22nd, 1950

Will September never end? It's a holiday month so being back at the bench I consider it over. It's been dreadfully depressing

---

7 'I thought I'd gone mad and he was dead' in heavily Italian-accented French.

8 British journalist.

9 I was there, aged about six, and remember the occasion well.

10 Keats, 'Ode to a Nightingale'.

11 Of bookplates and photographs.

since you left. I can't do without your support and affection, besides there's nothing to scold. We dropped Rai and drove home in splendid speed. The headlights are the best we've ever had. My room could have set ice cream. I woke up feeling ill–all–overish and melancholy and ashamed at 5 a.m. and remained so, too listless to do anything, even radio, nor garden or Norah or tidying – nothing – speechless too. The stove was lit in my bedroom and straight to bed I went in complete warmth. Papa read to me *A Town Like Alice*. We found it dreadfully dull. At last I took my temp. and found it over 100 and felt much better and less ashamed. This was good old *grippe* caught from Norah and explained a lot. Papa was put away downstairs and Noémi produced some seda-tives belonging to Mireille which I very much suspect, since they were as big as marbles, roughly made and navy blue.

Nancy's just rung me with a spicy story about Cyril Connolly. For a long time he's had a mistress called, I think, Miss Skelton. She is now the 'unidentified blonde' to whom the Pharaoh Farouk[12] has taken a shine. Figure to yourself – Cyril dashed down to the Midi to be in at the slaying and had a wonderful time on other men's gold. The King gave her £100 a day for clothes and made her buy £100 worth extra at one go, so she bought rolls of stuff and I suppose good stuff for Connolly. The result was a kindling of Cyril's passions and a determination to marry the breadwinner. He's trying with registry office now and from the day he lands her she'll bring home no more bacon.

Chantilly
October 4th, 1950

Lunch on Monday with Dolly and Mogens. They are going to Uruguay to escape concentration camps.[13] They call it an explora-

12 King of Egypt.
13 You may well ask.

tory journey but they are taking all their servants and I suppose the Rubens. I should love to leave myself, because I like moving on and new continents and blue skies and a new life, but I couldn't leave you and Papa, and Dolly only has Mogens who will follow. Kind friends tell her a revolution is imminent in Uruguay and that they are taking their money out of the country. I told her that I'd heard they were going to have atomic experiments in that part of the Atlantic, but she's only afraid of the camps, I think.

There was a dinner with the Windsors the night before. Just the eight – Dudleys, us, Vinses[14] and two Yanks. Wallis dreadfully over-animated and I don't somehow think it's drink – benzedrine rather. She repeats herself embarrassingly. That night you were the refrain – you at *Monseigneur* – over and over and very nice about you. I talked to the Duke after dinner (a particular agony) about the Bahamas. 'It was a bit difficult for me, you see, I'd been King Emperor and there was I, a third-rate Governor.' He says things like that so simply – no boggle, no laugh, no inverted commas. My agony began before I left home. I've only got one smart dress (or dowdy one for that matter) so I had to be got into it willy-nilly. Pierino was called to help with getting the zip together. Hiccups started as soon as I was fastened and kept its hick up until my return. Now hiccups can be arrested, even postponed, by very severe pressure on the palms of the hands. I dug my thumbnails therefore into my lines of life and fate and came home with bloody stigmata and at last free of the hicks. Louise has come back for good with another *chef-d'oeuvre* written. She has a well-paid difficult job – to buy antiques for Marcus,[15] a mammoth store in Texas. Everyone has heard of it but me.

I am at Chantilly with St. Martin's summer going on outside but I'm abed with 101 temp. and only hoping it isn't going to be bronchitis – and the *Arc de Triomphe* party arriving today. I

---

14 Try saying 'Windsor' in a French accent.
15 Neiman Marcus in Dallas.

walked Papa round the dahlias at Sceaux yesterday and didn't feel too bad, but by the time I got down here I was really ill. Better this morning and I sent for an old peasant to apply *ventouses*[16] and I hope – how I hope – it will be thrown off by tomorrow.

Post just arrived. Very brilliant Evelyn Waugh's new book *Helena* – special copy of thickest paper, widest margins and bound in white. A letter announcing her arrival from Freya.

Chantilly
October 10th, 1950

So Papa's gone to London. It's been the hell of a day. Papa's not at all used to trouble. It's funny for one who is never out of it to see the stranger swept in a twinkling into that horrid country, not knowing the language or what defences to use. First he found on arrival here two letters, the first from his partners in that firm he doesn't know anything about complaining that they'd waited for him at a business lunch. As this is the third time he's forgotten it's begun to frighten him.

The other letter was from the Director of Naval Intelligence saying a 'buzz' was going round that a book from Papa's pen was due to appear on the subject of *Operation Mincemeat*. If it was true, he would like to make it clear that he would oppose its publication with all he'd got. Very upsetting – I've always expected it. Papa the optimist felt sure he'd get away with it and consulted the man who'd arranged it and he consulted Antony Head on the W.O.[17] Board. M.I.5 is all right and Winston told the story at a dinner party. If the D.N.I. succeeds in banning it, it will be too bad for us and cruel to Rupert Hart–Davis, who will necessarily lose a lot as it's due out on November 2nd so

16 Cupping.
17 War Office.

all printed and bound. Compton Mackenzie wrote such a splendid piece in the little Book Society paper – try and get it. It was made alternative Book of the Month too. So I'm alone in the house.

Next morning: took a death dose and slept like the Seven only to be woken at cockcrow by a telephone *erreur*. Papa has rung up to say the D.N.I. has disappeared to the golfing suburbs and left his underling to help. The idiot was accepting this and going to see the flea of the flea, because the D.N.I. is not the body – he's only a huge flea. So I yelled and swore and begged him to dig out the Big Flea. The little flea will only send in a report that will be returned marked 'No', whereas Duff could read his book aloud to the D.N.I. and wring tears from him and melt his heart and break his pigeonholes and burst his red tapes. I begged him yesterday not to go without making quite sure his target was reachable, but Papa always knows best.

Chantilly
October 21st, 1950

P.L.'s back, a dream of bronzed beauty, bearing *petits fours* and a nice doggy smile. The child is in him still and I've made a profound discovery about our country and this one – nobody has the child in them here. Winston, Max, Papa, Belloc, Maurice, Antony Head, most nice women (not Nancy) but Jenny and Freya and Pam and Barbara, etc. And why none of the French (except Louise) have that precious vestige is because they've never had it in crawlers or sailor suits. They've always looked and been knowing and suspicious adults, without the child's honesty and generosity and vagary.

I've discovered that Prince Paul is tremendously greedy. He

was so austere at *La Reine Jeanne*[18] that I thought of him as an ascetic hypochondriac – still, the greediest of us went slow on that menu. Here yesterday he ate twice of everything plus a Stilton I'd managed to buy in London plus all the *petits fours* he could lay hands on. K. Humbert[19] said he'd always been the greediest boy he knew. A nice King, very *de la bande*,[20] and bald as a coot, and twenty years ago I left him maned like a lion. Everyone I introduced him to seemed to live in Italy – Auberon in Portofino, Bertie Landsberg[21] at Malcontenta, Freya might have been there and that would have been another, at Asolo. All may return but him, poor thing.

Two nice days alone with Papa – gardening, working and reading aloud *The Outcast of the Islands*.

Chantilly
October, 1950 (Saturday)

I've been in bed eleven days. I don't get a bit better – always 100 temp., always an appalling migraine through the endless and hideous night. A nurse exactly like Margaret Rutherford gives me a morning injection in the buttock of something as simple as Friar's Balsam, for the bronchial tubes that the doctor guaranteed clear. Can you beat it? She sweeps all the tables clear of their objects with the tide of her cape and tells me that doctors have lost their intuitive powers on account of too many aids and tests. My doctor hasn't been near me since he first saw me six days ago. Yesterday in a rage I got him on the telephone. He told me *qu'il était grippé*,[22] but he'd come all the same. He didn't, neither has

---

18 Paul-Louis Weiller's seaside house near Le Lavandou.

19 King Umberto of Italy, now living in exile.

20 One of us.

21 Owner of the Palladian Villa Malcontenta just outside Venice.

22 That he had the flu.

he telephoned this morning so if my spirit has the force I'll call him and ask him his temp. and his respiration and if his bowels have been open.

Papa came back after his happy day with you and dark delightful nights at the Dorchester. Here he has me migraining and moaning and wringing myself out of sweats and having a bath and asking him to read me to sleep again.

The Pretender of France[23] and his eleven children have been allowed to settle in Paris. 'The noble County Paris.' Mogens said 'Ve are vondering who the Parises vill go around with.' I bet a lot are vondering. A play came out two nights ago by an *homme du monde* called Fabre–Luce about the Resistance, debunking it. *Mort pour Rien* it's called. Aren't they pets?

Chantilly
January 24th, 1951

P.L.W. summoned me to Versailles to meet Eisenhower, visiting the Mendl house to 'get a perspective' also to revisit his headquarters of 1944 – *Le Noviciat*. Van der Kemp[24] was invited too but he arrived early, squatted down in the *salon blanc*, where sleep overcame him and out he stretched yawning just as it was all over. I didn't think Ike was a bundle of charms – though he tries to please. He told us of a murder plot during that last German effort in 1944–5 and how his garden was bristling with protecting guns and 'tecs and hand grenades ready to throw at the assassins. Meanwhile an unfortunate double was found – a man to stand in for him – to be dolled out in C.-in-C. uniform and medals and to be driven round in a motor car followed by armed jeeps to be shot at. What an unpleasant role to be cast with! But he answered my sympathy with 'The double came to see me and I was horrified what an ugly

23 The Comte de Paris.
24 Gerald van der Kemp, curator of Versailles.

little fellow they'd chosen to represent me.' Not very funny but all he said.

We dined with the Burckhardts to hear Louise read her new story aloud. *Madame de* it's called. I finished and adored Enid's book.[25] Papa doesn't think it so good as I do. It's not a bit like me, and I fear he has told her so. My fault for telling all and sundry that it was to be a photographic study of me in age. Lady Maclean (God's teeth) and Ruby too (what an appalling name) never comes to life. The central figure she is meant to be is a noble serene shadow, almost my opposite, with no fears and frailties, panics, pains. She loses her husband not by death and has a strained relationship with her only child. Pray God these two horrors are not in store for me. There are some splendid character sketches of others in the cast, and a lot of the writing touches me deeply – but O the name! It makes one long for an oven to put one's head in and have done with the struggle called living.

Chantilly
February 12th, 1951

So, Graham Greene rang up in his surprising way and said come and lunch with Katherine[26] at Véfour. He always does it on arrival in France, it's always an enormous success, the meal rollicks; and then no other come-togethers – no correspondence, no telephone enquiries – no plans till the next sudden message from Paris. So we came to Chantilly after a lunch of oysters and beef for them, and a dish for me of such richness that never again can I even think too hard about it. *Tranche de foie gras* hidden in frothy creamy sauce – wonderful, but it took two days discomfort and calomel pills, salts and bed and veganin to get on top and then rid of it.

25 *The Loved and Envied*, a fictional portrait of my mother.
26 Walston, his long-term mistress.

435

Party yesterday. When Graham Greene arrived I could see he was in terrible shape. He told me at once that he had been up till 5 a.m. discussing a play in French adapted from *The Power and the Glory* with Jouvet[27] and others and a lot of whisky. I took him alone to the drinks room to ask what palliatives he needed. Alcohol he thought. A stiff gin he hoped would steady his hand enough to get the glass to his lips without the help of his other one. I suppose the truth is he's a big double drunk and that's why he looks like Sinclair Lewis and as though he had been *seared*. I can't make out about his faith. I think it's guilty love has put him all out. Hence *The Heart of the Matter*. He said he hadn't spoken to Padre Pio[28] (you know, Auberon's saint in S. Italy). He'd been to his Mass which had lasted an hour and a half, tho' he and everyone else thought it had taken the usual twenty minutes – but he was frightened to talk to him as he feared he might alter his life.

Hugo walked with him after lunch and bombarded him with journalist questions such as 'tell me Mr. Greene, is *The Heart of the Matter* autobiographical'. He admitted to Hugo that he would welcome death but that may have been due to alcoholic depression or desire to be free of Hugo's questions, or again the only road to repentance. I think he is a good man possessed of a devil and that Evelyn contrary to this is a bad man for whom an angel is struggling.

27 Louis Jouvet, leading French actor.
28 A monk in the monastery of S. Giovanni Rotondo in Apulia. His hands bore the marks of the stigmata and he was revered throughout Italy and beyond as a living saint. He was canonised in 2002.

Villefranche
February 22nd, 1951
Papa's 61st birthday

I wonder if you have heard of the car tragedy? After a very successful journey bathed in rain as far as Aix, in sun, mimosa ever since, we came first to Eddie's superb hotel not far from Cannes. After a nice evening, a visit to Opio the following day – lunch at the *Vol au Vent* in Cannes Harbour – we arrived at Monte Carlo to board Daisy's yacht. A bit of a disappointment for me that Daisy had not put me into her *cabine-de-luxe* but in an ordinary underwater bunker. I suppose natural really – but otherwise very pleasant and independent.

We went up to dine with her that first night, and we came back at 10.30. I parked my car along with many others on the quayside – rather far from this ship because Papa hates backing.

At 1 a.m. we heard steps as heavy as Noémi's run above us on deck and half an hour later the steward in unattractive *déshabille* came to say the car was in the water. Nothing to be done, no good staring into inky depths – full fathom five. Next morning the diver arrived to salvage the poor monster. It took about four hours and in the doing of it everything seemed to give, so the hood[29] disintegrated completely – the triplex windscreen shivered – the bonnet and fenders in frills and tatters and God knows what of the engine. It was hauled off to the garage. I have not yet had a report – the wreck looks total to me.

Undaunted, in my own inimitable way I bought a second-hand Simca the following day. It cost 300-odd pounds and is a dear tough little thing – it will do as a Paris runabout or for you in England – it is 3 h.p. Cruises at 80 kms. if given time – holds two, luggage and is advertised as having an *appétit*

29 It was a convertible. A month or two later I drove it back to Paris.

d'oiseau.[30] Also it's so small it'd cost nothing to transport abroad.

Wonderful sun, icy cold. Dinner last night with Willie Maugham, his minion Alan Searle and Raymond Mortimer. Literary conversation at which Papa did not let Willie get a word in. Papa has taken on to please Caroline all the gains and losses and liabilities to Opio to save the rich Duffs the trouble. He never consulted me, but it will be me who has the sweat and strain. Josette and husband[31] had all the complaints ready, the chimney had fallen in and all but killed the baby, olives untended, etc., etc. I might have been back at Chantilly. Norah writes that Noémi has taken her dismissal calmly, but means to leave immediately. I'm rather glad – but aren't they all *shits*? I wrote to her to say I had done nothing about a successor and that she was to stay as long as she liked – anyway until she found a really good place.

Villefranche
Feb. 25th, 1951

I dined last night on the *Vanguard*.[32] Daisy's yacht sailed from Monaco – the owner aboard. Such a bustling and banging and sliding down companions dragging anchors, heave-hoing, abafting and all aboards from dawn till 8.30 when she arrived. The crew hasn't been out since September so it's a liberation for them. Daisy in seaman's jersey, divided blue short skirt, scarlet jacket and netted hair looked just the thing. The boat rolled pleasantly enough, the sun glittered and we sat under its slight warmth till after a gay little nursery lunch on board when the mistral took over with rain and depressing skies.

---

30 Appetite of a bird.
31 Caretakers at Opio.
32 The Navy's most recent and fastest battleship, flagship of the Mediterranean.

Vian[33] came to visit us as soon as we anchored – *Vanguard* sent up signals of loving welcome which we misread and sent up an answer that didn't fit and wrong at that – a solecism drawn immediate attention to by the Admiral to Daisy's discomfiture. He came with an invitation to dinner, which we didn't want but being caught unprepared with an excuse found we had to accept. He also came to thrust upon us the responsibility of the First Sea Lord's programme of pleasure. He showed himself the *autoritaire* martinet he is supposed to be. I obediently wrote out suggestions for each hour of the thirty-six. To invite S. Maugham and Daisy to lunch at the Château de Madrid, to go dancing at Cannes for dinner with Duff, me and any girls I can induce to dine there that night, for Lord Fraser to swing round with. The ship was a fair treat, a huge Nelson column as a table centre and some kind lady in Lisbon had presented a flock of small glass pigeons to make the board more Trafalgar-Square-like.

The other night we dined with Esmond Harmsworth in that house of hideous[34] and happy memories. After, Daisy and I sat for twenty minutes while the men caroused with Esmond's daughter, Lady Errington, a great beauty of twenty-eightish, very English, middle class, Swan & Edgar and curiously uninhibited – for in answer to questions about her three children she told me, unsmilingly that she did not like her daughter (aged seven) because she smelt so badly. 'Yes, from birth we never liked her smell – now the boy (aged four) smells all right. Rolly and I agree on it. The baby – well he's 50–50'.

Sister Anne[35] is as top heavy as a ninepin, the sea is blue glass and all the objects have been laid on the floor and I can hardly keep my seat.

---

33 Admiral Sir Philip Vian, First Sea Lord and Commander-in-Chief, Mediterranean.
34 Where my father had fallen so ill in 1947.
35 Daisy's yacht.

April 25th, 1951
69 Rue de Lille

Papa went to Paris in the p.m. to fetch Lord Linlithgow — a man I've always loved, not only for his brontosaurian shape but for his odd humour and fund of information.

So all our outlook and our spirits were coloured and warmed by spring and the next day broke more lovely than the last with a light hoar frost at 7 a.m. Who can all those who came to luncheon have been — I can't think of a name or a face yet we were eleven. Little walks were taken to the cascade — little drinks — large and generous admiration by all for the Battersby panels. That evening we all motored up, me in a diaphanous crinoline naked to the waist, Ld. L. and Papa laden down with orders (Lord L. is a Knight of the Garter) in the *camionette* with Mum at the wheel. We looked rum I can tell you, Pierino crouching in the luggage section.

St. George's dinner at the *Cercle Allié* was the occasion. I sat next to Oliver Harvey and Brontosaur. Every one spoke — the Consul told a story — Papa spoke best. Over and back to the truck, crinoline shoved in, crosses clanking.

On Tuesday Lady Brontosaurus came down to lunch — she's of the same race — she brought and left Jenny and took her own dear beast. The weather was still as lovely. The border is not half bad. Norah is beaming and ineffectual rather, Jenny dreadfully spotty, Susan Mary brought Bill and a Boston brute called Charlie Adams. She must have died of shame, the whimpering snarl that he uses for talk was only heard once.

May, 1951
69 Rue de Lille
Paris

I had an evening of historical honour that needs telling before it's forgotten. I went to dine with the Windsors — alone since

Papa was at Ascot. It was a large friendly dinner – a prelude to Elsa Maxwell's orgy at the Restaurant Laurent. Evangeline of course the loveliest in a Dior dress of white tulle draped in roses and elegant as a Third Empire picture. She went up in flames after dinner, no one rushed to help with rugs or knocked her down and rolled her in the carpet. She put her own fire out and had to go upstairs to have the charred ends cut out. Meanwhile Bestegui knocked over a glass with the tail of his coat and broke it resoundingly enough for the Duchess to run across the room and brush the pieces of glass sticky with stale cocktail, with her white ostrich fan – it was a gesture of grandeur, but the contaminated fan should have been handed over for destruction to the liveried blackamoor, and not kept to coquette with.

Dinner was as usual excellent, ending as an oxymoron savoury – slices of thinnest crispy bacon coated dryly in toffeesque molasses. Elsa's party cards told guests to dress as they felt their best. I had a new off the floor sober tho' ample dress from Griffe – so this I wore as the *belle(?) jardinière*[36] with large straw hat and basket of beautifully arranged Chantilly flowers on the arm. In spite of a baby's rotten nappy in the bottom of the pannier I put so much moss soaked in water to keep the flowers fresh that I left trails and pools where'er I walked. Always I'm like the unpopular man victim who was asked to go to the nudist dinner, went starkers and found all the others in *grande tenue de soir*.[37] So I was the only one dressed up. True, Wallis had had her hair blue powdered and spangled – a *chef d'oeuvre* really. She wore a short expensive white satin dress, common twinkly feet and the soiled fan, but looked remarkably fresh and alarmingly over-excited, jitterbugging, talking too fast and too repetitively and, with only her pure face to deny the supposition, hopped to the teeth. Mrs. Donaghue – the mother of the beastly young pansy

36 Literally *The Lovely Lady Gardener*, a picture by Raphael of the Virgin, Child and St John, now in the Louvre.
37 In full evening dress.

who Wallis has selected for her scandal and presumably for her lover – was present, as was the scandal himself.

At Elsa's next the party was fast, furious and photographed, Elsa Maxwellian in short – with all the photographing let to *Paris-Match* alone – so that other photographers crowded the sidewalks and got insulted by the Duke of Windsor and knocked over and out by Aly Khan. By two I was yawning and longing to be gone. Charles,[38] still bright and good for more, shamed me. I caught Marie-Blanche who was girding her loins and she agreed to take me. But I was reckoning without Wallis. Laura Dudley and I waiting on the pavement were victims of her not being able to listen to our excuses. No, no we must all go on to *Monseigneur*.[39] But Wallis, we've had every fiddler of *Monseigneur* deafening us here for three hours. We must go on to *Monseigneur* – the Duke would like it, so don't argue. She seldom calls him the Duke now but rather 'My Romance' with a funny tone – not sneery but not straight. We are for it, me and my leaking basket, Laura, Wallis and the Romance on the box swung off to Montmartre.

The pitch-black chamber (for me of horrors) was half empty and we naturally made a bit of a sensation putting ourselves on a centre room table. The orchestra swarmed round, singing Windsor favourites. Champagne popped open – but there was a cloud of displeasure on Wallis's countenance, dispelled twenty mins later when Jimmy Donaghue[40] arrived with Eric Dudley. Followed a really embarrassing scene. If it had been college boys with a millionaire in tow, some pretty cocottes, etc. – but for all these elderlies to be animated by this insane young addict of bad taste. Eric, pretty tight, was whispering 'We're witnessing the end of another chapter, we saw the end of one and we're seeing another, I can't help liking the guy.'

Meanwhile huge bunches of red roses were being carried in

---

38 Sir Charles Mendl, well into his nineties.

39 A nightclub.

40 Gay – but nonetheless scandalising – escort of the Duchess of Windsor.

for the ladies, also bottles of scent graded according to rank (I got the biggest after Wallis). Jimmy was busy, shouting, singing and yelling 'hit it up, hit it up'. Then he was up to the piano playing Rachmaninoff's Prelude. You couldn't tell if it was good or bad because of the twenty-five other instruments playing all out. The Duke looked neither pleased nor shocked – Wallis was waving her martini-soaked fan and saying look at the Prince of Wales's feathers in Mr. Donaghue's roses. Mr. and Mrs. Henry Ford II had arrived by then (more roses, scent) and Mr., who is gross to a degree, confided to Laura he would never do it again or go to the Windsors' house again. At last it ended, Wallis remained sitting with Jimmy after we had all left the table. 'Come on,' the Duke said to Laura. 'Why bother with them, the boy's drunk anyway.' So Jimmy was deputed to take me home.

In the car he came quite clean. 'Lady D.', he took to calling me, 'Do you hate me for all the scandal? – it's not our fault you know, it's the newspapers. Isn't Wallis your favourite duchess? She is mine – or would you rather have Alice Gloucester? I adore Wallis – she knows she's only got to call on Jimmy and I'll do anything for her. I *love* her – like my mother you know – not any other way because I'm not that sort', etc., etc. I don't write what I answered, it seemed useless to say much to someone quite beside themselves. I said the indiscretion of it all was idiotic and wounding and unsuitable to the Duke. Isn't it all desperately sad? He showed nothing, I have to admit, on his royal wizened face but if it's true and he learns it, the wife is gone, the legend dead, he'll have to throw himself off the Empire State Building.

The Harveys are throwing a party tomorrow. We are asked, and Daisy is asked, at 10.30. I met that attaché David? [sic] who told me it was a *mondain* party, or was meant to be. Eighty to dinner but that they'd been obliged to ask three hundred bores after. 'I'll see you' he said 'but from afar, as I shall be *bout de table.*' 'I haven't even made that,' I said, 'I'm one of the bores.' He, looking uncomfortable, passed on. The Duke at dinner asked me if I was invited. Yes, I said, but with bores after. 'We've been asked at

10.30' he said. I told him he oughtn't to go – but that I'd make doubly sure. I did – he's not going now. I hear that the Bruces have also been asked after, so what Labour *crème* can they have got to dinner? Lady Harvey now goes to Dior, spends her whole day in a beautifying mask. Talking of Dior, that great dressmaker has made me a present of a dress (to measure) called *Cecil Beaton*. It's not what I'd have chosen – but I'm awfully pleased. I'll wear it to the Travellers Ball. Conversation here in *our* set is confined to missing diplomats.[41]

May 10th, 1951
Chantilly

I'll write you an extremely indiscreet letter for my own amusement and I hope for yours, as well as for posterity's who will smile perhaps to hear of how age grabbed after youth.

Chapter 1. I have for a long time been over-conscious of a hideous pouch in the upper inner corner of an eye. One eye pouched worse and I took it some time ago to Sir Harold Gillies,[42] aged seventy-odd. He put me under Evipan, said he'd cut it out, left a scar and within a month or two it was as bad if not worse. Today off I hurried to 53 Rue de Longchamps where I was first put into a waiting room crowded with people and children clearly not in search of rejuvenation and later on to a little stool in the lobby from which point of vantage I was able to see the beautiful Mrs. George Annesley – wife of Papa's partner in the business of which he is totally ignorant (doesn't even know its name, but attends regularly – keeps mum) – issue from the consulting room. She caught my eye so we both caught each other out. M. Boivin was a nice dark gentleman

---

41 Guy Burgess and Donald Maclean, two members of the British Foreign Service, had just fled to Moscow.

42 The father of plastic surgery.

– spare and serious and a bit of a blab. He told me in the three minutes that I had with him that a) my job was a trifle that he would do it any day I asked him, b) that we'd met before with Claude Alphand and did I not think he'd made a good thing of *her* face – and that he did not think much of Sir Archibald McIndoe aesthetically – as a surgeon of plastic necessities, wonderful, but not good for beauty. I should just see the Queen of Yugoslavia's breasts. What a mess was there!

Chapter 2. I made a date for last Tuesday. I knew that I should be demonisingly ugly for ten days and thought old home week (Michael [Duff], Caroline, David, Jamie Caffrey, are Sunday's guests) would be the best time. That morning I was lunching with David and J. and Alvilde and they all thought me looking so well. The abominable glue-nosed Marguerite said she'd never noticed the pouch and I was sore tempted to postpone and not spoil an agreeable-looking week. But then it was icy cold, raining, Papa was away, so in the end I stuck to my plan – not seeing it really any worse than a dentist's. I drove the *camionette* to Ave. des Roules, the clinic, thinking to drive it back two hours later and was admitted into Paradise – a large garden led to a pretty, large, Georgian house, spacious, fresh and painted sky blue from top to toe. The nurses, all pretty, were dressed to match with ethereal blue organdie caps.

I was shown to a large hospital room and asked to get into bed. 'I've brought nothing, not even a nightgown.' 'Here is a surgeon's overall,' so I put that on and obediently went to bed. I felt no apprehension, only amusement and surprise. A blue angel came in and stuck a needle in my thigh before I was aware. She had turned the bed-clothes down 'So that you don't bleed too much'. The first sinister note. What nonsense, no one's ever died of having a pouch taken out of their lid. The theatre men arrived next, dreadfully white and swift. I became the parcel I was to remain for some hours, lifted from narrow bed to narrower trolley, from it to narrowest operating table. O I've forgotten the best event. While waiting in my blue room an unusually beautiful woman with a look of Bobby Helpmann[43] dressed in operating white with a turban twisted with Schiaparelli art came to my bed and announced herself as Dr. Boivin II *et sa femme en plus*.[44] 'I hope there will be no scar' I ventured. Dr. Boivin never leaves a scar she said. '*Il vient de démenager ma poitrine – j'ai nourri mon enfant et ma poitrine avait beaucoup souffert – voulez vous que je vous la montre?*'[45] In a jiffy her white overall slipped from her shoulders to her waist and exposed two first-class breasts, small, firm, *retroussés*, with very palpable scars, flat and scarlet, that will surely go. I felicitated her and au revoired.

Back to the op. theatre. We are going to cocaine round your eyes they said. Panic. 'Is it novocaine?' 'Yes.' 'But I react very often in the most terrible way – it's like death.' 'It won't be this time.' 'I must have a hand to hold.' 'Here it is' a million candle power poured down on my closed lids while they pricked around with the stuff that I knew would nearly kill me. The reaction came – not as bad as it can, but terrible. I gasped and sweated and mutilated the kind hand. The doctor said 'Has she had a shot of morphine?' 'No.' 'But why? We always give it. Bring it, quick.' So that went in and gave me another panic, but I calmed down at last and bore with great courage the painless agony of hearing the scissors cut your flesh and worse, see the dazzling light not shaded by the red that is its lid but only by a thin membrane. I suppose the globules they were going to remove – globules they were for he showed them me, whitish caviar, and the extraction of each gave the sensation of immense pressure on the eyeball though he was not touching it.

'Now I'm going to sew you up', and there was the nursery noise of Nanny's needle and the thread being pulled through, and next – O anguish remembered! – 'The other one will not take so long'. 'No – please not the other!' but there was no appeal. 'Your

---

43 Sir Robert Helpmann, ballet dancer and choreographer.

44 'And also his wife.'

45 'He's just cleaned up my bosom. I breast-fed my baby and my bosom had a bad time. Would you like me to show it to you?'

eyes will no longer be symmetrical. You'll be back in a year to have the other caviar removed', so I let them have their way. The morphia had got its strong soft arms round me and I was a Koestler case already. It wasn't so bad – no element of surprise and nerves numbed. I was parcelled back into my pretty room, left to cool or to set or subside for an hour or so. But the thought of leaving it and returning with two poached egg eyes, a muzzy mind and an empty flat prompted me to stay the night. Three whacks of peri-cline were given almost without waking me and next morning I was out, bespectacled and lunching with Papa. That was the Wed. Today is the Thurs. and I'm very clever at concealing the eggs with specs and veil on the day and becoming blind old lace at night. Papa notices nothing fortunately. The stitches come out tomorrow but even then I dare not show eyes that I may not paint up and look exactly like a pig's. FINIS.

Chantilly
Sept. 14th, 1951
Read, corrected and approved by Papa

This day twenty-two years ago I was leaving Gower Street in tears for the nursing home: it was a Saturday, and Noona and others were all pretending to be cheerful – and so was I, but as usual deathly fear was in my heart and knees as I drove off with a last lingering look behind me at the house we had made to be so happy in – drove off to Lady Carnarvon's Nursing Home, and next day you were carved out of me, and I couldn't remember for hours what sex you were (I asked four or five times). Papa sobbed and howled (quite untrue, D.C.) when he was told you were there and had not got a hare-lip as we expected, the grasspuss[46] having crossed the road before our car two days before. So with that opening I'll wish you many happy returns of the day and get back to my saga.

46 Old country slang for 'hare'.

When you left us [in Venice] we dined on board the *Sister Anne*. The crust was breaking up on every side – goodbyes echoing – Sunday a 'clear up' at the Lido – lunch at Harry's beach with Fulco and Judy and *Streetcar Called Desire* film in the evening. My 'upset' interfered with my enjoyment. Vivien is wonderful – as you see she got the prize for individual acting – but she looks pretty ugly (deliberately) and the sound track curiously bad and the whole production 100 per cent fiercer and more sordid than the play, so can you imagine? We lunched delightfully in a piazza at Ferrara in the shade of the gigantic palace, of the d'Estes I suppose – they were the Dukes in Ferrara and a daughter Isabella went to Mantua when the Gonzagas ruled and Beatrice d'Este married Ludovico il Moro – a Sforza of Milan. Over the Apennines and down over Montecatini, bigger, smarter, more Spa than I expected, pretty though, with flower beds and plenty of fiacres drawn by jet horses. The streets are like *Ben Hur*. The well-conditioned horses are either hopped up or fed on corn which they are not able to take. The old cabbies are hanging on to their mouths with all their senile strength, unable to hold their horses. Bella Vista Hotel above the agglomoration was quite to my liking but Papa hankered after the fleshpots and frou-frou, so after two days we moved down to Vanity Fair.

It's a lovely Tuscan country, high Apennines, cypresses, peaceful citadel, townlets mountain-built,[47] and many famous towns within reach. Our day is to rise with the sun at seven and with a glass-handled tumbler in our several hands stride briskly to what look like the Baths of Caracalla in their hey-day. Gigantic colonnades, halls, courts, awnings, marble on marble, a full orchestra scraping abominably (chiefly Verdi, who lived here). It costs 5/- to go in but once in there are shops, post offices, picture galleries, typewriters for passengers' use, loos *en masse* and *en série*, and many thousand milling round with their tumblers filling and refilling themselves from gold taps and inlaid marble bars,

47 Keats, 'Ode to a Grecian Urn'.

with five different thermal waters each stronger than the last, they must be taken *à petites gorgées*[48] ambulatorily. The five glasses must be spaced over thirty mins. Or more. We get rather irritated – the crowd naturally stare at me on account of my clothes and Papa on account of a large dark scab on his nose and because the drinks are so revolting, hot, salt and greasy.

Three days later this plan was changed and we go to another pump room, more select. Papa at eight where he has a carbonic monoxide bath – followed by an inhalation – they wrap him up in white linen and rubber, a hideous woman tends him with laughing affection but she let him bang his poor nose disfiguringly on the apparatus. We meet for the water sipping (five pints of sip) at nine. I meanwhile have had my mud bath in another magnificent bath house. I go into a marble room and a robot arrives wheeling an enormous container of blue-black mud, steaming hot. A comely signora in impeccable white lies me naked on a sheeted bed and slops the mud in heaping handfuls under my back and legs and over my legs and thighs – it's piping hot and delicious and the sheet is wrapped over this living mud pie – blankets piled on, and it's left to stew for twenty minutes. Back comes Signora, undoes me, puts me in a hot bath while she sloshes back the mud into the pail and remakes me a clean bed. I scour away at my legs with a sponge. It comes off all right but there are layers of it. Thus cleansed I'm wrapped up again in white linen and rest for half an hour utterly exhausted.

This treatment, with the water and an hour on the loo, finishes the daily cure. Lunch generally as you like it, siesta afterwards till four and expeditions till dinner, after dinner Italian film. *Anna Karenina* we saw, wonderful to me and so easily understood. Life of 'Sonny Boy' Al Jolson in gorgeous Tech. dubbed with English songs, Al played by a man of twenty-six. I blushed for our Americans, shamefully stupid it was. Last night an Italian film called *Virginità*. Too difficult for us so we left halfway. The cinema

48 In small sips.

is out of doors and we are forced into it because in our beds we hear every word twice as loud by amplifier till 12.30 at night.

Expeditions. The first ciceroned by a Jewish cosmopolitan Italian, called curiously enough Dino Philipson – rich once, politically powerful, nice, tho' a bore of course. We went to Pistoia, a beautiful unspoilt little town. The mayor, Communist, received us on his stomach. From Pistoia on to Dino's villa in the hills for dinner – heavyweight evening, but bearable. The next day we were taken to a house belonging to one Torregiani, marquis, his wife not at home but rather having a nervous breakdown on account of her mongrel's paralysis. What a house. The best of its style – or perhaps of any style – imaginable with a garden full of water jokes designed by Le Nôtre, and an old gardener who delights in sousing the guests. I enjoyed this outing more than I can say and as always in cases of enjoyment and seeing perfect things, I missed you dreadfully.

Yesterday an hour's drive to Florence in search of *The Times*. One copy found, and a visit to the English Tea House. Campari not spirits. This brings me to today, your birthday, in fact to where I came in and to where you came in twenty-two years ago. It's mid-day. I haven't had a promised letter from you, only a p.c. I pray it comes soon, but I've suffered disappointment too often to hope. We'll send you a telegram and then go to a peaceful citadel for lunch, with a *funiculi funicula*.

Chantilly
October 20th, 1951

It's been a year of gain. I've inherited Emerald's handsome cultured pearls, which everyone takes to be real, also her paste and diamond bracelet which is thought to be emeralds – a mass of objects and pictures which I shall take back in the *camionette*, which brings me to London Monday 22nd. Over and above this wealth Sugar Daddy Weiller has given me an Aleutian mink (the best) coat from Dior costing £4,500. I like people to know he

gave it to me.[49] I consider it gives him credit, but I do not hold
to anyone knowing the price. Anyway it's paid for and delivered
and Papa thinks it looks like any other fur coat and now my
troubles begin. Rising above the misery that wanting motor cars,
carpets, stone paving tiles for the terrace, ten dresses and a less
expensive mantle, instead of the Aleutian, it entails being chained
to it, insuring it, not sitting on it, having to have better hats,
gloves, and bags, always thinking it's lost or stolen, storing it all
summer and ultimately being murdered for it, receiving in-
adequate insurance at its loss or being driven to sell it for £200.
Stables of gift horses all gaping so I must keep my eyes shut.

I've started the delightful habit of going to bed with the sun.
Papa works rather gloomily at his Early Life so I creep into my
bed with my inarticulate radio, embroidery and books and there
keep warm and rested till dinner comes up to us both. Last night
I slept only one hour and read nearly two books thro' – one
exceedingly indecent by Julia Strachey and one about Hazlitt by
Hesketh Pearson called *The Fool of Love*. He's just written a new
one about Disraeli I'm anxious to read: in the afternoons I do a
hard two hours in the garden, scraping paths or pulling up huge
weedy growths rooted in Australia. Then there's a daily dash to
Paris – Louise very ill as usual – third pneumonia this year. She
moved into that morgue American Hospital in order to be operated the next day and have her hips loosened or stiffened, but
the fever caught her at once so the op. is postponed. She looks
like death, cries with weakness. No rules there, so she opened
her eyes *in extremis* to meet those of Prince Pierre de Monaco
right at her bed foot.

I'm having myself as Cleopatra[50] put on my new passport and
French *permis de circulation* – that will be unlike other identi-
fication portraits.

* * *

49 Later it was always known as 'the coat of shame'.

50 A photograph by Cecil Beaton in her costume for the Bestegui Ball in Venice.

February 12th, 1952
Chantilly

Just in time. You left me on a Sunday, I talked to you from my bed, sadly ailing. I went to France without any improvement. I rather naughtily didn't write out of a peevish, bronchial nastiness, wondering just how long you would let me languish. As I will probably see you before this letter reaches your poor myopic eyes it's just as well that I can no longer reproach you with unrelieved heartlessness. Whenever you are in pain of heart or body or in despair of jams, dishonour, disillusion, nervous apprehension, drink or blackmail, you may rely on your mother trudging thro' snow, thro' bars, to perjure, to betray, to murder or – most difficult of all – behave courageously to help you – but in your own smooth days I must be courted and petted and needed or I can't react. I was ever so, with lovers too, neglect never roused me; only true love and cosseting got good exchange. I could write daily to Conrad because he would have pined without his ration of loving words. I can't expect you to pine without yours, it wouldn't be in your nature, but there is a 'mean' (B.M.T).

On D day (D for dead)[51] I went to lunch with Poor Louis[52] and Louise and Prince Paul at Maxim's. There Paul broke the sad news and from then to now, and still, I listen to French and English news and accounts. I read the English, French and American press cover to cover. The French papers are as densely packed as the English – much more embroidered *à la française*, full pages day after day. As for the B.B.C., it has surpassed itself. I don't suppose you listened to the *Tradition of Kingship* – mourning and something like resurrection only not – wonderful verse, wonderful selections and music, very Third Programme. All three stations in one makes a big difference to the expatriates as the 'light' penetrates like a ray thro' jamming. 'Death came

51 The death of King George VI on 6 February.
52 Paul–Louis (joke).

like a friend' was, as you say, the wonder of Winston's oration. Evelyn of course tries to spoil it all by writing 'W. Churchill made an excruciating speech on B.B.C. about King's death. Platitudes enlivened by gaffes – the most painful was (roughly) "During the war I made a point of keeping the King informed. He showed quite an intelligent interest. I even told him military secrets and he never once blabbed."' We know poor Evelyn to be possessed, but I wish he didn't make me feel like a baby's cake of Pears' Soap. He goes on to say 'We are in fact the undoing of all the work of recent historians who have exposed the wickedness of Elizabeth Tudor. "It has begun today in all weekly papers – REBUNKING."'

We've just had such an onslaught of *pompes funèbres* on account of de Lattre. No one really cared a pin, or rather didn't care as much as you or I did,[53] but the *obsèques* were magnificent in size and Napoleonism. Our tradition is Chaucer in the villages. The heralds going from one to another – cutting red cords as they go '*Oyez, Oyez*'. Papa went over to the Privy Council and thought the Queen was a moving figure of pale dignity – her voice like her mother's bell and all the horrible elders (himself included) with vice and greed stamped on their features surrounding her frailty. Bobbety said 'Our beloved Princess Margaret'. I liked that but I do hate her no longer being *la fille du Roi* and having got more into the Aunt strata.

Prince Paul has been asked to the funeral. For him it's tremen–dous – back to England a real royalty after his disgrace and exiled Kings. I've had to get him his visa, trembling I was that obstacles might persist like lumpy seas.

I'll talk to you tomorrow about whether you want to go to War Office window for the funeral. I remember as a very little girl thinking King sounded so funny and actually Nanny saying Mr. Brown will be K.C. now, and not knowing what it meant.

---

53 My mother and I had accompanied him on a memorable tour of the French front in January 1945.

February 18th, 1952
Chantilly

Lovely journey, calm and foggy. It passed in a flash. I spent a very happy hour marking the programmes in my *Radio Times*, hearing them (fortunately) in anticipation, for they turned out to be records of the past week of the King's funeral. The little Simca was waiting on the quay. I was the only first-class passenger among a dozen other classes. I paused at the cake shop, ate a meringue and a *baba au rhum* and a small pyramid bar of Toblerone and set off for my wintry ordeal. No snow to start with; nothing much at Beauvais and at Creil. In our region quite a bit, not enough to make me late – so I was bitterly disappointed to find at what compares to your 5.45 an empty house shuttered up so darkly, no Papa, no nothing but cross-faced Mireille. There were a few letters, one from John Huston, a film producer who I had written to because Iris Tree had asked me to. He wrote from Vineuil to my surprise and asked me to come over for a cocktail. I did right away – very attractive man who did *The African Queen* and a pretty young wife – next door. He is working on *Moulin Rouge*, a story about Toulouse-Lautrec to be shot here and in London, so that is a flutter of excitement. There was a letter too from Paddy Leigh Fermor asking me to go and have a meal with him at Passy s/Eure, so that's another flutter and I shall go Friday next when Papa is gallivanting in Paris and talk about Voodoo and Toussaint l'Ouverture.[54] It's dreadfully cold and this French house has no *confort anglais*. No open fire that is more than a little black hope, no squelchy chairs to draw up, no room that isn't all doors and windows and passage. It means I just go to bed and stay there and get haunted by the thought of heating this huge house and then sitting in a small bedroom with a stove.

We read *Villette* aloud in the evening and first class it is – staggered one is by the sophistication of the vicarage-cum-moors' girl's

54 Patrick Leigh Fermor had just written *The Traveller's Tree*, a study of the Caribbean.

style and outlook. She's such a suspicious censorious prig to boot, but it is frightfully good. I miss the King on the radio quite dreadfully. Division of programmes, only one of which one gets and that the most frivolous. Why are my Eroicas and Donnes and Heralds, my coming up like a flower, my friend death, and my glorious Resurrection all blotted by *Have a go, Over to you?*

I'm bored, John Julius – sad isn't it? This is not a life I could ever tolerate, from early childhood I was always praying for excitement. Nature provides it in summer, but in winter the Monday morning stretches out interminably, no garden, no babble or effort. I'd be better in Paris with theatres and concerts and friends, but darling Papa's happy enough and busy with his 'past' delving and his book writing. I ought to put my letters and Conrad's and my life in order too – but there's no inclination and no room that has a table and sufficient warmth. I am going to try to keep a diary to you again. The cook's bedroom-grown amaryllis are show worthy – four mammoth red, white or pink megaphones on one stalwart stalk.

February 20th, 1952
Chantilly

Well, darling fool – *où sont les neiges d'antan?*[55] Gone, thank the Lord. Papa and I are to sneak off and lunch at the village of Montgrésin not ten kms away. All yesterday I pored over papers and letters, my own to you, and Papa's and brother John's. The latter writes me twenty kind pages about not marrying Papa. In it there is a piece that the poor boy did not realise was to be so soon disproved. John, a bit of a misogynist, wedded to his Uncle Charlie (Lindsay) – very girl-shy, fell deeply deeply in love with the girl of girls Rosemary Leveson–Gower, the best I have ever known. She was boy-shy (what ghastly expressions) and accepted his proposal of marriage and unending adoration with hesitation,

55 Where are the snows of yesteryear?

almost reluctance. The engagement was announced, jewels bought, everyone over the moon, when she took ill and was operated for appendicitis. During convalescence, weakened and apprehensive, she told her mother[56] to get her out of the promise.

Milly, a true Edwardian schemer and large-scale liar for the public good, sent for John and told him with tears that the doctors having peered into all parts of his beloved bride-to-be said biologically she was infantile and quite undeveloped and would never have children. John loved her so much that although to him this was the worst of handicaps he prepared to swallow it all. But Rosemary broke the engagement with determination and plunged poor Johnnie in desperate melancholy. Two or three years later they both got new spouses, Eric Dudley and Aunt Kakoo Tennant, and in this letter to me he tells me of his joy and relief at having been preserved from a fatherless fate – and advises sacrifice of true love in favour of good sense. Shortly after Rosemary bore Eric three bouncing sons, and was the most perfect of wives till she was killed at the age of thirty-six. John, deeply unhappy, took Belvoir's whole garden to her grave at Henley.

Feb. 21st. I never slept a wink last night, got over-excited about a book by Gallico about a pussycat.[57] I can't listen for a bit to the radio – saturation point was reached in London and now it's too frivolous and cheap. Tomorrow I'm out on the razzle dazzle with my boy Paddy Leigh Fermor, cross-country – but I'm not used to *tête-à-têtes* and I feel nervous.

Chantilly
Feb. 22nd, 1951

Just off for my jaunt to Passy s/Eure to spoon with P. Leigh Fermor. Shy, fluster.

---

56 Millicent, Duchess of Sutherland.
57 Paul Gallico wrote five books about pussycats. I don't know which this was.

Sunday. Well the gallivanting was a red letter. It took me a good two hours cross-country by Pontoise and Mantes. Strange little village house in which he lives – the loan of a Lady Smart – was warm and welcoming and I really felt myself back in the pond I was raised in. Conversation *très agréable* with a male man who delights in one. Paddy was superb. Cultured, funny, saga-ed, zealous. We had a charming filthy little lunch over the stove of sardines, Pernod and vin ordinaire and afterwards we walked for two hours over low wooded downs in sparkling sun, talking ten to the dozen about people, grievances and enthusiasms.

I was tired with motoring and enjoying myself but flogged myself to please Papa to *La Régence* for a bite of supper. There he did everything to irritate that's possible, ordered nine oysters and ate six, allowed me to order for him (as I was past eating) some chipolata sausages and wouldn't eat them, ordered himself an omelette, left half. We had a bottle of Traminer out of which I forced myself to drink half a glass, then another was uncorked without my noticing. Then to put the bottom on cruelty's cap at 12.15 when I'm tantrumming a bit, that it's his birthday and he likes a bit of celebration and he'd been alone all day while I was philandering, etc., etc. Ignoble, don't you think. I could have philandered any other day. I'd have given him a present and not been tired and cross. 'It is just as I feared' – one only has to be consciously happy, sunny, to be sure of an approaching drenching thundercloud. So I went to bed furious. Simca was too and stalled to demonstrate and we had to be bumped into *démarrage*[58] by a kind couple who sat next us and no doubt watched the row. Next morning Papa couldn't wake up, thanks to two whole bottles of Traminer, so I continued to be ill-tempered, naturally thinking he was going to be ill and die. Then we lunched at a charming restaurant *du quartier* – found by Auberon, *La Petite Auberge* (A1) and came back here to rest and warmth and a bath and *Villette*.

58 Starting.

Chantilly
March 3rd, 1952

(A blunt pencil and at the coiffeur so nothing to be done.) So much to say. Our lovely looked-forward-to weekend is a bit spoilt by Sheila Milbanke bringing as escort Rupert Belleville, semi-reformed alcoholic, instead of darling Tony Rosslyn her son. No matter. Nancy R. will be here and you'll get Papa's room and Tucker a bed at Norah's if he comes. The other sensational news is that Mireille and Jean are leaving our spoiling service. It's an 'unhappy ship' and the cause is Jean – no one can take him, he has no friend but his mistress, and also we can't afford the steadily rising books on account of the system (i.e. the more you buy the more commission for the buyer). Mireille being *du midi*[59] with dashes of Wop blood *cannot* resist listening at doors – always a direct method for self-inflicting wounds. I had an appalling scene with Jean, in which almost too much came out from me and not enough came back from him, then a charming one with Mireille who is far more intelligent and sensitive and admitted, half to save my pity, that she had always wanted an inn, an independent inn, in the mountains, so that's what now they will find, fortified by some handsome economies drained from us over five years. What will the unknown devil be like? Jacqueline is perfect and Pierino would be if not so *bousculé*[60] by Jean. (Pencil hopeless, just found another in the bag.) Then the Poles who are absolutely deaf and dumb because of language are said to be the source of all intrigue. Language on both sides was a little veiled. '*Vous allez vous installer comme restaurateurs il paraît.*' '*Où Milady a-t-elle entendu une telle histoire?*' '*Mais partout, Jean – dans la ville et dans la forêt.*'[61]

---

59 From the south.

60 Knocked about.

61 'I gather you're going to set up in a restaurant?'
    'Where did Milady hear such a story?'
    'Oh, everywhere, Jean, in the town and in the country.'

Poor things, I hate their fall — though it was they who consciously laid the last straw on my hump. Today comes my boy Paddy Leigh Fermor and his girl Joan Rayner, also Liz. We've had Wu alias Bo for a few days, he left yesterday for Rome and Capri. I'm pledged to meet him at Monte Carlo on 31st inst. and motor quietly home. Shall I be happy? — all is better when we're alone together and he has learnt how impossible he is as a provoker-cum-sulker — I think he'll try. I'm looking for a sort of Tony Pawson to drive the bat's-bath down — as I hate Pierino as a two-day companion. He criticises my driving and spends 1200 francs on his lunch.

The houseful now (Sunday a.m.) is delightful — all amusing, all pretty. Liz in inkiest black with too black hair. David and Jamie bent double over their several *petit-points*. Paddy I adore. His father was an expert on snowflakes and has three named after him. Three is the operative word. Joan Rayner charming, not unlike Joan of Arc. Lunch is to be darkened a bit by Bob Thayer (in love with Liz) and wife Minka, daughter of Pips Shey who befriended Paddy for a month at the age of nineteen in Bratislava.

———

My father had just been offered a peerage — a viscountcy to be exact — and there had been endless discussions on the title he was to take. My mother characteristically wanted the romantic or the jokey: St Vigil (from their love for San Vigilio) or Lackland. Templar and Tabard were also considered.

———

Chantilly
June 10th, 1952

Papa's all out for *Norwich* now. Man-in-the-Moon would be better. Norwich spells porridge to me.[62] He thinks St. Firmin spells vermin, but it also spells ermine. I'm so tired of being congratulated on my big step down.[63] Nice for Papa though, I must go on saying that. I don't know about you, you dear little boy.

Luncheon with P.L. for Margot Fonteyn. Twenty strong, very amusing, Orson Welles all the rage and in love with Lulu – who still lies in her plaster armour in hospital looking lovely. Then beastly Polly Palffy[64] comes and makes her cry and sob by reminiscing on past happiness. He does it in order to make her pay him to go away.

Conversation palpitante last night next to the Duke of Windsor. His mother he says is quite gaga; thinks the Queen is Queen Victoria, she thinks in her more lucid moments that the young Queen is abominably educated. His sister-in-law[65] is called 'Cookie' by them, the Windsors. The sad part is, he said, that his mother and his *beautiful* wife, whom he loves every day more and more, and 'it's sixteen years now', would get on like lovers. He described meeting his nieces for the first time after sixteen years, thought the 'Maggot' had something. 'Cookie' had been very nice, though he'd refused to take a drink with her. I think he was a bit tight or he couldn't have said so much.

---

62 *The Man in the Moon came down too soon, and asked his way to Norwich;*
They sent him south, and he burnt his mouth by eating cold pease-porridge. (Old nursery rhyme.)

63 From Lady Diana Cooper – she bore the title in her own right, the inclusion of the Christian name denoting a duke's, marquess's or earl's daughter – to Lady Norwich, simple Lord Norwich's wife.

64 Louise's second husband.

65 Queen Elizabeth the Queen Mother.

Epilogue

This is not the end of the letters, but it marks a milestone. My Oxford days were over, and in the autumn of 1952, a newly married man, I began my life as a member of the Foreign Service that was to continue for the next dozen years. For the first three of these I was stationed in London, going backwards and forwards to Chantilly whenever possible and speaking to my mother most days on the telephone. The letters consequently almost dry up; it was only when I was posted to Belgrade in January 1955 that they once again come thick and fast.

As I read them now, for the first time in well over half a century, how do they strike me? To begin with, they come from a different world, a world in which the presence of servants was a matter of course – and by no means only in families of the relatively rich and privileged. The perfectly ordinary middle-class family with whom I lived in Strasbourg, for example, a couple in their early thirties with two children, employed a staff of three – a cook and two maids – and still brought in caterers when they gave a dinner party. At Chantilly my parents must have employed six or seven at least; and, as the letters make all too clear, they frequently seem to have been a good deal more trouble than they were worth. Not that my mother was a difficult employer: Miss Wade, who plays a considerable part in the early letters, remained devotedly with her for over fifty years and was lovingly looked after for the rest of her life – though she proved, alas, untransportable to France.

To a large extent, of course, servants were indispensable. Vacuum cleaners, though still of a fairly elementary kind, were already in common use; but our primitive refrigerator at Bognor was operated by gas, while dishwashers, blenders, microwaves, deep freezes and the thousand other devices which we now take for granted – suitcases on wheels also come to mind – were still non-existent, as were supermarkets with their copious stocks of precooked dishes. This, perhaps, still fails to explain why my father, his friends and contemporaries needed personal man-servants for every day of their lives, valets who would automatically accompany them whenever they went away for the weekend and whom their hosts would expect to accommodate. Standards of dress were admittedly far more demanding than they are today; certainly until the Second World War, my father would expect to wear white tie and tails three or four times a week, and always when going to the theatre. After the war, white ties became a lot less frequent; but he still changed into a dinner jacket almost every night of his life,[1] and at Chantilly – which was, let me emphasise, considered pretty informal as such houses go – we never sat down to lunch or dinner without the butler, Jean, standing in the corner supervising the service.

Then there is the matter of transport. After the war the age of civil aviation gradually resumed, but at least until the middle 1950s aeroplanes remained unreliable. It was not that they tended to fall out of the sky; already they were probably safer than cars or even trains. But they were irregular and unpunctual, hideously so during the winter. When my father came to London in December 1944 to pick me up and take me back to Paris, RAF Transport Command made us wait four days in London before the weather permitted a cross-Channel trip; we arrived only on Christmas Eve.

There was one other enormous difference to our way of life sixty – nearly seventy – years ago. No television. I wonder whether my father ever in his life watched that tiny, flickering, black and white screen – not that it had much to offer in those days. Certainly we never had it at Chantilly. At weekends when people came to

---

1 At Belvoir Castle my uncle, the Duke of Rutland, who died during the war, was known to insist on white tie for dinner every night. When he was once asked if he never wore a black one, he replied, 'Only when I am dining with the Duchess alone in her room.'

stay, there might be a rubber or two of bridge, which he loved; otherwise we just talked, or occasionally sang to my guitar or around the piano. On all other evenings we read aloud, usually Dickens or Trollope, but sometimes short stories – by Kipling, perhaps, or Somerset Maugham, or – for me best of all – P. G. Wodehouse.

Mention of my father raises another question. To those who never knew him – and by now there are relatively few who did – I wonder how he emerges from these letters. Self-indulgent certainly: he loved all the good things of life and made sure that he got them whenever possible. 'It's always cheaper in the long run', he used to maintain, 'to stay at the Ritz' – though in fact he personally preferred the Dorchester. He was, on the other hand, anything but soft or effete. His physical bravery he had shown by winning the Distinguished Service Order in the First World War; his moral courage by his resignation from Neville Chamberlain's Cabinet after the Munich agreement of 1938. He was astonishingly well read in history and literature; his biography of Talleyrand has been consistently in print for the past eighty years. He also had a passion for poetry, which he could recite for hours at a time; Shakespeare he knew virtually by heart; he even wrote a short, light-hearted book about him. Thanks largely to a superb sense of humour, he was wonderful company – though if he was bored, he was incapable of concealing it.

None of this, of course, comes out in these letters. Why should it? I knew him already. The picture painted here strikes me as slightly mocking; but the mockery, such as it is, is clearly a sign of affection. This is made clearer still by the genuine anguish that my mother felt whenever he showed the slightest signs of sickness. He was, as we know, seriously ill in April 1947 and, as I have already said, I believe he never quite recovered. By the 1950s he was on a strict diet, which after a few early lapses he conscientiously followed; but it was too late. On New Year's Day 1954 he died of a sudden violent haemorrhage – at sea, on his way with my mother to a Caribbean holiday.

It took her a long time to recover from his death. She had had one or two light-hearted affairs, but he was the only man she had really loved. He, on the other hand, had had a great many throughout their married life; but she never minded except when she believed that the lady concerned was unworthy of him. 'Mind?' she once said to me. 'Why should I mind if they made him happy? I always knew: they were the flowers, I was the tree.'

Thanks to the support of friends and family, she gradually regained the will to live. Henceforth, inevitably, her entire life centred on me and my family. She hung on for another six years at Chantilly, on the grounds that the Foreign Office might post me to Paris. Over and over again I tried to explain that this would not and could not happen; that, if it did, life for my chief the ambassador – and still more for his wife – would be impossible; as the letters make all too clear, she had made things difficult enough for the Harveys. Of course she refused to listen, of course she pulled all the strings she could, but – thank heavens – to no avail. When, in January 1955, I was posted to Belgrade and my wife Anne and I lived for the first six months in one tiny hotel room, she took care of our two-year-old daughter Artemis at Chantilly, giving her daily lessons as she had given me; later she came to visit us, once to Belgrade, two or even three times to Beirut.

Finally, in 1960, I returned to London, with every prospect of remaining there for the next four or five years; and she gave up. The Château de Saint-Firmin was returned to the Institut de France, and she rented a house a few hundred yards from ours in Little Venice, where she was to live for over a quarter of a century. By this time my son Jason had been born; she took over his education too. No grandmother, I feel sure, ever got more fun out of her grandchildren; they adored her in return.

Despite everything we could do, her last three or four years were, I'm afraid, unhappy. Her great joy had been driving her little Mini around London; while she was mobile she was content; she could go shopping, take friends on errands or her grandchildren to the cinema. She would leave notes for parking wardens tucked under the windscreen wiper: one, I remember, read 'Dearest warden, have gone to dentist 19a. Look like 85-year-old pirate. Have mercy.' We were all surprised by how often they worked. Then, one day when she was eighty-nine, she hit a traffic island in Wigmore Street. She drove straight home, locked the car, went up to bed and never drove again. 'I never saw it,' she told me later, 'it might have been a child.'

She never left her bed again; there was no point. She had, thank God, no dementia; but failing eyesight gradually made it impossible to read, and increasing deafness to enjoy the television. 'You can't imagine what it's like', she said to me once, 'just staring at the same bit of wallpaper – and with nothing to look forward to.' I would call in every evening on my way back from the London Library, hoping that there would be no other visitor; three-way conversations were beyond her.

She died – quite simply of old age – on 18 June 1986, a few weeks before her ninety-fourth birthday.

Directory of Names

Albert	Lord Ashfield. Head of London Transport and in love with my mother.
Alex	Alexander Clifford, journalist. Married to Jenny Nicholson (*q.v.*), also journalist, daughter of Robert Graves.
Ali	Alistair Forbes, journalist.
Altrincham	Lord and Lady (Ned and Joan), fellow-directors of the Wagons-Lits Company.
Alvilde	Married 1) Anthony Chaplin, 2) James Lees-Milne.
André (Bonnot)	Huissier, white-tied door-opener at the Embassy.
Angleseys	Charles Paget, Marquess of Anglesey, married my mother's eldest sister Marjorie. Their children were Caroline (m. Sir Michael Duff), Liz (m. Raimund von Hofmannsthal), Rose (m. John McLaren), Mary, Katherine (Kitty, m. Charles Farrell) and Henry (present Marquess, m. Shirley Morgan).
Ann, Annie	Ann O'Neill, married 1) Lord Rothermere and 2) Ian Fleming.
Annabel Jones	Daughter of Pandora and Timothy Jones, later to found Jones, the jewellers. Married William Astor, mother of Mrs David Cameron.
Anne	Anne Clifford, whom I was to marry in 1952.
Ashfield, Lord	See Albert.
Ashley	Ashley Clarke, Minister in Paris under my father and later Ambassador in Rome. Married at that time to Virginia, later Surtees.

467

Asquith, Katherine	See Katherine.
Auberon	Auberon Herbert, a Roman Catholic eccentric, had been rejected by the British Army at the outbreak of war and had instantly joined the Polish one.
Ava	Lady Anderson, later Waverley. Her husband, formerly Sir John Anderson, had been Chancellor of the Exchequer and Home Secretary.
Barbara	Barbara Hutchinson, daughter of St John and Mary Hutchinson, married 1) Victor Rothschild, 2) Rex Warner, 3) Niko Ghika.
Barbie	Barbie Wallace, married to Euan (*q.v.*).
Baring, Maurice	See Maurice.
Barley	Barley Alison, on the Embassy staff, later a London publisher.
Beaton, Cecil	See Cecil.
Beaverbrook, Lord, Max	Proprietor of the *Daily Express*. My godfather.
Bébé	Christian Bérard, illustrator and designer.
Bedbug	Baroness Moura Budberg. See Moura.
Belvoir	Belvoir Castle, Leicestershire, ancestral home of the Rutland family.
Bendern, John de	My father's one-time secretary in Paris.
Benson, Jeremy	See Jeremy.
Bernstein, Henri	French playwright.
Berry, Pam	See Pam.
Bertram	Bertram Cruger, an American Anglophile friend of my mother.
Bestegui	Charlie de Bestegui, Mexican multimillionaire and connoisseur.
Betty	Married to Robert (Bobbety), Lord Cranborne, later Marquess of Salisbury, (*q.v.*).
Bill	William S. Paley, President of the Columbia

Broadcasting System (CBS) in whose house on Long Island I spent all my holidays during my wartime evacuation.

Bloggs   Wyndham Baldwin, son of the former Prime Minister. I think he and my mother had a gentle love affair, 1944–5.

Bobbety   Lord Cranborne, later Marquess of Salisbury. Married to Betty (*q.v.*).

Box   See Coalbox.

Brendan   Brendan Bracken MP.

Bruce, David and Evangeline   See Evangeline.

Burckhardt, Carl   See Carl.

Bulbridge   Juliet Duff's house at Wilton.

Carl   Carl Burckhardt. Swiss writer and diplomat, later Swiss Minister in Paris. Had a brief affair with my mother before the war.

Caroline, Cary   Lady Caroline Paget (later Duff), my mother's niece, greatly loved by my father.

Cat, the   See Kaetchen, below.

Cecil   Cecil Beaton, photographer and designer.

Cecil, David   Lord David Cecil, Oxford don.

Cecilia   Cecilia Hay, a distant cousin.

Charteris, Hugo and Virginia   See Hugo.

Chips   Henry Channon, MP socialite, snob and superb diarist.

Churchills, the   Winston and Clemmie. See also Colonel, the; Duckling. Their youngest daughter, Mary, married Christopher Soames. Their son Randolph married Pamela, who later married Averell Harriman.

Clarke, Rufus   See Rufus.

Clemmie	Lady Churchill.
Coalbox	Lady (Sibyl) Colefax, famous interior decorator.
Colonel, the	Winston Churchill (wartime alias).
Conrad	Conrad Russell, a bachelor friend of my mother who farmed at Mells, Somerset. He and my mother kept up an almost daily correspondence for perhaps a quarter of a century.
Cranborne, Bobbety and Betty	Later Marquess and Marchioness of Salisbury.
Cripps, Fred and Violet	Friends of my parents.
Curie, Eve	Daughter of the discoverers of radium and a dedicated *résistante*.
Daisy	Daisy Fellowes, another old flame of my father's.
Daphne	Married to Lord Weymouth, then to Xan Fielding.
Daphne	Wakefield, née Marler. My father's long-time secretary in the late 1930s, and a friend for ever after.
Dashwood	John Dashwood, Eton school friend.
David	David Herbert, son of Lord and Lady Pembroke (q.v.), delightful gay friend of my parents, living in Wilton and Tangier.
Ditchley	Magnificent seventeenth-century house in Oxfordshire, owned by Ronald Tree MP. Regularly used as weekend retreat by Winston Churchill during the war.
Dodgems	My mother's tiny little wartime car.
Doll, the	My mother's oldest friend, Iris Tree, daughter of the actor Sir Herbert Beerbohm Tree.
Dolly	Princess Radziwill, married to Mogens Twede.
Dorothy	Married to William S. Paley (q.v.). Their house on Long Island was my home in America.

Drian	Etienne Drian. Celebrated French artist, principally in charcoal, also a designer.
Duckling	Winston Churchill.
Dudley, Eric and Laura	See Eric.
Duff, Juliet	See Juliet.
Duff, Michael, Sir	Juliet's son.
Duncannon, Eric	See Eric.
Emerald	Lady Cunard.
Enid	Enid Bagnold, novelist, author of *National Velvet*, married to Sir Roderick Jones.
Eric	Earl of Dudley, married Laura (née Charteris).
Eric	Duncannon, later Bessborough. My father's private secretary at the Embassy.
Ernie	Ernest Bevin, Foreign Secretary 1945–51.
Esmond	Esmond (formerly Harmsworth) Lord Rothermere, proprietor of the *Daily Mail*.
Euan	Euan Wallace MP.
Evangeline	Evangeline Bruce, wife of David Bruce, US Ambassador in Paris.
Fara	Fara Bartlett, young English guardian of Milo Cripps in Canada.
Farmer, the	See Conrad.
Felix	Gardener at Chantilly.
Fellowes, Daisy	See Daisy.
Février, Jacques	Concert pianist and friend.
Forbes, Alistair	See Ali.
Frank	Frank Giles, Paris representative of *The Times*. Married to Kitty (q.v.).
Franck, Jacques	See Jacques.
Freya	Freya Stark, writer and traveller.

Fulco	Duke de Verdura, Sicilian jewellery designer, very amusing friend.
Gaston	Gaston Palewski, right-hand man of General de Gaulle and lover of Nancy Mitford (Rodd).
Gaulle, Pierre de	Brother of General de Gaulle, Mayor of Paris.
George	Lord Gage, another old family friend.
Giles, Frank and Kitty	See Frank, Kitty.
Godley, Wynne	See Wynne.
Guy	Guy Benson, husband of my mother's sister Letty.
Harmsworth, Esmond	See Esmond.
Harvey	Sir Oliver and Lady. My parents' successors at the Embassy in Paris.
Henry	Marquess of Anglesey, son of my mother's oldest sister Marjorie.
Herbert, David	See David (*q.v.*).
H.G.	H.G. Wells.
Hilary	Hilaire Belloc, writer and poet.
Hoffs, the	Liz and Raimund von Hofmannsthal (*q.v.*).
Hoytie	Miss Mary Hoyt Wiborg, a long-term American resident in Paris.
Hugo	Hugo Charteris, representative of the Continental *Daily Mail* in Paris.
Hutchie	St John Hutchinson, K.C. Married to Mary, *q.v.* His son Jeremy married the actress Peggy Ashcroft.
Hutchinson, Jeremy	See Jeremy.
Iris	Iris Tree.
Isaiah	Isaiah Berlin, Oxford philosopher.
Jacques	Embassy staff.
Jamie	Jamie Caffrey, friend of David Herbert.

Jean	Czech butler at Chantilly.
Jenny	Jenny Nicholson, journalist. One of my mother's greatest friends. Daughter of Robert Graves, and married to Alexander Clifford, another journalist.
Jeremy Benson	Son of Guy Benson and my Aunt Letty.
Jeremy Hutchinson	Son of Hutchie (see above). Married to Peggy Ashcroft, actress.
Jeremy Tree	Son of Ronnie and Nancy.
Jerry	Jerry Koch de Gooreynd, Anglo–Belgian man-about-town, long-term lover of Laura (*q.v.*).
Jimmy	Vincent Sheean, American journalist.
John	John de Bendern.
Johnny	Lord John Manners, my mother's nephew.
Jones	The gardener-handyman at Bognor.
Jubags	See Juliet.
Judy	Judy Montagu, daughter of Venetia (*q.v.*). Later Mrs Milton Gendel.
Juliet	Lady Juliet Duff, old friend of my parents.
K	See Katherine.
Kaetchen	Dr Rudolf Kommer, known as Kaetchen, or the Cat. One of my mother's oldest friends since her days acting in Max Reinhardt's famous production of *The Miracle*. Living at that time in New York, he was my official guardian when I was evacuated to the USA and Canada, 1940–42.
Kakoo	(Pronounced Car-koo.) Duchess of Rutland, married to my mother's late brother John.
Kat	See Kaetchen.
Katherine	Katherine Asquith, widow of Raymond Asquith, daughter-in-law of the former Prime Minister. A fervent Catholic, and one of my mother's oldest and dearest friends.

Keswick, Tony	Far Eastern expert (Jardine Matheson, Hong Kong) who accompanied my father to Singapore.
Kitty	Lady Katherine Giles, married to Frank (*q.v.*).
Kitty	Lady Katherine Farrell (née Paget), daughter of my mother's sister Marjorie, married to Charles Farrell.
Kommer	See Kaetchen, above.
L.L.	See Louise.
Laura	Sister of Ann Fleming, successively Countess of Dudley and Duchess of Marlborough.
Laurence, Larry	Laurence Olivier, actor, married to Vivien Leigh.
Laurian	Laurian Jones, daughter of Enid and Roderick, (*q.v.*).
Lavington	The Sussex country house of Euan Wallace MP.
Lawrence, Gertie	Musical comedy star.
Leigh Fermor	Patrick, Paddy. See Paddy.
Leonardo	Walsh, proprietor of the Locanda San Vigilio, Lake Garda.
Letty	Lady Violet Benson, my mother's sister.
Lipmanns, Walter	Highly distinguished American journalist.
Liz	Lady Elizabeth von Hofmannsthal, married to Raimund (*q.v.*). My mother's niece, daughter of her eldest sister Marjorie Anglesey.
Loel	Loel Guinness, rich yachtsman, owner of 69 Rue de Lille.
Loelia	Duchess of Westminster. One of the four successive wives of Bendor, 2nd Duke.
Louise	Louise de Vilmorin, L.L., Lulu. Mistress of my father and close friend to all our family.
Lulu	See Louise.
Major	Maurice Baring. See Maurice.
Manners, Johnny	See Johnny.

Marguerite	My mother's maid at the Embassy.
Marie-Blanche	Marie-Blanche de Polignac, head of Lanvin (*haute couture*). A fine amateur musician and singer.
Marjorie	Marchioness of Anglesey. My mother's oldest sister.
Marler, Miss	My father's secretary. See Daphne Wakefield (her married name).
Martin	Martin Charteris, later Lord Charteris of Amisfield and Provost of Eton. My mother's nephew, second son of her sister Letty.
Mason	A. E. W. Mason, novelist.
Maud	Maud Nelson, partner of Oggie (*q.v.*).
Maugham	W. Somerset Maugham, writer.
Maureen	Maureen Stanley, wife of Oliver (*q.v.*).
Maurice, Mumble Major	Maurice Baring, writer. A victim of Parkinson's disease, he was bedridden at his house in Rottingdean, Sussex.
Max	See Beaverbrook (*q.v.*).
Maxine	Maxine de la Falaise, one of the most beautiful women in Paris.
Maxwell	Elsa Maxwell, American gossip columnist and famous party-giver.
McEntire, Rosemary	See Rosemary (*q.v.*).
Mendl, Elsie	Nonogenarian wife of Sir Charles Mendl, formerly Press Attaché of the Embassy.
Millard, Guy (wife Ann)	Members of Embassy staff.
Milo	Milo Cripps, son of my father's friend Fred Cripps and nephew of Sir Stafford. He was with me at Upper Canada College.
Mireille	Cook at Chantilly. In love with Jean.
Mogens	Mogens Twede, a Danish architect and painter living in Paris, married to Dolly Radziwill.

Moura	Baroness Budberg. Russian, mistress of Maxim Gorky and later of H.G. Wells. Suspected Soviet spy. Great-great-aunt of Nick Clegg.
Mumble	Maurice Baring (*q.v.*).
Muselier	Admiral Emile Muselier, Commander of the Free French Naval Forces.
Nancy	Nancy Mitford, novelist – Mrs Peter Rodd.
Nancy	Tree, married to Ronnie (*q.v.*).
Nanny	Alice Ayto, who looked after me from a few weeks after my birth, and who took me to America.
Nicholson, Jenny	See Jenny.
Nicky	Prince Nicholas of Yugoslavia, son of Prince Paul. A close friend until he was killed in a motor crash at twenty-six.
Noémi	My mother's maid in France.
Noona	My maternal grandmother, Violet, Duchess of Rutland.
Norah	Norah Fahie, secretary-gardener at Chantilly.
Oggie, Olga	Olga Lynn, a former singer and singing-teacher, and very old friend.
O'Neill, Ann	See Ann, Annie.
Osbert	Sir Osbert Sitwell, writer.
Paddy	Patrick Leigh Fermor, writer and war hero. A close friend of my mother from 1951 until her death.
Pagets	See Angleseys (*q.v.*)
Paley, Dorothy and William S.	see Bill, Dorothy.
Palewski, Gaston	See Gaston (*q.v.*).
Pam	Lady Pamela Berry, later Lady Hartwell.
Pan, Pandora	Pandora. Clifford, my sister-in-law, married 1) Timothy Jones, 2) Michael Astor, 3) Philip Lebon.

Pattens, the	Bill (*q.v.*) and Susan Mary (*q.v.*). He was attached to the US Embassy in Paris.
Paul	Prince Paul of Yugoslavia, former Regent, but by this time in exile. Father of Nicky (*q.v.*).
Peter	Peter Quennell, man of letters.
Phyllis	Countess de Janzé (née Boyd).
Pickford, Mary	Silent film star, married to Douglas Fairbanks Sr.
Pierino	Pierino Chitto, young Italian valet-chauffeur.
P.L.	Paul-Louis Weiller, multimillionaire, Sugar Daddy.
Polly	Polly Cotton, a much-loved lesbian cousin of the Paget family.
Prod	Peter Rodd, extremely unsatisfactory husband of Nancy Mitford.
Quennell	See Peter.
Rachel	Lady David Cecil.
Raimund, Rai	Raimund von Hofmannsthal, son of the Austrian poet and librettist (*Der Rosenkavalier*) Hugo von Hofmannsthal, was married to my mother's niece Liz (Paget). They were perhaps my parents' closest friends.
Randolph, Randy	Randolph Churchill, son of Winston.
Regnier	Gardener at Chantilly.
Rex	Rex Whistler, painter.
Rodd, Nancy	See Nancy.
Rose	Lady Rose McLaren, my mother's niece. One of the five Anglesey daughters (Caroline, Liz, Rose, Mary, Kitty).
Rosemary	Rosemary McEntire, my father's secretary at the Embassy. After Paris she was posted to Mexico.
Rothermere	See Esmond.

Rothschild, Victor and Barbara	See Victor, Barbara.
Rufus	Rufus Clarke, formerly Assistant Military Attaché at the Embassy. Later lover of Louise de Vilmorin.
Russell, Conrad	See Conrad (*q.v.*).
Russell, Claud and Gilbert	Brothers of Conrad (*q.v.*).
Russell, Martin	My father's secretary/adviser in Singapore.
Sachie	Sacheverell Sitwell, writer and critic, married to Georgia.
SHAEF	Supreme Headquarters, Allied Expeditionary Force. After the Liberation of Paris based in Versailles.
Sheean, Jimmy	American journalist.
Sherwood, Hugh, Lord	Family friend. Lover of Daisy Fellowes (*q.v.*).
Sitwell, Sachie and Georgia	See Sachie.
Stanley	Edward, Lord Stanley of Alderley.
Stanley	Oliver, wartime minister, and Maureen.
Susan Mary	Mrs William S. Patten, Attaché at the US Embassy, Paris. Later Mrs Joseph Alsop. Mistress of my father, by whom she was to bear a son.
Teddie	Teddie Phillips, Comptroller at the Embassy, later Paris man-about-town.
Tree, Jeremy	See Jeremy.
Tree, Ronald,	MP. Married to 1) Nancy and then 2) Marietta. Owner of Ditchley Park, Oxfordshire, where my parents frequently stayed. During the war it was also used as a weekend retreat by Winston Churchill, whose own house at Chartwell in Kent was considered too vulnerable to German bombing.

Tucker	Dominick Jones, son of Enid Bagnold (q.v.), and my best friend at Eton.
Twedes, The	See Mogens, Dolly.
Ursula	Lady Ursula Manners, daughter of my mother's brother John, Duke of Rutland.
Vaniers	General and Mrs George Vaniers, Canadian Ambassador in Paris.
Venetia	Venetia Montagu, my mother's very old friend.
Victor	Lord Rothschild. Married 1) Barbara Hutchinson, 2) Tess Meyer.
Vilmorin, Louise de	See Louise.
Virginia	Virginia Charteris, married to Hugo.
Virginia Clarke	Married to Ashley.
Vivien	Vivien Leigh, actress, married to Laurence Olivier.
Wade, Wadey	Kate Wade, who had been my mother's maid ever since her marriage.
Wakefield, Daphne	See Daphne.
Wallace, Billy	Son of Euan and Barbie.
Wallis	The Duchess of Windsor.
Waugh, Evelyn	See Wu.
Weiller, Paul-Louis	See P.L.
Westminster, Loelia	See Loelia.
Weymouth, Daphne	See Daphne.
Winston	Winston Churchill.
Wormwood Charlie	General de Gaulle ('Wormwood and Gall')
Wu, Mr	Evelyn Waugh.
Wynne	Wynne Godley, economist and oboeist. Later married Kitty, daughter of the sculptor Jacob Epstein.

Acknowledgements

All my thanks, as always, go to my wife Mollie, who has put all these letters (and many others) on to the computer and has given me endless help and advice. I am also hugely grateful to Hugo Vickers and Claus von Bulow, whose memories succeeded when mine failed. And all my thanks, too, to Becky Hardie, my editor at Chatto, for her hard work, unfailing enthusiasm and inspired suggestions.

Index

Rothschild (*née* Meyer), Tess, 198
and n25
Rothschild, Victor, 91, 94, 101, 106,
175, 176, 187, 198 and n25, 232,
233, 265, 479
Rotterdam, 139, 151
Rottingdean, 35, 37, 55, 234, 246, 248
Rousseau, Jean Jacques, 319
Rowsley, 251-2 and n63
Royal Arthur, HMS, 227
JJN describes life on board, 224
Royal Navy, JJN in, 9, 195, 224, 226,
227, 260, 282, 290
Royaumont, 305-6, 407
Rubio, Gloria, 425 and n3
Rufus *see* Clarke, Rufus
Russell, Aliki, 403 and n2, n3
Russell, Claud, 54, 249, 478
Russell, Conrad (the farmer)
takes action in the face of
expected invasion, 36
accompanies DC to plays in
London, 52, 95
and guerilla warfare, 52
relationship with DC, 111, 219-21
visits DC at Bognor, 111, 112, 113,
114, 115, 119, 123, 127, 130
on the point of death, 212 n68,
216-17
and Roman Catholic Church,
216-17
death, 218-19
DC's memories of, 219-21
DC reads letters of, 249, 253
frequency of correspondence
with DC, 470
brief references, 1, 19 and n8, 23,
34, 88, 97, 169, 199, 212, 238,
246, 313, 452
Russell, Diana, 249, 312-13 and n40
Russell, Ethel (Essie), 403 and n4
Russell, Flora, 249, 312-13 and n40

Russell, Gilbert, 102, 478
Russell, Sir John, 403 and n2, n3
Russell, Martin, 149, 478
Russell, Maud, 236 and n24
Russia/Russians, 16, 128-9 and n16,
169, 283
Rutland, Henry Manners, eighth
Duke of, 1
Rutland, John Manners, ninth Duke
of, 455-6, 462 n1
Rutland, Kathleen Manners(*née*
Tennant), Duchess of (Kakoo),
396, 415, 456, 473
Rutland, Violet Manners, Duchess of
(Noona), 1, 4, 83, 99, 102, 252,
275, 319, 324, 447, 476
Rutland, Henry Manners, eighth
Duke of, 1

Sabang, 150
Sachie *see* Sitwell, Sacheverell
Sackville-West, Vita, 240 and n33,
279 n38
St Bartholomew's London, 7
St George's Hospital, London, 40,
41-2, 48, 74, 86
St John and St Elizabeth's Hospital,
London, 329, 337-8
DC writes from, 338-48
St Lawrence river, 21
St Margaret's, Westminster, 2, 386
St Marc, Baron, 419
St Maxime Abbey, 414, 415-16
St Paul's, London, 80, 271, 272-3
St Peter's Rome, 317, 320, 321, 322
St Petersburg, 7-8
Salisbury, 307, 308, 379
Salisbury, Lady *see* Cranborne, Lady
Betty, later Lady Salisbury
Salisbury, Lord *see* Cranborne,
Robert, Lord (Bobbety), later
Marquess of Salisbury